# Perpetual Jeopardy

# Perpetual Jeopardy

The Texas Gulf Sulphur Affair:
A Chronicle of
Achievement and Misadventure

by Kenneth G. Patrick

AN ARKVILLE PRESS BOOK
THE MACMILLAN COMPANY, *NEW YORK*
COLLIER-MACMILLAN LIMITED, *LONDON*

Collier-Macmillan Canada Ltd., Toronto, Ontario

Library of Congress Card Number: 70-143515

*printing number*
1   2   3   4   5   6   7   8   9   10

STUDIES OF THE MODERN CORPORATION
*Columbia University Graduate School of Business*

IRVING PFEFFER, *editor*
  *The Financing of Small Business: A Current Assessment*

STANLEY SALMEN
  *Duties of Administrators in Higher Education*

GEORGE A. STEINER
  *Top Management Planning*

GEORGE A. STEINER AND WARREN M. CANNON, *editors*
  *Multinational Corporate Planning*

GEORGE A. STEINER AND WILLIAM G. RYAN
  *Industrial Project Management*

GUS TYLER
  *The Political Imperative: The Corporate Character of Unions*

CLARENCE WALTON AND RICHARD EELLS, *editors*
  *The Business System: Readings in Ideas and Concepts*

## STUDIES OF THE MODERN CORPORATION
*Columbia University Graduate School of Business*

The Program for Studies of the Modern Corporation is devoted to the advancement and dissemination of knowledge about the corporation. Its publications are designed to stimulate inquiry, research, criticism, and reflection. They fall into three categories: works by outstanding businessmen, scholars, and professional men from a variety of backgrounds and academic disciplines; annotated and edited selections of business literature; and business classics that merit republication. The studies are supported by outside grants from private business, professional, and philanthropic institutions interested in the program's objectives.

RICHARD EELLS
*Editor of the Studies*

# Contents

# Introduction

NOTWITHSTANDING the anguished cries and strident disagreements likely to arise from lawyers, litigants, journalists, and not so innocent bystanders, this is basically a simple story concerning a corporation, various arms of government, and a substantial sampling of human beings—domiciled mainly in the United States and Canada—who found themselves involved, one way or another, in an interesting, provocative, and somewhat dismaying series of events.

Scholars and active formalists in our society—such as executives, professors, lawyers and judges, bankers, accountants, and editors (but not reporters)—may be offended by the designation "story." For their greater academic comfort it may also be termed a study, braced by the necessary documentation and a generous dose of research. Whether or not it is in truth "simple" may be open to argument.

Nothing is very simple in the second half of the twentieth century. Certainly the business corporation is not, except for the straightforward provisions of its charter. The government of the United States becomes increasingly complex and unmanageable as the centuries spin by, and this complexity is accurately reflected, if somewhat tardily and awkwardly, in the workings of the judicial system, that sturdy third leg upon which the republic stands. The

United States has no patent on complexity, for that matter. We have only to look around us, aided by the instantaneous playback afforded by modern communications. Other nations either aspire to our problems or have already surpassed them with short cuts of their own.

If this is truly a simple story, it is only because human beings conspire to keep things that way. The pattern of their ambitions, love, hate, greed, strength and weakness, envy, honesty, forthrightness and deviousness, sentimentality and stoicism, fear and courage remains reasonably constant in every age. In the end such standard qualities make things easier for any observer by supplying familiar norms of performance by which men and their deeds can be judged, or at least sorted out.

This account must of necessity present two faces, which should help to endow it with a realistic three-dimensional character. Since time is also a continuing factor, there may be logically entailed a fourth dimension, for this is a chronicle. It ends but does not finish. It has no symmetry.

First, there is the case history, or factual recital, of what happened to the Texas Gulf Sulphur Company, a United States corporation born in the closing years of the First World War. After it had achieved a monumental ore discovery in eastern Canada, the company immediately found itself the target of an investigation by the federal Securities and Exchange Commission. It was put against a wall and menaced with a silver bullet known as Rule 10b-5, complete with trial, judgment, and appeal to the higher courts of the land, including the people's court of public opinion. There followed, of course, a horrendous number of derivative or related legal actions, some seeking to wrest title to the mineral property from the company; others seeking astronomical monetary damages for shares of stock sold during the critical period between discovery and disclosure. In a sense the whole picture also involved litigations, investigations, and events which in fact preceded the action brought against Texas Gulf in 1965 by the SEC, but which find their place in the broad canvas. At this writing, if ever, the end is not yet in sight.

With the practical judgment characteristic of corporate management, the company chose meanwhile to go about its business, although not as if nothing had happened. In the prime action the corporation was not alone at the defendants' bench. It sat in company with thirteen individuals—directors, officers, and employees.

Not included in the complaint, but hovering in the background, was a sizeable company of others who were more or less on target. Unlike the *persona ficta* of the corporation, these were people, subject to the responsibilities and motivations and at least some of the standard traits listed earlier. If cut, they would bleed personally, whereas corporate bleeding is a somewhat more complex phenomenon, although just as painful. During the proceedings one of them died and one ran away, while others continued to work at their assignments and went on to new achievements, new responsibilities, and increased rewards, among other things. Whatever happened, or happens, they are the walking wounded and it is likely that they will never forget their experience. Perhaps the same can be said for the accusers and the witnesses, who are also human beings, whether acting as agents of the law or in a private capacity.

Case histories such as the one under examination here do not occur in a vacuum. As the proverbial stone cast into a convenient pond creates waves, so do the issues and decisions growing out of such a case affect the lives and fortunes, practices and policies, of many organizations and individuals. The nation and the economy—the pond—become disturbed. Change is wrought, although, as in this instance, the directions, terminal points, and durability of the change may teeter on the edge of costly uncertainty. In its other phase, therefore, this account must concern itself with the waves, a secondary but larger aspect.

What are the implications of the Texas Gulf Sulphur affair for the entire business community? What are the facts, and where now stands the law in respect to business corporations, their directors, officers, and other employees; or in respect to stockholders as a class, ranging from the long-term investor to the hot-tip speculator? What restrictions and guidelines have seemed to settle upon sellers, buyers, and professional dealers in securities, from bankers to brokers? In a case at law, when does a fact become "material" as it passes from person to person or swiftly makes its way over the intricate network of modern communications? In fact, when does it become a *fact*? How competent are the courts, irrespective of their unquestioned jurisdiction, to make major alterations in the working machinery of the business world, where practicing economists either fear to tread or are in wild disagreement over theories and practices?

Our treasured due process of law is an expensive and cumbersome instrument, and its blessings do not fall freely upon all who need them. They must be sought, and the seeking is fraught with peril. The court sitting in judgment is likely, if not exactly privileged, to invoke the hindsight unfortunately denied the participants in the heat of battle, and the weight of hindsight is heavy indeed. Does the Congress, in the deliberate exercise of its legislative function, establish until further notice the intents and boundaries of a law, or do the agencies which it creates to administer that law feel free, with the passage of years and the exhilaration of their task, to extend the intent, and breach the boundary, without any effective restraint? Who is calling the shots?

One of the subjects thrust into the spotlight by the Texas Gulf Sulphur case is "insider trading" in securities—broadly, the use of information by those who have it against those who do not have it, presumably for financial gain. This constituted the heart of the complaint against the defendants, although the fuse ran to many other subjects before it was exhausted. One mature critic, however, has held that Congress has never adopted an absolute prohibition on insider trading, that such a rule does not exist, and that if it did exist, it would be a threat to the survival of our corporate system. The arguments on all sides—there are more than just two—reach deeply into the functioning of the financial marketing system, and along the way raise for debate a number of legal and moral issues.

There arises necessarily out of the trial of such a cause, and out of the derivative actions, the old question of whose ox is being gored. Do aggressive and punitive actions of this kind on the part of such an agency as the SEC shield and enrich the speculator and chartist and opportunist of Wall Street and Bay Street instead of the long-term investor, whose real damage must be measured by the damage to the corporation itself?

The other provocative question coming to the surface in this affair involves where the line should be drawn between the employee as an individual and his corporate employer. Where rest the obligations of the director, the officer, the manager, or of any employee—to the corporation, to the government, to the public, and finally to themselves? The distinction is a hard one, and much of the homework remains to be done.

There is more than a suspicion that the modern corporation has not completely or effectively explored its relationships with its shareowners and turned them into assets, and that its failure of communication rests upon lack of understanding as well as upon lack of follow-through. Business managers have a lot on their plate.

The whole system of developing, implementing, and disclosing corporate information to the various publics, both directly and indirectly, through such media as investment analysts and trade, professional and scientific publications, would seem to be threatened to the point of extinction, or defeated in its purpose, by judicial findings prevailing at one critical point in the Texas Gulf case. Is this desirable, is it absurd, is it even possible, or is it what anyone wants? Such a policy of silence, under the threat of liability for disclosure, leaves a company literally defenseless. Granting the jurisdiction of the appropriate courts, and the necessary processes and evidentiary practices of the law, any action which pinpoints an alleged violation also has the unfortunate result of proceeding without regard to a defendant corporation's *total* activities, responsibilities, and motivations and its role in the continuing guarantee of a healthy economy.

These are but some of the waves which reached the shore of the pond as a result of the Texas Gulf case, commanding the attention of the wary and the unwary alike.

The TGS affair, in its ramifications, spanned one continent and one ocean, linked the Gulf to the Arctic, and metallurgically tied sulphur to copper, zinc, and silver. It brought to the stage a cast of characters including the Queen of England (she issued an order in council), judges, lawyers, corporation executives, customer's men, civil servants, miners, investors, engineers, speculators, financiers, drill riggers, ministers, core-grabbers, journalists, politicians, public relations counselors, map-makers, investment analysts, deans and professors, at least two rather unusual husband-and-wife teams, brokers, at least one fugitive from the law, scientists, fakers, hard-sell artists, and secretaries. The scenario featured at various times a ship that sank without a trace, a cracked-up helicopter, a tragic mine explosion, and all extremes of weather. It put on the record men who were honest, aggressive, distinguished, scholarly, and eloquent, as well as others who did not quite measure up, and a few who were downright rascals. To top all of this, for the first time in any courtroom within the memory of man, an adjournment was taken while human beings walked on the moon.

The remedy sought by the Securities and Exchange Commission, and made possible by the judgment of the majority of the United States Court of Appeals for the Second Circuit when it overturned the findings of the lower court, would "not only be inappropriate but would be destructive of fundamental rights," declared Circuit Judge Leonard P. Moore, in his stinging dissent. He then proceeded to put into his opinion the words "perpetual jeopardy" to describe the result. They also served *Barron's* in its issue of August 19, 1968, when it employed them to headline its "Angry Note on the Texas Gulf Sulphur Case."

Perpetual jeopardy, it might be said, is not much more than a succinct description of man's life on earth. Obviously Judge Moore (and *Barron's*) had in mind something rather more specific. Our system of laws does not exactly countenance jeopardy, but it is not above using it to make its point. The philosophical approach, and the more specific legal approach, to the conceptual abstraction labeled "perpetual jeopardy" may be at opposite ends of a spectrum, but they concern the same thing—the prospect of a continuing threat. The minimal purpose here is to view the prospect, as carefully and conscientiously as possible.

Generous—some might say overgenerous—use has been made of direct quotations from court opinions, testimony of witnesses, official pronouncements, newspaper and periodical texts, and corporate statements, as well as from law journals and similar recorded proceedings. It is hoped that this will not so much suggest laziness or lack of conviction on the part of the author as it does his desire to lay out as much of the evidence as possible, and in the exact words of the speakers and writers. Such takings constitute the only true record, after which the conclusions are largely up to us.

One final word—when a man is brought to trial on specific charges, the record begins to roll at that point and is limited by the rules of procedure to those words and acts which are relevant to such charges. What happened before and what the future may hold are strictly excluded, and relevance is a matter for the judge. A business undertaking stands in the same position, of course, and this is entirely proper for the purposes of the judicial process. Yet a defendant is not born at the moment he steps before the bar, nor is a company. Life has been going on for quite some time and the responsibilities and opportunities, the defeats and achievements of the normal world, and the whole business of getting on with the job have a relevance and importance to the case at bar which refuse to be shunted aside by any rules of evidence. To those in the gallery such facts sometimes help to explain the inexplicable. In this chronicle a certain amount of the history of the Texas Gulf Sulphur Company and the industry of which it is a part seems necessary to a proper setting of the stage. It is provided in the opening chapter. Those who lean only to the action and are content to waive history and environment, who thirst for the Packers and the Globe Trotters but who have little interest in Green Bay or Harlem, are duly warned.

In all fairness, something should be said to pierce the paper curtain which separates any book from the reasons and circumstances behind its execution. Texas Gulf people, eventually somewhat frustrated by their overwhelming load of mixed blessings (a fabulous mine, costly diversification into new fields, the SEC investigation and trial and all of its connected and concurrent actions at law, and finally a growing awareness of the fallout of confusion upon the financial, business, and legal communities resulting from conflicting court decisions and wide publicity) hoped that as much as possible of the action might be rendered down into a single account. At almost the same time, the Program for Studies of the Modern Corporation, having its home base within the Columbia University Graduate School of Business, became intrigued with those aspects of the conflict, noted earlier in this Introduction, which seemed to pose problems and have consequences for all business. The chronicle which follows resulted from these dual interests. Texas Gulf Sulphur Company provided funds for initial exploration, research, and writing, while the program at Columbia reviewed the project and undertook publication. Neither Texas Gulf nor the able people at Columbia leaned on, or in any way pressed the writer, at any stage of the proceedings. Any judgments, opinions, and language, unless otherwise indicated, are his alone. The undertaking, where it depended upon special knowledge of the mining industry, required substantial advice and counsel, and thorough factual checking, and these services were supplied freely and cheerfully by a host of people at Texas Gulf. The only real pressures upon the writer, working some 1,600 miles from Wall Street and Foley Square, were those gentle and beguiling ones offered by the Caribbean.

Blue Horizon                                    KENNETH G. PATRICK
Jamaica, West Indies

# Perpetual Jeopardy

# 1
# The Mill

I

$S$ULPHUR, along with carbon, was known
to the ancients, and to it were attributed strange properties. It is
the brimstone of the Bible, and it was employed by the priests and
witchdoctors of primitive peoples. It received a mention from
Homer in the chronicles of Ulysses; it contributed to the weapons
of the legions of Rome; and it exploded as gunpowder upon the
medieval battlefields of Europe, with an earlier assist from the
Chinese.

The history of the sulphur industry in the United States (and,
to be truthful, the history of the Texas Gulf Sulphur Company
also) certainly begins with a stocky German chemist from Würtem-
burg named Herman Frasch. Appropriately celebrating his 43rd
birthday, Frasch spent the Christmas Eve of 1894 testing a theory
in a Louisiana swamp—a startling idea that sulphur could be
melted and mined with hot water. Three days later he proved it.
About 72 years later, and 52 years to the month after Frasch died
in Paris, his name and his revolutionary method for mining sulphur
were destined to bemuse judge, counsel, participants, and spectators in a federal courtroom in Foley Square, New York City, during
the course of a trial. The ramifications of this proceeding would
engender confusion and chaos in the breasts and brains of much of
the legal, business, and financial communities of the country. All of

1

these people then had to wait for some eligible agency such as the Securities and Exchange Commission, the Congress, or the Supreme Court, to drop the other shoe.

After several thousand years, the long fuse of the "stone that burns" is more active than ever and its end is not in sight. Surfacing in Foley Square was only one more exciting and disturbing incident in its long and important lifetime, since sulphur is today a vital mineral used at some stage in the production or processing of nearly every product for modern living. It has been said that sulphur consumption closely parallels the Federal Reserve Board's index of industrial production and that its per capita use is a good indicator of the living standards in a given country. With the highest living standard of any, the United States, in 1967, used 106 pounds per person—up 30 pounds in ten years. Nearly half of the consumption now goes into fertilizers essential to food and fiber for the world's ever growing population, and the cumulative deficit between free world sulphur production and consumption in a recent five-year period was about three and a half million tons. In short, with more people and increasing use, the world is always looking for more sulphur.

It is all the more interesting in the light of the foregoing, although perhaps not surprising, that the quest for this bright yellow non-metallic element should come to have such a specific bearing on an argument over insider trading on the stock market, the timeliness of corporate disclosures, the prevalence of hindsight in judicial determinations, the propriety of stock options, the relations between a company and its stockholders, and what constitutes a material fact, among other things. On its classically hell-bent course from ancient times to the beneficent outpouring of the modern day, sulphur still has the capacity to pop a button now and then in the face of man.

Sulphur is widely and abundantly distributed in nature, and is present in the ores of many metals—one of the facts which eventually led to the legal proceedings in Foley Square and elsewhere. The element occurs uncombined in volcanic regions in various parts of the world, and in large deposits beneath the surface of the earth in Sicily, in Texas and Louisiana, and in Mexico. Sicily provided the world's principal source of supply from the days of the Roman empire until the later developments across the Atlantic. In fact it was the economic problem posed by the low cost of pick-and-shovel methods in Sicily, as compared to the application of similar methods by higher-priced labor in the United States, which drove Herman Frasch to seek an engineering solution in the Louisiana swamp.

Fortunes had been sunk and human lives lost in futile attempts before the turn of the century to mine sulphur. Frasch's idea was to penetrate through cap rock to the sulphur deposits, melt the latter with superheated water, and pump the liquid product to the surface. Put that way, it sounds easy. Volumes have been written describing the painful, expensive, and often discouraging development of the method, but viewed simply from the vantage point of more than 70 years, it comes down to this: three pipes, one inside the other, are sunk to the bottom of the sulphur bed. Water heated under pressure to a temperature well above the melting point of sulphur is conducted down the outer pipe, and air under pressure down through the innermost pipe. Their combined action melts the sulphur and forces it to the surface through the middle pipe, from which it is drawn off. Thus does time solve many intricate problems.

Today Texas Gulf Sulphur Company operates five domestic sulphur mines in Texas and one in Louisiana. Its net investment in property, plant, and equipment represented by all of its undertakings, after depreciation and amortization, is probably in excess of $300 million, yet it came into being with the deviousness usually associated with the docking of a small ferryboat under inexpert handling, and in spite of the fact that some of the men on deck were possessed of famous names. In fact, the earliest parts of the story seem to be more directly related to the founding of its chief competitor—Freeport Sulphur—as told by the industry's most prominent historian, William Haynes.[1]

The year was 1909 and one Francis Pemberton, son of the Confederate general who had defended Vicksburg, became interested in the sulphur activity in Texas and Louisiana while making investigations of timberland. His interest developed into an option on a property in Texas known as "Bryanmound," an historic landmark near the mouth of the Brazos River. Because the project was going to require substantial financing, Pemberton and his associates approached J. P. Morgan the elder. Morgan indicated that he would be interested if the sulphur deposits were as good as Pemberton believed they were. At this point Bernard Baruch, whose

[1] Williams Haynes: *Brimstone—The Stone That Burns*, D. Van Nostrand and Co., Princeton, N.J. (1959).

name had become well-known through the development of western
copper properties, was asked to explore the proposal, and he, in
turn, consulted the well-known mining engineer, Seeley W. Mudd.
Together, Baruch and Mudd journeyed to Houston and on July 4,
1910, met there one of Mudd's trusted assistants, Spencer Browne.

Browne had been on a scouting trip in order to familiarize
himself with oil drilling methods and to obtain some reliable
samples of sulphur. During the course of the trip he learned of a
dome called Big Hill, near Matagorda, 60 miles from "Bryanmound"
and close to the Gulf. As things turned out, the report on "Bryanmound" raised no enthusiasm on the part of Morgan back in New
York. Baruch had inadvertently described it as a "gamble"; Morgan
replied that he never gambled. Browne then remembered his
favorable impressions of Big Hill, and thereby became a key man
in the early moves which were to lay the foundations for Texas
Gulf Sulphur Company. "Bryanmound," which went on in history
to become a Freeport Sulphur property, nevertheless produced the
first sulphur ever mined in Texas.

As an oil producer Big Hill had been a conspicuous failure,
but failure—like some other qualities—is in the eye of the beholder.
A. C. Einstein and John W. Harrison had come to Texas from St.
Louis looking for sulphur, not oil, and they liked what they saw at
Big Hill. Returning to St. Louis they enlisted Theodore F. Meyer,
president of a drug company, in their scheme and organized what
they called the Gulf Sulphur Company, with Einstein as president.
The date of this incorporation was December 23, 1909, sufficiently
close to the anniversary of Herman Frasch's birthday to attract the attention of the lighter type of historians. Before too long it would seem
that Texas Gulf acquired an early habit of receiving significant
Christmas gifts. But, not to anticipate history, it developed later
in the cold new year that the expense of drilling was going to be
higher than the Missouri combine had expected, and the investment for a necessary steaming plant would require more capital
than they had available. The company had been capitalized at
$250,000, and it was said that one man owned all but 80 of the
25,000 shares—a fact which, if true, might make second thoughts
remarkably persuasive.

It was at this point in time that Spencer Browne recalled his
good impressions of Big Hill, and although nothing happened
immediately, the interest of Mudd and Baruch, aroused by one
prospect, was rekindled by another. In 1916, which now seems like

a rather long time in which to nurture such an interest, negotiations with Gulf Sulphur were climactically reopened, with Morgan and Colonel William Boyce Thompson lending their support in the background. Baruch and Mudd obtained control of the property and reorganized the company, this time with Mudd as president. Quietly, efforts were begun to acquire the whole dome area of Big Hill, and in 1918 the corporate name was changed to Texas Gulf Sulphur Company and capitalization was increased to $3 million, as Wall Street superseded St. Louis.

It will have been noted that 1918 was a year significant in many respects, and the heavy hand of World War I laid on some changes. For one thing, sulphuric acid became a critical material for military uses, and for another, Baruch was appointed chairman of the War Industries Board, which imposed certain strictures upon his relationship with the sulphur business. Colonel Mudd also went into war work, and in as president of the company came Walter H. Aldridge, who was to hold the post for 34 years. Texas Gulf was now exploring further its Big Hill property, and had projected a plant in blueprints. After a period, during which the importance of sulphur to the war effort was urged and examined, priorities for construction of the plant were obtained, and the work was begun on August 13, 1918. Charles Biesel, an associate of Aldridge, became general manager and stayed in charge of all TGS mining operations until his retirement in 1928. Ten years after the incorporation of the predecessor company production was finally commenced at Big Hill in March, 1919.

The famous dome was to yield more than 12 million tons of brimstone. However, when the war ended the munitions demand vanished, industrial activity slumped, and farmers were cutting down on their acreage and their purchases of fertilizer. Excess stocks were being dumped on the market, and the sulphur business —all too soon—seemed to be facing dark days. Considering this rather grim prospect, Aldridge nevertheless launched an intense educational campaign throughout the fertilizer industry, and while waiting for results proceeded to build a sound sales organization. Eventually industrial production revived. In the words of Haynes:

> The arrival of the "third competitor" had not upset the domestic market. The price war everyone dreaded never materialized because during the booming 1920's American consumption of sulphur grew greatly. Conditions for this expansion were trebly propitious. First, it was a period of extraordinary industrial activity

and the direct use of brimstone in paper, insecticides, and rubber increased enormously. Secondly, the switch of acid makers from pyrite to brimstone came just when the two greatest sulphuric acid users, fertilizers and petroleum, were enjoying a great boom. Finally, the decade was one during which phenomenal chemical progress in this country demanded many more tons of sulphur.[2]

Thus the initial period of organization and hectic scrambling came to a close on a promising note. In 1921 production at Big Hill had reached a million tons, and a time of expansion began, highlighting the fact for the first of many times that reserves appeared inadequate and further geological scouting would be necessary. A field office to polarize such activity was established by TGS in Houston in 1925. Among the regions studied was the coastal area west of Houston, including the Boling area, which had received the attention of various oil companies. In 1926 Texas Gulf became the world's leading sulphur producer, a distinction that was to continue, and a year later it obtained the sulphur rights on Boling Dome.

## II

Boling Dome became the largest and richest sulphur deposit the world has ever known—a fabulous mine. More than five miles long and three and a half miles wide, it is the largest of the shallow Gulf Coast salt domes. The sulphur formation has a maximum of 200 feet in thickness and ranges from mere traces to a sulphur percentage of more than 50 per cent. On March 20, 1929, production began at Boling, and during its first 30 years it produced more than 50 million long tons of sulphur, or about 38 per cent of all sulphur raised by the Frasch process since the Christmas Eve experiment in the Louisiana swamp in 1894.

One thing had to be clear: TGS was predominantly a *sulphur* company, and this conviction would be repeated and would dominate company thinking and operations for a long time to come. Sulphur was king, and would remain so whether the market was sick or booming. What was perhaps not so clear at the time was that a successful sulphur company—if it stays alive—inevitably must become involved in diversification because of the nature of its primary tools—research, exploration, the relationship to other

[2] *Ibid.*, p. 106.

types of depletable natural resources, the organization and staffing and equipping of mines, processing methods, transportation, and markets. Given the passage of time, changes in circumstances of industrial production, and the steady employment of the tools and skills necessary to a successful sulphur operation, diversification follows as day follows night. As it developed, diversification could be costly and discouraging for Texas Gulf Sulphur, or for any other mining company, and it could also be the royal road to increased earnings.

In one sense, even before it has attained the status of a conscious and announced policy, diversification begins with exploration for new sources of raw material and with improved methods. After World War II, Texas Gulf brought in four sulphur mines in Texas to supplement Boling (Moss Bluff in 1948, Spindletop in 1952, Fannett in 1958, and Gulf in 1965, site of the original production in 1919) and in 1968 one in Louisiana called Bully Camp, 40 miles southwest of New Orleans. But other sources of sulphur were continually sought. Around 1938 the company began investigating the removal of sulphur from the hydrogen sulphide contained in sour natural gas. This investigation led to the completion of a sour gas sulphur recovery plant at Worland, Wyoming, in 1950, and by 1959 it was producing from this source 60,000 tons a year, an important drop in a big bucket. In mid-1959 a similar recovery plant began production at Okotoks, Alberta, operated and 42.5 per cent owned by TGS. It exceeded 50,000 tons by the end of the year, and soon was operating at an annual rate of 130,000 long tons. Incidentally, this rate also allowed the recovery of 4.5 billion cubic feet of sweet gas.

In August of 1949 Texas Gulf became the first company to negotiate a contract for sulphur production with the Mexican government, and its basic terms then established the industry pattern. Plant construction began in 1955, when sulphur prices were higher, but production did not start until 1957, when prices had sunk, and no shipments were made since costs were too high compared with domestic production. The whole operation was suspended in 1960 as a matter of economy, with a substantial net loss. This was one of the bumps not unknown to mining enterprises, although by 1968 production had resumed at Nopalapa mine in Mexico, on the Isthmus of Tehuantepec, under a different arrangement.

What might be labeled, with hindsight, as the first of the substantial diversifications came in 1952 with an interest in oil, accelerated by production at Boling, Spindletop, and Moss Bluff. By 1958 oil production was running at 380,000 barrels; it peaked in 1960 with 596,000 barrels, but from this point fell steadily to 289,000 barrels in 1968. Complementing the oil interest was one in gas production. In a 1959 historical review Texas Gulf touched lightly on the gas from the Worland and Okotoks plants, and then only in connection with the location of new sulphur sources. The company continued to prospect and evaluate various oil and gas properties in the United States and Canada, including the Texas-Louisiana Gulf Coast, Kansas, Kentucky, Utah, and western Alberta. It had a 50 per cent participation in the drilling of a sour gas recovery well southeast of Calgary, and 40 per cent in another in the Wildhorse Creek area of western Alberta. Other wells were drilled in Texas. In Sudbury, Ontario, it was operating a pilot plant to determine the economic feasibility of recovering elemental sulphur from smelter gas. From an initially reported gas production in 1959 of 990 million cubic feet, the gas component of the business grew steadily to a figure of 10,034 million cubic feet in 1968. In December, 1963, the company had acquired all of the Delhi-Taylor Oil Company oil and gas properties in Canada and the net 230,000 acres accruing from this, added to a prior major interest in 300,000 wildcat acres, made for an important position across the border.

A somewhat more substantial indication of the coming diversification is documented by the fact that in 1957 claims for metallic ores were first staked at Baffin Island in the Canadian Arctic, probably one of the most northerly explorations in the world at that time, while two years later TGS optioned several lithium-bearing properties in North Carolina and set about studying the extraction process. Mineral evaluation studies were being made in Australia, Germany, Sicily, Iraq, Iran, Egypt, and Ethiopia. More immediately important, as it turned out, was the development of a helicopter mounted with special electromagnetic gear to survey anomalies and detect potential ore deposits from the air, and it began to be used in British Columbia and the Canadian Shield area of eastern Canada.

Shareholders were told at the close of 1959—rather conservatively and for the first time—that the company's "search for new sulphur supplies over the years has resulted, naturally, in exploration for other mineral sources. This is in keeping with the company's policy of eventually broadening its operations into materials other than sulphur." It was the kind of "insider" statement that could become very questionable in the next half-dozen years as the Securities and Exchange Commission mounted its new crusade in behalf of investors, but at the moment nobody was looking, and it probably created not a ripple in Washington, New York, or Toronto.

As historian Haynes had pointed out, the key to revolutionary changes, as always in the steady evolution of sulphur, is the market action and the chemical reactions of sulphuric acid. Sulphur has one major use, and it is the production of sulphuric acid, a not very glamorous commodity. Approximately 80 per cent of all sulphur is converted to acid. Prior to the First World War much of the acid produced in the United States was derived from pyrites, or metallic ores, and there were few big buyers of elemental sulphur in the chemical industry. The purpose of the Aldridge educational program launched after the war was to demonstrate to large acid producers the advantages of switching from pyrites to Frasch sulphur, and this was achieved.

In its drive for expansion to meet market demands Texas Gulf had to make operating efficiency a prime goal in cost control. Operating its various mines as a single unit, it constructed headquarters buildings, a large machine shop and warehouse, and a company personnel community known as Newgulf, which served as central headquarters. Beginning as a barren pasture, it became a town of 2,000 residents, with a hospital, churches, library, and recreational facilities. When Boling came "on stream" as the first of the unit mines, a powerhouse to supply superheated water, compressed air, and electricity; mining facilities; water disposal units; and transportation facilities were built. As each new mine came into production, site construction would include only essentials, and techniques were perfected to centralize operating control—systems of telephone and radio communication and local airstrips, as well as a central warehouse. The machine shop built special equipment and performed major overhaul jobs. Eventually a new shipping terminal in Texas on the Neches River south of Beaumont was completed, and these facilities were equipped to handle both liquid and solid sulphur shipments, domestic and overseas.

With the maintenance of adequate sulphur reserves a necessarily firm policy for an extractive company in the natural resource industry, TGS had to strengthen its exploration and research programs. The active airborne electromagnetic exploration program was projected in 1959 with the aim of continuing searches in geologically favorable areas, and following, when the indications warranted it, with ground geological and geophysical surveys and core drilling. To improve its techniques in this direction the company established a small research laboratory in Stamford, Connecticut, to study equipment and methods, advance field practices, and to interpret data. The innate skepticism of sulphur miners, it is said, derives from the difficulty in determining reserves with any accuracy. It is hardly possible to descend to the sulphur section of a salt dome, study its structure, and estimate its core content. Also, the mining equipment is very expensive, and state tax levies on supposed deposits can be very inequitable. An early Louisiana company is reported to have paid taxes on a million tons of sulphur that did not even exist. Such traditional skepticism doubtless underlay the official attitude of Texas Gulf some years later, on the occasion of its spectacular mineral discoveries in Canada, and for which it was criticized by some judges and government investigators. Since the constructive complement of skepticism is research, however, the Stamford laboratory devoted itself to improvements in existing processes, efforts to commercialize new sulphur sources, and research of a fundamental nature involving studies to improve methods of extracting associated metal values. The last-named function again pointed to diversification, a tag line that would more and more become associated with the names of Claude O. Stephens and Dr. Charles F. Fogarty.

Stephens is one of those top executives for which American corporations have a special fondness—all his business life was spent within the company which eventually elevated him to its chief executive post. During his summer vacations as an engineering student at Louisiana State University he worked for Texas Gulf Sulphur as an operator drill helper, and before he finished college had worked in every phase of sulphur mining. After his graduation in 1932 his employment became permanent rather than spasmodic, and he was a field engineer when World War II caught up with him, took him as a second lieutenant for the Pacific theater, and discharged him as a major after occupation duty in Japan. Stephens' way to the top of TGS proceeded through the managership of the Worland gas recovery plant in 1948, and he went to New York as manager of the new gas department, became vice president and manager of production, and was elected president in 1957 when problems for the industry were becoming aggravated but had not yet assumed dismal proportions. During the trial to come, senior director Thomas S. Lamont would testify that Stephens ". . . was imaginative, able, he was alert, he was aggressive, and he was a man of unquestioned integrity."

Fogarty ideally complements Stephens in many ways, but his approach to TGS was even more conventional. A Denver native, and an orphan, he graduated from Colorado School of Mines in 1942, served with the Army Corps of Engineers until his 1946 discharge as a major and spent the ensuing four years as senior geologist with Socony Vacuum in Colombia before returning to his alma mater to work on his doctorate in science. Receiving his doctor of science degree in geology in 1952, he then joined Texas Gulf as a geologist in Houston and later headed the exploration department, obviously a beckoning frontier, and one which led him through three degrees of of vice presidency—plain, senior, and executive— to the presidency in 1968, long after the "troubles" had erupted. Fogarty's job not only involved him widely in travel around the world, but also brought him—with Stephens—to prolonged sessions in court as defendant and a key witness in the legal actions which were the sequential but unhappy outcome of spectacular diversification on the company's part. These results were not limited just to Texas Gulf. They created havoc and dismay in the entire business and financial community before running their course.

However, the company which Stephens headed in 1959, after its half century of corporate life and 40 years of sulphur production, presented some provocative statistics. Taking the years 1920– 22 as an average, when record-keeping really came of age, its sales had risen from $7.7 million to $63.6 million; the high point had been $93.6 million in 1955, after which they had steadily fallen off due to low prices and excessive supplies. In the same period earnings had proceeded from $3 million to $13.3 million in 1959, actually the lowest then since 1944–46, having attained $32.4 million in 1955 and then slid downward. Quoted year-end sulphur price per ton had begun the measuring period at $15, peaked at $26.50 in 1954–5–6, and then settled to $23.50. Between 1920 and 1959 the company's total assets rose from $12.3 million to $124.5 million, and its working capital from $7 million to $100.7 million. Its shareholders—in 1920 a guess at 223—had now become 74,168 and were holding 10,020,000 shares. The company had no funded debt —a situation obviously subject to change—and its budgeted capital expenditures averaged $5 million a year over the past three

years—a level soon to rise dramatically. In 40 years there had
been no work stoppage attributable to labor trouble, and the average
length of employment was over 15 years.

It was a mixed bag, perhaps, but all in all a rather promising
one despite the problems inherent in the sulphur business, as the
company concluded its first half century and toed the mark on the
next.

## III

Those "problems inherent in the sulphur busi-
ness" will bear examination, both as a matter of history and as a key
to what was to come. Texas Gulf had become the biggest supplier in
the free world sulphur market, but that market had turned soft with
a vengeance, and this had been duly reflected in company sales and
earnings. From the 'twenties into the late 'fifties TGS was just a
sulphur mining company. It produced nothing but sulphur and
dividends, and both in large amounts. Beginning in 1956, as sales
and earnings declined, it began to fall on hard times.

Until the mid-'fifties the U.S. Frasch producers filled virtually
the entire domestic needs for elemental sulphur under conditions
of tight supply and exported about 30 per cent of their annual production to world markets. Suddenly sulphur became available from
three new large sources: Mexico, France, and Canada. The rise of
French and Canadian sulphur resulted from the discovery of large
sour natural gas fields in these countries, whereas in Mexico the
Frasch method of extraction was employed. The rapid increase in
production for some eight years, especially in sulphur recovered
from sour gas, resulted in oversupply and depressed prices. In 1959
the posted price of sulphur was only 47 per cent above the level
that had prevailed during the depression of the 'thirties, while the
average wholesale price of metals and metal products was 147 per
cent greater than in 1939, and the average of wages in the United
States was 257 per cent greater.

Domestic producers, such as TGS, also found their profits ad-
versely affected by a federal law which prohibited the use of for-
eign-flag vessels for shipment from one domestic port to another.
This meant that sulphur movements to domestic ports from the
Gulf Coast incurred freight charges considerably greater than those
applicable to Mexican supplies reaching domestic ports by foreign
transport. All of the adverse factors, of course, were subject to slow

correction as world consumption of sulphur increased, but the new productive capacity abroad was in the meantime deferring such an adjustment.

As the price of sulphur dropped from around $28 a ton in 1956 to below $20 in 1963, Texas Gulf's earnings dropped every year, from a high of $3.23 a share in 1955 to a low of 93 cents in 1963. The dividend rate, which had been $2 a year in 1955 and 1956, was cut in half in 1957–8 and descended to 40 cents in 1962. Part of the reason for the last cut, according to the management, was the high cost of diversification now under way. On the market the stock had dropped from a high of 45 in the mid-'fifties to a low of 11 in 1963.

Named chief executive officer of Texas Gulf at the close of 1960, Stephens found himself addressing the stockholders in somewhat defensive and unusually explanatory language—reaching a bit for good things to say which would take the edge off lower sales and earnings. Oil and gas production were up, but the company had decided to delay active field work in Australia until a later date, and had completed its lithium studies in North Carolina with no immediate plans for development. Up in the Canadian Arctic, however, an important lead–zinc prospect had been discovered and claimed at Baffin Island, and a drilling and evaluation program was to be undertaken over the next two seasons to determine tonnage and grade. Canada, in fact, continued to be the main target in a number of ways. Exploration crews were using the highly sensitive airborne magnetic equipment, and areas that showed traces of commercial type minerals were being further checked by geological, geophysical, and drilling tests. What appeared to be an important find, a new gas field, had turned up in that Wildhorse Creek area in Alberta.

The most important fact Stephens had to report was the company decision to diversify into the expanding potash field, and the place was Moab, a mining town of 6,000 in southeastern Utah. Rights to 11,400 acres, part of a federal reserve, had been acquired, and it was expected that $30 million would be expended in development and the construction of mining and processing facilities, in the hope of being on the market by the close of 1962. Underway was a 36-mile railroad spur from the plant site to the main line of the Denver, Rio Grande and Western. At one point the track would tunnel through a canyon wall for 7,200 feet. The plant, on which construction began in March, was designed to make it one of the largest domestic producers, and the initial capacity could be increased half as much again. Major diversification number two—if oil and gas could be listed as number one—was thus founded on the apparent need for feeding the growing world population, which was expanding at the rate of 150,000 new mouths per day. Keystone of the effort was artificial plant nutrients, and potash was a basic ingredient. United States consumption had increased sixfold since 1939 and 90 per cent of all potash produced in the country was going into the fertilizer market. It was also a natural complement to the sulphur market.

Unlike sulphur, potash is mined underground by the traditional method of sinking shafts. At Moab the shaft had to go down 2,800 feet. It was circular, 22 feet in diameter, and lined with concrete, and it was one of the largest and deepest shafts ever sunk in North America. Underground development work was not completed, but by the end of 1962 world potash consumption had increased five per cent, exceeding production by some half-million tons, as TGS prepared to enter the market with an initial productive capacity of three per cent of the world demand. While there had been labor troubles in the potash mining area of Carlsbad, New Mexico, and a marked decrease in production from the second largest producer, West Germany, Canada was resuming production, and this was shortly to become a notable factor in the world picture.

Both potash and sulphur set new consumption records in 1962 throughout the world, for the reason that they were essential materials, agriculture taking 94 per cent of all potash. Three-fourths of the sulphur produced went into acid, and 40 per cent of that was needed for chemical fertilizers. Obviously the growth rates for each followed the growth rates for agriculture and industry. The trick was to clear up the problems intervening between mine and user.

One of the significant developments in 1961 had been the upward trend in shipping sulphur in liquid form. It was welcomed by the customers because of the advantages in handling and storing. Half of the TGS shipments were now in this liquid form, compared to one-fifth the preceding year. In January the company had placed in service the first ocean-going vessel to be used exclusively for the transport of liquid sulphur, a 15,000-ton tanker named the "S.S. Marine Sulphur Queen." The ship was operated for Texas Gulf by the Marine Transport Lines. Unfortunately, this was not the last time the "Queen" would be mentioned in dispatches.

On Baffin Island another ocean-going vessel delivered several hundred tons of equipment to the lead–zinc prospect on Strathcona Sound. The crew commenced drilling at once and continued until operations were suspended for the winter. Resumed in the spring, the drilling aggregated 40,000 feet, including a large number of holes, but additional investigation seemed to be necessary to determine commercial worth.

Although the market for lithium did not then justify commercial development, all was not lost in North Carolina. A year of drilling in Beaufort County proved the existence of extensive phosphate deposits, options were secured, and phosphate was designated in 1962 as a development prospect involving mineral, engineering, and market studies, as well as a pilot plant operation. In Alberta, Canada, wells completed at Panther River and Hunter Valley showed substantial gas flows, with possibilities of sulphur recovery, and like the early wells at Wildhorse Creek were capped for later production. Meanwhile the dividend had been cut, and what management would term an "eventful year" was at hand.

## IV

It has been said that in 1963 Texas Gulf Sulphur was at the nadir of its fortunes. It was involved in expensive ventures which, if successful, would still not pay off for some time to come. It had financed them at first from retained earnings but subsequently resorted to borrowing. Sulphur sales were up slightly but earnings were down by about a quarter, partly because of a decrease in export price and partly because of the higher delivery costs—the latter for a reason charged with drama and mystery. Two years after it had been placed in service, in February of 1963, on its 64th voyage en route from Beaumont, Texas, to Norfolk, Virginia, the "Sulphur Queen" was lost without a trace and with all hands in the Florida Straits. In her brief career she had carried over 900,000 long tons of sulphur. Oddly enough, the only clue to where the tanker and its crew of 39 disappeared was supplied by a common seaman who called his broker in Tampa and requested the latter to buy him 5,000 bushels of wheat on the Chicago Board of Trade. The message was signed off at 9:36 P.M. on February 3, and a reply sent the next day was not received. The story of this rather faint clue came out during the SEC's investigation of insider trading on the stock market when a Texas Gulf director was discussing the purchase of company stock by down-the-line employees.

This was not the only dramatic setback in 1963. On August 28 a fatal explosion in the shaft of the potash mine at Moab cost the lives of 25 men employed by the contractor. It also disturbed plans to begin limited production during the year. The mine was essentially undamaged, although certain equipment and machinery had to be replaced and more than a year of time was lost. Economic loss resulting from two such tragedies in a single year could be accepted and countered, and it was, but the loss of so many lives threw long shadows over the men engaged in these undertakings, which would persist for a considerable period to come.

Although the "Sulphur Queen" had been chartered rather than owned by the company, the management took the trouble of investigating and answering the host of rumors and misstatements which naturally followed the tanker's loss. Some of these, coming up during the Coast Guard hearing at Beaumont, were that the ship had a "weak back"; that it had been operated in disregard of regulations; that corrosive conditions and improper maintenance had contributed to the tragedy; that liquid sulphur would explode violently on contact with sea water, and that it was inflammable and explosive. The Coast Guard report issued later, however, was critical of the owners for not giving proper instructions to the ship's master on transporting molten sulphur, and for failure to keep itself informed on matters affecting the vessel's safety. It was noted for the record that ten T-2 tankers had broken apart in the past.

Actually the ship was probably the strongest tanker of her class afloat, having been converted by Bethlehem Steel at great cost and in accordance with Coast Guard recommendations. It had been frequently inspected, and the crew and officers were held in high regard and commended for their efficiency by witnesses at the Beaumont hearing. It was established that there could have been neither a chemical nor a thermal reaction between liquid sulphur and sea water that could have damaged the ship in any way. The industry had handled over 150 million tons of liquid sulphur without serious explosions or fires. None of the debris recovered over a wide area of the Atlantic, and consisting for the most part of life preservers and miscellaneous items, showed any evidence of fire, although much of it could not definitely be attributed to the missing vessel. Even the storms that beset the ship's course were not as severe as those she had previously weathered.[3] The mystery remained.

In spite of the tragedies, in spite of the setback to the potash project, in spite of the fact that the phosphate project was only in a pilot state, and in spite of the fact that the airborne explorers had been mapping anomalies and had drilled 65 of them without any luck, there was another cast to the TGS story in 1963. Utilizing hindsight, the company's position appeared to be almost the reverse of its position in the 'fifties. A decade earlier it had fine earnings but poor prospects. In 1963 it had poor earnings but fine prospects. The incoming tide in its affairs was widely heralded in the fall and winter by a number of announcements, none of which, it was later to seem, had ever been read by either the staff of the Securities and Exchange Commission or the judges of the appellate court. But more of that later.

The October quarterly report said that production and consumption of sulphur were running ten per cent ahead of the year before. On October 29 it was announced that the Barber Oil Company had bought 300,000 shares of TGS in August and September. On November 14 the company announced that its by now $35 million potash mine was near completion and would begin production the following spring. On the occasion of setting up a new phosphate division on November 15—diversification number three—it was pointed out that the North Carolina phosphate reserves were estimated to be ample for many decades and contained high grade ore. On December 16, TGS announced that it had bought a substantial interest in almost 600,000 acres of oil and gas lands in Alberta and British Columbia and called this "another step in the company's diversification program." On December 30, President Stephens' year-end statement reported that "sulphur consumption and production . . . set new records in 1963," and added that "as a result, the outlook for higher prices brightened."

The "M. S. Naess Texas"—the world's largest liquid sulphur tanker, with a capacity of 25,000 long tons—was launched on December 31. It would carry the product to European ports. A sister

[3] The ghost of the "Sulphur Queen" was revived in June, 1969, in federal court in New York, at a hearing before Judge John M. Canella. Before the court was a petition for limitation of liability by the owners, Marine Transport Lines; claims estimated at about $5 million filed by families of the lost crew; and claims for the lost cargo, worth $480,000 and owned by Texas Gulf Sulphur.

ship of the same size was already under construction. The company had also contracted for the "S.S. Marine Texan," with a capacity of 23,670 long tons, to replace the lost "Sulphur Queen."

On February 20, 1964, the company reported that its 1963 sales rose to a four-year high, and expressed its belief that "1963 marks a turning point in the present trend of declining earnings." It again reminded its readers of its potash project in Utah, phosphate in North Carolina, sulphur recovery in Alberta, and even something new—trona in Wyoming. Trona is sodium carbonate-bicarbonate, convertible to soda ash, a basic industrial chemical. Test drilling was about to begin under rights acquired in government land in the Green River area.

On April 1, 1964, TGS announced an important two-dollar mark-up in sulphur prices, the first since 1953. Two days later it said it was going ahead with a $45 million program in North Carolina phosphate, with an open pit mine at Lee Creek on the south bank of the Pamlico River, and soon expected to ship potash from the new Utah mine. It thereupon declared that when phosphate production began in 1966, it would be "the only company in the free world supplying all three of these essential fertilizer components,"—sulphur, potash, and phosphates.

The next important release came on April 12, and it was the one that began all of the company's troubles with the SEC. *Not* announced, and for good reason, had been the fact that on November 12, 1963, after four days of drilling, a crew of the company in the bleak mining country near Timmins, Ontario, had pulled out the final section of a drill core 655 feet long—and it looked good.

It should be noted at this point that stock options under an incentive plan had been granted to 17 key employees back in 1961, at a market price of $24.50, but they had not been exercised for obvious reasons. At the moment the price was hardly an incentive. New options would be granted in 1964 to 26 officers and employees, at a market price of $23.81, and these would be cause for argument.

During the wintry months betweeen November 8, 1963, and April 1, 1964, TGS stock moved up from 17 to 26½; Freeport Sulphur moved from 31½ to 36⅞; and Pan American Sulphur moved from 16⅝ to 31¾. If Texas Gulf stock moved up somewhat faster than that of its largest competitor, Freeport, it could have been because of the blossoming of the diversification program.

V

Having tagged 1963 as an "eventful" year, Stephens did not hesitate to label 1964 as "unusually eventful" for Texas Gulf Sulphur. The distinction was compounded and the accolade awarded on the basis of a number of factors—sales and profits, the exciting fruits of long exploration, substantial moving ahead in the major diversifications, improved marketing and transportation facilities, and the first touch of legal troubles.

TGS followed its regular meeting of the board of directors on April 16 with a press conference to announce a major discovery of zinc, copper, and silver at what it had decided to call its Kidd Creek Mine, 15 miles north of Timmins, Ontario. The announcement, which launched officially an historic scramble for land and shares, had in fact been preceded by an unofficial scramble of rumors and feverish activity, principally in the Canadian mining community, never noted for the slow measures of the minuet when something appeared to be brewing. Back in November, after its first careful and educated guess that it might be on to something good, the company's problem had been at least twofold—it had to prove the guess to its own satisfaction before setting in motion an expensive and possibly hazardous drilling and development program, but first it needed to acquire the rights to more land in the neighborhood for geological testing and core drilling—the initial hole had proved to be uncomfortably close to the boundaries of its present operating area. All of this took a little time, almost right up to the opening moments of the directors' meeting.

Finally it was clear that the metals business, spearheaded by the development of the Kidd Creek Mine, would be diversification number four, and work proceeded on many fronts, including testing and engineering studies, construction of an access road to the barren winterbound site, a survey for railroad connections, and plans for production facilities. In June a metals division was established, and a preliminary reserve estimate of 55 million tons of ore was announced, enough to permit mining for many years. Over 100,000 feet of drilling had been completed. All was not progressively serene, however, because before the year was out two lawsuits were filed in Ontario questioning Texas Gulf's right to retain ownership of the ore body. One of them asked for damages of $50 million, plus handing over the property, or—alternatively— payment of $450 million. The other sought reversion of title for a critical part of the mining area.

These rather substantial clouds on the Canadian horizon undoubtedly gave management cause for thought as it reviewed the
spiraling costs of its other businesses. Stephens took occasion, while
highlighting the spectacular success of the exploring team in Ontario, to point out that ". . . it should not overshadow significant
events of the year in other areas of our planned program." All of
the company's achievements were related and complementary, and
the company's business was not only the production of minerals,
but selling and delivering them to the customer, in which transportation played a major role. The development of major natural resources "involve related technologies and experience in exploration,
mining, processing, transportation, and marketing." For really the
first time "on stream"—as the mining engineers say—TGS was announcing that it was no longer just a sulphur company.

Nevertheless, the consumption of free world sulphur in 1964
had exceeded production by nearly a million tons, and for the company the price increase of two dollars a ton, getting back to the
level of 1957, was the prime reason for a 23 per cent improvement
in profits. In the next four years earnings would multiply six times,
and sales would more than quadruple. The ability to serve customers was further improved in 1964 as most of the sulphur was
delivered in liquid form by ships, barges, tank cars, and trucks, and
the network of shipping terminals was increased to twelve. Liquid
sulphur service was extended overseas as a terminal was established in Rotterdam and another was under construction in Dublin.
Two overseas tankers went into service.

That was not all. The Cane Creek potash mine finally began
operation in the latter part of the year near Moab, in the scenically
spectacular canyon lands along the Colorado River. The decision
to proceed from pilot plant to major operation at the Lee Creek phosphate mine in North Carolina involved considerable rearranging of
the landscape, digging new channels to divert existing streams and
filling new areas for an airstrip and buildings. Production would
begin at the rate of three million tons a year. With capital expenditures in excess of $30 million for the year, and a lot more to come,
it was necessary to obtain $55 million in long-term financing, and
no wonder.

In fact, TGS spent almost $60 million for capital purposes in
1965 and was looking forward to topping $100 million in 1966,
as it moved along on all of the new fronts. For one thing, it had
tentatively agreed, subject to later ratification, to pay $24 million

under an arrangement with the Curtis Publishing Company (which was having troubles of its own) to acquire all of the Curtis property in Ontario's Kidd Township, including a ten per cent interest in part of the Kidd Creek Mine. This would mean the acquisition of 110,000 acres of mineral and timber lands in Ontario, and 141,000 acres in Pennsylvania.

In North Carolina plans to double the phosphate capacity had been announced even before the start of its first full-scale production, and now TGS decided to add facilities for turning half of the Lee Creek Mine's output into wholesale fertilizers. This increased the total investment to around $80 million and made it one of the largest mines in the world to be brought into commercial development in recent years. The company's fifth Frasch sulphur mine was completed in late 1965 at Gulf, Texas, the site of its original sulphur production in 1919, while the first year's operations of the Cane Creek mine at Moab confirmed it as one of the largest and most important sources of potash in the United States. That, as things turned out, could be a mixed blessing. In Wyoming, evaluation of the trona deposits had been completed, and plans were made for a mine and processing plant. Building a concentrator and related facilities at the Kidd Creek Mine would push the company's metals investment there to around $60 million.

Lest it seem that everything was going without a hitch in the latter 'sixties, however, the rough side of the ledger produced some unhappy entries. At the end of 1965 a number of companies had successfully bid and paid a total of $33.7 million to the U.S. government for leases and the right to explore for sulphur on 72,000 acres of underwater lands in the Gulf of Mexico. TGS, together with the Gulf Oil Corporation, acquired in a combined bid 10,080 acres for $2.5 million. This offshore exploration was completed in the fall of 1966, when 14 holes were drilled without finding sulphur in commercial quantities. The leases were returned to the government and all costs written off.

Then again, after several months of questions and answers and the other accoutrements of investigation, the Securities and Exchange Commission, somewhat unexpectedly, brought a complaint against the company and 13 individuals on April 19, 1965, in the United States district court for the Southern District of New York, charging violation of Section 10(b) and Rule 10b-5 of the Securities Exchange Act of 1934. The government agency sought to enjoin the corporation permanently from "making or omitting to make" untrue or true statements of material facts, respectively, concerning its activities and operations; to enjoin the individual defendants from buying or selling securities on the basis of inside information not available to others; to order the latter to rescind transactions already made and, in certain cases, to make restitution to those from whom they had purchased TGS stock; and finally, ordering nullification of all stock options issued to the individual defendants, unexercised as of a certain date, and to return any profits obtained. Essentially, the SEC claimed the company's release on April 12, 1964, to have been false and misleading in respect to the discovery of the ore body near Timmins, and that several "insiders" had profited unfairly by purchasing stock and giving tips to others before the true state of affairs had been disclosed to the public.

Hard on the heels of this development, the company and others were named defendants in numerous suits by former stockholders who sold shares during the period in question. Taken together with the suits already filed in Canadian courts questioning title to the mine, the SEC and stockholder actions made it certain beyond a reasonable doubt that Texas Gulf Sulphur was in for another major diversification—this time in the courts. What was not so immediately apparent was that the proceedings would involve and affect the entire business and financial community, and mobilize lawyers, directly and indirectly, from all over North America, in frenzied efforts to untangle and interpret the state of the law as a result of recent findings.

Meanwhile, at the close of 1966 the total revenues of TGS were the highest in the company's history and earnings were up 55 per cent. Capital expenditures had also reached an all-time high —approximately $140 million—and this required further outside financing, bringing the total at year-end to more than $146 million. As the concentrator at Hoyle began late in the year to produce the first dividends from the new mine in the form of zinc and copper concentrates, and the outline of the Kidd Creek open pit mine took shape, both mine and concentrator were transferred to a wholly-owned subsidiary, Ecstall Mining Ltd., with Fogarty as president. The new company derived its name from the first Canadian mining property acquired by Texas Gulf in 1937.

Bringing the company at least a limited amount of cheer, Judge Dudley B. Bonsal, in the New York federal court, dismissed the charges brought against it and eleven of the individual defendants by the SEC. That agency, and the remaining two individuals, immediately appealed, as hearings continued in Canada on the civil actions disputing title.

Sulphur, which had continued to account for most of the company's earnings as prices continued to recover from the depressed levels of the past decade, for the first time saw its position challenged. With sales and earnings in 1967 the highest in the company's history by a wide margin, the greatest increase was from metals. Ecstall, the new subsidiary, mined and milled more than its design capacity of three million tons of ore, although the facilities were not yet at full speed during a full year. It was ironic that, at least in the public view, progress in realizing the fruits of the spectacular mining discovery in Canada went largely unnoticed. The big news about Texas Gulf Sulphur, for almost everybody except the company's management, was stalled back at the first drill hole of November, 1963, as legal actions waxed and raged and public media batted the story back and forth. While time stood still in the courtrooms and editorial offices, the landscape around Timmins had been so drastically altered as to make it unrecognizable as some $55 million was poured into new facilities. All of this, of course, had something to do with the hindsight judgment that would soon affect official and unofficial convictions.

Not all of the action was in Canada and the Texas sulphur country by any means. In North Carolina the phosphate mine and plant complex now included six different operations, each of which had demonstrated its ability to operate at design capacity or better by late 1967. A substantial inventory of phosphate rock was available to supply fertilizer materials plants at Lee Creek, and it appeared that the world-wide demand for the mine's products might double or triple in the ongoing decade.

Out at Moab the potash operation mined and milled considerably in excess of its initial goal of 4,000 tons per day, and production costs were greatly reduced, but gratification at these developments was tempered by severely depressed prices resulting from large increases in Canadian production. Prices had broken as much as 35 per cent in two years. The outlook was hardly encouraging since even more facilities were getting into the act in Canada. At the end of 1968 the division operated at a loss despite important improvements in efficiency and reductions in operating costs, because of the flood of low-cost potash from Saskatchewan and Europe. In a move to join, if it could not beat, TGS examined some

prospects in Saskatchewan, and acquired and explored three extensive blocks of land, while with the other hand it investigated the
chances of buying an interest in a going Canadian potash mine.
In April, 1969, it acquired a 40 per cent ownership in the Allan
Potash Mine near Saskatoon, paying $6 million in cash to pro-
vide some low-cost competitive production to hedge its bets at Moab.
And in 1970 the decision was made to convert to the more economical solution mining process, with completion expected in the
middle of the following year. This meant that the present mine
would be flooded with water, the resulting brine containing both
potash and salt would be withdrawn through drilled wells for solar
evaporation in specially constructed ponds, and the results would
be processed. Moab, it seemed, had played a rather unhappy obbli-
gato to the Kidd Creek Mine, where good progress was now being
made on underground installations and the construction of a zinc
plant. But that's mining.

Near Black's Fork River in southwestern Wyoming work had
begun at the close of 1967 on a 1,500-foot mine shaft for the trona
deposit. This depth was reached in 1969 and shortly test mining
would proceed. The 140,000 acres of Pennsylvania woodland acquired from the Curtis Publishing Company had now become the
Armstrong Forest division. The area affected was not only valuable
timberland but embraced some oil and gas production. Another
wholly-owned subsidiary, the Australian Inland Exploration Company, with headquarters in Perth, was granted a concession to
prospect for nickel, lead, silver, zinc, and copper in 540 square
miles of crown land by the government of Western Australia. In
1968 it carried out airborne geophysical surveys and geological
studies, and extensive drilling was done on a copper-zinc-silver
prospect at Mons Cupri. The word here, as it had long been at
Baffin Island, was "more drilling will be required."

Fifty years after its incorporation, Texas Gulf Sulphur was still
very strong on exploration. Discovery was the sharp edge of the
knife that later might be dulled by accidents, depressed prices, new
competition, or excess stocks. These were problems for another
group, in another part of the forest, and would be met when they
showed their heads. From its headquarters in Toronto, the exploration division under Walter Holyk (who had also made the scene
as a defendant in the SEC action) directed activities in Houston,
Calgary, Tucson, Vancouver, Carlsbad, Mexico City, and Antofo-
gasta. It was drilling in west Texas and New Mexico and in the

Blind River area of Lake Huron—the latter confined to a season when ice would support the drill rigs. It was about to investigate a 1,330 square mile tract in Newfoundland, and the company was beginning to become interested in exploring for oil, gas, and minerals in Africa. The annual meeting of stockholders had approved a three-for-one stock split, and Dr. Fogarty, the friendly and loquacious moving spirit behind most of the exploratory expansion and diversification, moved up to become president of the company, as Stephens became chairman.

Back at the "first hole" the lengthy litigation brought by two Canadian companies challenging title to the Kidd Creek Mine came to an end in the Supreme Court of Ontario, and on November 29, 1968, was decided in favor of Texas Gulf. Management drew a long breath of relief, which was needed both for morale and for somewhat sturdier reasons, because the Second Circuit court in New York, situs of the appeal in the SEC proceedings, reversed in most respects the trial court's decision, which had favored the company and all but two of the individual defendants. It was what Chairman Stephens might have termed a "most eventful" decision.

Another wry note arose from the circumstances of the "other" Canadian lawsuit challenging title. Trustees for the Hendrie Estate were contesting, since 1966, the company's rights with respect to a *portion* of the Kidd Creek Mine. During 1968 the income from that portion of the mine represented approximately one-third of TGS' consolidated net income, and this was duly noted in the annual report, a somewhat unorthodox touch but one intending, no doubt, to put the shareholders on notice that they had better keep their eye on the box score.

Four categories of figures, covering the ten years from 1959 through 1968, documented the longtime performance and league standing of Texas Gulf Sulphur, although it could be said that the play-by-play accounts were considerably more exciting. Sales had gone from $63.6 million to $310 million; earnings from $13.3 to a low of $9.4 million in 1963, and then up to $70.5 million; total assets had been $123.6 million in 1959, and were now $523.6 million; plant, property and equipment had risen from $33.3 to $293.4 million. In this time the stockholders' equity had improved from $111,625,000 to $296,867,000. There were now 62,000 stockholders, and something over 30 million shares outstanding after the split.

Students of the modern corporation who tend to doodle during the recital of statistics, and who perhaps are more interested in the play-by-play than in the league standings, might have been somewhat intrigued by the portrait studies of Stephens, first as president and later as chairman, which were usually a feature of the company's annual reports. In 1959, in fact, there had been no portrait, but the ice was broken in 1960 with a group photograph of Stephens, Fogarty, and Frank Tippie, the project manager at Moab, as they leaned somewhat cautiously over a table model of the potash mine. It was a side view and the expressions were equivocal, justifiably so as things turned out. The year 1961 presented a black and white, and markedly sombre, portrait of Stephens alone, but with no lines of worry showing. The 1962 representation was in sepia, with an added degree of sobriety—earnings were down, the dividend had been cut, and a ship had disappeared before the annual meeting. In the eventful year of 1963 the president was very sober in black and white because earnings were down more, costs were up, new financing was being arranged, and there had been a tragic explosion at the potash mine. Stephens appeared in full color in a blue suit and red tie in most eventful 1964, still sober in mien, but he appeared to be waiting for something. There had been the spectacular Timmins discovery, sulphur prices had gone up, the step into phosphate had been undertaken, and there were the first legal actions filed questioning ownership of the mine. "At Bay" would have been a good short title. The portrait went to black and white in 1965, possibly because of the SEC complaint. Other things were beginning to break, sales and earnings were up, and diversification was proceeding. From then on it was all full color; 1966 exhibited his relaxed smile and satisfaction with the highest revenues in company history. Also the SEC complaint had been dismissed, although appeal was coming on. In the following year the smile was even better because Kidd Creek Mine was making money as well as trouble, while 1968's smile was pointed slightly at heaven, as befitted a successful chairman. All three of the last years featured a green suit and a green tie, which might raise a question as to whether the chief executive of TGS was superstitious. Or, harking back to the sales and earnings, it may just have been the color of money.

As for 1959, there may have been no picture to titillate the shareowners when they first opened the company's annual report, but there had been quite a picture in the mind of Dr. Fogarty. The onetime Denver orphan had made considerable progress and there were now eight children in the suburban home in Rye on Christmas morning. After the early morning excitement, father retired to his room and locked the door. There he stayed until a late hour working on a memorandum which he was later to style his "Christmas plan." It had much to do with changing the future course of Texas Gulf Sulphur.

Dr. Fogarty's sense of urgency in committing his vision of the future to paper was sparked by a business proposition which had been put before the directors, and which the latter were seriously considering. Another company was proposing a merger in which TGS might have been swallowed up and its identity lost. Stephens and Fogarty made a keen analysis of that offer, and the company's capabilities and its long-range goals, and did not care much for it. "We sincerely believed that our shareholders would benefit far more by letting Texas Gulf follow its own route rather than being merged," Fogarty said.

> In 1959 our stock was low, and the sulphur picture wasn't as bright as it could be. During this period Texas Gulf was often looked at by other companies as an attractive acquisition. The company could have been acquired for relatively little money. This would not have been in the best interest of the shareholders because our reserves in the ground were not being given their true value. Neither were our assets in people. We had skilled people in mining, in exploration, in management ability, and in sales. We felt we had the opportunity to make Texas Gulf into a great basic natural resources company.

The "Christmas plan" proceeded to set out the expansion of exploration activities into related resources, naming phosphate, potash, oil and gas, and sulphide ores containing valuable minerals. In one section Fogarty wrote: "Long-range exploration may be costly and fraught with many failures. Money will be spent on projects which prove valueless. Other projects may have to be financed that will not be productive for several years. It requires patience, perseverance, understanding, and foresight. Nothing, however, is so rewarding as a valuable mineral discovery."

The last ten words had already turned out to be rather pertinent. Christmas had come and gone in the Fogarty home, and also in Kidd Township in Ontario, and it would take quite a while to unwrap all the presents.

# 2
# The Mine:
# Stage One

I

$\mathbf{S}$OME eight to ten thousand years ago, when the last continental glacier had receded from what is now eastern Canada, it left behind a vast lake covering tens of thousands of square miles of the smooth and flattened surface later to be known as the Canadian Shield. Streams carried billions of tons of fine sediment into the lake, where it settled to the bottom and built up clay beds, which, in some instances, are more than 300 feet thick. This clay belt, on the authority of Hugh D. Carlson, resident geologist for the Ontario department of mines, obscures bedrock geology throughout a vast region which acts as host country for deposits of copper, zinc, silver, gold, nickel, asbestos, and magnesite.[1]

Although Champlain may have reported the presence of iron and silver as early as 1604, in the Precambrian rocks forming part of the Canadian Shield and covering much of Ontario, the mineral wealth of that province went almost unexploited for nearly 300 years. Even then accidents seemed to play a major role in dis-

[1] *Report of the Royal Commission to Investigate Trading in the Shares of Windfall Oils and Mines Ltd.*; Hugh D. Carlson: "Brief History of Mineral Exploration and Development in the Porcupine Area, Ontario," Appendix A, 1965, p. 123.

covery. Mining and prospecting is that kind of business, or was, until the advent of modern scientific methods. In 1909, for example, gold was discovered in the famous Porcupine Camp when a prospector stumbled, while a few years earlier an engineer's mistake led to the discovery of great nickel deposits. Porcupine Camp lies along the southern edge of the so-called clay belt of northeastern Ontario and northwestern Quebec.

The construction in 1903 of the Temiskaming and Northern Ontario Railway, which was designed to aid promising agricultural and lumbering undertakings, led to the discovery of rich silver veins, and the result was the development of the famous Cobalt silver district. Earlier still, the location engineer for the Canadian Pacific Railway had mistakenly, it is said, run the new line north of Lake Ramsey, instead of south of it, as planned, and the grading crew uncovered a considerable deposit of mineralized rock. That led to the Murray mine at Sudbury, and an eventual development that became the source of more than half of the free world's nickel output. Finally, in 1909, it was also told of a prospector named Harry Preston that he slipped on a moss-covered rock knoll, his heel scraped off the moss, and there was revealed a quartz vein flecked with gold. The Preston prospecting group followed a wide 21-foot ledge along to a dome-shaped outcropping, and after the moss had been stripped off, it glittered with gold. Ultimately this became the Dome mine, famed as having a "golden stairway" because the vein was so rich it was quarried rather than mined. Dome Mines Ltd. is still the biggest gold mine in the area, with an annual output close to $7 million.

The first really big mining boom had come at Cobalt, however, and miners who had learned their business there fanned out to range the whole Shield, thus paving the way for the gold discoveries. In the past half century more than a score of mines, according to Carlson, have produced upwards of $1.5 billion in gold from the Porcupine, making it far and away the most productive gold mining district in the western hemisphere. The Dome, together with the Hollinger and McIntyre mines, which all developed from surface showings uncovered by venturesome prospectors, comprised three of the greatest gold deposits in Canada. The Timmins brothers, who had made their fortunes at Cobalt, took over the Hollinger mine, and Noah Timmins founded the town bearing his name, which included the mine in its boundaries. The Hollinger mines are now closed down. Prior to its birth the town area had

been a wilderness, but before long the producing mines developed
a community of some 30,000 people and for a half century fed its
prosperity. Inevitably all mines decline, as ores are depleted and are
less profitable to work, and after 50 years the ore reserves of these
major mines were nearing exhaustion. Timmins, in the late 'fifties,
was rapidly becoming a ghost town and its future was not very
bright. Not until 1964 would the prospecting fever again run
high.

In order to promote colonization and encourage the early development of agriculture in this region, early in this century, the
provincial government had made generous land grants to veterans
of the Fenian Raids, the Boer War and the First World War. These
grants included surface rights, plus timber and mineral rights.
Some of the land grant properties were never farmed, because of
the harsh and unfavorable conditions, and some are still held by
heirs and descendants of the original grantees. Many of them,
during the years of depression, were acquired at low cost by
lumber companies. The long lag in successful mining exploration
in more modern times, in the region lying to the north of the
Porcupine gold camp, has been attributed to the fact that much of
the region was privately owned and was thus not available for
public staking of claims. Also, difficulties arose because the bedrock was extensively covered by a thick mantle of glacial debris.

It was in this historic mining territory that the exploration
team of Texas Gulf Sulphur Company made its first successful
drill hole in 1963, on land that had been given to a veteran of the
Boer War. Uncounted and nameless prospectors spent much of
their lifetimes in this area, most of them reaping disappointment
and some dying in the field. One of these, according to local legend,
froze to death seeking a very rich lode which he was sure was
nearby. He had lived for years in a cabin about 700 yards from
the spot where TGS sank its first hole, and the hut and his
abandoned belongings were found by the first Texas Gulf staff
people to arrive on the scene in 1959.

This spectacular discovery of metal-bearing ores, added to the
growing suspicions of its imminence, touched off a chain of events
of wide consequence. For one thing, it resparked the primeval urge
for quick wealth, the unquenchable optimism of the mining fraternity, and the hopes of the people of Timmins, now resurgent, for
a new lease on life for their community. There followed a staking

rush [2] with frantic efforts to acquire property. Some hard evidence of this can be found in the files of the mining recorder at Timmins; in 1963 there had been filed about 1,995 claims, but in 1964 there were over 20,000 claims, at least half of them occurring in the first four months.

Of the many mining companies whose shares, following the TGS discovery period, left an erratic and disturbing record of market fluctuations, those of Windfall Oils and Mines Ltd., were without doubt the most spectacular. The rise in the shares during July of 1964 was almost unparalleled in height and duration, and their sudden drop left many shaken and poorer for the experience. The direct result, in fact, was the appointment by Queen Elizabeth II of a Royal Commission to look into the matter in August of that year.

It was later pointed out, in the introduction to the so-called Windfall Report, that while the "softening effect of urbanization, and the increased emphasis on technology in prospecting, have somewhat dulled the sense of personal participation which marked the earlier mineral discoveries," this has been balanced by the increasing number of persons involved in mining development by the purchase of shares. "Thus, in addition to the 'rush' to the scene of the mineral discovery, there follows a secondary rush to the stock markets; and through the merchandising methods of the financial industry, there is a widespread effort to secure as buyers of mining company shares, willing people who would not otherwise become involved in mine finding and mine making." [3] It was this "secondary rush" that would be a major factor in the unrolling of the Texas Gulf case, and not alone in Canada.

## II

In the succinct words of Chief Justice George Gale of the Supreme Court of Ontario, following the trial of one of the thornier issues that was to follow the Texas Gulf discovery, [4]

---

[2] Mining claims on crown land and mining rights which are crown property may be staked by the holder of a miner's license, obtainable by anyone over 18, on payment of $5 and written application in prescribed form. Each licensee may stake 90 mining claims (each of about 40 acres) in a license year (April 1 through March 31) but not more than 18 in any one of Ontario's 14 mining divisions.

[3] *Op. cit.*, p. 38; p. 1.

[4] From the Opinion, p. 4, *Leitch Gold Mines Ltd. & Mastodon Highland Bell Mines Ltd. v. Texas Gulf Sulphur Co. & Ecstall Mining Ltd.* (1968),

"A mining exploration program is an ever-narrowing process of selection, beginning with the choice of certain large areas for aerial survey and ending with the selection of a drill site." It was an apt text.

Under an earlier management, under different conditions, and some 23 years before the emergence of the Fogarty "Christmas plan," the hard beginnings of the Texas Gulf activities in the exploring and mining of metals probably date from 1936, when the company had acquired a property on the Ecstall River in British Columbia. The name would survive as the trail led eventually to Timmins and Kidd Township in Ontario. In any concentrated and detailed account of a single important venture, such as the Kidd Creek Mine, it is inevitable that observers will lose sight of the fact that this was only one of many undertakings being carried on simultaneously by the company, and not at first a very important one. In the main, the thrust of the search was always for more sulphur. And even more in later days, amidst the various legal uproars that pursued the sinking of a drill hole in the barren and wintry country near Timmins, the same observers could be pardoned for losing sight of the total industry picture. At this point their company also included members of the judiciary and many unofficial commentators.

Texas Gulf's exploration in British Columbia in 1936 did prove the existence of large bodies of pyrite copper-zinc ore, but the venture was interrupted by the frenetic confusions of the Second World War. Geologic work was resumed in 1952, and in 1957 and 1958 some interesting sulphide ore prospects were discovered on this property. But there had also been a sulphide prospect in Mexico, in 1951, and a pyrite property was optioned by TGS in New Brunswick in 1953. The latter was dropped after some drilling, however. These were the beginnings of the geologic program, as such.

Baffin Island, in the Canadian Arctic, made its appearance in the company records about this time. Richard D. Mollison, then manager of exploration, recalls that there had been obtained from the office of the Canadian Geological Survey certain reports of abundant pyrites in this region, leading to its first consideration in 1955. Two years later the first trip was made, and Baffin Island claims were staked for metallic ores. Fogarty dates the company's official exploration program for mineral sulphides in northern Ontario from 1957, as the company was again seeking alternate sources of sulphur—the old refrain. He describes the Canadian Shield area as extending for hundreds of thousands of square miles, and notes that for this effort the chain of command then extended from him to Mollison as manager of exploration, then to chief geologist Holyk, then to geologist Dr. Leo Miller, whose job was field evaluation. All of them were destined to move up in the organization as a direct result of their teamwork here. Holyk, who would figure largely in events to follow, was from Revelstoke, British Columbia, and had been a World War II flying officer with the Royal Canadian Air Force. He graduated from the University of British Columbia in geological engineering but obtained his doctorate in geology from Massachusetts Institute of Technology. Eventually he would become vice president in charge of exploration. Mollison would become a vice president and head of the forthcoming metals division, while Miller would become president of an Australian subsidiary. Fogarty himself would become president of the parent company. But all of this was over a big hill.

Aerial reconnaissance, as an effective modern tool for surveying the rocky and muskeg-covered areas, had been considered and adopted by the company—it was certainly the farthest cry from the heel-scrapings of the early prospectors. After some experience with contract flying employing the planes of others, Mollison came to the conclusion, in the spring of 1957, that airborne electromagnetic surveys constituted the most effective method of looking for metallic sulphides, and that they would gain much greater flexibility if the exploration group owned its own equipment and could assign it freely. Fogarty approved, and H. V. W. Donohoo, Texas Gulf's chief geophysicist, was in charge of the project in which steps were taken to have the electronic components of the electromagnetic system designed and built into a helicopter by Varian Associates of Palo Alto, California. Donohoo, who later became a vice president, had broad electronics experience with the U.S. Army in World War II and the Korean War.

The procedure was that recommendations would be submitted by the exploration group; these would be studied and evaluated by others in the department, and a decision to fly an area might result. The decision might not be final, and it would sometimes be altered because geological considerations might influence them to extend the direction and scope of the area. In this manner, as Justice Gale was to recall in his opinion on the Leitch case, 19 areas in Ontario and Quebec were established for airborne examination over a period of three years by Texas Gulf. This was part of the closing-in, the "ever narrowing process of selection." These areas varied in size and shape from one, termed "Groundhog River," which measured eight by four miles, to one called "Holliday La Flamme," which was ten miles wide and 112 miles long.

For the flight survey, aerial photographs would usually be purchased, possibly from the government, and pieced together in a mosaic. The boundaries were then drawn in, and also the proposed flight paths, about a quarter of a mile apart. The direction the aircraft would take would be indicated. The mosaics were then cut into "flight strips" for convenience in handling in the plane. Flights were made, as a matter of policy, at a constant air speed and height, so far as possible.

The helicopter used in the aerial surveys held two persons, a pilot and a navigator. Its equipment was designed to find locations which produced electromagnetic responses indicating mineral deposits, and included an aerial camera, a recorder, and an intervalometer. The latter served to provide the time relationships for the pictures and the electromagnetic information put on the tape. Any deviation from the norm was termed an "anomalous reading" and the ground point became an *anomaly*—a word which would be added to the vocabularies of many non-miners during the next few years. The navigator maintained a flight log, and it was TGS practice to keep the camera in operation at all times after ferrying the helicopter from its base. The result showed, therefore, all shifts from one flight strip to another. Weekly reports were prepared with a summary of the airborne data, as well as anomaly evaluation sheets, and these were sent from the field of operations to the exploration department headquarters. Finally, an AEM, or airborne electromagnetic map, would be compiled, and all such data was labeled and stored for future use and reference. If details such as these seem boring to the general reader, they should at least warm the cockles of TGS shareholders, since they helped to save almost a half billion dollars in Ontario's Supreme Court.

Some of the other methods employed in moving up on prospects—or at least *potential* prospects, since "prospect" is a term of rather precise definition in this business—are worth noting. These would include ground exploration methods, gravity tests, and drilling. They also belong to the second phase of the activity, in the sense that aerial reconnaissance may be carried on *without* staked claims or property options, whereas very much in the way of ground follow-up, and certainly drilling, has as its condition precedent the right to invade such ground. Considerable time may elapse between air and ground operations.

A ground exploration crew, having taken off the shelf the airborne survey, could conduct tests at plotted locations, to see if they were correctly positioned on the map, and to determine, if possible, the cause of the anomalous readings obtained from the air. In this process grid lines are customarily cleared on the earth's surface, and investigations are then conducted with reference to them and in order to relate to the airborne survey. In the *magnetic test,* the magnetometer employed will respond to deposits of iron ore and iron sulphides. The *gravity test,* on the other hand, employs a gravimeter to find shallow and massive sulphide deposits. It is thus able to distinguish between sulphide deposits and graphite, whereas the magnetometer cannot, and the method is therefore useful in appraising the *value* of an anomaly. There are other types of ground electromagnetic methods. Texas Gulf's crew only rarely used a *geochemical survey,* which will analyze several soil samples for copper and zinc content. Mollison has said that the gravity method is theoretically attractive, but that in the experience of TGS its utility seemed somewhat limited in terms of results. In short, drilling is the quickest and best way to get an answer.

And if the other investigations are favorable, drilling will almost certainly follow. The holes are placed in relation to the grid lines. The location and angle of each drill hole are decided in advance, but the depth of the hole will depend on what is found as the work progresses. The drilled cores are generally in the range of ten to 20 feet long, and are one and one-eighth inches in diameter. When brought out, the cores are then broken to fit into core boxes, are immediately placed in such boxes, and are logged by a geologist according to rock type, mineralization, and similar characteristics. In effect, this is a rough assay performed on the spot. The cores showing any significant mineralization are split in half lengthwise, one half being sent for assay and the other kept for reference and further study. As Justice Gale was also to note in his opinion, "It is the assay results which finally determine whether or not an economic mineral deposit has been discovered." The drilling of several holes on a promising site is what eventually determines the depth and the dimensions of an ore body, and it is at this point that the second phase of successful exploration has come to its logical close.

In 1958 Dr. Miller prepared a general report to the company recommending nine areas which he deemed of first priority for field examination in the Canadian Shield. One of these he called the "Alexo Basin"—it was some 40 miles long and 12 miles wide, and included both the Timmins and the Prosser-Geary areas. Miller had done his field work early in the summer of this year and made his report on July 17. On one page of it he referred to a sulphide zone in the northeastern part of Kidd Township, 1,000 feet long and 50 feet wide. One day soon it would prove of the greatest significance to his company. Mollison, as head of the exploration department, evaluated it along with chief geologist Holyk and chief geophysicist Donohoo, and they approved an aerial survey. Miller's name for this area gradually changed to the "Timmins area," although earlier it had also been termed "Sulphides 88." Several hundred feet east of an emergent rock formation called the "Martin outcrop" there would someday soon be a mine. It the meantime aerial photographs were ordered from the Ontario department of lands and forests. Because these had originally been taken in 1946, and there had been intervening lumbering activities which altered the topography, there would be some problems later in locating the anomalies on the ground. Next year was problem year.

The new helicopter, now fully equipped, finally arrived in Toronto on February 11, 1959, and after it was checked over by the exploration staff it reached Timmins on March 2. The next day four "test" flights were made, one of them passing over the Kidd zone. But on March 4 the helicopter crashed, putting an abrupt although temporary ending to the proceedings. Eventually the airborne surveys were resumed on June 5, and were completed for the whole area on July 3.

Actually the anomaly which later turned out to be the Kidd Creek Mine was detected on three occasions in 1959. First of these was the Miller "test" flight on March 3, before the crash, and the second detection was on June 17, after flights had been resumed. The second detection left some doubts, however, because the geophysicist, Richard H. Clayton, was acting as navigator and had been adjusting the equipment at the time. To clear the situation Clayton went along on a reflight on July 2. As a matter of historical interest, the anomaly was detected two more times during the following year. While doing flights over nearby areas the exploration group thought it might be possible to add to their information, and did so. After that the crew moved many miles away, to the James Bay area, for other surveys. In August of 1961 a magnetic test of the anomaly produced negative results, and this seems to have discouraged some of the personnel. Three and a half years later, months after the details of the mine had officially been made known, other magnetic tests yielded favorable results.

By the winter of 1961–62 the exploration of all anomalies which Texas Gulf proposed to examine had been completed, except for those on patented lands. From this point, until October of 1963, no exploration work was done in the Timmins area, the TGS personnel and equipment being engaged for the most part at Baffin Island. Interest had necessarily shifted to the Arctic, where claims had been staked, for a very practical reason—the number of people available for these tasks was somewhat limited, and operating decisions were largely controlled by the budget for the work. This was the time of declining earnings, low sulphur prices, and reduced dividends. Air reconnaissance, and some ground exploration, had picked up conductors in the Kidd area, however, and those selected for drilling were on private lands. One of the landowners was the Curtis Publishing Company, then awash with serious troubles of its own. Sometime after the March flights in 1959 attempts had been made to ground-locate the anomaly which had attracted special attention, and this was done more accurately now during the summer and fall. Kenneth Darke, one of the geologists in the exploration group, had made sketches and reported his conclusions. Complementing the sketches, Dr. Miller sent a memorandum to Mollison on April 2 in which he set out the names of the owners of the two half-lots containing the Kidd anomaly.

What later came to be the mine ore body, although its determination was still well in the future, lay partly in each of the following properties in Kidd Township:

—The south half of lot 3, originally granted to the Boer War veteran, was owned by the Roberts Estate.
—The north half of lot 3 was owned by the Murray Hendrie Estate, and the executor was the Royal Trust Company of Toronto.
—The south half of lot 4 was owned by T. S. Woollings and

Company Ltd., which was a subsidiary of Curtis Publishing Company.
—The north half of lot 4 was owned by the Elliott Estate. As matters turned out, it does not yet contain any part of the mine, but was nevertheless acquired in the land program.

With the completion of his evaluation, Dr. Miller had finished his particular assignment, moved on to the company's new phosphate project in North Carolina, and out of the developing Canadian picture. He was a Californian, with a doctorate in geology from Columbia.

During the summer of 1959 Texas Gulf had seen fit to alter its policy in respect to land acquisition, and it adopted a practice that was generally used by the Canadian mining industry. This practice was to offer a land vendor some cash plus a net profit interest as a consideration for an option on the property. Subsequent negotiations for the land in the Kidd area were carried out with this practice in mind.

As Fogarty said, getting land is critical, otherwise there can be no drilling. On July 27 Holyk began his cautious efforts, telephoning and writing the solicitor for the Roberts Estate, W. J. S. Knox, and expressing an interest in optioning the property. The caution, which also reflected the fact that Texas Gulf actually had at this time no real knowledge of an ore deposit, shows in the terms of the first offer—a suggested two-year agreement at a price of $25,000. There would be a down payment of $200, followed by $300 on the renewal for the second year. The balance would be paid on actually exercising the option, if this were done. Nothing happened right away, in any case, and many more attempts would be made.

## III

What might now appear to be an inexplicable hiatus in pressing the search for metals in the vicinity of Timmins —at least to those following only the story of the Kidd Creek Mine— was not in fact that at all. In 1960 Texas Gulf was busy following up its lead-zinc prospect at Baffin Island and contemplating a two-season drilling and evaluation program there. It was also looking into matters in Australia, and in Canada, north of Calgary, it had discovered a new gas field at Wildhorse Creek. It was doing research on hydrocarbon gases. And it was beginning a slow, almost stately approach to acquiring land in Kidd Township, as has been noted.

On January 24, 1961, Holyk telephoned the people at Royal Trust who were trustees for the Hendrie Estate. They negotiated gently back and forth for more than a year until February 14, 1962—Valentine's Day—at which point the draft of a proposed option agreement was sent to A. E. Love, of the trust company. He retained it until May, when several new points were raised regarding the terms. Early in June TGS agreed to the changes and sent a revised agreement incorporating them. Nothing happened until the *next* Valentine's Day, in 1963, when Holyk once more petitioned Love, whose name so neatly coincided with the date. On March 1 the secretary of Royal Trust, F. M. Henderson, replied to say that they were still considering an option and hoped to reply definitely "within a couple of weeks." The weeks stretched until May 24, when Henderson sent back another revised draft featuring several changes. He suggested that if it were acceptable, it should be executed and returned with a check for $500 as consideration for the option. It was then returned on June 10, with the requested check, but approved and initialed several days earlier on May 27— Fogarty's birthday, incidentally. Texas Gulf now had its option on a critical piece of land and could proceed to see what might lie beneath it, but this did not end the negotiations with Royal Trust. Subsequently Texas Gulf tried to buy back the ten per cent interest. These attempts were abortive, however, and eventually Stephens exercised the option and purchased the land on April 9, 1964, just a week before what was to become a rather famous meeting of the board of directors in New York. The whole process had taken three years and two months after Holyk's first telephone call.

It should also be noted, in view of what was to come later, that in September of 1961 there had been launched some conversations between Texas Gulf and representatives of the Canadian mining company, Leitch Gold Mines Ltd., which would first lead to a contract, and eventually to the Supreme Court of Ontario. The conversations were innocent enough—Leitch was interested in participating in the TGS airborne survey program in several areas, having no helicopter of its own. In exchange for such services, and for the resulting data which TGS, presumably, might not be interested in pursuing, Leitch would offer the usual ten per cent of any net profits in any discovery. So far, however, there were only conversations, as the Royal Trust negotiations were in early stages.

Meantime, in October of 1961, Holyk and his associates in the exploration department were instructed by headquarters to press the negotiations, already begun in July of 1959, with the Woollings Company. Talks were opened on November 6 when Ken Darke visited the lumber company's office in South Porcupine. This promised to be another stately minuet. James Reid, the general manager, was most receptive, and the first proposal was made a day or so later covering lands owned in six townships, including Kidd. Numerous conversations carried over to Valentine's Day of 1962—and it was probably no coincidence. Texas Gulf now had two preliminary irons in the fire and could sit back and see which one heated up first.

The terms suggested to Woollings were quite complicated, enough so that it was not until April 25 that the president of the company, A. L. Bennett, accompanied by Reid, visited the Texas Gulf office in Toronto and spoke with Mary Hoyt of the exploration group.[5] Bennett casually mentioned that they had been approached by another company with similar aspirations, and expressed the view that there was little to be gained by his organization from the present suggested draft. He hoped changes could be made. On July 19 Reid wrote to Miss Hoyt and again mentioned the interest of another company. This, in turn, may have influenced Holyk to take action, because he replied on July 25 with quite a different proposition. He declared that TGS had changed its policy and now proposed optioning several specific pieces of land at fixed prices per acre, with a ten per cent interest in the net profits to be retained by Woollings. On August 7 Reid answered that they were willing, whereupon there then ensued another one of the seemingly inexplicable delays so often encountered in this business, unless it be construed that the explanation lay in the progress of negotiations with Royal Trust. It was one year and five months later, on December 27, 1963, that Mollison telephoned, and then wrote, to Bennett with a new proposal. By this time TGS had acquired the Hendrie option and Mollison could say that the company "was working in the area" and would still like an agreement. Texas Gulf, to antici-

[5] As a matter of interest, Miss Hoyt became the wife of Hugh Clayton, the geophysicist, and did consulting work for TGS. She would appear in another capacity in Clayton's testimony during the trial to come.

pate matters, had also drilled its first hole in the Kidd area and was in the new position of seeking more land. It had banked its knowledge, and its educated guesses, and was proceeding with what might be termed all deliberate speed.

The option agreement with Woollings, anticipating Valentine's Day by ten days on this occasion, was executed February 4, 1964, was for three years, and the price was $11,588.50. One-third of the land covered was to be released each year except for 1,920 acres to be selected by Texas Gulf. Actually the terms did not matter too much, as events transpired, and whether or not any option payments were made did not matter either, because eventually the company purchased all the shares of the Woollings Company and owned the land. The price of that deal, negotiated with the parent, Curtis Publishing Company, was $24 million.

To complete, more or less, the orderly account of Texas Gulf's land acquisitions again necessitates jumping ahead in the story of the mine itself. It will be remembered that the first approach to the Roberts Estate was made by Holyk back in 1959, when he telephoned the solicitor Knox and suggested an offer. Many more attempts were made, but the lawyer was playing hard to get and all were unsuccessful. In any case the business of the other options was proceeding. The end result so far as the Roberts Estate is concerned was best described by Chief Justice Gale in his opinion in the Leitch case, when he noted that a "caution" dated April 13, 1964, had been registered sometime later against the property purporting to show binding agreements of purchase and sale, and three option agreements, made with the beneficiaries of the Roberts Estate. Unsuccessful with the lawyer, TGS had ultimately gone around him to the principals and made a deal, sometime in 1964.

Justice Gale also supplied a quotable comment on the whole land proceeding. Although it was offered somewhat later in time, as part of the Leitch proceedings, it is pertinent here. During argument the plaintiff (Leitch) had criticized Texas Gulf for being so negligent in pursuing its land options that it had seemed no longer interested in, and as if it had abandoned, the anomaly which was now the subject of litigation. Not at all, said the Chief Justice, "for obviously Texas Gulf could not push the negotiations too hard without causing the prospective vendors to suspect that a discovery had been made, in which event either purchases would have become impossible or prices grossly inflated. Under the circumstances, I believe that Texas Gulf did what any prudent mining company would have done to acquire property in which it knew a very promising anomaly lay."

### IV

While 1963, the year of discovery, may properly be said to have begun with the obtaining of the option on the Hendrie Estate land in June, it was late fall before things really began to happen. With the right to proceed on this patented land now established, Darke returned in October to begin line cutting and other work on the north half of lot 3. Holyk's decision to drill K55—the Kidd Township area originally spotted by Miller—came out during the later SEC investigation when he was discussing the purposes of aerial reconnaissance generally. The survey had reflected the presence of an electrical conductor and the existence of rhyolite and andesite. Clayton had also returned to Timmins to begin the geophysical work. Just before the the drilling began, the reconnaissance electromagnetic ground survey had produced, said Clayton, the best reading he had ever seen. He further interpreted it as indicating not one, but three separate conductors, running generally in a north–south direction, of undetermined width and with a steep dip. The nearest outcropping of rock was probably a thousand feet away from the property. Darke fixed the point of this diamond drill hole number one at a point where it would intersect the easternmost conductor, starting about 60 feet east of that charted indication. The hole was drilled westerly, at an angle of 60 degrees because of property boundary problems. The date was November 8, 1963.

Texas Gulf had been following up its aerial survey results, and had as of this time drilled more than fifty anomalies, with one or two holes for each one, but the first prospect resulting from all of this effort was the one at K55. After the first 150 feet of drilling Darke had made only a hasty examination of the core. But on November 12, after more than 650 feet of penetration, his visual inspection seemed to indicate massive sulphides containing copper and zinc—enough so that when he got back to Timmins he telephoned Holyk in Toronto, 450 miles away, and the exploration manager arrived the next day to take his own look. The crew was really working in a swamp, he recalls, with the water table almost at the surface. They would travel to the site by jeep to a turn-off point, and then proceed the rest of the way by muskeg tractor, if one was available, or on foot. In November the trip from Timmins took about an hour and a half. By the following April it would take this long just to get to the turn-off point, with five miles still to go on snow, making about a four-hour trip. Once they left at 8 in the morning and did not arrive until 4:30 in the afternoon.

Hole number one was drilled to a depth of 655 feet. Holyk and Darke took steps to hide it, moving the drill rig away and sticking cut saplings in the ground to conceal its location from snoopers. They also proceeded to drill a second hole—K55-2—off the anomaly in order to produce a barren core, although there is not complete agreement on this fact, even though the purpose was clear. Most of those concerned admit that the hole, at such a location, was a deliberate misleader, for the benefit of any competitors who might come or fly around, but Clayton insisted later that it was not entirely a ruse but a genuine exploration effort. He added —and this was probably more to the point—they also wanted to keep the drill occupied and the drilling crew out of Timmins as long as possible.

More important, the company imposed the usual exploration security measures regarding discussion of the hole on the part of those who knew about it, or any announcement to those who did not know, and returned with new vigor to its land acquisition program. The core from K55-1 was split longitudinally and sent off to the Union Assay House in Salt Lake City, Utah, for chemical assay. Texas Gulf received reports on it in mid-December, and for its 600-foot length the hole averaged in excess of one per cent copper, eight per cent zinc, and nearly four ounces of silver, per ton of ore. Still, it was only *one* hole, and one hole did not make a mine by any means. Until April 16, 1964, when it first became possible for TGS to announce that it had indeed come up with a mine, these were the only chemical assay reports received by the company on any drill hole.

Later, during the questioning, Fogarty said that "after drilling many holes, one showed great mineralization. It was close to the southwest corner [of the northeast quarter-section] and we did not own the land for the next significant east-to-west hole. . . . Here we were with this good show and no land. In the best interests of the stockholders, and they should be real proud right now of the accomplishment here, we set about to acquire the adjacent and adjoining land." As for the matter of security and keeping secrets, he was asked whether or not he had told his wife about the first hole and replied, "No. I've learned years ago to discuss very little business. With eight kids, we have a lot to talk about other than business."

Stephens did his talking for the record in the 1963 annual report. After some references to continued activity on Baffin Island he said, "We have continued our metallic sulphide exploration activities in eastern Canada. The program has included geological and surface geophysical surveys and related drilling, all of which will be intensified during 1964. We have also staked claims on crown lands and obtained options on patented acreage." Actually, he then had the Hendrie Estate option, Mollison was pressing the Woollings inquiry, and the Elliott Estate property, which did not contain the ore body, had been acquired some time in December.

At the year-end very few people knew about K55-1—certainly not the stockholders or the directors of TGS, nor even more than a handful of its employees. No one, with even fewer exceptions, knew or cared anything about the Leitch mining company, although TGS had finally signed a contract with them back in February, agreeing not to explore or mine in certain Canadian areas, and to turn over certain data. And with the work on K55 stopped, but not completed, Ken Darke, the exploration geologist, went off to spend some of the Christmas holidays with old friends in Washington, D.C.

# 3
# The Mine:
# Stage Two

I

ON MARCH 31, 1964, with several feet of snow on the ground, and with seasonal alternations of freezing and thawing weather, Texas Gulf moved four drills into the Timmins area. Rights to operate on the land were assured and it was time for action. The drills did not go through the town but were driven up a side road, yet could hardly go unnoticed in such country as this, what with rigs, helicopters, and men on snowshoes moving north. The moccasin telegraph carried the news, and there had been some leaks. A helicopter pilot-mechanic had said he was not allowed to see the cores, although there was nothing unusual in that. One of the drillers went out to Kirkland Lake, 70 miles from Timmins, for Christmas, and started a little talk. On February 27, the influential weekly journal, *The Northern Miner*, had declared that:

> A real staking spree appears to have developed based on rumors concerning the local activities of TGS. . . . This well-known American major has been carrying on a modest program on a spread of ground centering around a point some ten miles due north of Timmins. The rumor machine has Texas Gulf obtaining some fat ore indications from its work. . . .

On March 31 the company invited *The Northern Miner* to come see for itself, setting a date of April 20 for the visit. Sitting in a bar with Holyk in Timmins, sometime in February, Darke had described the interest of a friend of his who was certain that TGS had encountered some mineralization. Regardless of what anybody thought, this friend and some associates were going to go in and stake some claims. At the time Texas Gulf was staking and restaking all of its old anomalies in the area but in such a way as not to focus attention on the Kidd 55 area, because there were rumors around and Holyk felt "we would prejudice our efforts to acquire the land if the promoters or the mining companies heard about it. So I at that time told Ken to go right into the Kidd 55 area and to stake all the claims that we need and to steer away his acquaintance, give him a helicopter ride or anything, just to get him out of the way."

The drilling program for additional holes came to its high point during the month of April, with six or seven rigs in operation, but this kind of activity was not possible in the beginning, despite the fact that additional equipment had been brought in. (The program was substantially *completed* only in March, 1965, with a total of 123 drill holes.) Prior to April 7 a shortage of water needed for drilling had prevented the operation of more than one drill rig. The second rig was put into operation on April 8, and the third and fourth rigs on April 10 and 12. On April 8 and 9 seven feet of snow on the ground impeded travel from Timmins, and the trip took as long as four hours. It meant that on those two days no geologists were available to inspect cores or make visual estimates. While this may not have seemed anything but routine at the time, it became a critical credibility factor during the trial, bearing on what was, or was not, material information then possessed by the company.

The rumor mill, however, was going full blast. There were press reports April 9 in the Toronto *Daily Star*, the *Globe & Mail*, and in *The Northern Miner*, on the TGS exploration work, with more to follow on the 10th and 13th in both of the newspapers. The April 9 account in the *Globe & Mail* bore the headline: "Wild Speculation Spree on TSE: Gigantic Copper Strike Rumored," and followed with:

> Rumors that one of the biggest copper deposits in North America has been discovered near Timmons have Bay Street agog.
> In the past couple of weeks the Toronto Stock Exchange has been experiencing its wildest speculative spree since the 1950's. Shares of penny mining companies with properties in the area have

been trading in the millions of shares and their prices have been doubling and trebling. . . .

    . . . rumors that Texas Gulf has made a discovery in Timmins of extreme importance. . . . Texas Gulf employees have been heavy buyers of the company's stock through brokerage offices in that town. . . . On the New York Stock Exchange . . . in the past two weeks the price has risen more than $5 a share. . . . The company has its own helicopter which flies between the property and Timmins with personnel and supplies.

Alarmed by the course the rumors were taking, Stephens on April 10 telephoned Thomas S. Lamont, senior director of the company and also a director of Morgan Guaranty Trust Company. This was the first time, according to his later testimony, that Lamont had heard of the exploration on the Kidd 55 segment. He advised Stephens to ignore the rumors unless they reached the New York press. The next day that very thing happened.

It was Saturday, April 11, and David M. Crawford, who had recently come to New York from Chicago to become secretary of the company, was on his way to Houston. He wanted to meet some of the TGS personnel in that office and begin arrangements for the forthcoming annual meeting. He was also planning to stop off in Chicago in connection with the sale or lease of his home in Lake Forest, because his family had moved east. In Newark terminal Crawford idly picked up the morning papers and, like Lamont, learned for the first time of what was going on near Timmins. On page one of the New York *Herald Tribune*, under a two-column headline, he read:

    The biggest ore strike in more than 60 years in Canada has stampeded speculators to the snowbound mining city of Timmins, Ontario. This time it's copper.

    Texas Gulf Sulphur Company Ltd., which reportedly has made an unparalleled find in the Big Water Lake area about 15 miles north of Timmins, would not confirm reports of the strike.

    The richness of the copper it discovered was so great that samples reportedly were flown out of the country to be assayed. The huge lode is supposed to consist of a bed of copper sulphide 600 feet wide, with a possible overall copper return of 2.87 per cent through most of its width.

The *New York Times* headline was on an inside page: "Copper Lode Cry Excites Toronto" and beneath this: "A rumor that a big United States corporation has made a sensational copper strike sent the [Toronto] tickers crazy." Crawford undoubtedly somewhat gratified at this evidence of spectacular activity on the part of his new employer, telephoned Stephens before catching his plane and gave him the news. His gratification might be somewhat tempered at a later date.

This time Stephens telephoned Fogarty, at his home in Rye, and the latter went out to get copies of the newspapers to check the stories. Both the president and his executive vice president were concerned and upset, for a number of reasons. In the first place, as they knew, it was not a "copper lode." One story said that "PCE Explorations, reportedly a key in the exploration work, slipped one cent to 46 cents after a huge rise of 22 cents on Thursday," but neither of them had ever heard of this company, which a later check revealed to be a Canadian flier in speculative penny stocks. Stephens and Fogarty were nowhere near as sure of what was being found in Kidd Township as were the rumormongers. Also, there was a New York Stock Exchange requirement for prompt clarification in such matters, and they *had* heard of that. There had been references in the newspapers to the fact that this "would come just at the right time for the copper industry, where demand recently began to overtake supply early this year, sending copper prices up." Fogarty immediately decided to get in touch with Mollison, now home from Timmins for a weekend in Old Greenwich.

Before leaving the Kidd site on the morning of Friday, April 10, Mollison had checked over the latest data available, as he was the one who was responsible to the New York management for the project. At the 7 o'clock closing the night before, the number 4 hole had encountered mineralization over 366 feet of its 420-foot length, and then hit barren material. On the next day, after Mollison left, the hole was completed to its length of 579 feet by 7 P.M., without any further mineralization showing. K55-3 had been finished on April 7, and had shown substantial copper mineralization. By Friday evening of the 10th, K55-5 had gone only 97 feet and had intersected copper over the last 42 feet. By this same time K55-6 had reached 569 feet, showing substantial copper over the last 127 feet. Holes K55-1 and K55-3 had been positioned on the basis of ground geophysical work, and the rest of the holes from knowledge gained as the work went along. Hole number two was a dud, of course. This, then, represented all of the information constructively available to Texas Gulf as of the evening of Friday, April 10—and Mollison would not have been completely up-to-date on all of that, since he had checked during the *morning* before leaving. There was no telephone at the site and no way of getting more information on a Saturday afternoon. Holyk, however, also left Timmins for a New York week-end on Saturday, April 11. As a witness later he would recall the drilling schedule—that it began March 31 with one rig. The second rig was started on April 7, somewhat later than planned because of the shortage of water required for drilling. The ground was frozen, there was three or four feet of snow, and they were pumping from a pond a half mile away. The third rig started Friday, April 10, before Mollison left. No core shack had been erected as yet.

As noted before, Mollison had written Graham Ackerley, of *The Northern Miner,* inviting him to visit the property on April 20. But now that the papers were carrying articles or news about the work which seemed totally unrealistic, he changed his mind and issued a new invitation. "There were a great many rumors in Canada as well as in the United States about our activities," Mollison was to recall, "and I think we felt we should try to clarify the situation. It seemed appropriate not only to issue a statement here [in the United States] but to further clarify it, have a representative of the industry present, the Canadian mining industry press, visit the property, see for himself what there was and write a story. . . . The easiest way to do this was to invite him to come a week earlier." This call had been made to Ackerley before Mollison left for Old Greenwich.

During his several talks with Stephens and Mollison on the critical Saturday the news broke in the New York papers, Fogarty was upset, admittedly, and not just by the reference to PCE Explorations as being associated with his company and partly responsible for the discovery. The news reports "gave figures of many percentages of copper," he was to say later at the trial, "that this was a fabulous copper discovery, when this wasn't so. . . . They made many statements in these articles, for example that we had moved in four drills and were moving in four more drills, and that this was the most sensational discovery since the Klondike days, and many others. In my opinion they were exaggerated and they could be misleading to the public."

In giving his evidence long afterwards, Mollison was urged by Judge Bonsal in federal court to recall the state of his mind during his conversations with Fogarty on that April Saturday, and it went like this:

    I felt that we lacked an understanding of what these sulphide
intersections meant at the time. I had in mind my own experience
and concept of this kind of thing. I had in mind the closest known
sulphide occurrence to this one that we were working on, one
twelve miles away, which was a series of small, disconnected
sulphide masses. I think there are probably a dozen or more of
them in this other mine. And in a new situation, with no geology
of our own—we were working through the muskeg with no help
from surface geology whatsoever, it was out in the middle of a
swamp—it is necessary to try to get any help from the closest possible source. Sulphide bodies are likely to have the same general
habit in a district, and this other occurrence twelve miles away,
the closest one, was extremely erratic, not only in the fact that
there were a number of small, disconnected bodies but in the
mineralization within those bodies. And that particular one was
one that had been known for years. A number of people had tried
to work it. It had been worked for a short time during World War
II as a War Production Board effort, I believe. I think the United
States government financed it. It was not a profit-making enterprise at that time, and it was only after two or more efforts that
finally the then operators were able to develop it into a producing
mine. And even after all these years of work the total reserves
there are probably not over five million tons in a dozen different
small bodies. I was simply unwilling to draw any specific conclusions to what we had [now].

Even now, said Mollison, they didn't know what they thought they
had. If anything, it seemed more in the way of zinc than copper.

    The company's current position undeniably leaned to the con-
servative side. It should be recalled that it had already discovered
two large ore bodies in Canada, one at Baffin Island and one in
New Brunswick, which it had not considered large enough to be
then worth developing. Some of geophysicist Clayton's later statements bear on the point. He declared that hole number three, the
one completed April 7, had not *confirmed* anything. The two holes
supplied a plane, "but you have no reason to know that if you go
a hundred feet north and a hundred feet south that you still might
have a sulphide body—we definitely have that situation out in Baffin Island, where we have high grade stuff and we put a hole next
to it and we got nothing."

    Finally—and whether the Texas Gulf executives knew it at the
time or not is not clear—the Securities and Exchange Commission
had taken the position on registration statements under the Securities Act of 1933 that ". . . three diamond drill holes are insufficient

to determine whether a commercial ore body is present, even though they should encounter a gold-bearing structure." [1]

So, having been told by Mollison that it was impossible at that time to understand the structure, to make projections from one hole to another, Fogarty went back to Rye and drafted his idea of a news release, characteristically, on the kitchen table. The result he took to a member of a public relations firm that served Texas Gulf, and who also lived in Rye, so that it could be put in shape for release the next day, Sunday. Fogarty had telephoned one of the company's lawyers, Earl Huntington (general counsel Harold Kline was also away in Houston on this week end, in connection with the annual meeting arrangements) and read his notes to him. Huntington made a few suggestions and then said he thought the release would be all right. On Sunday Mollison was checked for any further thoughts and then instructed to get back to Timmins as soon as possible to "move things along." Fogarty and Robert Carroll, the public relations man, completed the final draft of the story at Carroll's house, after which Fogarty telephoned Stephens and read it to him. Stephens asked some questions and suggested minor changes, then requested that the release be issued promptly so that it would be put on the wires Sunday afternoon.

There was, of course, no legal requirement that the corporation issue this or any other release. There was the New York Stock Exchange rule requiring the clearing-up of any such situations as this promptly. There was Lamont's rather backhanded advice about waiting until the news hit the New York papers. And there was the executive uneasiness over the crop of wild rumors that had swept down from Canada, plus a feeling of responsibility to shareowners and the financial community, to state—but not overstate—the facts as they saw them. Under date of Sunday, April 12, and directly quoting Fogarty, the release said:

> During the past few days, the exploration activities of Texas Gulf Sulphur in the area of Timmins, Ontario, have been widely reported in the press, coupled with rumors of a substantial copper discovery there. These reports exaggerate the scale of operations, and mention plans and statistics of size and grade of ore that are without factual basis and have evidently originated by speculation of people not connected with TGS.
>
> The facts are as follows: TGS has been exploring in the

[1] *Pan-American Gold Ltd., 31 S.E.C. 141, 147–8* (1950).

Timmins area for six years as part of its overall search in Canada and elsewhere for various minerals—lead, copper, zinc, etc. During the course of this work, in Timmins as well as in Eastern Canada, TGS has conducted exploration entirely on its own, without the participation by others. Numerous prospects have been investigated by geophysical means and a large number of selected ones have been core-drilled. These cores are sent to the United States for assay and detailed examination as a matter of routine and on advice of expert Canadian legal counsel. No inferences as to grade can be drawn from this procedure.

Most of the areas drilled in Eastern Canada have revealed either barren pyrite or graphite without value; a few have resulted in discoveries of small or marginal sulphide ore bodies.

*Recent drilling on one property near Timmins has led to preliminary indications that more drilling would be required for proper evaluation of this prospect.* The drilling done to date has not been conclusive, but the statements made by many outside quarters are unreliable and include information and figures that are not available to TGS.

*The work done to date has not been sufficient to reach definite conclusions and any statement as to size and grade of ore would be premature and possibly misleading. When we have progressed to the point where reasonable and logical conclusions can be made, TGS will issue a definite statement* to its stockholders and to the public in order *to clarify the Timmins project.*

The italics indicate what many expert readers of the often-quoted release believe to be the salient points, but considering the time given to it on Fogarty's kitchen table, and by others closely concerned, it is fair to say that the entire announcement might be read to reach an understanding of the company's state of mind and its future intentions. This applied especially to the final "bullish" paragraph which was destined to be so widely ignored. In any case it was taken around to the newspapers and wire services late on Sunday.

With the stock exchange rule for clarifying of confusing situations high on their minds, Texas Gulf executives kept one eye on the market to measure the effectiveness of their communication. The company's stock had closed on Friday at 30⅛. It opened on Monday at 32, a seven-year high. It slowly sagged on Tuesday and Wednesday, but so did that of Freeport and Pan-American. (Even so, the closing price on Tuesday for TG was still higher than its close on Friday.) The *Herald Tribune* on Monday passed its own judgment by saying that the release was confirmation of "preliminary favorable results, sufficient at least to require a step-up in drilling operations."

It would seem that any stockholder who sold TGS stock on these three days could have known—if he wanted to know—that the company would soon bring out an important announcement, possibly quite bullish. The release said as much. Up at the mine site on April 11 they were beginning to drill number eight—a "mill test hole" with a core two and a quarter inches in diameter and in this respect unlike the smaller regular cores. It was intended to be used for metallurgical testing to determine the amenability to milling of the material encountered. No log or visual estimates were made of it, and although it was completed on the 13th, no testing results were immediately available. A gravity survey would not be made until summer.

In addition to the planned statement to stockholders and the public which the April 12 release anticipated for some future date, two other announcement efforts were now in the making. After receiving his call from Mollison, advancing the date of his planned visit, Ackerley, of *The Northern Miner*, arrived at the site on Monday, the 13th. He had participated in earlier discussions and suspected some kind of announcement might be forthcoming—in fact, he had been promised first crack. Holyk and Mollison had hurried back from New York to get as much information as possible for the forthcoming New York release, and Ackerley met them, and Darke. He was allowed to examine portions of drill cores from K55-1 selected by Holyk and was given assay figures. Subsequently he wrote his story and turned it over to Mollison for review and comment, having been promised that he would have it back when the time came to release it. That time now appeared to be rather soon. If good news came along from the cores, the company had hoped to make an announcement at the annual meeting in Houston on April 23, but now the results had come up so fast that it was decided to issue the news release as part of a press conference following the regular directors' meeting in New York on Thursday, April 16. That would also be publication day for *The Northern Miner*, as it happened.

Mollison read Ackerley's draft on Tuesday and changed nothing, merely suggesting the addition of one or two names. He disagreed, he said later, with a statement that two holes established the ore zone, but, "It was his article, it wasn't mine. I was not passing judgment on it." Darke, however, said in later testimony:

"I recall at the time that I certainly didn't agree with all aspects of the article. I disagreed with some of the language used. I thought it was certainly written in a way to be sensational, which I also felt was not unusual for a reporter to do this. I felt that he was making many, many generalities in his conclusions and felt that it was not, frankly, what I would have reported." Part of the article was to appear in paragraph 92 of the SEC complaint when it was filed.

The article was flown to Toronto and Mollison handed it over to a taxi driver for delivery to the editorial offices around noon on Wednesday. Here it became a part of the next day's issue, on the streets of Toronto at 8 A.M. and delivered to brokerage houses by 9. The latter promptly telephoned any highlights to their correspondent houses in New York. Among other things it said that K55-1 was "one of the most impressive drill holes completed in modern times. For a core length of better than 600 feet, the hole had averaged in excess of one per cent copper, eight per cent zinc, and nearly four ounces of silver." It confirmed a mine in the making, estimated its dimensions, sketched the location in Kidd Township, and included the log for the first drill hole. The issue also contained an editorial on the subject by the editor, John Carrington.

This issue would have a circulation of about 7,000 in the United States, of which some 1,200 would go to New York. And it was coming out practically on the heels of the annual convention, from April 13 through 15, of the Canadian Institute of Mining and Metallurgy, which was held at the Queen Elizabeth Hotel in Montreal, attended by about 600 mining people, including some from the United States. Timmins had been the leading gossip topic, as might be imagined, in the corridors and bars. Among those attending were the Ontario Minister of Mines, the Honorable George Wardrope, and his deputy minister, D. P. Douglass.

Earlier on, Holyk, as a Canadian citizen, had felt that the exploration department should have some contact or exchange with political people and with the department of mines, as a matter of good provincial relationships, and had urged this on Mollison.[2] If it were going to be done, it had better be soon, and accordingly a

[2] Excerpt from Fogarty's pre-trial examination, p. 71: ". . . We decided also that since this is Canada, we are a foreign company in a foreign country, as far as Canadians are concerned. [That] out of due courtesy to the Canadian public and to the Minister of Mines, to whom we looked for everything in the future—everything we do in one way or another we would have to go through the Minister of Mines, roads, taxes, lots of problems. . . . You have the Minister of Mines and his people against you, your life will be much more complicated, and in my opinion this is a great factor for Texas Gulf stockholders, if he is for you or against you. . . ."

meeting was arranged in Montreal for Wednesday, April 15. Holyk and Mollison were going to fly Wardrope and Douglass back to Toronto in the company plane, and Mollison was also going to deliver *The Northern Miner* article for release, as promised. It was a busy day.

The conversation was general during the flight to Toronto, with Mollison talking to Wardrope on one side of the plane and Holyk conversing with Douglass on the other, showing him some cross-sections of drill holes and assay reports which he had with him. "Their response was complex," Mollison recalled. "They were happy that we had found something. They wanted to make some statement about it from the department. This would be something the mines minister would put out." And in response to such a request, Molllison wrote out a brief statement for him:

"Information now in hand . . . gives the company confidence to allow me [the Minister] to announce that TGS has a mineable body of . . . ore of substantial dimensions that will be developed and brought to production as rapidly as possible." The minister had a dinner and speaking engagement that evening, just out of Toronto, but said he expected to be back in the city so that he could make a radio or television announcement at 11 o'clock. Accordingly Mollison had marked his rough draft "for 11 o'clock" and later reported the whole business back to New York. His conclusion, then and later, was that Wardrope intended to make a late news broadcast.

Back in the company offices in New York, of course, the most important third leg of the triple announcement was being readied— the release for the press conference following the next day's board meeting. Crawford, the company secretary, who had been absent in Houston during the preparation of the first release, had returned. Together with Stephens, Fogarty, and a man from the public relations firm, they tackled the job. Crawford, in addition to his responsibilities as corporate secretary, was manager of government and public relations, and Fogarty handed him a copy of the statement Mollison had prepared for the Ontario Minister of Mines, to use as material for the release. Late in the evening Crawford telephoned the exploration office in Calgary and read to the manager there the text of the announcement, also telling him that the Minister of Mines intended to broadcast the news that same evening at 11 o'clock in Toronto. In this latter respect it turned out that he was wrong, but nobody in Texas Gulf discovered the mistake until about a week later. On the next day Stephens told the directors that the

broadcast had taken place. But for some reason Wardrope postponed his announcement until about 9:40 A.M. Thursday, April 16,
at which time it was handed to the reporters in the press gallery
of the Ontario parliament. For the record, Crawford was to make
still another critical decision that night. He placed an order for
some Texas Gulf stock.

There were thus three forms in which the good news to stockholders and the public regarding the Kidd Township developments
were to issue—the supposed broadcast or telecast on Wednesday
night, April 15; the weekly issue of *The Northern Miner;* and the
press conference release in New York on the 16th. Some 21 representatives of wire services, newspapers, trade and business periodi-
cals, and some brokerage house publications were invited. The
directors met at 9 A.M. as scheduled, and sometime before 10
o'clock the reporters were invited into the board room and given
copies of the press release, which in its first paragraph announced
a major discovery of zinc, copper, and silver. It went on to give
lengthy details of the official assay report of the first core, and said
that the relatively slight extent of the overburden would make possible easy mining by the open pit method.

After the fashion of business executives from time imme-
morial, the president read the release, and after the fashion of
reporters for just as long a period, some of the press people did
not wait, but rushed for telephones, thus paying the best tribute to
the importance of the news. The wire services of the brokerage
firm of Merrill Lynch, Pierce, Fenner and Smith, and of the Canadian Press Service, were the first to carry the story—both at
10:29.[3] For a strange reason which has never yet been unearthed,
the Dow Jones broad tape did not carry it until 10:55. In the meantime some slides were projected for any who cared to stay around
and look. The Dow Jones broad tape said in part:

> Preliminary data indicate a reserve of more than 25 million
> tons of ore. The only hole assessed so far represents over 600 feet
> of ore, indicating a true ore thickness of nearly 400 feet. . . . The
> overall interval of mineralization which could be mined in an open
> pit operation averaged 1.18 per cent copper, 8.1 per cent zinc and
> 3.1 ounces of silver over a core length of 602 feet.

[3] The bulletin by girl reporter Norma Walter (who would later appear
as a trial witness) was carried on the teletype news service of the country's
largest brokerage firm to its 159 branch offices. Although the Canadian Press
wire service carried a bulletin at the same time, Miss Walter's story broke from
10 to 25 minutes ahead of those reported to major U.S. newswires by competing male reporters who attended the same press conference.

On Wednesday, the day before the meeting, the market for Texas Gulf had closed at 29⅝. It opened Thursday at 10:06 A.M. at 30⅛, and 20,500 shares were bought in the first ten minutes of trading. By the time the Dow Jones broad tape carried the story, the stock had traded 80,000 shares and was up to 32⅝. By the close of the day it had gained 7 points, or nearly 25 per cent. At about 10:20 A.M., after the press conference announcement, a TGS director, Francis G. Coates, had telephoned a buy order to his Houston broker, who also happened to be his son-in-law. At about 10:40 Lamont had a telephone conversation with an associate at Morgan Guaranty Trust Company in which he advised the latter that he should "watch out for news of TGS on the tape," whereupon the firm, without further ado, put in a substantial order for the stock. And at 12:35, after leisurely proceeding downtown, Lamont put in an order for himself.

It is perhaps noteworthy that during the approximate time the initial drill core for K55-1 was kept *confidential*, from November 10, 1963, through April 10, 1964, a total of 2,562,000 shares of Texas Gulf's outstanding ten million shares had been bought and sold on the New York Stock Exchange. During this time, officers of the corporation—for whatever reasons—bought only 3,400 shares. This adds up to just one-tenth of one per cent of the "action." For purposes of comparison, Freeport Sulphur officers and directors bought during this time 8,520 of their outstanding 7,652,000 shares. Between December 1, 1963, and March 31, 1964, Pan-American Sulphur officers and directors bought 16,487 of the 4,710,000 shares outstanding. It should not be forgotten that the sulphur business was once more doing very well.

In Washington, on the day of the board meeting, an observant female financial analyst for the Securities and Exchange Commission, in charge of the ticker room, noticed the time of the broad tape report and the climb of the stock.[4] She compared the news releases for April 12 and for April 16, and after the market had

---

[4] Ingrid Nelson, called as plaintiff's witness during the trial, was asked why she had written "10:55, April 16" on the release coming over the DJ ticker. "I had been watching Texas Gulf Sulphur stock rise for several days, and especially on the morning of the 16th. So as I got up and looked at the Dow Jones ticker in order to cut the tape, I saw the headlines coming through Texas Gulf Sulphur and I thought the Commission might be interested in this release, particularly after I read the first few words, or the first few lines of the zinc and copper ore findings, remembering the statement of Monday which had said that the rumors were exaggerated and that there had been no find." *Joint Appendix, Vol. 1, U.S. Court of Appeals for the Second Circuit; SEC v. TGS et al. (1966)*, p. 399a.

closed telephoned the Commission's New York office. The next day
an investigation began, and continued for several months.

## II

       The investigation aside, things began to hap-
pen in the company and at the mine site almost immediately. In June
TGS established its new metals division, which confirmed, as only an
organization chart can, that the company was now definitely in the
metals business, and Mollison was named the vice president in
charge of it. The new division was staffed with Canadian experts.
Holyk became manager of exploration. There ensued metallurgical
testing, engineering studies, road construction, and a survey for a
railroad site. In June, also, a preliminary reserve estimate of 55
million tons of ore was announced, up from the 25 million figure
of April. Over 100,000 feet of drilling was completed, adding to
the tonnage estimates and confirming the ore values. The ore body
included substantial sulphur as pyrites, which might be ironically
construed as making the company an honest man for all of its earlier justifications of its exploration program. In fact, Stephens
declared in the annual report for 1964 that "TGS plans to utilize
the substantial sulphur values from its Canadian mining operation
and to integrate this with its phosphate operations." The grade of
ore determined from 17 drill holes was 7.08 per cent zinc, 1.33 per
cent copper, and 4.85 ounces of silver per ton. It was clear from
the plans underway that the first phase of development would require a multi-million dollar investment.

       Plans advanced rapidly for the open pit mine, and for a con-
centrator to be built in a township better suited for transportation
purposes. The concentrator would have an initial capacity of two
million tons of ore annually, but could be readily expanded to three
million—9,000 tons a day. In the beginning the metal concentrates from this installation would be refined by custom smelters,
while the possibility of a major investment in roasting and smelting
facilities was studied further.

       The generous cooperation of various Canadian government
departments, which had been foreseen as necessary by Holyk and
Fogarty, was in fact made available. The departments of highways
and mines, in Ontario, and the access roads committee, made it
possible for a Toronto contractor to complete a 13-mile section of
hard-surfaced access road in October, and additional miles of link-

ing roadway were also built. At the end of October access was available for heavy equipment, and work was begun to ditch the mine property and drain the heavy muskeg-covered surface so as to remove soil. Test trenches were dug so that the potential bidders for soil-removal work could evaluate the characteristics of the clay overburden. The latter ranged from five to fifty feet in depth. In November a Calgary-based engineering company began stripping the estimated six million yards of overburden from the ore body. This was expected to take more than a year, before production could begin, but it did not in fact take that long. Finally, in December, the Ontario government approved plans for the construction of a 16-mile spur line of the Ontario Northland Railway from the mine site to a point several miles east of Timmins.

At another level of corporate concern, and in bland disregard of all the work and money being lavished on the development in the Kidd Creek Mine, two lawsuits had been filed against Texas Gulf in Canada. One arose out of the contract the company had signed with Leitch Gold Mines Ltd., and its associate, Mastodon Highland-Bell Mines Ltd., on May 22, 1963, alleging that the property which was the mine site was subject to an agreement not to acquire mining claims in certain designated Canadian areas. TGS immediately replied that the discovery was *not* in any of those areas, and pre-trial discovery got under way. The other suit was instituted by Royal Trust in behalf of the Hendrie Estate, and presumably on the supposition that the Leitch claim was valid, it alleged that the purchase by TGS of the property in question, under the option agreement, was beyond its authority and title should therefore revert.

In February of 1965 the Royal Commission for the Windfall matter, which had been appointed late the preceding summer, began its hearings in Toronto and in Timmins. They concluded in June after examining 144 witnesses and 416 exhibits, plus the results of questionnaires sent to 800 small stockholders. Although these hearings were concerned with the affairs and actions of a Canadian company and with sidebar explorations into the functions and activities of the Toronto Stock Exchange and the Ontario Securities Commission, the chronology began with the first drillings by Texas Gulf in Kidd Township, and most of the story that subsequently unrolled found points of reference to that event and its spectacular conclusion. Significantly, representatives of the U.S. Securities and Exchange Commission attended the hearings, and it is a fair assumption that what transpired may have helped to determine the SEC course of action.

In any event, one year and three days after Stephens officially announced the major discovery near Timmins, the SEC filed a complaint in federal court in New York against Texas Gulf Sulphur Company and 13 individuals—the president, executive vice president, two directors, two vice presidents, the corporate secretary, a company attorney, a geophysicist, a geologist, the exploration manager, an office manager, and an accountant. The complaint charged violation of certain Commission rules, and sought an injunction and various remedies. In the main it was concerned with an alleged failure to disclose to the investor public, prior to purchases of stock by company people, deemed "insiders," what had been going on, and with the issuing of a "false and misleading" statement on April 12, 1964. Not surprisingly, a number of stockholder actions against the company followed closely.

Nothing daunted, the development of the mine and its facilities moved along. Production capacity during the year was increased to three million tons annually. More than 85 per cent of the muskeg and clay overburden had been removed so that, starting in October of 1965, ten thousand tons of ore per month were mined for the bulk pilot testing at the nearby Kam Kotia mill. A similar program was in prospect for the following spring, using the neighboring Broulan Reef mill. Such tests were necessary to develop metallurgical knowledge before building the new company concentrator in Hoyle Township, adjacent to the main line of the railway and 15 miles from the mine. Contracts were awarded for the railroad spur to the new concentrator site, and by September of 1966 it would be ready to haul ore from the primary crusher that was now under construction at the mine. The company's estimated investment at this point appeared to be around $60 million—for the mine, access road, concentrator, and related facilities. Part of its expense would be the $24 million to be paid to the Curtis Publishing Company covering the Woollings land, the ten per cent interest in the part of the mine offered for the option, and mineral and timber lands in both Ontario and Pennsylvania.

While the lawyers in New York and Washington, as noted earlier, would still be concentrating their attention for some time to come on the first hole drilled in the barren wilderness of the Kidd area, the actual scene had begun to change remarkably. Preparation for open pit mining first involved the stripping of millions of yards of muskeg and clay from what was roughly an oval area a mile long and a half mile wide. The mine area included the perimeter roads extending a hundred feet beyond the crest of the open pit. The entrance road to the first "bench," where mining operations began 40 feet below the surface, was completed. Three types of concentrates were to be produced annually—one containing about 50,000 tons of copper, another for 250,000 tons of zinc, and silver values would be recovered primarily in the lead and copper concentrates. So far the ore had proved to be very complex, but it was expected to produce concentrates with a high rate of recovery. In 1966 mine employment would increase from 100 to 350, all Canadians.

The trial of the SEC action against the company began on May 9, 1966, and was concluded on June 21. On August 19 Judge Bonsal dismissed the charges against the corporation and all but two individual defendants, whereupon the SEC—and the two defendants—filed an appeal in October in the United States Court of Appeals for the Second Circuit. On October 31 Chief Justice Gale began hearings in the Leitch case in the Supreme Court of Ontario.

By the year's end sulphur continued to account for most of the earnings of Texas Gulf, but two of the major diversification projects—metals and phosphates—were approaching the stage of full-scale operations. A series of strikes against the contractor had delayed the construction of the Hoyle concentrator, but operations began on November 16, and the smooth start-up of the first circuit, designed to process copper-zinc ore, was thought by the management to be unusually successful. Copper concentrates were being shipped for smelting and refining in Canada, and the zinc concentrates were being custom-smelted in the United States, in Europe, and in Japan. On January 1, 1967, the Kidd Creek Mine and the Hoyle concentrator, having outgrown their spawning bed and acquired a production personality of their own, were transferred to a new wholly-owned subsidiary, Ecstall Mining Ltd., with Fogarty as president and Mollison as executive vice president. This was a Delaware corporation, and its name had some historical significance to TGS, since it was borne by the first Canadian mining property acquired by the company in 1937. Mollison, a Minnesotan, was celebrating his twentieth year with the company by being promoted, and in another somewhat wry sense, by being defendant in a lawsuit.

In January and February of 1967 the two other concentrator units were completed. Development and construction work at the mine site had been finished, and the rail line to the concentrator was built. All equipment for moving ore was installed, tested, and put into operation. As the outline of the mine took shape, TGS was training the operating personnel and completing its marketing arrangements. During the year the company expected to produce at an annual rate about 100 million pounds of refined copper. Significantly, during the year copper production in the free world declined 1.3 per cent, while consumption had increased 8.1 per cent. As one of the unavoidable signs of prosperity, Texas Gulf had a 22 per cent increase in its costs, and more than half of it was accounted for by the start-up of its metals and phosphates divisions. By the end of 1967 sales and earnings were the highest in the company's history by a wide margin. Sales were up 91 per cent and earnings up by 121 per cent—$6.15 per share compared to the previous $2.80. And while sulphur was still the mainstay, the greatest increase in earnings was from metals. This gave rise to two things—the exploration budget was increased, and more suits were filed by stockholders, now some 90 in all.

Details on the increased earnings from metals stemmed principally from the achievement of the Ecstall subsidiary in mining and milling more than its design capacity of three million tons in less than a full year. Actually it produced 3,093,000 tons in 1967, which included 432,000 tons of 52 per cent zinc concentrates, 205,000 tons of 25 per cent copper concentrates, 43,000 tons of copper-lead concentrates, and 7,800,000 ounces of silver.

The scene in Canada continued to change markedly in 1968, as the open pit mine had progressed satisfactorily to its fifth "bench" and preliminary studies were begun to develop the eventual underground mine that would supplement the pit. After blasting, the broken ore was being loaded by six giant electric shovels into a fleet of eighteen 50-ton trucks, which carried it to the primary crusher on the rim. There it was broken into six-inch pieces and taken by a conveyor to a 6,000-ton loading bin, whence it was sent 17 miles by rail to the Hoyle concentrator. Here winter temperatures sometimes dropped into the minus-50 degree range. Unloaded into a 2,500-ton dumping pocket, the material was then moved to later stage crushers which reduced it to pieces smaller than three-quarters of an inch. The nerve center of the concentrator is a control room, utilizing continuous metal analysis by x-ray and computer, the pride of the whole establishment and presenting the most dramatic contrast to old-time mining. Whereas standard chemical assaying requires a two-hour delay for analyzing mineral proportions, the new instruments can provide quantitative analysis of five elements at a given point in 60 seconds. Three sets of rod and ball mills grind the ore into water slurry, to separate the minerals from the waste. The slurry, in turn, moves through flotation cells and on to large concentrate thickeners resembling swimming pools. The concentrator itself covers an area the size of six football fields.

There had been nothing very mysterious about the way Texas Gulf had pinpointed its mine and brought it into being, as contrasted with the efforts of early prospectors. It was the result of years of patient work and great investment, and using the latest in exploration equipment and methods. If all of this was a gamble, it had to be the kind of calculated gamble with a tremendous ante that is characteristic of modern industry. What these experts found, declared *Engineering and Mining Journal*,[5] was "a base metal concentration of enormous value. The orebody is, in fact, so rich and varied that the Kidd Creek complex is the largest zinc mine in the world, the largest silver producer in the world, a potential major source of cadmium, and that, when operating at capacity, its daily concentrate output surpasses anything in the world."

With all of its new machinery functioning smoothly, the company in 1968 again established new records in sales and earnings —and in stockholder suits, which had grown to more than a hundred. But it was hard to worry about such matters when Ecstall had milled more than 3,600,000 tons of ore, increasing the total of each type of concentrates and recovering 13,396,000 ounces of silver. The sales of lead and zinc, less smelting and refining charges, were 19 per cent greater than in 1967. While Frasch sulphur and that recovered from gas operations accounted for the greatest part of the year's earnings, metals contributed most of the increase in net income. As mentioned before, there was a slight *caveat* here for the management and the stockholders—about one-third of the consolidated net income proceeded from that portion of the Kidd Creek Mine for which title was being disputed by the trustees of the Hendrie Estate. On the other hand, on November 29, the lengthy litigation brought by Leitch in the Supreme Court of Ontario was

[5] Finn B. Domaas: "Kidd Creek—A Huge Mining Success in Ontario," *Engineering and Mining Journal*, April, 1969.

decided in favor of Texas Gulf. After reading the opinion of Justice Gale, and presumably after taking counsel with counsel, the plaintiffs decided not to appeal. That decision caused considerable anguish to some of the Leitch stockholders, who had been tasting in advance the delights of a $450 million payment, or alternatively of $50 million in damages and the mine to boot. They made a fuss but were outvoted in a special meeting. Mr. Justice Gale's secondary finding that Texas Gulf had committed two breaches of its agreement with Leitch was cold comfort, for these breaches were not connected with the mine itself and the damages payable to Leitch would not likely be large. The amount of these damages was referred to a Court officer to assess, and there the matter rests today.

At the end of 1968, as the sun slowly set over the widely scattered scene of the various undertakings of Texas Gulf Sulphur Company, and in particular as it seemed to be casting its golden rays over the bustling site of the Kidd Creek Mine and its related facilities, there was just one matter that was still confined to limbo. On August 13 the majority of the judges of the United States Court of Appeals for the Second Circuit, speaking from various combinations on various points, had nevertheless reversed most of the findings of the lower federal court. The result, for an unforeseeable but no doubt lengthy period, approached chaos, and it was chaos of much wider dimensions than the corporate boundaries of Texas Gulf Sulphur encompassed. Its effects spread throughout business, financial, and legal circles.

Specifically the case against Texas Gulf and many of the individual defendants was remanded to Judge Bonsal for further action along the lines laid down by the Court of Appeals. The nature of that "further action" would not be disclosed for 17 months. On the other hand, two of the individual defendants set out on the long trail to the United States Supreme Court. How all of it happened is a different kind of story, and necessitates an examination of its own.

# 4
# Investigation

IT has been suggested, earlier in this chronicle, that the legal action brought by the SEC against Texas Gulf Sulphur Company and a number of individual defendants came as something of an unpleasant surprise. A little over a year had passed after confirmation of the discovery at the press conference in New York when the complaint issued. While it is true that the Commission staff in New York plunged into the investigation the very next day after the news was published, there is some question about what they expected to find, and even in which direction they were pressing. They were simply hungry hunters. "The whole investigation started off as a routine surveillance," one SEC official was quoted as saying later, "but we hit pay dirt."

The kick-off came as a result of two news releases by the company four days apart—the first having an obviously negative cast, although promising a later report, and the other confirming the discovery of a rich mine. Then there were the violent reactions of the stock market. The Commission's first concern, oddly enough, appeared to center on whether or not the company could support its April 16 claims for such a large mine. A skeptical memorandum from the chief mining engineer in the SEC division of corporation finance said, on April 30, "We do not have sufficient data to ascertain whether a commercially mineable ore body of any size exists at the property." It must be remembered that the Commission's hard-eyed experts and analysts were usually on the trail of those who claimed too much, rather than not enough. It was not until the first estimate of ore reserves at the new Texas Gulf mine had been more than doubled—from 25 to 55 million tons—in the June

statement by the company that the SEC apparently concluded that
if the April 16 release was not too bullish, then the one on April 12
must have been too bearish. With such a conclusion the needle
swung around and pointed at those who had bought and sold stock
in the company, and timing of the transactions. Trained teams set
out to go through the records of brokerage houses looking for the
names of Texas Gulf people who had bought large or small blocks
of TGS stock.

The man immediately behind the gun, from the moment
Washington called and set off the whole business, was Edward
C. Jaegerman, the chief investigative counsel for SEC in New
York, and right behind him was John T. Callahan, special counsel.
It was their custom to work as a team on investigations and prose-
cutions. In 1938 *Fortune* magazine had described them as the
"Rover Boys" and the name stayed with them. Callahan had been
twice captain of the Yale football team in his youth, but he would
now retire, at 70, after the TGS investigation was concluded. Both
men were colorful characters. Jaegerman had been with the
Commission since December of 1936 and had participated in more
than 500 investigations, moving steadily up the ladder from
senior trial attorney to chief of the office of special investigations,
and—since 1963—to chief investigative counsel. The younger of
the team, Jaegerman had graduated from Yale in 1935 and was
admitted to the New York and Connecticut bars the same year.
"I am one of the few people able to do it; passed both at first
crack," he somewhat unblushingly declared in his own deposition
before trial of the TGS action. Labeled by Vartanig V. Vartan,
of *The New York Times,* as a tough and tenacious investigator over
three decades, he had since the 1950's figured prominently in such
spotlighted cases as those of Alexander L. Guterma, Lowell M.
Birrell, Walter F. Tellier ("king of the new issues") and Earl Belle
("boy wonder of Wall Street").

The executives of Texas Gulf, and their legal counsel, apparently offered every cooperation to the Commission's investigators, who went through records, obtained copies of documents,
interviewed personnel at great length, and flew to Canada in a
plane provided by Texas Gulf to inspect the discovery site. As early
as April 29 Jaegerman brought Benjamin Adelstein, chief mining
engineer for the SEC, to the TGS board room for a meeting that
lasted five or six hours. Adelstein had been with the Commission
since 1937, and since 1941 he had reviewed substantially all of

the mining prospectuses, proxy statements, and similar documents related to mining which had been filed there. He estimated the number of these as more than 4,000. This was a conference, however, that would be reviewed and chewed over during the later trial. Fogarty recalled that "we pretty well discussed the entire Timmins project. We discussed the geology, drilling, the tonnage estimate. There [was] some—and I don't mean to convey the wrong impression—skepticism on the part of these individuals . . . that we even had a discovery at all, and they were there in a sense to establish that our 25 million ton estimate was accurate or reasonable. At that time we were really trying to convince them . . . that we had a 25 million ton ore body."

Another incident at that first get-together involved the initial TGS news release of April 12, the one begun in Rye on Fogarty's kitchen table, and which the SEC was to hold as "materially false and misleading." The Texas Gulf executive vice president said that at the end of the conference, "after we had reviewed things . . . and as we were leaving, Mr. Adelstein made the comment to me that he thought the April 12 release was accurate and he probably would have done the same thing if he had been in my position." When these words got into evidence at the trial later, Adelstein was recalled, and denied making *that* statement, although he shuffled a bit: "The answer as to what I said to him was that this release did not appear to be an overstatement, that it was, if anything, on the conservative side." Adelstein also said that he could not have determined whether it was "correct and accurate" because he did not then have the vital data. TGS officials, however, maintained he *did* have the data, including everything available up to April 29, and had been given anything he requested.

As things went along, the investigators swiftly became more and more concerned with building a case around the significance of the first hole sunk at Timmins—the discovery hole—and what they felt to be the deliberate withholding of information on the part of "insiders" while buying TGS stock and giving tips to others. Jaegerman showed a remarkable interest in the doings of Ken Darke, the geologist. Another one of the unnamed SEC "officials" told the reporter for *Life* magazine, "It seems to us where you have inside people telling only their friends, it opens the door to back-scratching—you give me a few tips about your company and I'll help you out. The public investor will really be getting diddled." While this may have underlined the nature of the Commission's theories about insider trading, it hardly fitted the circumstances that were alleged in the TGS matter, since none of the so-called "tippees" represented anything but themselves.

As for the significance of the first hole, Alvin W. Knoerr, the editor of *Engineering and Mining Journal,* had sent off a letter to the *Wall Street Journal* in which he said:

> When a diamond drill hole hits good ore in virgin territory, this initial discovery does not constitute a mine. Many more holes have to be drilled to determine the extent of the ore body, its value or metal content. Normally this takes months or even years of work.

And Darke, when being interviewed by *Life* writer Chris Welles in Timmins, declared: "In my opinion those three holes [as of April 12] confirmed about four million tons of ore at most, which is nothing for Texas Gulf. Hell, Texas Gulf has five million tons up in New Brunswick they haven't even touched yet." Four months after the complaint was filed, Darke wrote to one of the lawyers for Texas Gulf, sending him clippings from Toronto newspapers which he hoped would help to show "just how asinine the SEC's charges really are regarding their allegations that one drill hole indicated a mine." He was referring to the case of the rise and subsequent fall of the stock of McWatters Gold Mines Ltd. Wrote Darke:

> This winter [November 1964] McWatters drilled a nickel zone located 18 miles southwest of Timmins—they have subsequently moved off the property. The initial diamond drill hole contained some outstanding nickel values. The press article contains the statement: *"Ore of this dimension and grade is seldom found in mining exploration in Canada."* The second and third drill holes also were very good, but subsequent drilling failed to prove an ore body. The stock hit a high of about $2.00 at the height of the speculation, and is now trading at about 34 cents. Obviously the *outstanding nickel values* found in the first drill holes did not indicate a mine—only an interesting speculation. The pathetically amateurish hindsight currently being displayed by the SEC on "their one drill hole equals a mine" nonsense with regards to the Kidd Creek Mine should be held up to the full ridicule that it so justly deserves.

The Toronto *Globe & Mail,* whose report had been quoted in Darke's letter, had said in a story on November 24, 1964: "Speculators gambling that a commercial nickel deposit has been found 18 miles south of Timmins in Northern Ontario yesterday gave the Toronto stock market its busiest day since April. . . . Exchange officials delayed the opening of trading in McWatters for nearly an hour as they matched a weekend accumulation of orders to buy and sell." But by the same newspaper's issue of January 2, 1965, it was saying: "Trading fire in McWatters shares continues to cool."

Jaegerman's interest in Darke did not extend to the latter's opinions in regard to the significance of drill holes, but was hung on other facts. Some of them came out during the hearings in the Windfall matter before the Royal Commission, which the chief investigator was attending. Richard Roberts, staff reporter for the Toronto *Telegram,* wrote in the issue of March 31, 1965:

> The Securities and Exchange Commission . . . is a keen observer at the Windfall Royal Commission public hearings now in their fifth week. . . . SEC is busily engaged in its own big probe. It is investigating, and has been for the past 11 months, share trading in Texas Gulf Sulphur Company. The Commission, according to Edward C. Jaegerman . . . who is attending the Windfall hearings in Toronto, is interested in "anyone from anywhere" who has capitalized on inside information to make a profit in trading in shares of Texas Gulf.

The Windfall hearings developed the fact that Nedo Bragagnolo, a Timmins real estate broker and prospector and a casual friend of Darke, had set up a partnership involving Darke, himself, and John Angus, manager of a local brokerage office, in January, 1964, in a venture to stake mining claims as close as possible to the Texas Gulf operation. At first reluctant to join, Darke came in on the basis that no ground which he wanted for Texas Gulf would be staked by Bragagnolo. The existence of the partnership was not disclosed, its operations being outwardly those of Bragagnolo, to whose name were transferred 241 mining claims recorded by various stakers. None of these claims ever became the property of Texas Gulf. Angus later withdrew, selling his interest, and Darke resigned from Texas Gulf as of June 30, 1964. The claims were mainly sold to purchasers who poured into Timmins after the announcement of the TGS discovery. One thing of interest, as the Windfall report noted, was that this group, through its activities, was able to stake, at a cost of some $7,000, properties which they later disposed of for an aggregate cash consideration of $900,000. Said the report:

> Due to the two-fold capacity in which Darke acted during this time, every one of the mining claims involved in the operations of this partnership comprised ground which he, alone or in concert with some other officials of Texas Gulf, had already concluded did not warrant further examination. None of these properties had any indication of airborne anomalies, and the only reason for selecting the particular properties was, as expressed by Darke, that they were as close as possible to the discovery area of Texas Gulf: in other words, as he states, it was the nearest available land." [1]

With this kind of information serving as general background, and no doubt spurred somewhat by Darke's scorn for the "single hole" theory, the SEC investigators pressed him for details of his Christmas, 1963, sojourn in Washington. It will be recalled that the geologist, having closed the first hole in November pending the TGS land acquisition activities, had gone to visit friends in the capital, as he had done on several other occasions. The friends were Madge Caskey, a 64-year-old clerk in the National Bank of Washington, and, in particular, her 34-year-old daughter, Nancy Atkinson, then employed as a secretary in the Department of Commerce. To them he was a family friend who dropped in from various parts of the world now and then. They knew, for example, that he had once broken his back in a plane crash going to Baffin Island. Darke enjoyed escorting Nancy (before the trial she was married and became, for the record, Nancy Atkinson Brown) and said that on several occasions he had recommended Texas Gulf to the family as a good blue chip investment in place of the Canadian penny stocks which Madge Caskey was fond of playing around with on a small scale.

Ultimately, before the trial, Darke was examined under oath in Toronto on March 11, 1966, by Frank E. Kennamer Jr., who would be the chief prosecutor. He freely discussed his conversations with Mrs. Caskey and her daughter in regard to investing in worthwhile stocks. He described what he thought was the future of TGS just in the sulphur industry alone, its current phosphate prospects, and declared he considered his company to be a tremendous investment in five different areas. He had made similar recommendations, he told Kennamer, to many other people,

[1] *Op. cit.*, p. 38.

including his parents. The latter had not acted on his suggestions and this had made him angry with them. On February 20, 1964, he had purchased 300 shares of Texas Gulf—his first ownership of the stock which he had for so long been recommending, although he had owned shares and calls in other companies. Subsequently he purchased 1,000 calls on TGS on February 27, another thousand calls on March 23, and a final thousand on March 30. That was the record. On the direct question from his own counsel, William D. Conwell, he declared that from November, 1963, until April, 1964—the critical period—he did not tell the facts concerning the exploration and drilling in the Timmins area to Atkinson, Caskey, his brother Ernest Darke, Bragagnolo, or other associates of the latter.

Stock purchases, and ownership, in Texas Gulf constituted, of course, much of the meat of the investigation. TGS directors actually held comparatively small amounts of the stock. On May 14, 1965, less than a month after the complaint was filed, they were reliably reported to own 0.2 per cent, whereas of the same date the directors of competitor Freeport Sulphur had an interest in 3.1 per cent of their company's shares. These figures were taken from the "insider" reports required by Section 16 of the Securities Exchange Act of 1934, applying to officers, directors, and ten per cent stockholders.

There is irony, and some enlightenment, in the fact that after the mailing of the 1963 proxy statement of Texas Gulf Sulphur, prior to the April annual meeting, letters had come into the company's offices criticizing Fogarty, by then elected executive vice president and a director, for holding so little company stock. He then owned 505 shares. In fact, in pursuit of his determination to become a substantial stockholder of the company, he had bought 200 shares in August, 1963, on the day before a tragic explosion in the company's new potash mine shaft in Utah. This was a distraction which occupied his mind for a considerable period, until another distraction came along. In October it was reported that the head of Barber Oil Company had acquired 300,000 shares of TGS, and there were rumors of a possible take-over. Fogarty then resumed his personal purchasing program on November 12 with 300 shares—the first of the 3,100 shares he would buy between then and April 6, 1964, and which would figure in the SEC complaint.

Questioned directly on this point by the judge during trial,

Fogarty responded: "Well, I figured, as a director the more stock I had the harder time—they would have a hard time getting rid of me, and at the same time others in our organization, because we hadhad built up a pretty good team at that time. So I resumed my purchasing on November 12th and I continued a pretty steady program of purchasing stock right up to April 6th. . . . I had a continuous program going with a set goal of becoming a substantial stockholder of Texas Gulf." The Timmins development did not especially affect these actions, he said, although, "As part of a total picture of total corporate information that I have, the answer is yes. . . . On the other hand, they didn't really play any part. If Timmins hadn't come along, I would have done probably exactly the same thing, maybe on different days. There is really no relationship between them except that I have to say I knew of Timmins."

When Jaegerman pressed him in pre-trial examination about why he had not bought shares or calls after April 6, and during the period prior to the public announcement on April 16, Fogarty's reply had been: "Well, eight kids, I'm a conservative individual anyway. I don't gamble particularly, I don't speculate. The few times I have speculated I've been unsuccessful. And this would still be in the class of speculation." As a matter of fact, Jaegerman should have understood this only too well. He had six children, two of them in college.

Throughout his preliminary examination by Jaegerman, Fogarty did a very consistent job of setting forth his own philosophy in regard to shareholders in the company. He took every opportunity to point out that he related the shareowner to the ongoing fortunes of the corporation, rather than looking upon him —as the SEC obviously did—as an investor who must be protected against trading losses. There was something to be said for each viewpoint, and the conflict was philosophical, involving no real clash of facts. As such it sharply set apart the two sides.

Jaegerman enthusiastically and vigorously processed both the "big" and "little" people during his questioning. John Hill, who had been chairman and chief executive of Air Reduction Company, had served as one of the Texas Gulf directors who were members of the stock option committee, along with Coates and Leslie M. Cassidy, former president and chairman of Johns-Manville Corporation. Hill described the option plan which had been approved by the TGS stockholders in 1961, covering 250,000 shares of stock. Some 57,000 shares were then granted to 17 officers and employees, at a price of $24.50 a share. The options became exercisable 18 months after the date of the grant, and would expire ten years after that. One of the ensuing problems was that the market price of the shares went down, instead of up, and it was the feeling of the company management that no new options should be granted under the plan until the market price had someday caught up with the price attached to the first batch of options. It was a quirk of fate that this did not happen until February of 1964— right within the period of time between the discovery hole and confirmation of the mine.

The duel between former Texas governor Allan Shivers and Jaegerman served seemingly to reveal the investigator's real intentions as to the effective time of press disclosure on the actions of purchasers. Shivers had been governor from 1949 to 1957, and was now chairman of the Austin National Bank. He was later to become president of the Chamber of Commerce of the United States. A Texas Gulf director since 1958, he owned 3,000 shares of the stock. There was some interesting by-play raising the question of how many shares had to be purchased to disclose an intent to do wrong. Speaking from his experience as governor, Shivers told Jaegerman there was no doubt in his mind that news became public the moment one gave it to a reporter, and he added that if the individuals at TGS involved in purchases had really known they had a sure thing, their purchases would not have been so small.

On his examination President Claude Stephens contented himself with presenting the point of view of the company's chief executive in regard to those projects he considered most important to the corporation. His relaxed responses on the record, in what might almost be termed a country boy style, seemed to confuse his interrogator.

Another director, Lowell Wadmond, a partner with White and Case, a firm with which he had been associated since 1935, could come down handily on the side of character, which he did. He had at various times been an assistant United States attorney in the Southern District of New York, special assistant to both the New York State and the United States attorney generals, and chairman of the committee on character and fitness of the New York Appellate Division for the First Department, which includes

Manhattan. This is the all-powerful committee which must pass on the non-legal qualities of every bar candidate before admission. As of the 1969 proxy statement, Wadmond owned 10,200 shares of TGS stock, and his firm was representing the corporation in this litigation. During his examination he had strongly stated his opinion that company secretary David Crawford had not violated Rule 10b-5 by his purchase of 600 shares on the day of the mine announcement, April 16. Crawford, after all, was a lawyer with an excellent background. Wadmond asked Jaegerman if he had any legal authority for holding the contrary point of view, but received no reply from the exasperated investigator who exclaimed, "I don't understand what a man's background has to do with whether a purchase of shares by him might be in violation of Rule 10b-5!" He didn't, and Wadmond did, and that was just the difference.

Cassidy, the Johns-Manville executive, since deceased, had been with his company since his graduation from the Wharton School of the University of Pennsylvania in 1926. He became a TGS director in 1958. Cassidy gave Jaegerman little on examination except to state, as the long-time chief executive of a mining company, that he knew reports of exploratory drilling in the early stages could be very misleading—in his experience it was never the practice to report results of a single drill hole.

Francis Graham Coates, 70-year-old attorney and a partner in the Houston law firm of Baker, Botts, Shepperd and Coates— counsel in the southwest for Texas Gulf—had, like Jaegerman, graduated from Yale, but in 1916. He had gone to Texas for his law degree, however, practiced in Fort Worth and Houston, and specialized in corporate and public utility law. Coates was a TGS director from 1949 until his retirement for reasons of health in 1968. He had made the fatal mistake, in Jaegerman's eyes, of purchasing 2,000 shares of Texas Gulf stock for family trusts by telephoning his son-in-law, a Houston broker, about 20 minutes after the April 16 press conference broke up. Coates, during his examination, tried hard to educate Jaegerman in the motives which influence corporations in granting stock options, but without any apparent success. On the record this was one of the roughest exchanges between any witness and the investigator.

The opinion of one Texas Gulf executive, who did not care to be identified, is interesting here nevertheless. He feels strongly, although Stephens and others disagree with him, that the SEC case was heavily influenced by the stock option element. There is a class of people, he believes, including lawyers, politicians, and key men in government agencies, who never get stock options and therefore regard them as a dirty word and are against the idea. They do not understand the motives behind the option system. In the case of Texas Gulf, the class of option recipients was unfortunately—but understandably—very small, because of the organization structure characteristic of mining companies. The nature of the business dictated that relatively few people would be highly aware of any outstanding business development, such as a promising mineral strike. Aside from the question of stock options, there were those who were convinced that the Johnson administration had been unhappy with the price increase in sulphur, and had leaned heavily on the SEC attack upon Texas Gulf. This rumor, unsurprisingly, could not be substantiated.

Almost without exception the directors who were interviewed presented an imposing front to Jaegerman and were deep in business experience, professional acumen, and prestige. Edward G. Lowery Jr., who resigned his Texas Gulf directorship in 1965, had been president of the General Reinsurance Corporation. A New Yorker, with degrees from Harvard, Oxford, and Columbia Law School, he had experienced federal service with both the Reconstruction Finance Corporation and the Treasury. It was Lowery, in discussing how far down the line one should go in considering stock-buying employees to be classed as insiders, who recalled that a common seaman on the ill-fated tanker "Sulphur Queen" had telephoned his broker to purchase wheat, and thereby provided a clue to the general location of the missing ship.

The senior director in point of service was Thomas S. Lamont, on the Texas Gulf board since 1927. A director of Morgan Guaranty Trust Company, he had retired as vice chairman. Lamont's association with J. P. Morgan was of long standing—he had become a partner in 1929. He was a fellow of Harvard College. In response to the investigator's questions he had generally described his feeling about Texas Gulf, what he had previously said about it at the bank, and how his associates there had become skeptical as to the possibilities of the corporation because of its declines in sales and profits in recent years. This expressed attitude had been "distasteful" to him, he admitted. Lamont was firm in declaring that he did *not* suggest a purchase of stock when he telephoned after the April 16 meeting of the board. After he returned to his office on that day, he had bought 3,000 shares for himself and members of his family.

On the other hand, there was Thomas Peter O'Neill, the Irish accountant whose salary was $775 per month, and who had come to the New York office of Texas Gulf by way of Canada. His current job was to handle billings for the Canadian activities of the exploration group. O'Neill gave Jaegerman an interesting account of how a young man in a corporate structure regards the operations of his company in relation to his own modest fortunes. He had indulged in cautious forays into the market at the nominal level he could afford in his circumstances, and gave forthright reasons for his actions. Actually a billing clerk, he declared that he had known nothing about the results of the drilling near Timmins, but had decided that Texas Gulf might be a good buy because of the rumors of a take-over bid by outsiders. This, he assumed, would raise the price of the stock. O'Neill, not unaware of the possibly favorable arithmetic attaching to calls, had bought 100 of them on December 17, 1963. On January 2 he purchased 100 shares outright, and then followed with calls on 500 shares on March 18 and 200 more on March 20. This was the extent of his plunge. Whereas Jaegerman repeatedly tried to nail down a prior knowledge of the Timmins strike as a motive for O'Neill's acts, the witness only served back the fact that he had acted on his own convictions and general knowledge.

Jaegerman showed his rough side in the questioning of Madge Caskey, constantly interrupting her replies in the attempt to get her to involve Ken Darke as a specific tipster on the discovery hole. Here, presumably, was the symbol of the small investor which the SEC was pledged to defend against the Wall Street wolves, but the investigator's tactics put this picture a little out of focus. Mrs. Caskey had purchased 3,000 calls on TGS on December 30, 1963, presumably as a result of Darke's arguments against penny stocks, and on March 30 she bought 100 shares outright and another 1,000 calls. Her daughter Nancy bought 50 shares and 200 calls on February 17, 1964, and then on March 30 purchased 400 more calls. From both the mother and the daughter Jaegerman repeatedly tried to get an admission that they had said they would "beg, borrow or steal" to put more money into Texas Gulf stock—it came to be a favorite phrase of the investigator but no one would admit to having used it. With both mother and daughter he also introduced the name of Herbert

Klotz, Assistant Secretary of Commerce in the Kennedy administration. Klotz, previously associated with an investment banking house in Washington, had been chief administrative officer for the department during the period regarded as critical by the investigators. His was, therefore, a "government" name carrying a certain publicity value. Klotz, however, was somewhat more difficult to bulldoze, and really gave the examiners little of any substance. Nancy Atkinson had telephoned her mother during office hours, in his presence, and discussed their common stock ventures. He said he had thus inadvertently had his interest aroused, subsequently did his own checking, noticed heavy trading with a price increase, and played his hunch by purchasing 2,000 calls on TGS the last day of March, 1964. Klotz later left the government service and became president of the Potomac Packaging Corporation. The Washington picture on stock purchases, except for a man named Miller, who bought 1,000 calls in February and March, was completed by the questioning of Stanley Westreich, a real estate man and another of the friends of Nancy Atkinson. He had first begun to think of Texas Gulf as an investment when Nancy went to him for advice in making her own purchases, and had bought 2,550 shares and 1,000 calls between January 16 and March 30.

Longstreet Hinton, the executive vice president of Morgan Guaranty, fell into a different classification. He had bought 10,000 shares on April 16 for the account of the Nassau Hospital and for other customers of the bank, including pension trusts, but explained his motivation as being based on many factors, not just the current press release. A couple of days earlier he had spoken with Lamont about the rumors in Canada, and was told that Lamont knew nothing more than had appeared in the press. Before leaving the Texas Gulf offices, after the press conference, Lamont had telephoned Hinton and told him that good news about the company would shortly be coming out on the tape. Hinton, however, did not wait for the tape but spoke with his trading department and was informed that the stock was active and up three points. Lamont, he declared, "didn't suggest that I buy any shares."

These were some of the people, and some of the matters, reached by Jaegerman and his staff during the period of investigation. Not all of the more than a year of days which intervened between the confirmation of the mine on April 16, 1964, and the filing of a complaint by the SEC on April 19, 1965, were filled with such specific matters as examinations and fact-finding. Many other things happened which were not necessarily on the investigation agenda or schedule, but which would bear significantly upon, or be reflected in, the oncoming formal legal actions.

As late as April 2, 1965, a memorandum to the Commission from its division of trading and markets made two points in respect to the Texas Gulf Sulphur file which so far had not been set forth in the draft of the complaint, but which the memo writers seemed to think might bear on the amount of information available to Texas Gulf employees prior to the April 12 release, and which might buttress the charge that it had been false and misleading.

The first point was that, on April 9, 1964, Texas Gulf had offered to purchase the ten per cent profit override from Royal Trust as executors of the Hendrie Estate, for $57,000, and had asked for a quick reply. Furthermore, the memo declared that the SEC had documents indicating active negotiations on this offer as late as April 15.

The second point was that on April 11 there had begun, at the site, the drilling of the larger-sized mill hole.

The inference, in each case, was that company executives already knew they had a rich mine, and then had proceeded to issue a disclaiming news release. Actually, April 9 was the day on which the option, obtained earlier from Royal Trust, had been exercised by Stephens. Although it might not know what it had, the management had decided to go ahead. The third hole had been completed two days before (the second hole had no significance and was planned to mislead) revealing substantial mineralization; the fourth hole had looked good in the beginning, but by the evening of April 9 had entered a barren stretch; the sixth hole had been begun the day before, and the fifth would not commence until the following day. Because of the absence of geologists from the drill site on April 8 and 9 due to bad weather, no visual estimates had been available. The offer to buy the ten per cent interest, although it proved abortive in the end, could be—and was—left open as long as possible, although obviously negotiations could not be carried on after the 15th since the mine was confirmed publicly the following day.

So far as the metallurgical testing hole was concerned, it was true that the decision to start it was made on Saturday, April 11—before the "misleading" release was issued—but the only information available in New York when the release was composed was for the period through Friday morning, after which Mollison and Holyk had left for New York.

Back on the subject of stock purchases, any significance which SEC might have attached to the 150 shares of stock purchased by Holyk and his wife on November 29 and December 10, 1963, would appear to be diluted by the fact that they sold the shares on December 31 in order to make a quick profit.

Fogarty, before the filing of the complaint, offered to transfer the stock he had purchased between November 12, 1963, and April 6, 1964—3,100 shares in all—to the corporation at his cost, and to surrender and cancel his options granted on February 20, 1964. This offer was accepted by the board of directors, which then passed a resolution commending his integrity and expressing its "gratitude and appreciation." His purpose was to offset any questions that might be raised in the minds of those benefited by hindsight, now that the mine had come in so spectacularly. His option was for 7,800 shares at 23 13/16. As noted earlier, the board had acted according to an option program of several years' standing, and had chosen to act in February, 1964, because the stock had returned to the price at which options had been granted originally, and because of what appeared to be an impending change in the tax laws.

Stephens also cancelled his options for 12,800 shares, despite the advice of counsel that all grants and purchases were entirely legal and proper. By this means he and Fogarty sought to shield Texas Gulf from any Commission criticism, through their voluntary actions which involved a good deal of personal sacrifice. It did them little good so far as warding off the complaint. Mollison and Harold Kline, general counsel, were among those granted options, each for 4,300 shares, and Holyk had been granted 2,000 shares. Mollison offered to return the 300 shares purchased by himself and his wife, and his offer was accepted by the directors. Kline chose not to return his options, although he did not exercise them for the present.

Crawford, the corporate secretary, had informed a representative of the New York Stock Exchange on the afternoon of April 16 that if he inadvertently or unwittingly had done anything wrong in buying his 600 shares—although he did not believe he had—he would be glad to do whatever was necessary to rectify the error. No such request was ever made by the exchange. Prior to the filing of the complaint his offer to transfer his shares was also accepted.

In this connection, counsel was to point out later that if Crawford had *wanted* to beat the news, he could have traded on the San Francisco Stock Exchange on April 15, the day before the announcement.

Then there was Ken Darke, who had freely admitted on examination that he had recommended TGS stock to several people, and had analyzed for them the company's overall prospects, but declared that he told them nothing about the first drill hole. Yet he, according to the complaint about to issue, was supposed in some way to have defrauded those persons who had sold stock on the open market to the various so-called tippees and sub-tippees. The Commission's position, apparently, was that because Darke *knew* the drilling results for one hole, he was barred from making recommendations, even though he had been doing this over a period of years. The SEC would ask Darke to make restitution of more than a million dollars for transactions which were of no benefit to him personally, and of which he was probably never aware. It was a demand that could make history, if granted.

Some other things in the interim period of the investigation helped to build up the atmosphere. On June 5, 1964, less than two months after the mine had been confirmed, a writ was issued in behalf of the Leitch and Mastodon-Highland Bell companies in Canada, challenging the ownership of the mine by Texas Gulf. Shares of both Canadian companies had been active in recent weeks on the Toronto exchange on rumors that this would happen. Leitch soared $1.15 a share on this day to close at $6.15. In early May it had sold as low as $2.39. Highland Bell shot up 95 cents on the news to close at $7.25. A week before it had closed at $5.55.

And on the same day the Pennzoil Company, of Oil City, Pennsylvania, liquidated its entire holdings of 150,000 shares of TGS at a profit of about $30 a share. President J. H. Liedtke told his stockholders, in effect, that the stock had been acquired in 1963 as an investment, and the profits could now be utilized for other purposes. Fair enough.

All of this might serve as a prelude to some comment on the way in which the actions of stock exchanges, and similarly the actions of the press, serve to set stages and produce results of their own, while quite independent of the formal procedures of fact-finding investigations and legal process. When the SEC brought its complaint in April, 1965—and surprised both the corporation and the individuals involved, as noted—all of the elements of a sure fire news story were ready and waiting. While recent Supreme Court decisions, capped by the Sam Shepperd case in Ohio, had focused much attention on the problems flowing from press interference with a fair trial in *criminal* cases, little attention had been given to similar obstacles to a fair trial in the court of public opinion in civil actions. When a powerful government agency lodges a complaint, involving a corporation and its people, and makes sensational charges of wrongdoing, press treatment almost invariably places the accused in a position of presumed guilt. Before trial, which in the Texas Gulf case did not begin until more than a year later, such charges are not only repeated but often distorted and capsulated in summaries over a long period. Acquittal or disproval, if it comes, usually finds its dreary way to the back pages.

In April of 1965 Texas Gulf had been for more than a year the highest flier in a high-flying stock market. At the start of 1964 the whole market was poised for the beginning of one of the most remarkable bull markets of modern times. Although TGS had nearly doubled in value since October, 1963, the rise in its stock did not seem particularly remarkable in the light of the market as a whole. As a leading sulphur producer through most of its 50-year history, with some handsome earnings performances and dividends, it did not seem so much a growth or speculative stock as it did a widows-and-orphans investment. But in 1956 things had slumped, with new sulphur sources, big inventories, and dropping prices. The dividend was reduced, in steps, and the stock went from a high of 45 in 1955 to a low of 11 in 1962. Things began to turn around again late in 1963, as the outlook for higher sulphur prices brightened and the attention to diversification was intensified. Such diversification promised growth, even though the company's entry into the potash and phosphate businesses caused little excitement.

Texas Gulf stock was not a special standout during the first months of the bull market in late 1963 and early 1964, although the company made frequent announcements in regard to its new properties and projects, and the improvement of its facilities. It rose from 18 to 22 while the stock of its biggest competitor, Freeport Sulphur, moved from 25 to 35. By the time the price of sulphur was finally increased on April 1, 1964, and this was followed two days later by the decision to invest $45 million in the North Carolina phosphate project, the stock had risen to 27 but still lagged behind the rising curve for the market as a whole as shown by Standard and Poor's averages for 425 leading industrials. Then began the Canadian rumors of a big copper strike near Timmins, and Toronto newspapers reported the stock exchange "flushed with speculative fever."

While the first Canadian reports were not published in New York until April 11, it should be noted that Texas Gulf was actively traded throughout the preceding week on the New York Stock Exchange, which was not so cut off from information as the Commission officially presumed. On Friday, April 10, there were 92,100 shares of Texas Gulf that changed hands, and the stock closed at 30⅛, the highest mark in seven years. Saturday brought the published reports in the *Herald Tribune* and *Times,* and Sunday, April 12, produced the company's statement on the Timmins situation as of the latest information available in New York. The release described the recent drilling, declared "more drilling would be required for proper evaluation of this prospect," and classified any conclusions as to size and grade of ore as "premature and possibly misleading." Most important, TGS promised to issue a definite statement when such conclusions were available.

The market opened on Monday, April 13, with TGS at 32 and the stock closed at 30⅞ after trading 126,500 shares. Tuesday's closing price was 30¼, *still higher* than the preceding Friday's closing price, and on this day 76,900 shares were traded. On Wednesday 43,800 shares were traded. The company's cautionary release apparently had produced the desired effect of stabilizing the stock in the face of unconfirmed rumors.

The real excitement began next day when the company confirmed its major discovery of commercially mineable zinc-copper-silver ore. The exact moment of disclosure was to become a central issue in the trial of the SEC's complaint against the company more than a year later, but from the time of the opening of the New York Stock Exchange at 10 A.M. there could be no doubt that a new spectacular had been launched in Wall Street. During the first hour 120,000 shares were traded, and 444,200 for the day. By 10:40 the price had moved up more than $3 a share from the previous day's closing—ten per cent of the stock's total value. It closed up seven points at 36⅜.

Although the SEC investigation began immediately, it was not publicly announced, and it continued for several months with the full cooperation of Texas Gulf officials. Meanwhile the company became Wall Street's—and Bay Street's—speculative favorite. The stock was traded in huge volume and prices-per-share bounced wildly. Nearly five million shares were traded in New York in the last two weeks in April. The stock rose to 42 on April 17, then settled back to 40¼. A week later it climbed to 48¼ in anticipation of further disclosures at the annual meeting in Houston, but when none were forthcoming it slumped a half dozen points. The rumors persisted, however, and at month's end it closed at 54¾, having once reached a high of 59.

In Canada there was a wild orgy of trading in penny mining stocks on the Toronto exchange, where one day's trading of more than 30 million shares set a North American record for all time. This added zest to the Wall Street speculative spirit without doubt. Traders eagerly bid up prices of any small mining company rumored to have claims on land within 50 miles of the Texas Gulf discovery, while in New York the stock of Curtis Publishing Company joined Texas Gulf at the top of the most active list when Curtis announced it would participate in the profits from the sulphur company's exploitation of adjoining Canadian timberlands.

The continuing violent swings in TGS stock a month after the announcement of the discovery are especially interesting in the light of a key point that would be argued two years later in the trial of the case. SEC took the position that company "insiders" should wait to buy the stock, not only until the news had been published in major media, but until "the investing public has had sufficient time to evaluate its significance."

It had not taken very long for some of that investing public to make its evaluation. One New York couple, as reported by a broker's representative at the trial, bought 1,500 shares at 10:09 on the morning of April 16, when the press conference at TGS had barely begun, and 2,000 more at 10:29. They sold them later in the same morning for a profit of $10,500. Some of the "difficulties" inherent in significant evaluation appear from the fact that the information on which the couple acted was obtained from the morning's report in *The Northern Miner*, published in Toronto. The broker could not find a copy uptown near his Madison Avenue office, but telephoned a friend in Wall Street and had him read the article, all before telephoning his customer.

About a month after this, the issue of *Forbes Magazine* for May 15 had this comment: "'Stock market gyrations aside, how valuable is TGS' find? That remains to be seen. Some mining men think it has been greatly exaggerated and that the rejoicing is premature. But others think the find will make TGS rich."

It was the "others" that kept things going. One broker's market letter estimated the company's ore reserves at 100 million tons with a "gross assay value of $3 billion." During the month of May a total of 5,747,000 shares were traded and the price bounced even more widely between a low of 46⅜ and a high of 60½, but closed the month at 54½. On the day the Leitch writ against Texas Gulf was filed, TGS closed at 50⅛. The legal action was announced after the market closed, but on the Pacific Coast the stock sold off sharply to 45¾ and trading was suspended for eleven minutes. In the middle of June, however, Texas Gulf announced its new preliminary estimate of 55 million tons of ore reserves, based on further extensive drilling, and said that it planned to proceed with a mine and a plant that would produce at the rate of two million tons a year. This seemed to stabilize the stock and during the summer it traded within a narrower range. L. O. Hooper, in *Forbes* in mid-July, said of TGS that it was "down from around 60 to the middle 40's, is beginning to look reasonably valued. The stock certainly is worth $10 to $15 a share more because of the new Canadian discovery, and I think the stock is worth 30 to 35 without the Timmins property. One never knows how long it will take to wash out the emotional camp followers who bought the stock heedlessly on the run-up." Despite such cloudy crystal balls extreme activity kept TGS on the hit parade and the year's volume totaled 24 million shares, more than twice that of Chrysler, the next most active stock of 1964. One year after the discovery was announced, Texas Gulf was still one of the most active stocks on the New York exchange and reached a high of 71, but the new headlines were made by the SEC.

After the complaint issued in the spring of 1965, the battle lines slowly began to sort themselves out. It could be observed, after the declaration of war, who were the attackers and who the attacked, and what were likely to be the issues in contention. For one thing, no matter who might be claiming to have justice and the gods on its side—and both sides did, following the standard pattern for any conflict—it was certainly clear that the spotlight was mainly on all those who had bought or sold shares of stock. They were at the heart of the provocation, of the action about to take place, and must be involved and affected by any solutions or results when the smoke had cleared away. As far as could be judged, the air was going to be smoke-laden for a very long time.

It hardly requires argument that the whole purpose of the various statutes and rules which formed and armed the Securities and Exchange Commission was to protect and defend the investing public. The common soldier in that rather nebulous and abstract army of buyers and sellers was the shareholder, and he came in all sizes. His tenure as the owner of one or more certificates signifying equity ownership might be very long, or extremely short. Although his spirit might be most frequently and popularly invoked in the shape of an individual (small investor, people's capitalist, widow or orphan, elderly pensioner, etc.) he also came in the shape of an institution, such as a bank, insurance company, pension trust, or corporation. It is part of popular mythology that there are many unsavory characters in both groups—sharpies, tipsters, get-rich-quick operators, market manipulators, cold-hearted and avaricious syndicates, and giant financial complexes. And since, in any such panorama of action there must be both "bad guys" and "good guys," conforming to popular jargon, it is widely assumed, and hoped, that federal administrative agencies and departments, such as the SEC and the Department of Justice, ride the white horses and break their lances for the latter group. The assumption, if not the hope, is somewhat encouraged by treatment accorded by the press, possibly for motives of its own.

The picture is not that simple, of course, and difficulties arise when the *genus* stockholder is closely examined and his reactions noted. The white knights may ride, and their efforts may prevail, buttressed by the decisions of the courts, but somehow in the process the objects of their affection—the buyers and sellers and holders of stocks—turn up dead, wounded, or indignant. When the battle is over, or temporarily subsides, the carnage can be quite substantial and the confusion measureable. Granted that some will prosper as a result of the fortunes of war, there is a real question as to whether the majority of the shareowners involved wanted to be so sharply defended in the first place, considering the cost. A defendant corporation, such as Texas Gulf Sulphur in this instance, is owned by its shareholders. If the corporation is made to bleed, it is stockholders' blood being spilled.

The war between stockholders and management, like the comparable war between men and women, is after all a family fight, and those most involved prefer to term it a "relationship."

Each party has its options and courses of action and does not always welcome or need outside intervention. The remedial machinery is built-in, established by contract, and enforceable by law.

Filing the complaint against TGS and 13 individual defendants was not more than a sharp skirmish opening hostilities, but it initiated the polarization process among stockholders. The very next day a retired publisher in Calgary, Alberta—C. V. Myers—who said he "owned several thousand shares" sent off a letter to the chairman of the SEC, with a copy to *Barron's:*

> Your action is couched in such terms as to suggest that it is aimed at the protection of investors. The action . . . has reduced the value of my shares on the market, has cast doubt on the integrity of the company.
>
> Certain shareholders of TGS may complain they sold their shares without knowing the full extent of the company's worth. I bought substantial holdings at the same time they were selling, without knowing any more. In fact, who knows the value yet? You complain because the directors bought 6,100 shares of TGS stock. I bought more shares than all the directors combined, on the open market. Surely there must be bigger things for the SEC to investigate.
>
> As a shareholder without inside information, and without personal acquaintance, I am immensely pleased with the directors of this company, and I believe the vast majority of my fellow stockholders agree with me. We do not feel we have been cheated. . . . The big damage in this case has been done by the SEC itself. It has slandered the reputation of a highly successful and efficient company by casting character reflection on able management. . . . Your action has reduced the value of my stock in the eyes of the investing public.

Myers was not alone, although he did more about it. Many letters were from small holders, from elderly people, and were hand-written. One stockholder, noting that company officers had returned their stock options, even suggested a method to the company that would restore what had been taken away. Whether the number of letters addressed to the Commission totaled in the hundreds or the thousands is neither ascertainable nor especially important, since no public referendum was being held and the action was proceeding on a plane that would hardly have been affected had there been one. Excerpts from some other correspondents, however, do provide some indication of *some* stockholder attitudes.

From Des Moines, Iowa: "What would have happened if Texas Gulf Sulphur had prematurely released news of a mineral discovery of magnitude and it proved otherwise? It would have precipitated a complaint of manipulation. I think Texas Gulf Sulphur officers' and directors' action was honest and prudent."

From Warrensburg, Missouri: "Is the Commission going to flood the courts with thousands of actions because some official has been too optimistic or too pessimistic? Your action in regard to Texas Gulf Sulphur makes one wonder if this is a police state of 1980 or the U.S.A. of 1965. . . . Your action . . . has certainly depressed its stock. Are you going to sue yourselves?"

From Tucson, Arizona: "The Pandora's box which this decision of the SEC now threatens to open for the business world tends towards a situation where every so-called investor who makes a mistake in buying or selling will want to sue some one. If the Monday evening TV doesn't tell him that the XYZ company sales were off 2 per cent in the preceding week, he will have a grievance."

And from Lake Hamilton, Florida: "If management is required to report a Timmins strike before it is thoroughly evaluated, then why should not management be required to report large sales contract negotiations, research developments, etc., *even while pending*? . . . The news of a large contract signed, sealed and delivered, or a new process completed, can greatly influence the market when announced and can make the previous day's seller of that particular company's stock wish he hadn't!"

"I just want you to know how much harm you are causing a poor widow, whose husband invested all his money in 200 shares of Texas Gulf Sulphur on margin just before he died of a heart attack on June 18, 1965," wrote one of the SEC chairman's correspondents from Jamaica, New York. "Due to the action taken by the Securities and Exchange Commission . . . the stock has dropped to this low value. It will be *only* a matter of time and the company's name will be cleared. In the mean time I will be sold out and will have lost my life's savings. For you $14,000 may not be a great deal but it is all my husband left me. He did not have an insurance. My only income is $101.50 a month from Social Security. While you are trying to help the people who sold Texas Gulf before the news of Timmins reached them, remember the people like me who had faith in the good reports they heard and read about and invested their money. If your aim is to protect the investors, protect the present investors."

The reply, to the Jamaica widow and others, was made by David Ferber, solicitor for the Commission, and it invariably stated that the SEC action was "solely in furtherance of its statutory mandate to protect the public interest."

Ex-publisher Myers felt that the Ferber reply was "highly revealing" in discussing the Commission's positions set forth in the complaint. He made an analysis, including his own comments, and sent it off to several thousand TGS shareowners at his own expense, urging them to write the SEC chairman, Manuel F. Cohen. To Ferber he responded: "If you win your case against us, you will have reversed the entire concept of free trading in securities in North America. Henceforth the losers will win, and the winners lose. . . . Surely this is not part of your mandate from the United States government."

On July 22, 1965, the campaign mounted by Myers bore some added fruit when it attracted the attention of the *Wall Street Journal*. The newspaper reported that he had spent $4,000 to date from his own funds in fighting the SEC action and was looking for help. In due course he established in Calgary a protective shareholder committee under the aegis of a local bank.

Not all of the shareholders enjoyed this point of view, and especially not all of the *ex*-shareowners. Many of them filed suits to recover their "losses" caused by selling their stock at the "right" time, but more of that later. The husband-and-wife team in New York, who had joined the Texas Gulf family for only a half day before selling out with a clear $10,500 profit, neither complained to the Commission nor filed for damages against the corporation. One might call them just enriched neutrals.

# 5
# Complaint:
# Bricks and Straw

I

**W**ITH expert timing, the Securities and Exchange Commission picked the spring Monday afternoon of April 19, 1965, to unleash the complaint against Texas Gulf Sulphur Company and thirteen individual defendants. It consisted of 102 numbered paragraphs and what the language of the law calls a prayer, although in this case the courts, not heaven, are the designated recipients and there is a certain lack of humility in the style.

The action against the company, incidentally, was filed less than 72 hours before the annual meeting of Texas Gulf stockholders in Houston on April 22, and the timing almost justifies a charge that the Commission is not quite as solicitous of the welfare of the corporate shareowners as it purports to be. The investigation of TGS had begun in April, 1964, and continued for almost a year. But on March 5, 1965, the SEC *approved* all of the proxy materials which Texas Gulf had submitted in advance of its annual meeting, and the material contained a statement that the management knew of no matters, other than those specifically referred to in the proxy statement, to be presented at the meeting. The SEC has a rule—X-14a-9—which prohibits "false or misleading statements" in proxy solicitations. In spite of the fact that the Commission had investigated TGS for eleven months and must have decided in that time that it would bring suit against the company, it approved the proxy material on March 5, 1965, and the material contained no reference to any forthcoming action. Then, 23 days after the material was approved, the SEC notified counsel for TGS that an action would be brought and the complaint issued four days later. Months later, in December, the SEC announced an amendment to its rules which in effect operated as a disclaimer of such responsibility. Among other things it said that, "The fact that a proxy statement . . . has been filed with or examined by the Commission, shall not be deemed a finding . . . that such material is accurate or complete or not false or misleading. . . ."

Be that as it may, the total cost to everybody of this challenging document has never been estimated, but the modest page-and-a-half SEC news release announcing the action (Litigation Release No. 3196) might be said to have borne a hundred million dollar price tag. In the immediate trading future it effected a decline of ten points in the price of TGS stock, and there were ten million shares outstanding. The complaint, like a rocket, was pointed right at headquarters, while its vapor trail, comprising the press treatment, hung around a very long time but gradually phased off in several directions. These substance and shadow aspects require separate examination.

The first of the 102 paragraphs named the corporation and the thirteen individual defendants who "have engaged, are engaged, and are about to engage in acts and practices" in violation of Section 10(b) of the Securities Exchange Act of 1934, and of Rule 10b-5, later promulgated by the Commission under the authority of that statute. The next 16 paragraphs established the jurisdiction of the federal court and described the defendants.

Paragraphs 18 through 20 told of the company's aerial survey program and the drilling, from 1959 through the completion of the discovery hole on November 12, 1963; the security measures taken by the company; and its land acquisition program. The next paragraph counted the shares owned prior to November 11 by Fogarty, Mollison, Clayton, and Huntington, and declared that none had been so owned by O'Neill, Darke, Crawford, Murray, and Holyk.

Then the complaint took off for 60 monotonous paragraphs detailing the shares purchased, and when, by the defendants and their friends, sandwiching in the fact that the first core had been assayed and that Darke had supplied information to the tippees— all these acts having been performed by those who had knowledge not known by the investing public.

Continuing onward, paragraph 82 described the stock options that had been granted by a committee of directors, from whom the information in regard to the drilling had been "intentionally concealed," while paragraph 83 noted the completion of the land acquisition, the further drilling of two more holes, and that, on the basis of the acceptance of visual estimates as of April 9, and assays of the original core, "the existence of a large body of commercially mineable ore of substantial value . . . had been established."

From paragraph 84 to the close, further stock purchases by individuals were detailed; also described was the "false and materially misleading" news release of April 12, known to be such by the TGS principals; the resulting lower stock prices; the story in *The Northern Miner* giving its estimate of the mine; the board meeting, press conference, and confirming release of April 16; the fact that the news appeared on the Dow Jones broad tape at 10:55 A.M. of that day (no mention of the earlier teletype distributions); and the fact that shares had been sold by those who would not have sold had they known the material facts. For the first time, this latter statement served to suggest the possibility of corporate liability in the form of civil actions, since there was no prayer in the complaint for damages from the company itself.

The final paragraph, 102, summarized the defendants' purchases from November 12, 1963, through 10:55 A.M. of the following April 16, as being 9,100 shares, 5,200 calls, and options on 31,200 shares. On reading this, one observer pointed out that the number of shares purchased by insiders seemed inordinately small if they really intended to make a killing. The SEC prayer, absent humility, sought five gifts from heaven's stand-in:

1. A permanent injunction against the individual defendants, "from employing any device, scheme, or artifice to defraud . . . in connection with the purchase and sale of securities." It then spelled out what it meant by "in the course of their corporate duties."
2. A direction to all individuals (except Lamont, Stephens, and Kline) to offer *rescission* to the sellers from whom they had purchased.
3. A direction to Darke to make *restitution* to all who sold stock to him and to those of his tippees named in the complaint; to Lamont to do the same for those who had sold to him and to the Morgan Guaranty Trust Company; and

to Coates to do the same for those who sold to him and those named as his tippees.

4. A direction to all defendants who received options to cancel and rescind the options granted during this period and to return to the corporation the unpurchased shares and any profits.

5. An order permanently enjoining the corporation "from directly or indirectly, by use of any means or instrumentality of interstate commerce, or of the mails, or of any facility of any national securities exchange, in connection with the purchase or sale of securities, from making any untrue statement of material fact or omitting to state a material fact necessary to make the statements made, in light of the circumstances under which they were made, not misleading, namely, from issuing, publishing, distributing or otherwise disseminating materially false, misleading, inadequate or inaccurate press releases and other communications and reports concerning material facts about Texas Gulf's activities and operations."

That last was quite a mouthful. In effect it seemed to be asking for a court adjuration to speak the truth, carefully circumscribed in just under a hundred words. Presumably taking a long drafter's breath and wondering what had been left out, the SEC then asked for "such other and further restitution and other relief as to this Court may seem appropriate."

While the defendants were busy composing themselves and their answers, the complaint attracted considerable attention in professional circles, because it seemed to have the Commission breaking new ground in all directions—in the persons cited, the actions complained against, the kind of relief asked, and the section of the law under which the complaint was brought. For example, the granting of any such permanent injunction against the corporation would make it liable to contempt of court if it ever put out a news release that would, by some subsequent tribunal, be judged "false or misleading." [1]

The complaint ran against ten officers or employees of Texas

[1] Alan R. Bromberg: "Texas Gulf Sulphur and its Implications," *Southwestern Law Journal*, 1968, Vol. 22, p. 737—"An injunction may be little more than a warning to behave in the future. But history suggests that law developed in injunction cases is later applied in liability and criminal cases as well. The injunction suit is often the camel's nose in the tent."

Gulf who had purchased the company's stock, or who had recommended it, or who had accepted options on it, between the dates mentioned, or before the "material fact" of the November core was made public on April 16. It also ran against one officer and two directors who bought stock on April 16, but who had not waited long enough to suit the SEC. And it asked for *rescission* to the sellers by all of those who bought, and *restitution* to those who sold to friends of the defendants, and even to those who sold to friends of *those* friends. Commented Henry G. Manne, the Kenan Professor of Law at the University of Rochester and a frequent critic of the Commission:

> The prayer for restitution to individuals selling to those who bought on the advice of insiders is most peculiar. The complaint does not even limit the liability to cases of sales to first-level advisees. . . . There is no attempt to include individuals advised by second-level advisees, though it is well-known that these did exist. . . . In going beyond liability to persons who sold to insiders the SEC has perhaps made the most unusual proposal. Clearly the number of shares an advisee purchases or causes others to purchase cannot be controlled by the insider. Thus, as an advisee and his friends become richer, it is more and more in their power to bankrupt the inside adviser if civil actions are brought against him by those who sold to the advisees.[2]

There must be limits to such a notion, Manne added, since out of a given number of fundamentally unreliable tips, a few are bound to prove correct. It would be the height of absurdity to hold speculators on the few occasions when their gambles paid off, but equally strange "to make the insider who told the first outsider an insurer for every seller's loss."

## II

From this point, and perhaps straining the reader's patience and eyesight, the backward paper trail is laborious but also illuminating and necessary to the story. As for the legal basis of the SEC charges, all of the wrong things, as stated in the complaint, had been done in violation of the so-called "fraud section"—10(b) of the Securities Exchange Act of 1934. Yet no

[2] Henry G. Manne: *Insider Trading and the Stock Market,* The Free Press, New York (1966), pp. 44–5.

such charges had ever been brought in a federal court under this section. As a consequence, no federal court had so far defined what, under this interpretation, is a material fact, nor decided the range of persons to whom this interpretation applies. No such court had so far ever legally defined when such persons might safely buy or recommend the stock after the material facts have been made public. Until the issuance of this complaint, it had been thought by most authorities that the only federal law applicable to a company's public statements was that pertaining to specific forms such as registration statements, prospectuses, and certain periodic reports. It had probably never entered anyone's head that press releases would be just as liable to federal attack under the securities laws, unless they involved fraud or *scienter* (the intent to deceive, or knowledge of falsity). But the SEC was now obviously assuming that it did not have to prove *scienter*, and that the statutory phrase, "in connection with the purchase or sale of securities" was in effect meaningless.

Up to now it had also been thought that the only section of the law applying to "insider trading" was Section 16 of the 1934 Act, the so-called "insider section." But this prescribes nothing against any of the individual actions described in the complaint. It applies to short-swing transactions—stock purchased and then sold within a six-months period by directors, officers, and ten per cent stockholders. Only six of the defendants, apart from their actions, came within this category.

The Commission was claiming, therefore, under Section 10(b), that *any* persons acquainted with material facts about the company, not known to the public, must either reveal such facts before trading, or not trade, and not recommend. The membership in the insider club had suddenly been expanded. Four questions were raised:

1. Was the April 12 release misleading and careless, and in violation of the law as a *fraud*?
2. What is a material fact?
3. Who is an insider?
4. When has a material fact been made *sufficiently* public for insiders to buy and sell stock safely?

The answers were now going to be applied to Texas Gulf and its people as guinea pigs, although neither Congress by statute, nor the courts by interpretation, nor the Commission by its previous rule-making, had laid down any guidelines or orders. In the instant case the SEC would argue that the first press release was misleading for calling the drilling results through April 9 only a "prospect," which meant something less than *probable* ore and still less than *proven* ore. It also suggested that Fogarty should have tried for more information before issuing it, or waited until he had more. There was the rather novel view put forth that the first core must have been a material fact because those who bought the stock must have thought so.

The Texas Gulf case was the first to attempt to define the time of disclosure as *sometime after* the information had been released to the press, if that can be called a definition. And it was under continuous revision. The SEC lawyers at first held that the news of the mine had become public at 10:55 A.M. on April 16, the time of its appearance on the Dow Jones broad tape being determining. More than a year later, and just before the trial opened in federal court, the SEC amended its complaint and shifted its position to claim that even this was not sufficient to cover Lamont's purchase at 12:33 P.M. Still later they insisted that the ban on buying stock must extend for a further unidentified period until investors could consult with their financial advisors, but they wanted the court to say when: "It is the Commission's position that even after corporate information has been published in the news media insiders are still under a duty to refrain from securities transactions until there has elapsed a reasonable amount of time in which the securities industry, the shareholders and the investing public can evaluate the development and make informed investment decisions." [3]

In their answers the defendants' lawyers—among other things —denied that Section 10(b) applied to any of the charges. They denied that the release was fraudulent, misleading, or negligent. They rejected the claim that the November core was a material fact and they declared that the news had already been made public when the market opened on April 16.

[3] After Lamont's death, the SEC withdrew its appeal of the trial court's findings in favor of this defendant in this aspect of the case, and therefore the ultimate question of time was not before the Court of Appeals. However, the majority opinion commented in a footnote that "in any event, the permissible timing of insider transactions after disclosures of various sorts is one of the many areas of expertise for appropriate exercise of the SEC's rule-making power, which we hope will be utilized in the future to provide some predictability of certainty for the business community."

This complaint constituted the most dramatic disclosure since the Pecora hearings of 1933, so far as Manne was concerned, and he said the case itself "presents in almost classic terms all of the factors that must be considered in a comprehensive treatment of insider trading. The resolution of the questions in this case may determine the law in this field for many years to come." [4]

Some three years after the bringing of the complaint, Professor Bromberg was to point out, in his review of the case, that the action against Texas Gulf was not an ordinary injunction suit since, from the outset, the SEC sought private relief against the individual defendants and asked the court to deprive them of the benefits of their use of inside information. Bromberg added that the answer to the question of who is an insider is no longer a matter of categories or boxes in organization charts, but of information-yielding relationships, and he offered a check list of such insiders, consisting of ten classes. "Anyone who gets information from a company is potentially an insider for 10b-5. This is quite distinct from Securities Exchange Act Section 16, which applied reporting requirements and short-swing profit recapture to a class of insiders defined to include only officers, directors, and holders of 10 per cent or more of a class of equity securities." [5]

While another commentator among the professionals limited his checklist of probable insiders to only three headings, he went further than Bromberg and included "government officials serving in capacities through which they necessarily obtain information relevant to a company's securities" [6]—which presumably would include the Commission itself. In his discussion of insider trading, Manne had said that "myriad government reporting requirements may make private policing of information by corporate insiders very difficult. The net effect of requiring disclosure to unpoliced government officials may be to deprive . . . the shareholders of the benefits they would otherwise receive." In justice he went on to point out, however, that the SEC makes unlawful the personal use of information filed with the Commission, through the statute creating it, and that it makes a continuing effort to prevent any abuse—but no other agency except SEC has regularly shown itself eager to police its rules. [7]

[4] *Op. cit.*, Note 2, this chapter, p. 40.
[5] *Op. cit.*, Note 1, this chapter, pp. 738, 740.
[6] *St. John's Law Review*, Vol. 43, 1969, p. 437.
[7] *Op. cit.*, Note 2, this chapter, pp. 183, 185.

It should be noted that victims of manipulation by corporate insiders were to some extent afforded a remedy at common law, but patent injustices often were the result. The background of the Commission's action against TGS could be said to begin with three rules developed in the state courts over the years. The *majority* rule, to which most of the states subscribed, set forth that there was no obligation on the part of insiders buying a company's shares to disclose information. Directors and officers under this rule deal at arm's length with stockholders, and the only limitation on this was fraud, which was difficult to prove.

Eventually certain states, such as Georgia, Kansas, and Nebraska—and, as one writer has noted, all were far from Wall Street or a stock exchange—saw fit to develop a *minority* rule which did create a fiduciary relationship between the corporation's officers and directors and the selling stockholders. In these cases, full disclosure was required before any dealing.

Finally there came along, at common law, the so-called *special facts* doctrine. It dates from a famous 1909 case, *Strong v. Repide*, which did not arise from the common law jurisdictions at all but from actions taking place in the Philippine Islands, in which a civil code derived from Spanish law was in effect.[8] The defendant here managed a corporation owning lands in the islands, and also owned about three-fourths of the shares. The land had become almost worthless as the result of guerilla activities, and this had been discussed in the press, but the defendant had negotiations underway with the government and apparently was convinced that the government would purchase at a handsome price. Through agents he approached the plaintiff to buy her small interest. The principal was never disclosed. The plaintiff ultimately sold her land for about one-tenth of what the government later paid. Although the Philippine court followed the *majority* rule and found for the defendant, the United States Supreme Court took a different view and held that the plaintiff would not have sold if she had known the defendant was the purchaser; that this was not a matter to be determined by the bare relationship between director and stockholder, but that there were special circumstances. The defendant, said the court, had a duty to speak, and it found strong evidence of fraud. While the *special facts* rule was born in the Philippines, many states have chosen to follow it as the common law rule. It would appear,

[8] *Strong v. Repide, 213 U.S. 419 (1909).*

however, that some substantial danger of fraud was a necessary element, such as undue influence.

However, the common-law approach to insider trading, where the shares of large corporations were listed on an *exchange,* still seemed clear—nothing impeded such trading with undisclosed information. In 1933 the Supreme Judicial Court of Massachusetts declared: "Law in its sanctions is not coextensive with morality. It cannot undertake to put all parties to every contract on an equality as to knowledge, experience, skill and shrewdness. It cannot undertake to relieve against hard bargains made between competent parties without fraud." [9]

This case, a writer would note some 36 years later, was "one which demonstrated how corporate officials who were privy to material inside information could easily take advantage of ignorant minority stockholders without fear of retribution, especially if the transactions involved took the form of impersonal and indirect dealings effectuated over a national exchange. To remedy this defect in the common law, Rule 10b-5 was promulgated as an expansive anti-fraud regulation. . . . The language of the rule is deceptively vague in its details, and thus remarkably broad in its scope. . . ." [10]

Before that, of course, there came upon the scene the Securities Act of 1933, the Securities Exchange Act of 1934, and the Commission itself. From October, 1929, to July, 1932, the Dow Jones industrials had dropped from 381 to 45. Then Congress passed the Securities Act of 1933, applying to the issuance of new securities. While it was being debated, and because it applied to registration statements and prospectuses, Wall Street called it the "truth in securities" bill. In 1934, following the exhaustive Pecora investigation and lengthy hearings and debates, Congress passed the Securities Exchange Act of 1934. It applied to *dealing* in securities, and it created the Securities and Exchange Commission. The now famous Rule 10b-5, promulgated under Section 10(b) of the 1934 Act, actually did not come into being until 1942. In that year markets had started turning upward from the depressed 'thirties, and the upturn prompted the rule. In substance Section 10(b) merely said it should be unlawful for any person in connection with the purchase and sale of any security to engage in any conduct that the Commission might, by rule, say was manipulative or deceptive. The

[9] *Goodwin v. Agassiz, 283 Mass. 358 (1933).*
[10] *Op. cit.,* Note 6, this chapter, p. 427.

entire TGS case is based on this section. As Professor Louis Loss, of Harvard, has pointed out, the section is not self-operative and makes nothing unlawful. Its entire legislative history resides in a sentence spoken by Thomas V. Corcoran, then the administrative spokesman before the Senate Banking and Currency Committee: "Thou shalt not devise any other cunning devices." [11] This is the rule: [12]

> It shall be unlawful for any person, directly or indirectly, by the use of any means or instrumentality of interstate commerce, or of the mails, or of any facility of a national securities exchange,
> (1) to employ any device, scheme or artifice to defraud,
> (2) to make any untrue statement of a material fact or to omit to state a material fact necessary in order to make the statements made, in the light of the circumstances under which they were made, not misleading, or
> (3) to engage in any act, practice, or course of business which operates or would operate as a fraud or deceit upon any any person, in connection with the purchase or sale of any security.

Section 16 of this statute, on the other hand, regulated insider trading. It applied only to officers, directors, and owners of ten per cent of a corporation's stock. It was passed, so it is said, for the purpose of preventing the unfair use of information which may have been obtained by such beneficial owner, director, or officer. This is what most of the TGS case would *appear* to be about. It was a very simple section, in three parts. The first part required the classes of persons named to report their holdings and transactions in their companies' stocks. The second required them to turn over to the company any profits made on less than a six months' turn-around. The third forbade them to sell their own company's stock short. That was all. It said nothing about employees' trading, material facts, tippers or tippees, undisclosed facts or any duty to disclose, nor about restitution or rescission to unknown sellers. The narrowness of Section 16 in regulating insider trading was deliberate. Seven years after its passage, in 1941, SEC Chairman Ganson Purcell testified that it was "eminently wise" that the section prohibited only the most prevalent form of the abuse of inside infor-

[11] Louis Loss: "Corporate Insiders and the Fiduciary Concept," an address before the American Society of Corporate Secretaries, Colorado Springs, Colorado, June 27, 1966.
[12] 17 C.F.R. Section 240, 10b-5 (1968).

mation—trading designed to take quick profits from short-term market fluctuations.[13]

It has often been said that probably the true purpose of Rule 10b-5 has been best crystallized by Chief Judge Leahy, of the federal district court in Delaware, in his often-quoted "equalization of bargaining position" rationale: [14]

> The rule is clear. It is unlawful for an insider such as a majority stockholder to purchase . . . stock of minority stockholders without disclosing material facts affecting the value of the stock known . . . by virtue of his inside position but not known to the . . . [seller], which information would have affected the judgment of the sellers. The duty of disclosure stems from the necessity of preventing a corporate insider from utilizing his position to take unfair advantage of the uninformed . . . [outsider]. It is an attempt to provide some degree of equalization of bargaining position in that . . . [outsiders] may exercise an informed judgment in any such transaction.

While the first judicial recognition of the applicability of 10b-5 to insider trading in a private civil action had come in 1947 [15] the 1951 case of *Speed v. Transamerica Corp.* which offered the Leahy doctrine was still not one involving a transaction across an exchange, but it went far beyond anything suggested in earlier cases.

Nine years after the rule was written, in 1951, Judge Jerome Frank wrote a decision for the Second Circuit Court of Appeals— the same court that would review the TGS case—which found that, "Proof of fraud is required in suits under 10(b) of the 1934 Act and Rule 10b-5. . . ." [16] And Frank had been an early chairman of the SEC.

Only the Securities Exchange Act of 1934 and one rather curious case decided in 1949, *Brophy v. Cities Service*, have ever maintained the position that insider stock trading injures the corporation, rather than the individual, and allowed recovery.[17] The case has seldom been cited on its merits, presumably because of the facts. One Kennedy, the confidential secretary of the Cities Service president, knew that the company was buying its own shares in the open market. Kennedy would buy before this was to

---

[13] *CrCl 30.*
[14] *Speed v. Transamerica Corp., 99 F. Supp. 808 (1951).*
[15] *Kardon v. National Gypsum Co., 73 F. Supp. 798 (1947).*
[16] *Fischman v. Raytheon, 188 F. 2d at 786–7 (1951).*
[17] *Brophy v. Cities Service, 31 Del. Ch. 241 (1949).*

happen, and sell afterwards. The court found this a violation of his fiduciary duty because he was using the information for his own benefit. The opinion did not make any analysis of the potential loss to the company, but simply held that the secretary could not profit by his confidential information, which belonged to the company and not to him.

Manne, whose stubborn advocacy of insider trading as *beneficial* to the economy often leads him into prodding both the SEC and the law experimentally, has posed this hypothetical problem under 10b-5: on the theory that corporations can violate the laws as well as individuals, a corporation which—unannounced—purchases its own shares and raises the market price in the process, presumably violates the rule. However, if it announced its intention beforehand, the cost of the shares purchased would be greater, and so would the loss to the shareholders who were not doing the selling.[18]

Section 16(b) is an explicit effort to equalize the bargaining position of insiders and other investors, and Rule 10b-5 combined the jurisdictional coverage of 10(b)—"any person" and "purchase or sale"—with the substantive aspects of 17(a) of the 1933 Act. In 1962 the case of *Blau v. Lehman* [19] gave the U.S. Supreme Court its first opportunity to construe the section, and the result put limits, at least temporarily, on how the Commission might push it. The case is mainly significant for this fact, at least for the purposes of this study. The action was brought by a stockholder of Tidewater Associated Oil Company against the Wall Street investment banking and brokerage firm of Lehman Brothers, a partnership, and against Joseph Thomas, a member of the firm who was also a Tidewater director.

Recovery was sought, for Tidewater, of short-swing profits alleged to have been realized by the defendants. The theory of the plaintiff's case was that the investment firm had *deputized* Thomas to act as its representative on the board, and that his inside knowledge had resulted in Lehman Brothers' purchasing and selling 50,000 shares of stock. Such profits, under 16(b), would inure to Tidewater. All three courts held against the plaintiff, however, the Supreme Court refusing to disturb the finding of facts below and holding that Congress did not intend that partnerships be included automatically whenever one partner was a statutory insider. The

[18] *Op. cit.*, Note 2, this chapter, p. 236.
[19] *Blau v. Lehman et al*, 368 *U.S.* 403 (1962).

Commission, as *amicus curiae*, had been pushing the point that the section should be extended to include *anyone* realizing short-swing profits based on inside information—not just the officers, directors, and ten per cent stockholders named in the Act. It was a definite rebuff for the SEC, since the court replied: "Congress . . . might amend 16(b) if the Commission would present to it the policy arguments it has presented to us, but we think that Congress is the proper agency to change an interpretation of the Act unbroken since its passage, if the change is to be made." Justice Hugo Black, who had been a senator during the consideration of the 1934 Act, wrote the decision.

It remained, finally, for another case to break some barriers, supply the Commission with needed ammunition, and later be hailed as the most important opinion in these matters until the Texas Gulf action came along in 1966. This was an administrative proceeding, *In the Matter of Cady, Roberts and Co.*[20] It was brought by the SEC as an action to discipline a broker and his firm for violation of 10b-5, but it did not involve any issue of money damages for individual traders. It was only a disciplinary action by the Commission. The respondents' offer of a settlement was accepted—the broker was suspended for 20 days and no sanction was imposed against the registrant—and the matter did not, therefore, reach the courts, but it has been said that its underlying logic would seem applicable to a private civil action. Said Manne, "*Cady, Roberts* laid to final rest the belief that Rule 10b-5 was still circumscribed by the older special-facts approach . . . its general tone as an attack on all insider trading was unmistakable."[21]

The facts were these: J. Cheever Cowdin, a registered representative of Cady, Roberts and Company, was also a director of Curtiss-Wright Corporation, whose shares had risen considerably as a result of recent publicity attendant upon a new engine development. Shortly after this, however, the directors substantially cut the dividend. During the increase in the price of the shares, one of the partners in Cady, Roberts had been buying for 30 discretionary accounts, including that of his wife. On the day before the dividend was cut he had begun selling, with some shares being sold short, and within a two-day period he had sold more than half of the holding.

[20] *In the Matter of Cady, Roberts and Co.*, Securities Exchange Act Release No. 6668, Nov. 8, 1961.
[21] *Op. cit.*, Note 2, this chapter, p. 39.

On the day of the board meeting, a recess had been called at about 11 A.M. after the dividend-cutting session, and at this point Cowdin telephoned the news to the partner. The directors had already authorized the transmission of the news to the New York Stock Exchange, as was ordinarily done, but the exchange did not receive it for another hour and a half. There was no explanation, except that the delay had been caused by typing problems. The Dow Jones broad tape was not given the information for 45 minutes after the recess, possibly from inadvertence. On the exchange trading had to be suspended after the news because of the sudden rush of sell orders, and the stock price plummeted. The Cady, Roberts orders had been executed 15 and 18 minutes after the dividend action. The action of the broker was found to be a willful violation of Section 17(a) of the Securities Act of 1933, of Section 10(b) of the Securities Exchange Act of 1934, and of Rule 10b-5.

In his opinion, Chairman William Cary of the Commission declared this to be a case of first importance in the administration of the federal securities acts, and said that liability under 10b-5 "rests on two principal elements: first, the existence of a relationship giving access, directly or indirectly, to information intended to be available only for a corporate purpose and *not* for the personal benefit of anyone, and second, the inherent unfairness involved where a party takes advantage of such information knowing it is unavailable to those with whom he is dealing. . . . Intimacy demands restraint lest the uninformed be exploited."

The respondents argued that 10b-5 was not intended to extend beyond the special facts rule in state law, that no special facts case ever found liability in a transaction over an exchange, and that some semblance of privity always had to be shown. The Commission rejected these arguments, saying cases under the common law special facts rule had no relevance, and that privity was not required in an action to discipline a broker.

The legal stage was now set for the trial of Texas Gulf Sulphur, except for the possible mention of two other pertinent points relating to tipping and materiality. It has been noted that courts in the past have been reluctant to apply the fraud provisions of the securities acts to alleged violations by tippees because neither party to the transaction is, at the same time, a recognized fiduciary of the corporation or one who directly benefits from the abuse. "It is much easier," said one writer, "to detect an untimely transaction by an acknowledged insider than to show that he has privately di-

vulged confidential information to a third person who is unknown
to the SEC as far as 16(a) reporting requirements are concerned."
Tippee fraud has rarely been proven. And the same writer points
out that the 10b-5 limitation on insider trading turns upon possession of material information. "The materiality of information becomes the key consideration in determining the point at which the
duty . . . arises." [22] End of paper trail.

### III

So far as the press-inspired vapor trail was
concerned, Texas Gulf people could have no complaint in respect
to volume, but it often seemed that every new development in the
SEC case against the company landed with a negative impact or
unhappy timing. The complaint itself appeared near the end of the
day on Monday, April 19, too late for any very careful study either
by reporters or company executives, but early enough for the tabloid
New York *Daily News* to sum it up in 120-point headlines:

### SEC SUES EXECS
### IN TEXAS GULF
### FORTUNE GRAB

and to support it with:

> The fabulous Canadian ore strike that sent Texas Gulf Sulphur
> Co. stock skyrocketing in one of the biggest speculative booms ever
> seen on North American exchanges backfired yesterday against 13
> officers and employees of the company.
>     In a civil suit filed in federal court here, the Securities and
> Exchange Commission charged that 12 of them had made a killing
> in "insider" operations in Texas Gulf Sulphur stock betweeen Nov.
> 12, 1963, when a first drill hole near Timmins, Ont., indicated
> the existence of a high-grade copper and zinc deposit, and April 16,
> 1964, when the news was made public.

Such colorful language as "fortune grab" and "insiders made
a killing" did not appear in the complaint, of course, but the *Daily
News* could reasonably defend its fair interpretation of the suit's
implications. Nevertheless, it is not too difficult to start the snow-
balls rolling. News of the complaint was carried on the Dow Jones
broad tape at 4:59 P.M. of the day of release. It had not yet been

[22] *Op. cit.*, Note 6, this chapter, pp. 439, 442.

received by Texas Gulf officers, and barely by the lawyers. It is not surprising that the wire services and the press would have some difficulty capsulating the charges. The New York Associated Press lead said, "13 top officials of the Texas Gulf Sulphur Company were accused by the Federal Government yesterday of buying thousands of shares of the company's stock while withholding information about a rich copper ore strike in Canada." And this single sentence was wrong three ways: not all 13 defendants were top officials; not all were accused of buying stock; and the SEC did not charge that all defendants withheld information.

The next stage in the snowballing is exemplified by the United Press International wire story published in Texas newspapers two days later. It was almost an open invitation to stockholders to bring suit against the company, since the lead said that Wall Street lawyers were predicting that the SEC suit would result in possibly thousands of individual legal actions. The next paragraph compounded the Associated Press error with new flourishes:

"The SEC has accused 13 officials of Texas Gulf Sulphur Company in a civil suit of keeping a $2 billion Canadian copper and zinc strike secret while they bought more than 45,000 shares of the stock in order to make a huge profit on the market. The stock tripled in price when the ore find became known."

The complaint did not mention $2 billion, or put any other value on the alleged discovery. The defendants bought a total of 9,100 shares. The stock rose about 20 per cent when the company confirmed the strike, although it had more than doubled in price more than a year later, when the complaint was brought. As noted elsewhere, it then went down ten points on the news of the complaint.

All of this time, the company had other problems of its own, which could not fairly be blamed on the press. When the complaint was announced, officers were busy preparing the agenda for the annual stockholders' meeting to be held in Houston on Thursday morning. They had little time to deny wrongdoing and had to concentrate on what to tell the shareowners two days later. But such is life in the large corporation. More bad breaks were to come, for the Sunday financial sections and the news weeklies were tuning up.

On Sunday *The New York Times* had four major feature stories on the topic, but because of its deadline missed the carefully prepared statement of President Stephens before the stockholders on Thursday. This had lasted 45 minutes and was greeted by a standing ovation and a vote of confidence for the management—but that was in Houston, not in New York. The editors of *Newsweek* apparently did not have time for a careful reading of it either, and reported on May 3 that the "Company's rebuttal was clearly sketchy. It did not, for example, mention the furious buying of call options by many officers. . . ." One reason for the omission may have been that no officers of the company bought calls, and the SEC did not so charge.

The president's statement received scant attention in the daily papers, perhaps because on the same day the SEC charges had created another news break, shifting the scene of action to Washington and thickening the plot with the name of Herbert Klotz, the Undersecretary of Commerce, who had become one of the so-called tippees through the proximity of a pretty stenographer in his office who was also a friend of Ken Darke, the geologist. The news elements of a sub-cabinet official, a "Wall Street scandal," and a pretty stenographer made things rather difficult for any airing of President Stephens' reasoned statement in Houston. The odds were too great.

Many of the points made by Stephens never did get published in the media, which had given prominent space and headlines to the charges. For example:

1. The total number of TGS shares purchased by company insiders during the period in question was substantially less than the number of shares bought by officers of the other sulphur companies during the same period, when the market as a whole was on the rise and improved sulphur demand, prices, and profits were being discussed in the financial community.

2. During this time a number of other good things were happening to brighten the TGS outlook, and the company had issued several news releases concerning them—rather strange conduct for officers now charged with trying to keep the company's stock depressed in order to "make a killing."

3. News of the initially successful drill hole was not deliberately withheld from the directors when they voted stock options on February 20, 1964, Stephens said. In fact, a single drill hole was *never*, as a matter of practice, reported to directors because—for one thing—it could be misleading without further evaluation. The reason for issuing options on that particular date was that the market price of TGS stock had just returned to the level at which options had first been issued in 1961, and the president had not thought it fair to issue new options until this level—about 23—was again reached.

Whether any of this was ever digested by news commentators or not, it hardly showed. Financial commentator Sylvia Porter still referred to the defendants "who profited enormously by buying Texas Gulf stock before the public was given news of its fabulous copper-silver-zinc strike," and a month later Drew Pearson peered into *his* crystal ball and predicted an unexpected bonanza for the Curtis Publishing Company. Texas Gulf, he said, "had hushed-up the ore strike while 13 inside officials made a killing. . . ."

Pearson also predicted that, based on the SEC complaint, "Curtis will now claim it is entitled to 90 per cent royalty, not 10 per cent. In addition, it owns 52,000 acres of unexplored land on which geologists believe there must be valuable ore deposits. . . . On the basis of 27 holes drilled on the 46,000 acres leased to Texas Gulf, this acreage alone is estimated to have 6,400,000 tons of ore valued at $319,000,000." He was neither the first nor the last of the amateur estimators to get into the game.

Curtis, of course, never made any such claim. It sold its property in the Timmins area, plus 140,000 acres of Pennsylvania woodlands, to Texas Gulf for $24 million, and the Curtis directors successfully defended their agreement in a stockholders' suit.

On the whole, it was not surprising that most reporters, aided as much as the courts by hindsight, tended to concentrate on two things in the case, despite the 102 paragraphs in the complaint. These were the idea of insiders making a "killing" in company stock, and the fact that everything was somehow related to a "false and misleading press release." By looking closely, they could have discovered that none of those involved in issuing the release— Stephens, Fogarty, Mollison, Holyk, and possibly Lamont—had bought any stock between the time it was issued and the time of confirmation four days later. In another aspect, the whole action hinged on one startling fact. How could a *prospect* requiring more drilling for proper evaluation become a *major discovery* within a period of four days? Adjectives and the meanings of words became an important factor from the outset.

The misleading characterizations of the complaint prevailed also in book form, when the *National Observer's* "Newsbook" entitled "A Report in Depth on the Stock Market" said the complaint was against "13 of its directors and officers," when six defendants were neither, and that "the alleged inside trading violations had been on an unusual scale, and so was the SEC's reaction." As pointed out earlier, the TGS insiders bought on a somewhat smaller scale

than those in competing companies, and although reported as
required by law, the purchases were so small that they never were
published in any newspaper.

Not all the loose reporting came from reporters and commentators. In 1969 a Republican President appointed Hamer H. Budge
the chairman of the Securities and Exchange Commission, but on
November 18, 1965, he was just one of the commissioners, speaking
to the New York chapter of the American Society of Corporate Secretaries on "The Texas Gulf Sulphur Case—What It Is and What It
Isn't." [23] After carefully qualifying his remarks by saying that ". . .
the final decision as to the facts and as to the legal conclusions to
be drawn from those facts properly lie with the courts," Commissioner Budge did not hesitate to dip into some rather colorful language and a few conclusions not yet litigated, item: ". . . it should
be noted that much of the corporate information concerned in the
Texas Gulf case was volunteered by certain insiders to their select
friends. It is the Commission's view that a leak of corporate information to a few buddies is quite distinct from the normal release
of corporate information."

Interestingly enough, it was *Life* magazine, rather than a law
or professional journal, which was one of the first to suggest that
the issues of this case might concern a much broader group than
just the defendants named.[24] An article appearing not too long
after the complaint was filed observed that the Commission

> has now set for itself the ambitious task of establishing the re-
> sponsibility of every individual with inside information. Most
> companies have elaborate rules limiting to the fewest possible
> persons dissemination of news about activities which could mate-
> rially affect the price of their stock. Restricting the spread of such
> knowledge is not easy. Every company has numerous dealings with
> law firms, public relations organizations, advertising agencies and
> banks, as well as other companies. There are thousands of analysts
> and researchers employed by brokerage houses, mutual funds and
> other investigating organizations, whose job it is to get as much
> information as possible about companies in order to predict future
> stock movements. . . . There is a very wide spectrum of people
> who have access to information not yet available to the general
> public. Obviously the SEC is not challenging all of them.

That remained to be seen.

[23] Reported in *Dun's Review and Modern Industry*, January 1966.
[24] Chris Welles: "Bonanza Trouble," *Life*, August 6, 1965.

Texas Gulf could actually find more comfort in some of the comments made north of the border, where perhaps the problems inherent in the mining industry were better understood. *The Northern Miner* had played a leading role in many of the events leading up to the complaint, and early in May, 1965, under the heading "This Should Never Happen in Canada," the Toronto journal called the TGS action essentially a sociological reflection of the times, pointing out that

> . . . many governments generally and particularly the United States government are so devoted to protecting the rights of the individual that their efforts are often over-zealous. Often they have left the margin of practicality far behind them. The end result is more harmful than the original offense if, indeed, there is one.
>
> In the current action, this seems to be the case. It opens the door wide to a succession of private suits (most of them bound to be parasitical) and could conceivably create a legal quagmire that might take decades to sort out. This is fine for the legal profession . . . but it does no good for the company, and it does no good for the vast majority of its stockholders who, everyone seems to forget, have benefited vastly from the efforts of the TGS management. . . . We would have to say that somewhere, somehow, something has got far out of perspective. Who can win what? [25]

Later in the summer, in another editorial, *The Northern Miner* contributed some of its special expertise to the debate on just what constitutes a material fact. It pointed out that, stripping the situation of legal technology, the case appeared to revolve on just how quickly Texas Gulf knew it had a major ore body.

> Actually, even the word "major" is inadequate—in this case, because Texas Gulf is a large and diversified company with established earnings from a variety of sources, it would appear to be a question of how quickly it recognized an ore body had been established big and rich enough so as to exert substantial leverage on the company's overall earnings potential. . . . After all, Texas had previously found two large ore bodies in Canada—one in New Brunswick, pretty well drilled off, and one in Baffinland, which is still in the evaluation stage. Both are major in terms of tonnage, but neither so far appears capable of influencing future company earnings on a sizeable scale.

The editorial observed that the SEC case tended to operate

[25] *The Northern Miner*, May 6, 1965, Toronto.

from hindsight, and shouldn't, if the Commission were more knowledgeable. It cited the practices of two other well-known mining
companies—Anaconda and Kennecott—operating in Canada, which
for a considerable period had indicated the presence of very large
ore bodies but have waited upon evaluation to tell the shareholders
of the possibilities. The charges against Texas Gulf, said this article,
were "born of a lack of knowledge of mineral exploration and what
constitutes an ore body. . . . [It] places management of publicly
owned corporations in the United States in a virtually untenable
position." [26]

A few days before the trial was to begin in New York, some 13
months after the complaint had been brought, there was the possibility that some of the defense points might be given equal time
when the publicity on the case resumed. But at this point the SEC
amended its complaint against Lamont, the best-known of the
13 defendants, and the new charge insured top billing for the Commission in the headlines once more.

Thomas Lamont, as one of the last links to the era of J. Pierpont
Morgan, the retired vice chairman of Morgan Guaranty Trust Company, and long an outstanding influence in the financial community,
was bound to draw substantial center-stage attention as one of the
defendants from any reporter worth his salt, even though he was
not charged with improperly purchasing stock of the company,
accepting stock options, withholding information, or taking any
action for personal benefit. It was just as inevitable that *The New
York Times*, itself something of a figure in the community, should
have been the principal instrument in singling him out and making
him a leading character in the Texas Gulf drama. He was the best-
known actor. Max Ascoli, the former editor and publisher of *The
Reporter Magazine*, recently defined *The New York Times* as "the
most authoritative organ of woolly thinking in our country,"—one
of those shafts which heals even as it wounds.[27] In any event, Lamont—who described himself as an admirer of the newspaper for
many years—prepared a 12-page complaint of his own, citing headlines and stories that had appeared in the paper from May 14, 1964,
through July 8, 1965. He declared that the *Times* "has over and
over again given special emphasis to me in its stories dealing with
the Texas Gulf Sulphur case, and it has in the instances cited by

[26] *The Northern Miner*, July 22, 1965, Toronto.
[27] Max Ascoli: "Campus Riots and the U.S. Government," *Wall Street
Journal*, May 27, 1969.

me misrepresented the charges made against me by the SEC. . . . I am bothered by this record of inaccurate reporting and careless editing."

This detailed document was handed to Turner Catledge, the executive editor, over lunch toward the end of December, 1965. Catledge replied by first turning the matter over to Clifton Daniel, the managing editor, and then going to New Orleans for the holidays. Daniel wrote what he termed a "preliminary response" which combined a confession-and-avoidance plea with professions of honest intent and continuing friendship. It contained one rather astonishing dictum:

> Headlines are by their nature concise, cryptic and incomplete. We must rely on the intelligence of our readers to make a distinction between headlines and news articles, and we believe they can do so.

In his own later "Dear Tom" letter, Catledge said there was nothing he could add, although "there were certain minor things such as headlines which I wish had been different."

There the matter rested. It was one more example of the fortunes of war which flow from the skirmishes between businessmen and the law as reported by the press, and it is doubtful if the result can ever be otherwise, given the positions and objectives of each party. In this case, the *Times* had the last handsome word. In its issue of April 11, 1967, it devoted almost three columns to Lamont on the occasion of his death the preceding day following an operation for open-heart surgery.

# 6
# All Hands Below:
# Trial and Judgment

I

FOLEY Square in New York City has a personality all its own. Lawyers and judges may perhaps look upon it as home grounds, but the members of the visiting team are often subjected to the same kind of traumatic effects as baseball rookies from west of the Hudson experience when making their first visit to Yankee Stadium. The federal building and its courtrooms somehow present a stranger and more sterile front than those of the State of New York nearby. The seats seem harder and the edge of the knife sharper. Not all of the landmark decisions which periodically change the life and alter the manners of the business and financial community of the United States begin here by any means, but a fair share of them do.[1] The games played are not very exciting for the spectators, but the scores go into the record book. Except for defendants in greatest jeopardy, the grind of the law in Foley Square can be very dull, and most of the businessmen involved are at least uneasily aware that they are spending a great deal of time away from the office.

The trial of Texas Gulf Sulphur Company and the individual

---

[1] The New York regional office of the SEC, while located in another "federal area" in Federal Plaza, is the largest SEC office outside Washington. While most regulatory policy is made in the capital, some of the biggest enforcement investigations originate in New York, and this office also deals frequently with the stock exchanges.

defendants finally got under way in federal district court on May 9, 1966, more than a year after the complaint had been brought and about two and a half years after the drilling of the discovery hole near Timmins, Ontario. On the same day presiding Judge Dudley B. Bonsal signed pre-trial order number six, which more or less set forth the ground rules that had evolved from the complaint, the answers, and the interrogatories. For example, it stated that "on April 13, 1964, there was not one sale of Texas Gulf stock on the New York Stock Exchange at less than the highest price at which such stock had been sold on the preceding market day, Friday, April 10, 1964." It will be recalled that April 13 was the day on which there had appeared the TGS news release which the Commission charged was false and misleading, and others had described as gloomy. But for the most part, the pre-trial order listed amendments of the complaint; schedules of stock purchases by the defendants and others; the positions held by the defendants; the stock options that had been granted; established facts and dates relating to events that had transpired; the members of the Ontario parliament press gallery, and the names of those who had attended the TGS press conference in New York; the geologists' logs; the documents pre-marked as exhibits—39 for the SEC and 104 for the defendants; and finally, the issues to be tried, as formulated by the Court. All parties waived a jury and agreed that trial should first be had on the issue of whether one or more of the defendants had violated Section 10(b) and Rule 10b-5, reserving for later hearing the issue of remedy to be applied in the event such violations were found. The attorneys had agreed to produce in court all of the defendants represented except Darke, whose deposition had been taken in Canada.

In his opening remarks,[2] Frank E. Kennamer Jr., the assistant general counsel for the SEC, made haste to take his text from a 1928 opinion of the late Justice Benjamin Cardozo [3] which set forth a standard of corporate morality characterized by fiduciary ties.[4]

[2] This, and all of the indirect and direct quotations appearing in the account of the trial before Judge Bonsal in a federal courtroom of the Southern District of New York are taken from the *Joint Appendix,* Volumes I, II, and III, pages 1 through 1,730, certified on the trial record to the U.S. Court of Appeals for the Second Circuit. The specific pages have not been cited, but the order of witnesses and exhibits has been followed in the text.

[3] *Meinhard v. Salmon, 249 New York 458 (1928).*

[4] Cardozo and his latest quoter, Kennamer, to the contrary, the Second Circuit had written this, in the year that Rule 10b-5 was written: ". . . so

A host of impoverished investors, said Kennamer, stand ready to attest that there are dangers in spreading about half-truths and untruths, that when such information is given currency in the market, shareholders, the investing public and the financial community lie at the mercy of the purveyors of such information or misinformation. He charged the defendants with serious misuse of confidential corporate information in order to enrich themselves, and then reached for another Cardozo quote: [5] "When wrongs such as those have been committed or attempted, they must be dragged to light and pilloried." Mr. Kennamer then declared that the Commission's objectives in bringing these proceedings before the Court were "to drag to light and pillory the misconduct of the individual defendants."

This fiery note drew an indignant response from Orison S. Marden (later to become president of the American Bar Association) who was representing the company and ten of the individual defendants: "Mr. Kennamer used adjectives, and the Commission, strangely enough, has used adjectives which, coming from the mouth of the Securities and Exchange Commission, to me are nothing less than astounding."

Kennamer's associate in presenting the Commission's case was Michael Joseph, attorney for the SEC in Washington. Thomas S. Lamont was represented by S. Hazard Gillespie, and Francis G. Coates by Albert R. Connelly. Gillespie kicked up a little fuss in *his* opening remarks. Until a few days before, the case against Lamont had consisted solely of his telephone call to the Morgan Guaranty Trust Company at about 10:40 A.M., following the press conference, as a result of which the bank bought 10,000 shares of TGS stock. But just before the trial the SEC had amended the complaint in such a way as to include the 3,000 shares that Lamont purchased for his own account at 12:33 P.M., and now his attorney was calling foul.

The fact, as well as the time, of this last purchase had been

far as we are able to find, no case has gone to the length of holding a director accountable to a stockholder in the purchase and sale of shares of stock except where fraud or some form of overreaching is shown as the inducing cause of the transaction. . . ."

The SEC appealed but the Supreme Court confirmed, saying: "As the Commission concedes here, the courts do not impose upon officers and directors of a corporation any fiduciary duty to its stockholders which precludes them, merely because they are officers and directors, from buying and selling the corporation stock." *SEC v. Chenerg Corp., 318 U.S. 80, 88 (1944).*

[5] *Jones v. SEC, 298 U.S. 1(17) at 32, dissenting.*

known two years before, said Gillespie, when the SEC investigator examined Lamont, and so this could be no mere inadvertence. The Commission's trial brief now demanded "a reasonable amount of time in which the securities industry, the shareholders and the investing public can evaluate the development and make informed investment decisions."

The new shift involved a very fundamental change in the plaintiff's policy, said Gillespie. Originally they had been claiming that the prohibitions of Rule 10b-5 were lifted after the news appeared on the Dow Jones broad tape at 10:55. Now the time had been extended indefinitely. Why? Said Gillespie:

> I think it can be laid to kibitzing . . . since the filing of this suit there have been no less than seven articles written on the subject of when information should cease to be inside information and become public, by law professors and others. It is a very poor bar association that hasn't held a panel to discuss the pros and cons of the Texas Gulf case and when news becomes public . . . it is not surprising that the SEC in this situation is unable to point specifically to any rule which it has adopted at any time to advise the public fairly and squarely of when insider information ceases to be inside information. Having started down this slippery slide of shifting position . . . as a matter of logic the SEC went on last Tuesday and on this theory said for the first time that they wanted to amend their complaint to include a claim against Mr. Lamont for the shares he had purchased . . . at 12:33 on the theory, presumably, that while buyers of over 240,000 shares that morning had been able to evaluate that information and every selling broker who sold shares to Mr. Lamont had had the Dow Jones broad tape . . . there was something tainted about the transaction. If it were not for the stigma that attaches to a person against whom a claim of this nature is made in an effort to pillory, if I may use the word of counsel for the SEC, . . . this would be a laughable matter the way the SEC has shifted their position.

Whatever the merits of the case might be, for either side, the defense was bound to be in a box about which it could do little. Each of the individual defendants (except Darke and O'Neill) were called as witnesses for the Commission. They could be examined by the attorneys for the defense only on cross-examination, and in effect their positive roles in the picture that TGS must try to paint would be limited by the rules of evidence to those points and subjects covered by direct testimony for the Commission. It was a little as though the home team was employing the leading players of the visiting team against their own club for a large portion of the contest.

The story as it would unroll in the courtroom was going to be somewhat disjointed and the audience would have to put the pieces of the jigsaw together as best it could. Crawford, the corporate secretary and manager of TGS government and public relations, led off. He had lately come to the company from Chicago, where he served as secretary and general counsel for Abbott Laboratories, and on the week end during which the April 12 release was being put together, he was off to Chicago, to try to sell his Lake Forest house, and then to Houston to get acquainted with the TGS people there and make arrangements for the forthcoming annual meeting. Having read the rumors of the Timmins strike in newspapers in Newark airport, he had called Stephens and relayed the news. Up to this time he had known nothing about the Kidd 55 area, he said. On his return a few days later he had been given the assignment, logically because of his job, of helping to write the April 16 announcement. At the end of that long evening, before departing to a Park Lane hotel room, he had called first his wife, and then a broker, also a friend, in Chicago, and placed an order for 300 shares of stock. Next morning, before going to the office, he changed his mind, again called Chicago, and changed his order to 600 shares. Attorneys for both sides asked him why. Tomorrow was going to be a busy day, he replied, and the night before was too long to allow much time for reflection. In any case, at the time he believed the news had been made public by the Ontario Minister of Mines. Subsequently he had borrowed from First National City Bank to help cover the purchase, rather than sell some of his securities on deposit in Chicago.

On April 17, the day after the board meeting and press conference, Crawford went, along with Fogarty and general counsel Kline, to a meeting of the stock list committee of the New York Stock Exchange. A member of the committee had telephoned him the previous afternoon asking whether any officers and directors of TGS had purchased shares on the 16th. Crawford said he did not know about others, but that *he* had, and if he had done anything wrong he would be glad to rectify it. The matter was never again brought up.

The Commission had later read into the record the deposition of Edward Hurd, the Chicago broker and Crawford's friend of seven years, who had helped him to settle in Lake Forest. Although it changed none of the principal facts, Hurd's statement may not have helped matters. He admitted that he had consulted his attorney before making the statement; that he had purchased shares of TGS for his wife's account and sold them later in the day. He over-stressed his lack of knowledge of Texas Gulf to a point that seemed unrealistic in the light of his business. Crawford's request to purchase some shares next day had been liberally interlarded with personal conversation relating to each other's family affairs.

John A. Hill, chairman of Air Reduction Company and a director of Texas Gulf, had served on the board's stock option committee. He spoke briefly of the workings of the option plan, and was followed on the witness stand by defendants Coates and Lamont. Coates, a director since 1949, had been chairman of the option committee, and Joseph questioned him about this, as well as about the specific events of the press conference on April 16. After the meeting the lawyer had telephoned his son-in-law in Houston, Fred Haemisegger, also a broker, requesting the purchase of 2,000 shares of TGS in behalf of four family trusts. The gist of the Coates message, in addition to the number of shares and a limit of $32 per share placed on the purchase price, was this: "I referred to a prior conversation or two that we had had about the unusual . . . market activity in Texas Gulf stock, and told him that I hadn't been able to give him any information about Texas Gulf because no public announcement had been made of this Timmins discovery and that I wanted to be very careful both as a lawyer and as a director . . . and that I was too old to get into trouble with the SEC."

The burden of the Coates testimony was that he had been aware of the various developments in the company and in the industry which had resulted in an increased market price for TGS stock and had felt that the price, by all professional standards, was "getting pretty high"—hence his decision to make additional purchases for the family trusts after the announcement of the spectacular Timmins strike. He advised Haemisegger that public disclosure had been made, on the basis of the [presumed] announcement the night before by the Ontario Minister of Mines, and of the announcement at the press conference, which had by then concluded.

With Lamont's appearance, Kennamer took over. After a rather detailed account of the banker's previous and present relationships with both Morgan Guaranty and Texas Gulf, it developed that the senior director had not known about the activity in Kidd Township until Stephens telephoned him on April 10, in relation to the rumors circulating in Canada. He knew no details until he read press accounts some days later, including the company's April 12 release. The Commission was mainly interested in conversations that might have taken place between Lamont and Longstreet Hinton, the bank's executive vice president with top responsibility for the portfolios of its trust accounts. Over the years, since Stephens had become president of Texas Gulf, Lamont had suggested to Hinton that "he might well look" at TGS. But in the year or two before the April 16 announcement, "he had disregarded any suggestions of mine, so far as I recall." Two or three days before the press conference, Hinton had queried Lamont about the rumors circulating in the press, but the latter indicated that he only knew what he had read in the newspapers. After the press conference concluded, on April 16, he recalled Hinton's conversation, telephoned him at the bank around 10:40 A.M., and suggested he look at the Dow Jones broad tape in regard to a "pretty good" announcement about Texas Gulf. He then visited with some of the officers of the company briefly, and "about noontime" drove to the bank's offices at 15 Broad Street. Here he inquired as to what was happening in regard to TGS stock activity, and on being told, placed orders for 3,000 shares for his own family accounts.

Not until 12 days later, incidentally, did Lamont learn that Hinton had bought 10,000 shares for various trust accounts prior to the announcement on the broad tape. And only later, at the stockholders' meeting in Houston on April 23, did he learn that the Canadian minister's announcement had not been made on the night of the 15th. He was followed to the witness stand by Hinton, whose testimony did little more than supply the "other end" of the Lamont telephone call and another version of the message: "Take a look at the ticker. There is some news—interesting news coming out about Texas Gulf Sulphur." Hinton, as it developed, did *not* look at the broad tape, but called the trading desk for his check, and then the orders were put in. He believed the news was public.

The next SEC witness was Mrs. Ingrid Nelson, a Washington employee of the Commission's branch of market surveillance. She had been watching TGS on the ticker for several days, read the April 16 announcement and remembered the statement of April 12 saying the rumors were exaggerated. Her report had triggered a telephone call to New York and the investigation was under way.

The parade of defendants as Commission witnesses resumed

with Kline, the general counsel; Huntington, also a TGS attorney; and Murray, the office manager. Kline had been one of those to receive a stock option on February 20, 1964, and as corporate secretary—before the coming of Crawford—saw to the drawing-up and distribution of all of the options. He was not charged with making insider stock purchases except in the special sense of having received the option without disclosing to the committee his knowledge of the discovery at the Kidd 55 segment. According to his testimony, he first learned of exploration in the Timmins area in mid-November of 1963:

> I was at a luncheon with Mr. Stephens and Dr. Fogarty, and the conversation turned to a favorable development connected with the hole at Timmins, Ontario, and there was a reference to a telephone call which had communicated the word of the favorable development . . . at the luncheon conversation there was a reference to the fact that the drilling had been done right on the boundary of such property as we had and that we would be interested in acquiring more property so that further exploration could be conducted.

But Kline then had no responsibility for land acquisition. And it did not cross his mind that it would be appropriate for him to tell the stock option committee what he knew of the single drill hole, which was very little in any event.[6]

For his part, Huntington had been involved in helping to obtain some of the land needed to continue the exploration work. He told how the Roberts property, one of the sections sought, was obtained by going around an obstructive attorney and dealing directly with representative interests; of some negotiations on the Woollings

---

[6] Excerpts from post-trial brief filed July 5, 1966, by attorneys for TGS and the individual defendants:

"The options were granted in consideration of the past and contemplated future services of the employees with the company and to increase the optionees' sense of proprietorship.

"The optionees did not bargain with the Stock Option Committee as to the size of their options. Indeed there is no evidence that defendants Holyk or Mollison even knew that the Board was about to grant options at this time. The amount of the options was not determined in any respect by whether or not a particular individual had knowledge of a drill hole or whether such a hole existed, but by a mathematical formula based on salary.

". . . it was not customary for persons receiving stock options to go to the Board or the Committee and tell them all the facts they know which might or might not be material. Thus the Board could not have relied on their failure to have done so as indicating that there were no material facts. There was no proof that the Board would have acted differently had it known of this project."

property; and he had helped prepare a letter of March 16 to the Royal Trust Company in regard to the estate of Murray Hendrie. TGS already held the option here, where the first hole had been drilled, but in effect was offering to pay another $57,000 for the remaining ten per cent interest in the land retained by the trustees. The effort was unsuccessful. On the same day Huntington had bought a call on TGS stock. Earlier he had purchased some shares outright, and the reason given for all of his purchases was his evaluation of the total company business and prospects. The idea of the call, which he had never heard of before, had come from a casual conversation with Holyk.

Murray had begun with TGS as an office boy in 1924, and worked his way up to become office manager on his predecessor's retirement. He declared that he had known nothing of the affairs at Timmins until the newspaper stories began appearing, but he had purchased calls for 400 shares of company stock on January 8, 1964. At the trial, as during his pre-trial examination by Jaegerman, there was an attempt by counsel to link Murray somehow with the absent Ken Darke, presumably to build evidence on Darke's alleged tipping activities, but the effort was something of a failure. He had told Jaegerman: "I am not a professional on these questions. I was confused. . . . I met him [Darke] outside of my office, because the men's room was right out there, and he was going by, and I think I told him that I had purchased four calls, and he said, 'Well, that's the way to make money.' "

Murray said the idea of calls came to him some years earlier when he was attending New York University for his master's degree. A fellow named Joe Sullivan gave him "a pretty good lesson." He, also, had previously purchased TGS stock, and other stocks, but did not consider himself a significant investor. He had been with the company a long time and liked the management and the way things were going.

At this point, before calling the rest of the defendants—who might be classed generally as those having the closest knowledge of the Timmins undertaking—the plaintiffs drew upon their experts, Adelstein and Edwin N. Pennebaker. The result, when combined with the testimony of the several experts that TGS would later introduce, constituted not only the largest portion of the total trial record, but a thoroughgoing cram course in mining, mineralogy, geology, geophysics, and mine management and evaluation for any who might care to be so enlightened. As might have been foreseen, there were challenges and disagreements, but the least that could be said was that the documented display of professional expertise was impressive, if a little on the heavy side. The Court, in a sense, was the only student who would be called to account in a final examination, but appeared to be an assiduous questioner and note-taker, deserving high marks for this venture into a new discipline.

It was clearly the assigned task of the plaintiff's counsel to employ Adelstein and Pennebaker to set up the Commission's case for the importance and significance of the first drill hole, and to put into evidence for the first of many times the definitions of a *prospect* and of *proved* and *probable* ore. This would also be the first opportunity for the defense, in its cross-examination, to make its "hindsight" charges and counterclaims. When the ensuing mountain of words had been mined, processed, and smeltered into what might then be no more than a very few hard conclusions, these would necessarily be vital conclusions indeed. They would bear upon the materiality of facts and the timing of disclosures, and thereby hung the case. Oddly enough, the testimony of the SEC experts also served to raise a somewhat unexpected issue of credibility, not as to the highly technical facts presented, but running to the integrity of the leading representatives of the corporation. The exchange enlivened the proceedings each time it occurred, but curiously had almost no bearing on the issues being tried.

Adelstein had served the Commission staff since 1937 and had long been its chief mining engineer. A significant and important part of his work, he said, related to the estimation of ore reserves and their dollar evaluation. The definitions were elicited early in his testimony:

"A prospect is a property where there is no assurance, from the information known, that a commercially mineable ore body exists. And . . . I mean profitably mineable."

Again, "Proven ore means a body of ore so extensively sampled that the risk of continuity of the ore within that body is reduced to a minimum."

And still again, "Probable ore is where the risk of continuity on the basis of the sampling done is greater than for proven ore, yet there is reasonable warrant for assuming continuity. In both

of these categories each can be considered as a commercially mineable ore body on a known basis."

As the proceedings moved forward into exhibits of logs and
drilling records, Marden, for the defense, objected to the inclusion
of some of the material, not so much on the question of its authen-
ticity as on the ground that it represented material going beyond
the critical date of April 16, 1964. Throughout the trial he would
continue to do so, and although the Court would in most cases allow
the exhibit, or the statement, as the case might be, the point was
made repeatedly that the defendants were not to be tried on hindsight. Over objection, Adelstein testified that the K55-1 "values over
the length that they occurred greatly exceeded anything that I have
seen of my own examination or anything that I have ever read of
in my perusal of technical publications." He went on to say that he
was familiar with open pit mining operations having a gross assay
value of five to six dollars a ton, but knew of none where such values
approached ten dollars a ton. Here, however, he figured the gross
assay value of the metallic elements discovered in the course of
drilling K55-1 to be about $32.03 a ton based upon chemical assay.

In the long courtroom struggle between experts as to whether
the core of the first hole was spectacularly outstanding or possibly
just doubtful—and what this might portend in respect to ore deposits as of this early date—the Commission witnesses introduced
the subject of "banding" on the theory that the bands indicated continuity of valuable deposits. The Commission's two experts had
spent more than 15 hours minutely examining the split and broken
sections of the first core with a protractor. This exercise (which was
never done by any of the Texas Gulf geologists and was admittedly
not normal practice) illustrated the desperate efforts of the Commission, said defense attorneys, to draw more meaning from one
hole than is ever attempted in practice, and more than was warranted. All of this took a great deal of time, also, and was violently
challenged, but in the end—as so often happens—had almost nothing to do with the final rulings. Much of the argument wound up in
occasional summaries, such as the following exchange between
Kennamer and Adelstein:

Q. Mr. Adelstein, as I understand it, it isn't your position, and never
   has been your position, that the drilling of K55-1 established the
   existence of a commercially mineable ore body?
A. That is correct.

Q. But it is your position . . . that bearing in mind all the factors that were known at the time K55-1 was drilled, it gave substantial promise, substantial indication, of developing into a wide, rich, mineable ore body?
A. It gave such indication.

It was Kennamer's fashion, in addressing almost every witness, to describe the hole, the core, the anomaly, the metallic elements, and the values in the richest of superlatives. That was *his* point.

Shortly before Marden took over for cross-examination, Adelstein stated that in his opinion, based on information received solely from TGS, the ore reserves as of 7 P.M. April 9, 1964, aggregated 7,700,000 tons having a gross assay value of $204,200,000. The latter figure, according to his calculations, then increased to $217 million as of 7 A.M. the following morning, and finally to $252.1 million by 7 A.M. April 12—the day of the release supposed to counter the wild rumors.

Marden hammered away, when his time came, at what he deemed to be the application of Adelstein's hindsighted conclusions to the knowledge actually available in the period of November 12 through April 9. He pointed out that the witness had expressed an inability to project a commercially mineable ore body *at all* on April 30, 1964, in a memorandum to an associate at the Commission; that in December, 1964, he had calculated the proven ore (as of April 9) at five and a half million tons; and that now, at the trial, the figure had increased to 7.5 million tons. Critical of the frequency with which "gross assay values" were being used, Marden asked the witness if any issuer of a security had ever been permitted by the SEC to include gross assay values in a registration statement. The answer to that was "No." In the argument over whether or not the first hole at Kidd 55 was an "unusual prospect" Adelstein interjected a quotation from an industry authority: [7] "Once in a blue moon you will see a prospect so obviously good that the probability is almost a certainty." At this point the Court interrupted: "How often do you have blue moons?" but the witness had no statistics. It was a feeble but perhaps pointed attempt to lighten a very heavy subject. Pennebaker came on next.

A 64-year-old geologist from Scottsdale, Arizona, Pennebaker had been retained by the SEC as consulting geologist and expert witness. His experience had covered Mexico, Cuba, Ecuador, South

[7] Hugh Exton McKinstry: *Mining Geology* (1948).

Africa, Venezuela, Australia, and Canada, and he had been employed in this instance mainly to estimate reserves and examine ore.
He had used slightly different methods than had Adelstein, and his
estimates as of 7 P.M., April 9, amounted to 5.5 million tons of
proven ore plus 1.1 million tons of probable ore. It was all very
straightforward, and Marden only brought out the fact, on cross-
examination, that the figures supplied by the witness were all gross
assay figures, and that no computation had been made as to net
values, after mining, milling and selling.

The first round with the experts was over, and now the plaintiffs resumed their direct attack, on defendants Clayton, Holyk,
Mollison, Fogarty, and Stephens, clearly the management group.
This completed the roster of defendants appearing as Commission
witnesses. Out of all this now finally came the detailed story of the
exploration and the Timmins discovery, for the record, with the
parts played by each. Also disclosed were the roles of each defendant in making the two news releases and—except for Stephens—
in their purchases of TGS stock. Operations, administration, and
motivation were duly revealed. As in a sentence of schoolboy German, the action words were coming at the end of the Commission's
case, and it was left to the defense attorneys, on cross-examination,
to complete the story as best they could with somebody else's scenario.

Richard Ward Hugh Clayton, 45 at the time of the trial, was
a Welshman who had served in the Royal Air Force. Now he was
a Canadian national, and a geophysicist for TGS. He had never been
served personally in this action, as he was either in, or on his way
to, Baffin Island, where there was no mail service and radio communication was faulty. Clayton's wife had done occasional consulting work for the company, and in fact had figured in some of
the conversations on land acquisition. On April 15, 1964, the day
before the press conference in New York, Clayton had bought 200
shares of stock through a Toronto broker. His reply to the inevitable
"Why?" was that he had been buying stock since 1962, had 1,260
shares at the time, and decided to buy more.

Clayton was reasonably successful in resisting Kennamer's
repeated efforts to force a jump to conclusions in respect to what
the exploration and drilling had established, to his own reactions
to the two news releases, and to his reasons for buying stock. He
had purchased 400 shares on February 24, 1964, and Kennamer
pressed somewhat sarcastically: ". . . what development within

the company except the fact that in the meanwhile the chemical assay of the core recovered from K55-1 had been received, and the company was aggressively engaged in picking up the other three quarter sections of this quadrant of land, influenced you in buying those 400 shares?"

"Well, sir, it wasn't a change in the company that . . . influenced me," replied Clayton. "It was a considerable change in my financial position. . . . I married a rich wife."

Then there were the 200 shares bought on March 26. Clayton said the price was rising, and it made sense to buy on a rising market. He recalled a negative development which was all news to the attorney, and did not exactly coincide with the SEC's allegations. Clayton announced that the Kidd 55 anomaly had a twin next to it—the Kidd 66. "And we thought at that time they were the same anomaly, basically. I mean they were along the same structure. And I think in March sometime we drilled three holes in it, and they were all almost barren. So that meant that we . . . couldn't assume or expect that the Kidd 55 anomaly would all be ore-bearing. In the same structure where we had one good hole we now had . . . three bad ones." He bought the stock, nevertheless, because the company was making big advances.

Asked at one point to agree that the ore body within the confines of the Kidd mine was tabular, Clayton replied that it was a pipelike body running down like a large turnip. There was a great deal of discussion regarding the surveying of the anomaly, and at one point the combined efforts of Kennamer and the Court fell afoul in trying to persuade the witness to say what *might* lie between the first two drill holes:

THE COURT: You know what is in the drill hole?
  WITNESS: You know what is in the drill hole and that is all you know for sure.
THE COURT: So you would assume that there ought to be another core out of these two holes, and there was nothing at all in between them?
  WITNESS: No, I wouldn't assume that. At this stage I wouldn't assume anything. I would just keep on drilling.

At this point they gave up, almost, but the results were disappointing. As for the management's estimate of 25 million tons in the April 16 announcement, Clayton did not agree, and thought they had gone a little bit overboard. "On April 16th I would say that we didn't have any certainty of a commercial mine. The release said 'indicated.'"

During his cross-examination by Marden, Clayton provided, in terms of his own judgment, an interesting and hitherto unrevealed insight into some of the problems of development faced by Texas Gulf, both in contemplating a mine and in making the April 12 release. He had been asked about the possible advantages of open pit mining as they might appear after the initial hole had been drilled:

> Suppose we assume that we have a small ore body, as we might have had on say, the 12th, or something like that, of five million tons, or whatever it might be.
>
> Well, in order to mine that by open pit you would have to strip off just about as much as you would for a large ore body. You would have that big wall of clay, which was, I estimated at the time, to be 100 feet, and that is a varved clay . . . that means it has little slip panes of silty material running through it, and it is the sort of thing that once it starts to move it runs almost like water.
>
> So if you have to move above five or seven million tons of this overburden, which would be very expensive, you would have to slope it back at a very shallow angle, and it just wouldn't pay to put in an open pit mine. If we look at it from the angle of a larger ore body such as we now have, I am still against it, although this may be largely hindsight. The stripping process has been very, very expensive. Having that hundred feet of clay around the edge is a dangerous position to be in. I don't mean that Texas Gulf hasn't done a good job in insuring that it is going to stay there, but we still prefer not to have it there.
>
> And furthermore, a lot of this so-called ore in this ore body, which looked barren when the hole was originally logged, proved to have low values of zinc or a little copper or a little silver. When the assays came back . . . from the assay values alone it looks like this stuff might be mineable and you could mine this whole thing as one ore body, but if you look at the ore body you will find that this ore is mostly graphitic or has a lot of pyrite in, and both of those materials are very hard to separate in a milling process and I think that a lot of this intermediate stuff in the holes is low-grade stuff. It is just going to be waste and you might have done better, I think, to go underground at first and mine the higher grade portions and leave this stuff behind.

So much for the Commission's gross assay values.

Walter Holyk, the TGS manager of exploration who had been chief geologist during the drilling in the Timmins area, took the chain of command a step higher. As was the case with Clayton, and others, Kennamer asked many questions about Darke, whose absence from the courtroom seemed to serve the purpose of building, rather than diminishing his importance to the Commission case. Holyk had been Darke's superior, had worked closely with him, and had eventually received his resignation from the company. With this out of the way, Holyk's testimony traced the now familiar path of the logs and the drill holes; his role in the preparation of the first news release; his participation in the meeting with *The Northern Miner* reporter and in the airplane flight from Montreal with Mollison, the Ontario minister, and the latter's deputy; and finally the stock purchases made by his wife and himself. The geologist had traded for some time and calls were not the novelty to him that they were to some of the others involved; at one point he was helping to instruct the Court in this variety of investment, at the latter's request. It appeared, in Holyk's responses both to Kennamer and Marden, as well as to Judge Bonsal, that while he was necessarily aware of the scope and progress of the business of Texas Gulf, its diversification program, and in particular of what was going on under his own direction in Timmins, his trading activity was inspired and paced by developments in the market itself. In short, when the Holyks made purchases or sales, they were watching the market, not the drill holes.

Mollison came on the trial scene as TGS vice president responsible for the new metals division, a position he had won in mid-1964, and quite logically, as the company had quickly moved to develop its newly discovered Kidd Creek Mine and consolidate its metals activities in a single component of the organization. In every respect Mollison was a key witness. He had been placed in charge of all exploration a few years earlier and, subject to Fogarty and Stephens, directed the activities which eventually led to the confirmation of the strike. Now, whenever he was not occupied with the SEC and the courts, it was also his task to get the minerals out of the ground and on the market. In the interval he had been concerned with the drilling program, with evaluation of the findings, with the acquisition of land, with relations with the Ontario government, with disclosures to *The Northern Miner*, and with the preparation of both the April 12 and April 16 news releases. He had also purchased Texas Gulf stock in November and December of 1963, and on April 8, 1964, as well as having received a grant of stock options from the directors. In fact, Mollison touched almost every base directly and significantly and was a true first-person witness for both sides.

It was, in fact, Mrs. Mollison who made the final purchase of shares on April 8. She had inherited some money from an uncle, and her husband had suggested that she just not leave it in the bank. Unaware of any details of the Timmins operation, he said, she had bought the hundred shares without his specific knowledge.

Kennamer bored in on the matter of the conversations with the Minister of Mines and the much discussed but not consummated radio and television announcement, unsuccessfully trying to obtain an admission from Mollison that he knew the minister had decided *not* to broadcast, and that it was "unseemly" for the latter to make such an announcement "before the directors of the company were let in on the secret." But the witness denied there had been any such agreement between the parties, and added that a week passed before he learned that the broadcast had not taken place at all.

One of the plaintiff's exhibits, presented by its experts, had set forth the "Progress of Drilling in Ore Blocks"—a concept that was to be treated by the defense experts with some scorn. When it was shown to Mollison, he started the ball rolling by declaring that the exhibit "is a measure of footage of drilling, but it is not a measure of knowledge or understanding. . . . I can't accept 'ore blocks' at that state. . . . That's a calculation of the percentage of drilling, but it means nothing to me." After this, the SEC counsel returned to the more familiar matter of stock trading, asking Mollison why he purchased shares three days after K55-1 was completed. He received this answer:

"I bought this stock as an investment. I had seen the price of Texas Gulf rise during the previous three or four or five months from about 13 up to 17 or 18. I had seen the prices of all the other sulphur stocks increase. I knew that the sulphur business was improving. I was aware of other operations of the company such as phosphate and potash. I was not blind to Timmins. I believed that it was desirable for responsible employees of the company to own stock, and I had the cash so I bought it." He declared the same applied to later purchases.

After spending considerable time in such places as Iran, the Middle East, Germany, and the Far East, Dr. Fogarty had arrived permanently in New York in 1957 as vice president in charge of exploration, the year in which the TGS program for seeking out resources other than sulphur really crystallized. And having roamed the world in comparative safety, he had now been ambushed in Foley Square by fellow citizens. Joseph led the attack for the SEC by moving the subject of the questions directly to Timmins. The drilling on K55-1 began on November 8, 1963, and on the 12th Mollison and Fogarty flew up to the site, "in the course of our normal duties." On this day, also, he had placed an order for 300 shares of stock. The record would show that he bought shares again on the 15th, 19th, and 26th of that month, on the 30th of December, on February 10, 1964, and on April 1 and 6. This pretty well covered the critical period from the time of the first hole until the release of April 12, composed on the Fogarty kitchen table on a Sunday, which began all the trouble with the SEC. The executive vice president had also, of course, been granted stock options in February, along with others.

After a telephone call from Stephens on April 11, Fogarty agreed with the president that a clarifying statement on the rumors would be in the best interests of the company and the public, and he made contact immediately with Robert Carroll, vice president of the Doremus public relations agency, in Rye. He tried to reach Kline, the general counsel, but eventually settled for Huntington, and did reach Mollison, who filled in what he knew of the drilling details up to the time he had left Timmins on Friday noon. The Court particularly wanted to know what Huntington, the company counsel, had said. Fogarty obliged: "He quizzed me in some depth as to the status of things and the accuracy . . . we wanted to make as clear a statement as was humanly possible to the people so there wouldn't be any misunderstanding or misleading information. . . . He made a suggestion or two and . . . told me that as far as he was concerned legally it was all right."

After church on Sunday, and after additional talks with Mollison, Fogarty went to Carroll's house and they completed a draft of the story and read it to Stephens, who then directed that it be released as promptly as possible. Mollison and Holyk had already been instructed to return to Timmins and move things along. At this point in the testimony, Judge Bonsal's concern was with what Fogarty thought when he wrote the release ("It was a very hopeful prospect,") and what was worrying him and Stephens about the rumors ("We were receiving phone calls from brokers, we were receiving phone calls from the press asking us what was the situation with these rumors in Canada, had we discovered the biggest—you know the adjectives that they used, and these things were causing us concern because we view our responsibilities very heavily, your Honor, . . .".

The decision to announce the discovery on April 16, at the board meeting, was made by Fogarty and Stephens on Wednesday, the 15th, which didn't leave much time for tactics or strategy.

There followed some testimony as to what information Fogarty and his associates had supplied to Adelstein at the investigation conference in the TGS offices on April 29, and this—almost inadvertently—erupted into the unexpected credibility issue referred to earlier. On cross-examination Marden asked what the SEC expert had said at the end of the conference, and Fogarty replied:

"As we were leaving Mr. Adelstein made the comment to me that he thought the April 12th release was accurate and he probably would have done the same thing if he had been in my position." This would come up again, before the Commission rested its case, during the examination of Stephens and in a recall of Adelstein. But for now the questions pertained to the Fogarty stock purchases. The replies of the witness followed the pattern of his pre-trial examination by Jaegerman—he had been embarrassed at stockholder criticism of his small holdings after becoming a director, and had set out on a systematic purchase program.

The drilling of K55-1 had not meant a mine to Fogarty, it could have turned out a liability, and he supplied examples, even though "it is embarrassing."

> One specifically . . . in the field of sulphur was what we call the Stewart Beach Sulphur Dome, which is a dome off the coast of Texas. We had located this dome by geophysical methods. It had been put up for competitive bid by the government, being in government waters. We knew there was a dome there. We could predict fairly accurately the depth to the caprock of the dome, and all that really remained was to drill it and to find out whether or not sulphur actually existed.
>
> The company bid seven million dollars on that dome, which was a fantastic figure to bid for a really unknown rank prospect, and we drilled, and the first hole was encouraging. . . . It had every indication of being a potential mine. We drilled other wells, and found they had no limestone or sulphur, merely gypsum. And to summarize, we drilled some 21 holes on that dome at a cost of another million dollars before we proved that there wasn't enough sulphur on that dome to be of economic or commercial interest.

There had been other instances, in Sicily and in Mexico, where first appearances had been promising but led to nothing. In re-direct examination, Joseph—somewhat carelessly as it turned out —again introduced the subject of the "banding" technique in examining cores which the SEC experts had so lengthily expounded, and Fogarty contributed his nail to the coffin:

> I know of no textbook, I know of no school that really teaches this type of banding or this method to determine dip that has been used and described before. I was really totally ignorant of it until I heard it described here in this courtroom.

Claude Stephens, president and chief executive, who went to work for TGS in 1930 and "subsequently performed every task or chore or job that the corporation has to offer anyone," was now finding himself performing one he had *not* expected as he assumed the chair as an SEC witness. After the usual background questions, Kennamer pushed into the matter of the announcement by the Ontario Minister of Mines once more, in the process displaying considerable naivete in respect to news broadcasting. The record is worth re-running:

> Q. Mr. Stephens, just how did you visualize that the Minister of Mines of the Province of Ontario was going to arrange for a radio or television broad-cast at some obscure hour late at night or early in the morning?
>
> A. I wasn't even concerned about how he arranged to make this announcement, sir.
>
> Q. Didn't it strike you as rather strange for the Min-ister of Mines of Ontario to be making an an-nouncement at eleven o'clock or at midnight or at some later hour with respect to a discovery made near Timmins?
>
> A. It didn't strike me as strange at all, sir.
>
> Q. By the way, sir, whom did you expect to listen to such a broadcast at such an hour?
>
> A. I didn't expect anyone to listen to it. I thought it would be a natural broadcast, if in fact it was.
>
> Q. You didn't expect anyone to listen to it, is that right?
>
> A. It never crossed my mind that anyone other than normal people would listen to it.
>
> Q. I don't know too many normal people sitting up at

eleven o'clock or twelve o'clock or two o'clock in
the morning in Ontario.

THE COURT: You don't know about Toronto. It might be a welcome change to whatever they listen to ordinarily.

THE WITNESS: I do a great deal of my listening after eleven
o'clock, sir.

THE COURT: But you are not listening for new strikes, are you?

THE WITNESS: I am listening to 'most anything, sir.

It may be that there was some obscure purpose behind this dialogue,
or it may just have been fatigue. In any event, there was something
about Stephens as a witness that more than once appeared to draw
Kennamer off balance. The "radio hour" was not the only example.
The prosecutor shifted his questions to the April 12 news release,
leading off by reading selected passages from a brochure of the
New York Stock Exchange entitled *The Corporate Director and the
Investing Public,* as follows:

> A corporation . . . is expected to release quickly to the public
> any news or information which presumably would materially affect
> values or influence investment decisions.
>
> It should be a corporation's primary objective to assure that
> news will be handled in proper perspective. This necessitates ap-
> propriate restraint, good judgment and careful adherence to the
> facts. Any projection of financial data . . . should be soundly
> based, appropriately qualified, conservative and factual. Exces-
> sive or misleading conservatism should be avoided.
>
> Occasionally it may be necessary for corporate officials to
> deny false rumors or clarify misunderstandings which are affecting
> the market in their company's stock. A quick, clear announcement
> to the press and wire services along with immediate notice to the
> Exchange is the most effective procedure under the circumstances.

Stephens was quick to agree with all of these policy statements, as might be expected, but would not go along with Kennamer's repeated assertion that "an official announcement by the
company to the effect that these rumors were wholly unfounded
or substantially unfounded" would affect the market price of Texas
Gulf. He pointed out, fairly, that this was not what the release said,
but finally, at the Court's urging, agreed that the release had a stabilizing effect. The SEC attorney made quite a point of the fact that
the drilling of the first hole in November, 1963, had not been
brought to the attention of the directors, stockholders, or anyone
until the 16th of the following April, and in fact that the stockhold-

ers had not been told face-to-face until more than a year after that, at the 1965 annual meeting, and after the SEC had brought a lawsuit. The witness acknowledged this charge, but obviously saw no pertinence in the point, unless it was in the fact that members of the exploration group had in the meantime been buying shares and calls. Of such purchases, he said, he knew nothing, except perhaps for those of Fogarty, and in response to the Court's restatement of Kennamer's queries, said that the company had taken no action against any of the defendants by reason of their purchases during the period.

In his cross-examination Marden referred back to the policy statements of the Exchange, which had been read, and put into the record the 16 press releases of Texas Gulf from November to April which *did* serve to keep stockholders and public informed of the company's affairs. The April 12 release had the same objective, Stephens said. He told Judge Bonsal that K55-1 was a rich, but not *unusually* rich core, that he had seen richer ones, and "as a matter of fact, I have cut a few."

In view of Fogarty's earlier statement to the effect that Adelstein had made a friendly and somewhat startling statement to him regarding the April 12 news release, at the close of a day-long conference in the Texas Gulf offices on April 29, 1964, it was no surprise when Marden returned to the point with Stephens as corroborator. By now there were two points in issue—whether any such statement had been made, and whether Stephens had been present in the afternoon. Parenthetically it seems fair to observe that Adelstein's alleged comment, if made, did not matter very much either way, any more than would the fact of Stephens' presence, but it obviously annoyed SEC counsel, who then chose to take out their annoyance in a diversionary attack upon the credibility of Stephens and Fogarty. Marden, with the Court's approval, put questions to the TGS chief executive which might indicate just how much of the day's discussion he had heard, and in the end Stephens repeated his version of Adelstein's comment, which corresponded to Fogarty's version. Kennamer, when he returned for redirect examination of the witness, went to considerable pains to shake the story, even demanding that Stephens repeat word for word what he had said to the conference group more than two years before. Even the Court felt constrained at this point to observe that a lot of time had passed in the interval. After a flurry of questions and answers, all that resulted was that Stephens repeated the Adelstein comment once more, and vouched for its accuracy.

Another result was that Adelstein was recalled, and the business of the conference was rehashed. Asked what consumed five hours of discussion on that day, he attributed this in part to the loquacity of Fogarty and Jaegerman. Finally came the question on the statement, as recounted by the TGS officers. The witness, speaking carefully, said, "I did not make that statement." But he then added that he did make a comment, which was: "The answer as to what I said to him was that this release did not appear to be an overstatement, that it was, if anything, on the conservative side." Then there was this final touch:

> Q. . . . was Mr. Stephens . . . present in the board room of Texas Gulf at any time on the afternoon of April 29th?
> A. No.

Hubert Norman, Adelstein's assistant, who had not previously been called, now was brought to the stand to corroborate the fact of Stephens' complete absence during the afternoon of the meeting, which he did. For good measure, apparently, Jaegerman, the chief investigative counsel for the SEC and the man who had put this show on the road, was also called. Although he himself had admittedly been "in and out during most of the afternoon," and for a great deal of the time making telephone calls in the anteroom, he testified flatly to the absence of Stephens during that time, and rounded off his brief testimony with a reference to a visit to Timmins and a conversation with Ken Darke. The issues of the Adelstein statement, and the Stephens presence on the afternoon of the conference, were left hanging right there. All that really mattered, of course, was what Judge Bonsal thought.

The Commission's case was about in, except for some exhibits purporting to show how long it takes for securities experts to evaluate the news, and some depositions covering the alleged tippees in Washington and Houston, and those of Hurd, of a Toronto broker named Roche—and of Darke. Said Kennamer:

"At this time, your Honor, the Commission renews its demand that the defendant Kenneth H. Darke be presented as a witness in these proceedings. I understand that he is a Canadian national, that he is now living in Toronto, and, of course, he is beyond the reach of ordinary subpoena. I believe, however, that the Court has the power to direct his appearance here in the event his counsel decline to produce him." Marden's response followed quickly. There had been two meetings with the Court on this subject, and on the record. Darke being a Canadian citizen, his deposition had been taken by the SEC in Canada for use at the trial, and Marden had offered on two other occasions to have further depositions taken if Kennamer wished to ask more questions but the Commission's counsel had declined the offer.

"Mr. Darke," declared Marden, "is the red herring in this case, the stalking horse. The most unhappy person in this room, if Mr. Darke were to come in, would be Mr. Kennamer. He is using Mr. Darke to try and prove the fraud that he has been unable to prove by any item of evidence that he has so far submitted to your Honor, and that is the only reason for this continuing harping about poor Mr. Darke. I now again offer to the plaintiff for the third time the opportunity of taking Mr. Darke's testimony, if they wish further testimony, in Canada. He has no obligation to come here. His deposition has been taken, just as happens so frequently with foreign nationals."

The Court said he would like to have Darke in the witness chair, but had no power to require him to appear. The SEC was about to rest its case when one of Kennamer's assistants handed him a note. Almost as an afterthought the SEC attorneys had recalled the *other* missing defendant, Thomas P. O'Neill. The former TGS accountant had been served with a summons and complaint but had failed to answer or appear. Apparently he had left the country, and either nobody knew why, or was not telling. The Commission now moved for a default judgment against O'Neill in a separate proceeding. The rest of the story would have to await Bonsal's opinion at the close of the trial.

With a fine disregard for any chronological step-by-step story, the Commission had hammered away at its "false and misleading" news release of April 12, at the charge that those with material inside knowledge had not disclosed it, and that all but two of them had purchased stock secure in that knowledge. The mass of technical evidence went to the point of the richness of the strike from the very first drilling, which raised questions of materiality and the timing of the disclosure. There was no proof offered that anybody had been damaged, since this had been left over by common consent until a later date.

## II

In one sense the defense now seemed a little skimpy, possibly because the attorneys had labored under the necessity of doing much of their work during the previous cross-examinations. The chief characters had already made their appearance on the stage at points, and under rules, not of their own choosing—except in one respect. There was now produced a battery of rather formidable expert witnesses who set out in workmanlike manner, under the guidance of counsel, to riddle in considerable telling detail, if possible, the evidence of the two SEC experts as to what constituted material knowledge of the mine on the eve of the first news release—the one the Commission charged was "false and misleading." In the end it would seem fairly clear, at least, that one hole did not make a mine.

In addition to the experts, a Lehman Brothers partner would be called to supply the total picture of Texas Gulf Sulphur activity in its various fields, as seen by knowledgeable people in the market. The manager of the Kam Kotia mine—a near neighbor to Kidd Creek—would discuss the environment in mining terms. A security analyst from New York University would report on his detailed study of the company and its business, past and present. The head of the Homestake gold mining enterprise would broaden the professional and technical picture of the mining business. And that was about all, except for some further argument on the credibility issue. In line with defense strategy, the TGS experts confined their studies of the facts to the period ending at 7 P.M. on the night of April 10, since the complained-of release was limited to that point in the information available in New York. The defense could then rest, except for the somewhat different cases of Coates and Lamont, who were represented by their own counsel.

After Mollison had been recalled, in connection with the identification of certain exhibits, the first defense expert made his appearance, in the person of Dean James D. Forrester, of the University of Arizona College of Mines. After substantial foundation-laying in terms of his experience, and specifically in terms of the logs and assay results, the witness declared that in his judgment neither proven nor probable ore had been established as of 7 P.M. on April 10. It was "an interesting prospect," but did not indicate the existence of a commercially mineable ore body. For good measure, he saw no significance of any consequence in the plaintiff's chart relating to ore blocks, and persisted in this opinion throughout cross-examination.

Alvin W. Pearson was president of Lehman Corporation and chairman of its portfolio committee. In the last months of 1963, after analyzing the prospects in sulphur stocks, his firm bought 75,000 shares of TGS, one of the controlling reasons being that the present management had shown aggressiveness in attempting to diversify the company. There also seemed to be substantial plus values. At this time nothing was known in the Lehman Corporation about the drilling at Timmins, but their decision to buy, Pearson declared, would not have been influenced one way or another by such knowledge. Pressed by Kennamer to acknowledge that K55-1 "by any standard is one of the most sensational discoveries within modern times," Pearson said that with his investment background he would be very loath to place value on one hole that would be sufficient to cover the vast sums required for investment and return of profit.

Charles F. Park Jr., professor of geology and former dean of Stanford University's school of earth sciences, was the second expert for the defense, and he offered substantially the same conclusions. He was followed by Gloyd M. Wiles, of Port Washington, New York, a consulting mining engineer of some 43 years' experience. He said that his principal concerns had consisted of evaluating mining properties through to the final cost and sale of the products, and his testimony provided insight into many of the hard details of processing ore after mining. When asked by Marden if he would have recommended purchase of the Kidd 55 property in November, after one drill hole, he replied that it would have been "an out-and-out gamble."

Confronted with the now familiar definitions of proven and probable ore, and the time limitation of 7 P.M., April 10, Graham Walkey, vice president and general manager of the Kam Kotia mine —12 miles away from Kidd—quickly declared his opinion that neither type of ore had been shown to exist in any quantity as of such date. His subsequent testimony chiefly concerned the geological environment of the area and the similarities between the two mine sites. In determining the continuity of mineralization, Walkey said their policy was to drill holes on sections no greater than 50 feet apart. When the talk got around to mine configuration, as it often did on cross-examination, the witness suggested the term "plugs" or cylinders, as characteristic of Kam Kotia, thus adding to the figurative nomenclature which had so far included turnips, carrots, string beans, and potatoes. Nevertheless Walkey demonstrated his substantial expertness even though—contrary to the traditional popular qualification—he was much less than 50

miles from home. The Texas Gulf parade of experts was now
drawing to a close, with a professor of finance and security analysis
from New York University, a professor from the University of
Arizona whose specialty was the localization of mineral deposits, a
Canadian mining geophysicist, and the chairman of the Homestake
gold mining company.

Douglas Bellemore, of the N.Y.U. graduate school of business
administration, had been teaching security analysis and portfolio
management for some 30 years, and had been requested to make a
study of Texas Gulf Sulphur stock at the end of 1963 and as of the
early months of 1964. Specifically he had been asked what value,
as a professional analyst, he would place on information from
the first drill hole. The thrust of Bellemore's testimony was to paint
a picture of the widespread activities of TGS and the effects of its
diversification program. As for the results of the single drill hole,
"I know of no way that I could have placed any earning power
on that, and my whole experience is that one drill hole doesn't
really prove anything. . . . I would consider it not material at all
in the valuation of the stock." Perhaps mindful of the consistent
attacks made upon the SEC case on the grounds of hindsight,
Kennamer chose to reverse the process in connection with Bellemore's projected evaluation of TGS stock as of early 1964, charging
him with having "projected himself backwards" and with employing "mental legerdemain." Such as this passage:

Q. Projecting yourself back in point of time, Dr. Bellemore, to
November–December, 1963, you found, did you not, sir, that
Texas Gulf was a very narrowly based company, at least in one
sense, that 97 per cent of its earnings were derived from the
sulphur business?

A. That they had been, but I was very well aware as of November,
1963, that they were going to diversify into an area which they
already well knew, fertilizers, and that they had made an
investment of $35 million already in a plant which would be
in operation the following year; that in the case of phosphates
they had . . . 300-year reserves, that they were operating a
pilot plant in which they had already invested two million
dollars, that the company had indicated from the potash alone
they could probably generate 50 cents a share in earnings. So
one of the very interesting factors that any analyst would have
seen at this point was not only diversification but in this case
it was unusual in that it was in areas where they had both
the fertilizer and the mining know-how.

Almost all of Kennamer's attempts to force Dr. Bellemore down into the "remarkable drill hole" and then to come back with evaluations or conclusions that would have altered his already stated opinion seemed doomed to failure. The witness, as a market analyst, was simply not impressed with one hole, no matter how good it may have been.

Professor Willard Lacy, head of the mining and geological engineering department at the University of Arizona, took Court and counsel somewhat farther along the path of a graduate education in the significance of what lies beneath the ground, but his conclusions as developed by Marden corresponded remarkably to those of the other experts. To estimate tonnage and grade of ore, he also would prefer "holes at 50-foot intervals because in the light of the extreme irregularity of the geological controls and our dearth of knowledge as to what these geological controls were, we don't have a background of geological experience to go by. So any projection at this point would be very misleading. It could be irresponsible."

The mining geophysicist was John B. Boniwell, of Port Credit, Ontario, and he found fault with the SEC exhibit which had attempted to measure the anomaly—"The method is incapable of providing such a measurement." Donald H. McLaughlin, a Californian who was chairman of the Homestake Mining Company, engaged in gold and uranium mining, a former chairman of the Harvard geology department and a former dean of the College of Mining of the University of California, batted last for the TGS experts. He also listened to the rules of the game which had been submitted to the others and pronounced the Kidd 55 property, as of 7 P.M., April 10, a prospect only, and said this was correctly stated by the first news release. The courtroom students were able to add a few last notes on the business of gold mining in the Black Hills of South Dakota.

Adelstein and Fogarty were recalled briefly, there was further argument concerning the material that had been supplied to SEC by TGS, and further argument as to what Adelstein had said to Fogarty and whether Stephens was present at the afternoon meeting, with no appreciable change by either side. Marden then rested for the defendants he represented.

Attorneys Gillespie, Connelly, and their associates, who were acting for Lamont and Coates, picked up the pace of the trial somewhat, perhaps because they were stuck with a more limited fighting front. Their two clients were charged with trading on inside information by purchasing stock before the disclosure to the investing public, and they marshaled a battery of 31 witnesses, 14 of whom appeared "live" and 17 by deposition. The presentation was divided roughly into two parts—testimony bearing on the role played in disclosure by *The Northern Miner,* and that bearing upon the press conference held in New York on April 16. The dramatis personae included an investment researcher, brokers in various locations in the United States and Canada, a security analyst, an eye witness to market reactions, a financial publisher, a circulation expert, an editor, a reporter, an investment banker, an arbitrage expert, a floor trader, a floor specialist in Texas Gulf, the head of the trading table of a large house, an expert in stock movements and timing, and a young law graduate who constructed a map as his assignment. It was a dazzling assemblage, an attempt to come up with the different pieces in a complex puzzle. At least in this first game in the match, it would be rewarded with success.

Gillespie began by reading into the record a series of admissions, covering the movement of TGS stock over a period of several days from April 10 through 15; that as of January 1, 1964, there were 3,553 Western Union stock quotation tickers located in 3,472 offices of New York Stock Exchange members in the United States and abroad; and that each stock brokerage firm selling stock to customers of Morgan Guaranty Trust Company on April 16, 1964, had in their offices of said date a Dow Jones broad tape. Robert A. Gilbert, a New York investment researcher, specializing in raw material securities, came on to recall a letter sent to clients on April 14, noting the TGS situation and suggesting further accumulation of shares. He had regarded the April 12 "gloomy release" as confirming a prospect, and whatever it said, he thought the prospect looked pretty good. Hyman Bluestein, of the Boston office of Francis I. duPont and Company, told by deposition of purchases made by clients on his recommendation, in the face of the release, because of the general nature of the Texas Gulf business, while Bernard Grishman, of Bache and Company, New York, produced unsolicited order tickets and his own thought at the time that the stock would move up.

In depositions, Geddes Webster, who was in the investment business in Canada, described the rumors circulating at the Montreal convention of the Canadian Institute of Mining and Metallurgy, while a Toronto broker, Alfred Vance, whose firm had tele-communications with its several branch offices and with Hayden, Stone in New York, also dwelt on the rumors. Kerry Donovan, a New York security analyst for F. S. Smithers and Company, recalled that he had available information on TGS prior to April 16 for anyone who called.

Perhaps the most colorful all-around account of the market reaction to the TGS strike rumors and news was supplied by the deposition of John M. Rogers, of Toronto, a partner in a brokerage firm for 30 years, and who had a direct wire to his correspondent New York broker, New York Hanseatic. Highly influenced by *The Northern Miner* accounts, he bought 3,000 shares of TGS on April 15 for around $90,000, "the largest position moneywise I have ever taken in a stock in 40 years." Toronto was buzzing with information, Rogers declared, and it dated from January. During April 13-14-15 his firm bought over 44,000 shares of TGS for clients. He said that a lot of this kind of information is generated by knowledgeable drillers who call other people—". . . I have seen drillers drop the goddam drill and beat it for a brokerage office . . . these *Northern Miner* guys are all in the market . . . they are great guys with the nose."

"I didn't write up General Motors or things of that nature," testified William Ramsay, former publisher of *Inside Wall Street*, and now doing oil and mining exploration. "I wrote up things that were unusual." He saw the happenings at Timmins as something that was "really mammoth, it could be considered one of the great empires of the world; but I didn't know this until well on into April 13, I think."

In his deposition, Charles D. McLachlin, circulation manager of *The Northern Miner*, supplied details: the publication was available at newsstands on Bay Street in Toronto by 7 A.M. each Thursday, and postmen delivered many more before 8 A.M.; newsstand sales in the United States run from 700 to 800 copies; total distribution of the April 16, 1964 issue was 29,847; some 540 copies went to New York City, exclusive of newsstands; the publication was often on the streets there by 9 or 10 A.M.; *The Northern Miner* circulation covered Buffalo, Detroit, Chicago, and Washington, and all states get copies.

The morning of April 16 was vividly recalled by Robert G. Matthews, an investment researcher of Toronto, who was leaving for Sault Ste. Marie to attend an annual meeting of a steel company. He picked up a copy of the *Miner* at the airport. He had "so many people interested and down my back . . . about Texas Gulf Sulphur" that he telephoned his office before 9 A.M., gathering from the article that TGS had released the information. There were others, from New York, Toronto, Hartford, Boston. One Canadian office had a call from Charleston, West Virginia. There was Ronald Killie, then of E. F. Hutton and Company, who had the temporary misfortune of being located "uptown" in New York City at 60th Street and Madison Avenue. No copy of the *Miner* was available there, and he telephoned a friend in Wall Street who read him the article. It was Killie who also telephoned one of his customers, the Cannons, who bought, sold, and made a profit of more than $10,000 during the morning.[8]

Testimony bearing upon the New York press conference and the timing of the disclosure began with a Toronto broker, Donald Angus, who read of the meeting in the April 16 issue of the *Globe & Mail* and requested that his New York office send a man. They did, and it was Andrew Kim, now also represented by deposition. Kim reported that Dow Jones would have the story and he was instructed to stay around for the question period. The deposition of Kenneth F. Smith, business news editor for the Canadian Press, noted that reporter Jim Peacock attended the meeting and transmitted the news at 10:29 A.M. with a follow-up at 10:32. It was here that the SEC attorneys learned, apparently for the first time, of the mechanics of "short takes" in wire news transmission, to add to the other facts they had apparently not known about eleven o'clock news broadcasts. Smith listed the newspapers served by their wire, plus seven private radio and television stations, all of whom got the message simultaneously on teletype.

The Court and counsel were by now meeting all kinds of people, and one of them was Norma Walter, occupation reporter, now on strike from the New York *World-Telegram* and working for *Business Week*. At the time of the events in question she was a writer-editor for *Investors Reader*, published twice a month by Merrill Lynch, Pierce, Fenner and Smith. Miss Walter was a nice change from the parade of male witnesses, or their depositions, and in fact she was more than that because her 62 words, dictated over the telephone, had scooped everybody else at 10:29 A.M. on the morning of the press conference. In an incident reported on page 2,427 of the court reporter's transcript on the sixteenth day

See P. 83, Chapter 4.

of the trial, the defense attorney asked Miss Walter to raise her voice and describe the circumstances of the "most dramatic spot news story" she had ever covered. The SEC attorney glowered and referred to it as a "fragment" and this brought forth the response: "Your Honor, I object to Mr. Kennamer's use of the adjective. . . ." Although it was a noun, Judge Bonsal responded that "I have gotten so many I am completely numb to all adjectives." Actually only two of Norma Walter's 62 words were adjectives. After the president of Texas Gulf had read his statement and answered a few questions, the lights were turned down for showing slides. She ran out a door and telephoned her story, and her testimony came to a close on this note:

> Q. Then what did you do after that?
> A. I stayed for the question and answer period.
> Q. And then what did you do?
> A. Then I left and went to a luncheon.
> Q. I hope you had a good lunch.
> A. Very nice.
> Q. Where was it?
> A. Twenty One.

Exit Norma. Enter William Karp, editor of the Merrill Lynch news wire, who had taken, written, edited and transmitted the TGS news to all of the company's offices in the United States and Canada— what was called a "three-bell" transmission. There was some by-play over the function of the bells in a teletype transmission, after which Karp was followed by the deposition of Jerry Bishop, the staff reporter for the *Wall Street Journal* who had attended the conference. His message, telephoned to the office, would normally have been on the broad tape within two or three minutes, he testified. Instead it appeared at 10:54 A.M., without explanation for the delay. None has ever been offered. In the beginning, this had appeared to be the official disclosure time for the news so far as the Commission was concerned, although it was later to change its mind. The time differential between the Merrill Lynch and the Dow Jones transmissions, for what it was worth, was underlined by the deposition of broker Charles Schultz, New York, who heard the news from a friend at Merrill Lynch, called a client, and ordered for him 100 shares at 10:31 A.M. There were other orders.

Of quite a different order was a call from another man at Merrill Lynch that morning to *his* friend, witness Herbert G. Wellington, investment banker. He had been buying Texas Gulf since January, bought 2,000 shares on April 13, and more on April 16. The friend had called to congratulate him for "being right for the wrong reason." After he had finished, Gillespie broke in to provide the record with two medium-light touches. The train from Toronto bearing *The Northern Miner* had actually arrived that morning three minutes early at Grand Central. And he submitted that, as of April, Merrill Lynch had 2,349 registered representatives. Kennamer, in a rare moment of generosity, offered to make it 2,350, but the Court refused to add to the Merrill Lynch overhead. The remaining witnesses, for the most part, added professional and technical details to the story. The Court found out what arbitrage was from John K. Redmond, who handles it for J. R. Timmins and Company, and who described it as a simultaneous transaction, buying in one market and selling in another and profiting by the differential. The point, for the defense, was that Redmond's operation kept going continuously a three-way telephone conversation between his office and the Toronto and Montreal stock exchanges, and he had been highly aware of the market activity.

The deposition of John W. Billings Sr., had been taken in Chicago, where he was an exchange specialist for Texas Gulf stock, had gone long on it, was concerned over the April 12 release, but didn't change his mind as to its prospects. Stuart Rafkind, a floor trader on the New York exchange, on the other hand, had been in Miami on holiday, where he had overheard hotel guests talking about Texas Gulf during a gin rummy game. He returned on April 15 and bought some of the stock. Harry Ness, a senior consultant with Standard Research Consultants, a Standard and Poor subsidiary, testified as to the sale of shares and the timing of orders on April 16. It remained for Daniel D. McCarthy, of Eastman, Dillon Union Securities, to complete the courtroom short course in securities trading. His job was to sit at a trading table, along with some 20 others, supervising and processing trading in large blocks of stock. Eight television cameras in this location are suspended from the ceiling so that every trader can see the tape. Using such expressions as "driving" and "heeling" McCarthy told how the bare news from the continuously moving tapes determined the trading, although he might not be specifically aware—in fact, had no time to be aware—of actual news statements in the usual sense. In short, news to McCarthy meant only *tape action*.

Daniel F. Kolb, a Michigan law school graduate not yet admitted to the bar but employed by Davis, Polk, Wardwell, Sunderland and Kiendl, had been commissioned by the defense to prepare a map which was now carried into the courtroom. As of 10:29 A.M., April 16, it showed black flags for the branch offices of Merrill Lynch in the United States and Canada; and brown, orange, green, silver, and blue flags for other houses, for *Miner* distribution, and for that of the Canadian Press Service, based on the testimony of previous witnesses. Kennamer made him count the flags, by colors, and the Court entered the act with this comment: "Isn't that beautiful—you did a fine job . . . but all it really is is an optimum. . . ." Kennamer kept calling the Merrill Lynch transmission "a fragment" and defense attorney Conwell retorted by having the witness point out that the map did not even include the press coverage by the Ontario press gallery.

Having run its zig-zag and somewhat exhausting course for six weeks, the trial had come to a weary close, but some of the excerpts from the summations are revealing. The Court pressed the attorneys, especially those for the Commission, aggressively but informally on the whole question of materiality. He asked Marden whether or not, if detailed information on the assays of the first drill hole had been circulated to *The Northern Miner* and the brokerage fraternity, it would have had an effect upon the stock. In such case it would have been material in a sense—"perhaps the wrong sense." But Marden replied that, "It would not be material from the point of view of the prudent investor, and these are the people they should look out for. They don't look out for the Bay Street gamblers."

Also Marden: "The Commission's proof . . . is 100 per cent hindsight. Both Adelstein and Pennebaker were armed with the drilling results after April 10th which was not the case with the experts we produced. We asked them to limit their examination to the facts as they were known to company management at the time we made these decisions."

And the Court, in respect to the April 12 news release: "They had to do this in a sort of a rush, didn't they, Mr. Kennamer? How strict a standard is it? Is the standard that you shall put out no press release unless you can put out one that really says everything that is reasonable to say in the situation?"

Kennamer: "Well, surely, your Honor, the standard must be sufficiently high to prohibit the management of a company from describing a major ore discovery as a mere prospect."

And later, the Court: "What about the argument that there isn't any standard provided, any rule, that it is too uncertain, that nobody knows how long they have to wait or, if they do have to wait, how long they have to wait before the news is reasonably disseminated to the public and the stockholders."

Kennamer: "I think that argument has been answered by the Supreme Court in the Capital Gains Bureau case. It would be, I think, your Honor, a nearly impossible task to formulate a rigid set of rules that would apply in all situations of this sort." [9]

There was considerable conversation about tipping and tippees, especially as it related to the alleged conduct of Darke.

THE COURT: "It was mostly conversation, wasn't it?"

KENNAMER: "There was nothing in writing that we know of, your Honor."

THE COURT: "No, I guess not, I guess not. But it sort of circulated around. As I remember, the old lady had some friend who handled her securities and the young lady had a boss in the government, and they didn't have very much to do because they were talking about securities."

KENNAMER: "Yes, your Honor. But the loyalty that the Court mentioned to his company was, in a sense, a newly-found loyalty and it was discovered—"

THE COURT: "I know. But how did they know that it was a newly-found loyalty?"

KENNAMER: "They might not, your Honor, they might not."

And the attorney for the Commission concluded in this wise:

This is to my knowledge the first case where the Commission has brought an enforcement proceeding involving the issuance of stock options. . . . I believe it is the first case where we have attempted to apply 10b-5 to the issuance by a listed company of a news announcement.

It had been a long trial, and it concluded June 21, 1964.

[9] *SEC v. Capital Gains Research Bureau Inc.*, 375 U.S. 180 (1963) arose under the Investment Advisers Act of 1940, which prohibits fraud by investment advisers. As Marden was to point out later, in the Utah stockholders actions, the *Capital Gains* case should be read in the context of the Act under which it was brought: "The Investment Advisers Act of 1940 thus reflects a Congressional recognition 'of the delicate fiduciary nature of an investment advisory relationship,' as well as a Congressional intent to eliminate, or at least to expose, all conflicts of interest which might incline an investment adviser—consciously or unconsciously—to render advice which was not disinterested." 375 U.S. at 191–2.

### III

As might be expected, Judge Bonsal's organization of the facts as set forth in the opinion, filed almost two months after the close of the proceedings in Foley Square, offered a somewhat more orderly pattern than had been made available to spectators at the trial itself. Events were rearranged in their proper sequence. Moreover the judge demonstrated that not only had he been a careful and critical listener throughout the long days of expert technical testimony, but that he was a translator and editor of a high order. His simple restatements of technical and scientific concepts and processes and objectives were brief, illuminating, and even refreshing. Judicial opinions, considered as a necessary class of the literature of communication, all too seldom provide clarity and effective quotability, regardless of their authority.

The editor of *The Northern Miner,* a publication which as both observer and participant in the trial, had earned its right to comment, declared the judge's conduct throughout the case was "an honor to his office," adding that there were audible sighs of relief in the business world when Judge Bonsal handed down his decision. His was "a particularly alert mind on the bench." [10]

The opinion began by outlining briefly the history of Texas Gulf Sulphur during recent years, giving specific attention to the reflection of its activities in the marketplace and the stock exchanges. It then summarized the company's burgeoning exploration activities on the Canadian Shield leading up to its particular interest in the Kidd 55 area, near Timmins, as early as 1959, and the acquiring of an option on the northeast quarter section in June, 1963. From here the opinion went directly into the drilling activity, beginning with K55-1, which terminated November 12, 1963, at 655 feet; the decision to acquire the other three quarter sections; and the imposition of security measures. There follows a hole-by-hole account of the later activities, broken significantly by a summary of known progress as of 7 P.M. on April 9, and by subsequent known results through 7 P.M., April 15, 1964. In this section the Court notes that the chemical assay report on the first hole, received in mid-December, was the only assay report on any drill hole received prior to April 16; also that the results of drilling through

[10] *The Northern Miner,* "Practical Decision on Critical Case," August 25, 1966.

the evening of April 10 were available to TGS when it issued its April 12 news release.

Here the Court left the Timmins scene, so far as mining results are concerned, and set forth the purchases of Texas Gulf stock and calls by certain defendants and tippees between November 12, 1963, when the first drill hole was completed, and the close of business on April 16, 1964—"the day on which TGS issued a press release announcing the discovery of a copper mine on the Kidd 55 segment at a press conference called for the purpose." The next sentence states that the evidence shows that the tippees purchased shares and calls on the stock "on the basis of advice received directly or indirectly from defendants Darke, Coates, and Lamont." The opinion then includes a table of all such purchases, giving names, dates, amounts, and prices.

With the mining and buying facts established, Judge Bonsal proceeded to the legal business at hand by stating appropriate sections of the Securities Exchange Act of 1934, including the promulgation of Rule 10b-5 under Section 10(b) of the Act, noting that the Commission contends that the defendants engaged in a "course of business" which operated as a "fraud or deceit" on the stockholders of TGS in violation of the section and the rule. Here a footnote points out that the SEC, in briefs and at the trial, made no distinction between the three sections of the rule, but that since the first two sections were not made the subject of any evidence, only the third section was applicable to the facts of the case. To the defendants' assertion that the Commission must establish the elements of common law fraud—misrepresentation or nondisclosure, materiality, *scienter,* intent to deceive, reliance, causation—Judge Bonsal said that recent decisions did not require proof of these elements in actions charging violations of Rule 10b-5, and cited decisions bearing this out, including language employed by the U.S. Supreme Court in the *Capital Gains Bureau* case.[11] Said Bonsal: ". . . the use of 'fraud' in Rule 10b-5(3) cannot be interpreted in its narrow common law sense."

To another suggestion of the defendants that Section 16 of the Act, relating to directors, officers, and principal stockholders, limits the liability of insiders to sanctions provided in that section, the Court replied that the provisions of Section 16 imposed no limitations on the enforcement of Section 10(b). On the other hand, for its part:

[11] See Note 9, p. 146, this chapter.

To establish violations of Section 10(b) and Rule 10b-5(3), the Commission must prove that the defendants engaged in a "course of business" which operated as a "fraud or deceit . . . in connection with the purchase or sale of any security." Questions arise therefore as to whether insider purchases based on material, undisclosed information constitute violations of Section 10(b) and Rule 10b-5(3); if so, who are the insiders; whether the statute and rule are limited to "face-to-face" transactions; and, finally, what constitutes material information.

Reviewing the principal cases, the judge concluded that insiders subject to the disclosure requirements of the section and the rule may include employees as well as officers, directors, and controlling stockholders who are in possession of material undisclosed information obtained in the course of their employment. He added that such an insider's liability for failure to disclose material information extends to purchases made on national security exchanges as well as to purchases in "face-to-face" transactions. To the point that it would be impossible for an insider trading on a national exchange to seek out the other party and disclose information, he replied that there are other ways of doing this job—and if not, the insider should forego transactions until the bar was removed. With these matters out of the way, he then came to the main point: the undisclosed information must be material. It was the occasion for a little homily.

There is nothing in the Act which precludes insiders from purchasing stock of their company or from being beneficiaries of the company's stock option plan. On the contrary, it is important under our free enterprise system that insiders, including directors, officers, and employees, be encouraged to own securities of their company. The incentive that comes with stock ownership benefits both the company and its stockholders.

Moreover, it is obvious that any director, officer or employee will know more about his company or have more specialized knowledge as to at least some phase of its business than an outside stockholder can have or expect to have. Often this specialized knowledge may whet the speculative interest of the insider, particularly if he believes in the future of his company, and may lead him to purchase stock. Purchases under such circumstances are not encompassed by Section 10(b) and Rule 10b-5.

An insider *does* violate these provisions, Bonsal declared, when he comes into possession of *material* information which he uses to his own advantage by purchasing stock or calls on the stock of his company prior to public disclosure, but the information is not material "merely because it would be of interest to the speculator on Bay Street or Wall Street."

There followed some definitions of materiality from leading cases and authorities. It was information "which in reasonable and objective contemplation might affect the value of the corporation's stock or securities. . . ." [12] Again, "It is information which, if known, would clearly affect 'investment judgment,' " [13] or "which directly bears on the intrinsic value of a company's stock."

Material information need not be limited to information which is translatable into earnings, as suggested by the defendants, the Court said. But the test of materiality must necessarily be a conservative one, particularly since many actions are brought on the basis of hindsight. The final reference was to a statement by a former member of the SEC staff: "It is appropriate that management's duty of disclosure under Rule 10b-5 be limited to those situations which are essentially extraordinary in nature and which are reasonably certain to have a substantial effect on the market price of the security if disclosed. A more rigorous standard would impose an unreasonable burden on management in its securities trading. Moreover, such a standard could involve the courts to an unrealistic degree in the determination of whether certain types of information might have an impact on the market." [14] So much for the law, the precedents, and the Court's interpretation. He now turned to applying these to the purchases of the individual defendants.

All of the individual defendants were directors, officers, or employees of Texas Gulf, and with the exceptions of Stephens and Kline, each had bought stock on a national exchange, so the jurisdictional requirements of the Act and the rule had been satisfied. It remained to be seen whether they had purchased with material information not disclosed to the public. To begin with, said Bonsal, Huntington and Murray, the company lawyer and the office manager, had no detailed knowledge about the work and hence were not in possession of material information. That was the first finding. It was two down and eight to go, and at this point the judge re-

---

[12] *List v. Fashion Park Inc.*, 340 F. 2nd 462 (2d Cir. 1965).
[13] *Cady, Roberts & Co.*, 40 S.E.C. 911 (1961).
[14] Fleischer: "Securities Trading and Corporation Information Practices: The Implications of the Texas Gulf Sulphur Proceeding," *51 Virginia Law Review 1271, 1289* (1965).

turned to the mine site, in effect. In respect to the remaining individual defendants he divided the critical period for the possession of material information into three parts: (1) from November 12, 1963 to 7 P.M., April 9, 1964; (2) the next period extended to 10 A.M. April 16; (3) the last period extended to close of business on April 16.

The Commission's experts contended that a mine had been established by 7 P.M. on April 9, while the defendants' experts unanimously agreed that the drilling of three holes to this time did *not* establish a mine. The Commission itself, in an earlier case,[15] had taken a position in regard to registration statements under the Securities Act of 1933 that three drill holes were insufficient to determine whether a commercial ore body was present even though they encountered a gold-bearing structure. The judge, having heard and considered the evidence in the TGS case, found that the drilling results up to 7 P.M. on April 9 did not provide such material information. "When considered in relation to the far-flung business of TGS at the time, it cannot be said that the drilling results of K55-1 and K55-3 constituted material information, the disclosure of which would have had a substantial impact on the market price of TGS's 10,000,000 oustanding shares."

In the succeeding discussion of the drill core of the first hole, Judge Bonsal thoroughly, but not lengthily, examined and weighed the statements of the several experts, taking from each what he apparently deemed to be significant points. It was an impressive performance—and it came down to the fact that one hole did not establish an ore body, and that no matter how good the hole was, no investment significance attached to it. So much for that, but it was also a Commission contention that the results of the one hole *were* material because of what they meant to certain of the defendants. From November 12, 1963, through the completion of K55-3 on April 7, 1964, defendants Fogarty, Mollison, Holyk, Clayton, and Darke had spent more than $100,000 in purchasing stocks and calls. They were experts, and might have had educated guesses. The question—was it material? The opinion said not:

> A similar question would be presented where an engineer in the research department of a publicly-held corporation believes that he may have invented a process which will substantially increase the corporation's earnings or where a chemist in a large

[15] See Note 1, Chapter 3.

pharmaceutical firm thinks he may have devised a chemical
formula which can cure cancer. In these instances it can be assumed that the insider, because of his educated guess, will be
enthusiastic and his enthusiasm may lead him to purchase stock
in his company and to recommend the stock to his associates and
friends even though his educated guess may turn out to be wrong.
It may be argued that such purchases are "unfair" to the outside
stockholders and come within the ambit of Section 10(b) and
Rule 10b-5. . . .

However, most insiders necessarily have educated guesses
about the prospects of particular company programs. If it is held
that purchases made on the basis of educated guesses are pro-
scribed . . . insiders who purchase stock in their company will
do so at their peril. If they announce their educated guesses before
purchasing and their guesses turn out to be wrong they would be
subject to suit; and if they purchase and keep their educated
guesses to themselves and they turn out to be right, they would
again be subject to suit. The creation of such a dilemma would
result in insiders not buying at all, though insiders should be encouraged to have a stake in the companies for which they work.

The outside stockholder can never match the knowledge of
the insider who necessarily knows more about the company and is
in a better position to evaluate its prospects. It may be that the
"fairness" overtones of *Cady, Roberts* indicate a trend toward the
elimination of all insider purchasing. But even were the Court
prepared to accept the proposition that all insider trading is unfair,
a proposition of doubtful validity at best, it would be deterred by
the admonition of Judge Learned Hand that it is not "desirable
for a lower court to embrace the exhilarating opportunity of anticipating a doctrine which may be in the womb of time, but whose
birth is distant." [16] Therefore the purchases prior to 7 P.M. on
April 9 were not based on material undisclosed information even
if the purchasers had educated guesses based on the results of
the first drill hole.

It was at this point that almost the only substantial reference
in the opinion was made to the geologist, Ken Darke, and his tippees, when the Court described Darke's visit to Washington late in
December, 1963. The opinion states that the evidence shows no
more than that Darke indicated to Atkinson and Caskey that he
thought TGS was a good buy, and there is no direct evidence that
he ever again communicated with them—but the record shows that
the tippees purchased substantial amounts of TGS stock and calls.

[16] *Spector Motor Service Inc. v. Walsh, 139 F. 2d 809, 823 (2d Cir. 1944).*

Bonsal said of this, "As the Commission points out, this is strong circumstantial evidence that Darke must have passed the word to one or more of his 'tippees' that drilling on the Kidd 55 segment was about to be resumed. But for the reasons hereinbefore stated, this information was not material." With which comment, the Court found no violations of the section or the rule on the part of any of the individual defendants who purchased—or recommended purchases—prior to 7 P.M. on April 9, 1964. That took care of four more defendants; there were still four to go.

Turning now to his second subdivision of the critical period, running to 10 A.M., April 16, Judge Bonsal examined the Canadian and U.S. rumor mills, the activities of *The Northern Miner* and its declared circulation, the announcement by the Ontario Minister of Mines (which was supposed to have been made on the night of the 15th but was actually made on the morning of the 16th), and the evidence that a number of brokers, speculators, and customers had picked up the information in advance. He was seemingly not too impressed with the aggregate weight of what had been described. He found that the material information about the mine had not become public knowledge prior to the TGS official announcement at the April 16 press conference, and declared that insiders who purchased stock prior to this time could not assert as a defense that the matter was already in the public domain. The immediate effect of this finding fell upon defendants Clayton and Crawford. Clayton, said Bonsal, kept himself fully informed about the Kidd 55 segment, and on the morning of April 15 had purchased 200 shares of TGS stock. It was immaterial whether he had intended to deceive or defraud anyone, since he had used his inside information to his own advantage, violating the section and the rule. Similarly, Crawford had become fully familiar with the contents of the TGS announcement on the evening of April 15. His purchase of 600 shares was executed on the morning of the 16th, and "it is clear that he sought to, and did, 'beat the news.'" These two, said the Court, were guilty of violations. That left Coates and Lamont, and the final subdivision of time.

Although Coates lost no time in telephoning his broker son-in-law in Houston, some 20 minutes after the press conference had begun, the Court found that the announcement had been made, and that this was controlling. "Coates, an experienced corporate lawyer, testified that he believed that the standard in the marketplace was that once the announcement is made, insiders were free to purchase stock or to recommend it to others." Coates, therefore, had committed no violation, and at this point the judge took off on the Commission's assertion, on summation, that the Court should fix a reasonable period so that the announcement can first be absorbed by the public.

> This could only lead to uncertainty. A decision in one case would not control another case with different facts. No insider would know whether he had waited long enough. . . . He would be subject to suit by the Commission (and to private suits brought by others riding on the Commission's coattails).
> The Commission has not supplied, nor has the Court found, decisions specifying a waiting period after a corporate announcement is made. After the action was instituted, Cary, the former Chairman of the Commission, and Fleischer, his former executive assistant, discussed a waiting period in policy terms. If a waiting period is to be fixed, this could be most appropriately done by the Commission, which was established by Congress with broad rule-making powers. Should the Commission determine that it lacks authority to fix a waiting period, authority should come from Congress rather than the courts.

After reviewing the time sequence and circumstances of Lamont's telephone call to Morgan Guaranty Trust Company, and his own later personal purchases, the Court noted that for reasons previously stated with respect to defendant Coates, the announcement had been made and Lamont was guilty of no violations.

Five defendants—Stephens, Fogarty, Kline, Mollison, and Holyk—had been granted stock options by the directors' committee on February 20, 1964, and the Commission had charged that they violated the statute and the rule because they had knowledge as to the drilling results and failed to disclose such information to the committee. The Court found that Kline did not have the necessary knowledge, and although the others did have it, they had been told not to divulge it. Stephens and Fogarty, while constituting management and having a duty to disclose material information bearing on the market value of the stock, were protected by the finding of the Court that the developments at the Kidd 55 segment were not material until 7 P.M. on April 9, some seven weeks after the option action. In view of the land acquisition program, said Bonsal, the security measures which they established were for the benefit of the company and its stockholders.

The final section of the opinion dealt with the controversial press release of April 12. In the only direct charge against the corporation itself, the SEC had argued that it was false and misleading. The story had been told in almost infinite detail during the trial, and the Court restated it in chronological order. Having done so, he declared that it was apparent that the purpose of the release was an attempt to meet rumors that were circulating, that there was no evidence that either TGS or the defendants who had participated in its preparation derived any direct benefit, and that it had produced no unusual market action. In the absence of such a showing, there was no violation.

Even if it had been established that the release was issued in connection with the purchase or sale of any security, said the judge, the Commission had failed to demonstrate that it was false, misleading, or deceptive. Fogarty and Mollison had been under considerable pressure.

> If they said too much, they would have been open to criticism and possible liability if it turned out that TGS had not discovered a commercial mine. If they said too little and later announced a mine, they subjected themselves to the charge that their press release was misleading or deceptive—and, indeed, this is what has happened. If they had announced the drilling results in terms of number of drill holes, footage drilled and mineralization intersected, they would have encouraged the rumor mill which they were seeking to allay. Perhaps they should have waited until they could have obtained more probative information before issuing a press release, particularly since developments were breaking so rapidly. However, as above stated, TGS must not be judged by hindsight. . . . While, in retrospect, the press release may appear gloomy or incomplete, this does not make it misleading or deceptive on the basis of the facts then known.

The complaint was dismissed against the corporation and ten individual defendants. Only Clayton and Crawford were found guilty of violations as charged. Thomas P. O'Neill, the TGS accountant, had been served but failed to answer or appear. Since the Commission had moved for a default judgment against him in a separate proceeding, he was not referred to thereafter.

But in a memorandum and order of the court filed September 27 the SEC motion for a default judgment was denied, without prejudice to its being renewed following final disposition of the appeal, which by then had been taken by the Commission. Judge Bonsal noted that O'Neill had made purchases of stock and calls, the last such being on March 23, 1964. All of the transactions had taken place before 7 P.M. on April 9. Fair comment might be that O'Neill might just as well have put in an appearance.

With the opinion handed down, the Commission appealed, and so did defendants Clayton and Crawford. Texas Gulf, against whom the complaint had been dismissed, was at least for the time being in good position so far as its legal affairs were concerned, but its luck with the press had not improved very much. The opinion had been filed after the market closed on a Friday afternoon, which meant that the news would appear in Saturday newspapers, generally regarded with a jaundiced eye by those in the urban business community who know only too well what happens to them on weekends. The New York *Daily News* had carried the original charges in big black headlines on page one, but buried the news of the vindication in the slim financial columns of the Saturday morning edition, while for *The New York Times* it was still Saturday morning and there were no extensive quotations from the opinion. For those, such as Stephens, Fogarty, and Mollison, who had been closely involved in the much-debated April 12 news release, there seemed little comfort in the coverage, although Judge Bonsal had devoted 1,800 words to the circumstances under which it had been written. All in all, Texas Gulf now dropped into relative news obscurity after the week-end.

"Considering the time, publicity, and the cost to both the government and the defendants, the trial of Texas Gulf Sulphur . . . accomplished virtually nothing constructive and in fact was a destructive procedure," *The Northern Miner* observed from Toronto. "Mining people are delighted to know the court recognizes an ore body is not drilled off with just a few holes—had the court ruled to the contrary, the present system of reporting and describing exploration results would be turned upside down and a process of misrepresentation would develop actually dictated by law. . . . All of this reflects a sociological disease of the times—a government agency, almost perpetually seeking to extend its authority, can be and often is irresponsible in pursuing what it considers to be its responsibility to the public." [17]

Most of the professionals in the law were not going to comment until much later, after they had glimpsed the whites of the eyes of the appellate court, but a week after the trial before Bon-

---

[17] See Note 10, p. 147, this chapter.

sal was concluded, Professor Loss, of Harvard, was lecturing a group which included the Chairman of the Commission, and observed that Section 10(b) was a "pretty slender reed." [18]

"Some law writers—perhaps some judges—have, I think, failed to appreciate that, just as it is important in the law to be able to march forward and not to have a static system, it is also important to see where you are going and to have an eye on the outer frontier. At some point," Loss declared, "the courts are going to stop. They are not going to let this rule take over the whole body of state corporation law as applied to relations between directors and their corporation's shareholders. But that is a line that has to be drawn gradually." He added:

> . . . . The time, I think, has come when the SEC has a further role to play. The SEC has, after all, a general rule-making power. We have lived now with this very general rule 10b-5 for almost 25 years, for a generation. . . . It is difficult, terribly difficult, to draft more specific rules, because the moment you draft a more specific rule you have given a blueprint to somebody for avoiding it. However, the Commission, it seems to me, after 20-odd years, should be thinking seriously of trying to answer some of these questions by making the rule more specific instead of leaving it all to the courts.

Loss had deftly anticipated part of the Bonsal opinion, but there was going to be a great deal more said on the subject.

[18] *Op. cit.*, Chapter 5, p. 99.

# 7

# Appeal:
# Mixed Chorus

I

SEVENTEEN months after the Texas Gulf
Sulphur trial wound up in federal district court in New York, with
the filing of Judge Bonsal's opinion, and four years and nine
months after the original hole was drilled near Timmins, the U.S.
Court of Appeals for the Second Circuit blew the top off another
publicity gusher by reversing practically every finding of the lower
court.

"It's going to have a hell of an impact on the financial world,"
declared Circuit Judge Sterry Waterman in releasing the opinion
of the majority—which he wrote. "Everyone in the United States
has been waiting for this." [1]

Like many another author, Judge Waterman may have exaggerated, or just overestimated, the size of the waiting audience,
but there was no mistaking his unconcealed enthusiasm for the
task in hand. Part of this may have been due to the circumstances
of the appellate review. On March 20 of the preceding year, and
about seven months after Judge Bonsal rendered his opinion in
the case, arguments on appeal were heard before a panel of three
judges—Waterman, Paul R. Hays, and Leonard P. Moore—and
the hearing lasted less than a day. What happened next, however,
lasted for 13 months, and must have entailed rather strenuous dis-

[1] *Wall Stret Journal*, August 14, 1968.

agreement, because after the opinions prepared by the panel judges were distributed to their associates on the court, it was ordered—on May 2, 1968—that the case should be considered *in banc* by all nine judges, without further argument by the parties to the appeal. Four more months went by before Judge Waterman surfaced with the opinion. It was a Tuesday—August 13—and the judge gave instructions that nothing should be made public until after all the markets in the country, including that on the Pacific Coast, had closed. Actually this gave the market another day, since the exchanges were then observing a Wednesday holiday each week in order to catch up on their paper work.

It was what later would be termed a "fractured opinion" because three judges signed the majority statement, four partly-to-wholly concurred, and two, including Chief Judge J. Edward Lumbard Jr., signed a strenuous dissent on all points. None of this appeared in the news releases, however, possibly because it was too early. The *Wall Street Journal* carried a rather lengthy story, but not one that tried to balance the six opinions which had been rendered and which ran to more than a hundred pages of typewritten copy. At first it referred to the "majority" opinion, and this was modified in later editions to read the "7–2 majority opinion." Nobody mentioned the dissent, or even the differences among the majority. In the weeks and months that followed, it might have seemed strange to an objective observer that none of the serious journals which featured lengthy articles, editorials, and discussions of the meaning of the Second Circuit's pronouncement ever got around to pointing out the diversity of views just in respect to the news release which was the basis of the Commission's case against TGS.[2] Only in October, in the monthly *Public Relations Journal,* did Henry Rockwell's article, "A Press Release Goes To Court," point out that the nine judges were in fact divided three, three, two, and one on the news release.

Judge Waterman's initial outburst had a good back-up in the follow-up story of Alan Adelson, of the *Wall Street Journal,* who interviewed the court's official printer and was told that the demand for printed copies of the opinion would put it on the best seller list. The paper gave *that* a top headline, but 24 hours later, when the response from Texas Gulf came along, its interest had cooled to a

---

[2] Part of Judge Friendly's opinion dealing with the news release ran to 2,000 words, while Judge Moore devoted more than 7,000 words to the subject, with the concurrence of Chief Judge Lumbard.

bottom-of-the-page headline which read: "Texas Gulf Sulphur to Appeal."

As for the point about the press release, Judge Henry Friendly agreed with the majority that "it did not properly convey the information in the hands of the draftsmen on April 12," but he also held that, "No one has asserted, or reasonably could assert that the purpose of issuing a release was anything but good." He concluded that "the company's motive in issuing the release was laudable; and the defect was solely a pardonable one of execution. If Judge Bonsal had denied an injunction on these grounds, I would see no basis on which we could have reversed him."

Two other judges—Irving R. Kaufman and Robert P. Anderson—concurred with Friendly on this point, and even Judge Waterman and his two associates in the majority of three said on this issue, "We cannot, from the present record, definitely conclude that it was deceptive or misleading to the reasonable investor, or that he would have been misled by it. Certain newspaper accounts of the release viewed the statement as confirming the existence of preliminary favorable developments, and this optimistic view was held by some brokers. . . ."

In his dissent, Judge Moore, with the concurrence of Chief Judge Lumbard, in one of a series of sarcastic sideswipes, said, "The majority offer suggestions for improving the press release, but, as their editorial skills and present appraisal of the then mining situation were not available when it was drafted, the relevant issue is whether the District Court was in error in determining that the release was accurate and not misleading."

Only one member of the Appeals Court, Judge Hays, held that the release was misleading as a matter of law. But all of this apparently never reached the commentators in the daily press.


II

The majority opinion was the big bang, of course, and in the days to come it would set off most of the hullabaloo among lawyers, academicians, financiers, business people, and writers—lay and otherwise. And in the legal clutch of Texas Gulf's troubles, the main ring was again obviously occupied by the Commission's action against the company and the individual defendants. Nevertheless, within the main tent, there were other related proceedings.

Any public corporation of any size is hardly ever free from some kind of legal proceedings. This is business as usual. But once in a while a polarizing action becomes of substantial importance to everybody in the business community and reaches both forwards and backwards, such as that proceeding brought against TGS by the SEC. Here there had been, and would be, important sideshows, and some attempt can be made here to cast them in the overall time sequence. In the center ring, the Commission had brought its complaint in the spring of 1965; the action had come to trial in the court of first impression in 1966; the appeal was argued briefly in 1967; and the Court of Appeals decision was rendered in the latter part of 1968. The first approaches to the United States Supreme Court, represented by two individual petitions for certiorari, received their negative reply in 1969, but no one then read this as finally definitive. Looming over everything, in the United States at least, was the high court—now a new Supreme Court under Chief Justice Warren Burger. For the moment the highest bench was hardly moving a muscle although it was certainly in a position to write a final chapter, as final as such things ever become under the American constitutional system.

But back in February of 1963, a Canadian mining company had made a contract with Texas Gulf Sulphur which would result in the issuing of a writ in June of 1964, challenging the title of TGS to the Kidd Creek Mine. Trial would begin in late 1966 (about the time Bonsal's lower court opinion would issue in the main case) and after 164 days would end in April 1968. An opinion in favor of the defendant would be handed down 7 months later, after the Court of Appeals decision in *SEC v. Texas Gulf Sulphur*. In 1966, also, another of the claimants to the land on which a major part of the mine was located—Royal Trust—filed a suit against TGS.

Back in 1964, as a result of generally wild speculation in Canadian mining stocks brought about by the TGS discovery, and specifically as a result of some spectacular and costly activity in the stock of another Canadian mining company, Elizabeth the Second of England had appointed a Royal Commission under the Public Inquiries Act of the revised statutes of Ontario, for full investigation of such matters. The first date in the published chronology of the Commission's report "to investigate trading in the shares of Windfall Oils and Mines Limited," was November 7, 1963, when TGS commenced drilling in Kidd Township. Hearings were held over several months of 1965—and not incidentally were attended by staff members of the U.S. Securities and Exchange Commission, then busily developing its complaint against Texas Gulf. The Royal Commission's report was submitted later that year. It was followed by much discussion and some changes in the structure and law of the Ontario Securities Commission, as well as by certain peripheral actions—such as the conviction in March, 1967, of Mrs. Viola MacMillan, influential in the affairs of the Windfall corporation, on charges of wash trading in shares of mining stock, followed in turn by the acquittal, in February, 1969, of Mrs. MacMillan and her husband, George, on charges of fraudulently influencing the price of Windfall shares.

Late in August of 1968, back in the United States, and just 13 days after the Appeals Court opinion was released in the TGS case, the SEC brought an action against the largest brokerage firm in the nation—Merrill Lynch, Pierce, Fenner and Smith—charging that it had improperly used "inside information" in 1966 to help some, but not all, of its customers make a profit in the stock of the Douglas Aircraft Company. In the foreground of the charges and replies, of course, was the now ubiquitous Rule 10b-5. Merrill Lynch settled late in November, and the settlement obviously moved forward the Commission's aggressive theories as to inside trading and public disclosure.

About the time the Court of Appeals in New York was moving from a three-judge panel to an *in banc* consideration of *SEC v. Texas Gulf Sulphur*, in the spring of 1968, a group of TGS stockholders was suing TGS in federal court in Utah for damages, and a goodly number of similar actions was accruing in federal court in New York, before Judge Bonsal. In June of 1969, the corporation would move for summary judgment on the latter, but the whole matter appeared to be waiting on further developments in the main case itself, which had been remanded. All of this was now moving in on the listening posts of the financial and business community, not to mention the bar association seminars and law journals.

## III

In its appeal brief, the Commission found that Judge Bonsal had been narrow, that he misunderstood, and that he was troubled in making his findings of fact, and it hastened to throw its protective mantle over the reasonable man as the injured party, while more or less branding the defendants-appellees as card sharks, runners on an inside track, and anything but reasonable men. The judge, it contended, took a "narrow view" of the factors that influence a "reasonable man" when he considers selling securities:

> The concept of a free and open market presupposes that neither buyer nor seller, neither investor, trader nor speculator, will be forced to trade with insiders on the basis of marked cards. . . . To maintain fair and honest markets, it is essential that no reasonable man . . . be placed at an unjustifiable disadvantage in his dealings with corporate insiders.

Then the SEC contended that Bonsal had misunderstood the Commission's position concerning the extent of public disclosure of information required before a corporate official might trade in his company's securities. It repeated its belief that "mere delivery of the announcement to the press would not have been sufficient disclosure to private investors to authorize sales by insiders," a belief founded on an earlier case.

The Commission brief restated its position on the business of the Dow Jones broad tape, and at the same time built a necessary bridge to an even longer disclosure period: "It is difficult to conceive of any situation where important corporate news is announced while the stock exchange is in session in which insiders should be permitted to trade before an announcement appears on the Dow Jones broad tape. Surely the securities laws must be construed to protect the ordinary investor, who does not have a Dow Jones ticker in his home or office." But at the end of the bridge it said that specific rules governing disclosure, however, would be "undesirable."

Finally, the court below was troubled by lack of a specific time limit, but "in many areas of the law men must guide their actions by a standard of reasonable conduct," since conscientious insiders who are not "trying to engage in a race to the market with the stockholders of the company should have little difficulty" in determining what is proper.

After all that had been said about fraud in the complaint, in connection with Rule 10b-5, the appeals brief of the SEC said: "The Commission is not required to prove *scienter* and intent to deceive in order to establish a violation of Section 10(b) and Rule 10b-5 in an enforcement proceeding such as this. . . ." It is interesting to note that in *Forbes* magazine for September 1, 1968, the SEC's general counsel, Philip A. Loomis Jr., had said: "By and large it is not necessary to prove *scienter*. It is possible to violate 10b-5 by being careless." Just 18 days before this was published, the Court of Appeals majority had anticipated his statement in its opinion which found that the deciding question about the April 12 news release was whether it was misleading, and not whether it was disingenuous or artful.

Crawford and Clayton, who had been the only individual defendants found in violation below, were also appealing, and their brief described them as "guinea pigs" because the SEC was not seeking to apply the securities laws enacted by Congress as they had been applied for more than 30 years, "but is urging *ex post facto* judicial legislation. . . . No court has ever before held that corporate personnel have any duty to disclose material facts in connection with a routine stock exchange transaction or that failure to make such disclosure constitutes 'fraud or deceit' upon the anonymous sellers of stocks."

The rule of law urged by the Commission, these appellants pointed out, would require an employee to sacrifice his right to buy the stock of his own company, or else run the risk of criminal penalties, extravagant damage claims, the stigma of a fraud finding, the uncertainty of what, in hindsight, might be claimed to be material. This, they declared, should not be a forum for debating policy questions, although the fundamental problems presented were not legal but legislative in character.

Justice Oliver Wendell Holmes had said, ". . . it is reasonable that fair warning should be given to the world in language that the common world will understand, of what the law intends to do if a certain line is passed. To make the warning fair, so far as possible the line should be clear." [3] No fair warning had been given as to the duty imposed on corporate personnel by Section 10(b) and Rule 10b-5 as interpreted by the Commission, and any such holding was unconstitutional by the appellants' standards.

They said further that they could not reasonably have anticipated, from a reading of the section or the rule, that their transactions were prohibited. Indeed, the novelty of the Commission's claim was demonstrated by the sensation it caused. The filing of the complaint had generated an unprecedented number of law re-

[3] *McBoyle v. U.S., 283 U.S. 25* (1931).

view articles and bar association forums devoted to divining what the law may ultimately be declared to be. "While these learned speculations proceed, Crawford and Clayton are deemed to have known the answers all along and are sought to be penalized accordingly. Such a result is unconscionable." But there seemed to be no way around it. Much of what was urged in the appellants' brief was pertinent to the larger issues and competently put, but they were doomed by their act.

"The basis for a finding of fraud is deception," their brief continued. "Yet the Commission does not attempt to define what it alleges the sellers of stock were deceived into believing or not believing by appellants' purchases. . . . Buyers and sellers of stock give their orders to brokers. The stock is bought and sold in such quantities that the actual buyers and sellers are not even matched. . . . Since no one has ever received any 'material facts' from the other party to such a transaction, it cannot possibly be contended that the failure to transmit such facts deceived anyone into a belief that there were no such facts to disclose. . . . The Commission's theory of fraud and deceit is based on fictional concepts which have no reality in the market place. . . . The Commission's real claim seems to be that . . . without equality of information there is fraud." It certainly looked that way.


IV

            Judge Waterman's opinion struck first and explained afterwards.[4] The lower court findings of violations by Clayton and Crawford were affirmed and remanded for a determination of appropriate remedy. The dismissal of the complaint against Murray, the office manager, was also affirmed, since he "had no detailed knowledge of the work."

In the matter of the stock options, the dismissal of the complaint against Mollison and Holyk was affirmed, since the SEC had not appealed the findings that they were not "top management" and had no duty of disclosure to the options committee, but Stephens, Fogarty and Kline were something else again, and the dismissal of the complaint below was now reversed. In Kline's case the Court also remanded with instructions to rescind his option and determine an appropriate remedy, considering him clearly to be

[4] *401 F. 2nd 833* (*1968*).

"top management." Stephens and Fogarty had surrendered their options, while Kline had not.

The dismissal of the complaint against Fogarty, Mollison, Holyk, Darke, and Huntington, who had purchased stock or calls between November 12, 1963, and April 9, 1964, was reversed and remanded for remedy. Clayton's purchases *before* April 9—which had not been explicitly excused by the district judge—were now implicitly *included* by the Court of Appeals majority, making him an appellee as well as an appellant, and the implicit dismissal was reversed. The dismissal of the complaint against Darke in the court below was reversed, as was that against Coates. Shortly after the appeal was argued, death had come to Lamont, and an order had been entered discontinuing his appeal and directing that the judgment dismissing the action against him be severed from that of the other defendants. That left the corporation, and here the finding below was also reversed and remanded "for a further determination by the district judge in the light of the approach taken in this opinion."

In his review of the "factual setting" Judge Waterman appeared to suffer somewhat from the malady alleged against the defendants in that he, also, did not disclose too fully. He more or less equated the testimony of the two parties as to the existence of proven ore, a rather doubtful conclusion when applied to the testimony given. He said that evidence as to the effect of the April 12 release was "equivocal and less than abundant"—quoting only the Canadian stockbroker who did not attend the trial, whose deposition was admitted but not read into the record, and whose business was largely in Canadian penny mining stocks. He ignored all the others whose depositions *were* read or who appeared before the court in person. This included the president of the Lehman Corporation, with $450 million in assets, and a professor of security analysis at the graduate school of New York University. He cited the Texas Gulf stock specialist in Chicago as becoming "concerned" over his long position in the market after the release, but omitted the fact that the specialist *continued* his position, nevertheless. He stated that Coates purchased before the release of April 16 had been "disseminated," without stating, however, that the announcement had been released at the press conference. And while reviewing the price of TGS stock from November 8, 1963, through April 15, 1964, he neglected to point out that the price had been substantially unaffected by the "gloomy" release.

As the majority opinion approached the stories of the individual defendants, its treatment of what was material inside information began with rejecting the conservative test of the trial court and inserting as a basic test whether a "reasonable man would attach importance." In a rescue gesture, Waterman added that the "speculators and chartists of Wall and Bay Streets are also 'reasonable' investors entitled to the same legal protection afforded conservative traders." He stated that materiality depended at any given time upon a balancing of both the *indicated probability* that the event will occur and the *anticipated magnitude* of the event in the light of the totality of the company activity, and then soared into the following value judgment:

"Here, notwithstanding the trial court's conclusion that the results of the first drill core, K55-1, were 'too remote' . . . knowledge of the possibility, which surely was more than marginal, of the existence of a mine of the vast magnitude indicated by the remarkably rich drill core located rather close to the surface . . . within the confines of a large anomaly (suggesting an extensive region of mineralization) might well have affected the price of TGS stock and would certainly have been an important fact to a reasonable, if speculative, investor in deciding whether he would buy, sell, or hold. After all, this first drill core was 'unusually good and . . . excited the interest and speculation of those who knew about it.' " In contrast, the opinion here said not one word about what the trial court had referred to as the far-flung business of Texas Gulf at that time.

The majority's disagreement with Bonsal on this issue, said Waterman, did not go to his findings of basic fact, but to his understanding of the legal standard applicable to them, and he declared that the majority's survey of the facts found below "conclusively establishes that knowledge of the results of the discovery hole, K55-1, would have been important to a reasonable investor and might have affected the price of the stock." For good measure he once more quoted the unread deposition of the Canadian, Roche: ". . . 600 feet is just beyond your wildest imagination."

The final factor in determining materiality of the first hole results, declared the opinion, was the importance attached to the drilling results by those who knew about it. The fact that they bought stock and *short term* calls "virtually compels the inference that the insiders were influenced by the drilling results. This insider trading activity, which surely constitutes highly pertinent evidence and the only true objective evidence of the materiality . . . was apparently disregarded by the court below in favor of the testimony of defendants' expert witnesses, all of whom agreed that one drill core does not establish an ore body, much less a mine."

Like Bonsal, who had taken the occasion of *his* opinion to say a few words about the importance of employees buying stock in their company, Judge Waterman also indulged in a slightly more jaundiced homily:

> Our decision to expand the limited protection afforded outside investors by the trial court's narrow definition of materiality is not at all shaken by fears that the elimination of insider trading benefits will deplete the ranks of capable corporate managers by taking away an incentive to accept such employment. Such benefits, in essence, are forms of secret corporate compensation . . . derived at the expense of the uninformed investing public and not at the expense of the corporation which receives the sole benefit from insider incentives. Moreover, adequate incentives for corporate officers may be provided by properly administered stock options and employee purchase plans of which there are many in existence.

Of course, he had just taken some of these away, but no matter.

It would be fair to conclude that Bonsal and Waterman did not see eye to eye on the matter of insider trading, since the former had described the proposition that all insider trading is unfair as of "doubtful validity at best" and backed his comment with the words of Judge Learned Hand. Waterman likened it to "secret corporate compensation."

The majority seemed a little disappointed that there had been "no definitive resolution below" of Darke's liability, since the trial court had brought him home safe, along with the several other defendants, on the April 9 deadline. Now, however, having decided that the drilling of K55-1 was material after all, it could hold that Darke had violated 10b-5 by "tipping" and remand for the appropriate remedy. Somewhat wistfully, the Court noted that the tippees were not defendants in the action, but rather threateningly then observed that their conduct could be equally reprehensible.

Coming to the question of when insiders may act, the opinion never really gives an answer. Crawford, Coates, and Clayton had conceded they were in possession of material information, but contended the news had been effectively disclosed. The Court disagreed flatly. Crawford's orders had been placed before the press announcement, while Coates should have waited "until the news could reasonably have been expected to appear over the media of widest circulation, the Dow Jones broad tape, rather than hastening to insure an advantage to himself and his broker son-in-law." In the interests of broader protection for the investing public, said the majority, the common law standard of *deceptive* conduct has been modified so that *negligent* insider conduct has become unlawful. The beliefs of Coates, Crawford, and Clayton, in respect to previous disclosure of the news, were to no avail because they were not reasonable under the circumstances.

In turning to the corporate defendant, the majority faced up to a rather thorny point. TGS relied upon the holding of the court below that the April 12 news release, among other things, was not issued "in connection with the purchase or sale of any security"— the specific language of Rule 10b-5. Judge Waterman felt that the district judge had used a standard that did not reflect the Congressional purpose which had prompted the passage of the Securities Exchange Act of 1934. A salient point in the majority argument appeared to be *its* interpretation of what Congress had been driving at in the securities laws, ". . . that all investors should have equal access to the rewards of participating in securities transactions. It was the intent of Congress (so said Judge Waterman) that all members of the investing public should be subject to identical market risks."

But this was not quoted from the preambles to, nor the hearings on, either law. The closest the majority came to substantiating its statement appeared to be in connection with its long discussion of the "in connection with" requirement. It quoted the comments of the *House* committee which had reported out H.R. 9323, a bill eventually integrated with a similar Senate bill, S.3420, to become the Securities Exchange Act of 1934.[5] These comments dwelt upon "honest publicity" and "true and accurate corporate reporting as an essential cog in the proper functioning of the public exchanges." Section 10(b) of the Act was taken, however, almost verbatim from the proposed *Senate* bill. This section, which had been specially concerned with *manipulation, deception,* and *fraud,* drew this comment from the majority: "Indeed, from its very inception, Section 10(b) and the proposed section in H.R. 1383 and S.3420 from which it was derived, have always been acknowledged as catch-

[5] *H.R. Rep. No. 1383, 73rd Cong., 2d Sess. 11 (1934).*

alls." They then quoted Thomas G. Corcoran's frequently cited explanation before the hearings of the House committee, that the subsection in question was "a catch-all clause to prevent manipulative devices." [6]

Oddly enough, the defendants had also quoted this to support the *opposite* side of the argument—that no one could sensibly call the April 12 release a "manipulative device," and that neither the corporation nor the authors of the release had bought stocks in the week that followed. Notwithstanding all of this, the majority summed up: ". . . the legislative history of Section 10(b) does not support the proposition urged upon us by Texas Gulf Sulphur that Congress intended the limited construction of the 'in connection with' phrase supplied by the trial court."

They couldn't leave it alone, however, and there was some further explanation on the majority's part. It seemed clear to them that the Congress did not really *mean* what the statute said. It only meant that the device employed be of a sort that would cause reasonable investors to rely on it when *they* bought or sold stock. If the statute meant only what it said—that the corporation or those issuing the release had to engage in securities transactions or act with wrongful motives—then "the obvious purposes of the Act to protect the investing public and to secure fair dealing in the securities markets would be seriously undermined by applying such a *gloss* onto the legislative language. . . . To render the Congressional purpose ineffective by inserting into the statutory words the *need of proving*, not only that the public may have been misled by the release, but also that those responsible were actuated by a wrongful purpose when they issued the release, is to *handicap unreasonably the Commission in its work*." The italics in the foregoing have been added, as it would seem that any other comment might be superfluous.

Two giant steps had now been taken: equating negligence with fraud, and eliminating the requirement of the purchase or sale of any security by defendants to bring the corporation within 10b-5. Little else remained for the majority to do except criticize the news release and suggest how it might have been written, after which it

[6] Corcoran, one of the draftsmen of the 1934 Act, said: "Subsection (b) says, 'Thou shalt not devise any other cunning devices.' I do not think there is any objection to that kind of clause. The Commission should have the authority to deal with new manipulative devices." From hearings before the House Committee on Interstate and Foreign Commerce on H.R. 7852 and H.R. 8720, 73rd Cong., 2d Sess. (1934).

remanded to the trial judge to decide whether the release was misleading and to take appropriate action as to an injunction.

In Waterman's view, any failure of the Timmins project as of April 12 was "a highly unlikely event." Toward the close of the opinion there occurs a long footnote which again exhibits a surprising lack of perspective. It is headed by the strangely significant words, "examined in retrospect" and it again quotes the Court's favorite Canadian mining stock specialist, Michael Roche, on how mines can be operated profitably even when they may have low percentages of mineralization. The note sets forth the calculation that there was good reason for optimism in the face of the "gloomy" release, because to judge from the drilling through April 10, "an ultimate profit could then have been established at more than $14,-000,000." Maybe so, but when even this is factored out, it should be noted (since the majority did not follow through on the arithmetic) it comes to a non-recurring total of only about $1.40 per share on the then outstanding stock, spread over five to ten years, and beginning a year or two in the future.

V

Representing what might be called the "second wing" of the Second Circuit's "fractured" opinion, Judge Friendly began by saying that he agreed with most of Judge Waterman's searching opinion, but would approach two facets of it differently. The first of these concerned the stock options. It amounted to not so much more than the expression of the judge's opinion, since the issue as he framed it was not before the court. The second facet was the press release, "transcending in public importance all others in this important case. This seems to me easier on the facts but harder on the law than it does to the majority."

As was the case with some of his associates, Judge Friendly's reasoning in the matter of the stock options proceeds on the assumption—patently invalid in the face of the evidence below—that some of the grantees must have known *in February* information "likely to produce a rapid and substantial increase in the price of the stock." And like those others he appears to disregard the positive reasons put forward by the management for awarding options at this time—that the market price of the shares had finally reached the approximate level it had enjoyed when the first series of options had been granted in 1961, and that changes in the tax laws affecting options were being seriously discussed in Washington. The company management had felt it would be unfair to award any new options so long as the purchase price attaching to the original ones—still unexercised—was higher than the current market price, but the two levels finally converged in 1964.

It is understandable that jurists cannot be expert at everything, but except for Bonsal in the court below, the learned judges involved in this proceeding seem to exhibit almost complete misunderstanding of the purposes and procedures of a corporate stock option program, which is a device designed to assist a corporation, and ultimately its stockholders, by attracting good people, by rewarding quality performance and helping to retain for the company valuable talent. Such a program almost always operates on a formula relating to the salary structure. The safeguards of an option program are carefully written into the instrument in the beginning, for all to see, and can hardly be jettisoned or redesigned at executive whim. It is for this reason that such a program is most often administered by a committee of directors. These are hardly back-pocket perquisites of top management, which can be used sporadically or stealthily for personal aggrandizement when the "right" opportunity comes along.

Bulwarked by his conviction that TGS had known in February what it did not announce until several drill holes later in April, Judge Friendly believed that this was "not the right time to grant options," and that the management of the corporation should have said so. He seems to cap his stance with this final observation: "I am not at all sure that a company in the position of TGS might not have a claim against top officers who breached their duty of disclosure"—this is legalese for not telling the directors—"for the entire damage suffered as a result of the untimely issuance of options, rather than merely one for rescission of the options issued to them. Since that issue is not before us, I merely make the reservation of my position clear." He then approached the second, and vastly more pertinent, of his selected subjects.

"No one has asserted, or reasonably could assert, that the purpose for issuing a release was anything but good. TGS felt it had a responsibility to protect would-be buyers of its shares from what it regarded as exaggerated rumors first in the Canadian and then in the New York City press, and none of the individual defendants sought to profit from the decline in price of TGS stock caused by the release." Still, he found it a wholly insufficient statement of what the corporation knew. Nevertheless it was a "needless exercise to require the district court to determine whether a reasonable investor would have been misled," since proof of what the investor would do could be found in the actions of the market itself. And now Judge Friendly was clearly demanding that the court below listen to him.

> I think the remand should make crystal clear that the issue whether this is a proper case for an injunction remains open . . . despite the principle that a violation of the securities laws or regulations generally gives rise to a private claim for damages, . . . violation of Rule 10b-5(2) may not do so under all circumstances, including those presented by the April 12 news release.
>
> The consequences of holding that negligence in the drafting of a press release . . . may impose civil liability on the corporation are frightening. . . . If the only choices open to a corporation are either to remain silent and let false rumors do their work, or to make a communication, not legally required, at the risk that a slip of the pen or failure properly to amass or weigh the facts— all judged in the bright gleam of hindsight—will lead to large judgments, payable in the last analysis by innocent investors, for the benefit of speculators and their lawyers, most corporations would opt for the former.[7]

The footwork of the majority opinion here comes in for some further questioning, and not only from the galleries, when Judge Friendly urges that the larger goals of the securities laws be furthered rather than frustrated.

> While I am not convinced that imposition of liability for damages under Rule 10b-5(2), absent a *scienter* requirement, . . . would not go beyond the authority vested in the Commission by 10(b) to act against "any manipulative or deceptive device or contrivance" and be so inconsistent with the general structure of the statutes as to be impermissible, it is at least clear that the April 12 press release would be the worst possible case for the award of damages for merely negligent misstatement, as distinguished from the kind of recklessness that is equivalent to wilful fraud. . . .

[7] Milton Cohen: "Truth in Securities Revisited," 79 *Harvard Law Review* 1340, 1370 (1967)—"One source of perplexity as to the appropriate bounds of the civil remedy for misleading filings is that any remedy imposed against the issuer itself is indirectly imposed on all holders of the common stock, usually the most important segment of the total category of investors intended to be protected."

The judge signed off by adding that this was not necessarily an appropriate case for granting any injunction as to future press releases. Judge Irving R. Kaufman concurred in the Waterman opinion, but agreed with Friendly that guidance should be provided to district courts with respect to private claims for damages based upon 10b-5. Judge Robert P. Anderson also concurred with Waterman, and with Friendly's discussion of the law relating to the news release. Judge Hays concurred generally, but thought an injunction *should* be granted. Judges Smith and Feinberg, composing the Waterman unadulterated majority, were not talking. And that left the last fraction—the dissenting opinion of Judge Moore, with Chief Judge Lumbard in concurrence. It was hardly likely that anyone would fall asleep over this one.

## VI

Judge Moore wasted no time in planting his feet or shadow boxing with any of the usual courtesies toward his associates. His opening sentence was long, scathing, but never dropped a stitch:

> In their opinion, the majority have become so involved in usurping the function of the trial court, in selecting the witnesses they (at variance with the trial court) choose to believe, in forming their own factual conclusions from the evidence (in disregard of Rule 52a),[8] in deciding with, of course, the benefit of the wisdom of hindsight, how they, had they been executives of Texas Gulf Sulphur Company would have handled the publicity attendant to the exploration of the Timmins property, in determining (to their own satisfaction) the motives which prompted each of the individual defendants to buy TGS stock and in becoming mining engineering experts in their own right, that I find it desirable —in fact, essential—to state my opinion as to the fundamental jurisdiction of the Court of Appeals and the issues properly before us. Primarily, our task should be to review errors of law.

While the SEC was a responsible agency of government, he pointed out, in the plaintiff's role it had to bear the evidentiary fair preponderance burden of *all* litigants, and be subject to the rule

[8] *Rules of Civil Procedure for the United States District Courts,* Rule 52(a): ". . . Findings of fact shall not be set aside unless clearly erroneous, and due regard shall be given to the opportunity of the trial court to judge of the credibility of the witnesses. . . ."

that the determination of what evidence is credible is for the trial judge. It was to this point that he first turned his attention, insisting that Rule 52(a) of the federal rules of civil procedure should be given particular weight where expert testimony must of necessity play an important role. In the instant case, the trial court had an opportunity not only to hear the qualification of the experts, but could form its opinion as to their credibility from their demeanor and responses. The importance of such an opportunity, where technical or scientific problems were before the court, had been. succinctly stated by the Supreme Court: [9]

"Like any other issue of fact, final determination requires a balancing of credibility, persuasiveness and weight of evidence. It is to be decided by the trial court and that court's decision, under general principles of appellate review, should not be disturbed unless clearly erroneous. Particularly is this so in a field where so much depends upon familiarity with specific scientific problems and principles not usually contained in the general storehouse of knowledge and experience." And later:

"It is not for this court (the Supreme Court) to even essay an independent evaluation of this evidence. This is the function of the trial court."

Reviewing the evidence of experts Forrester, Park, Lacy, Wiles, and Walkey, Judge Moore sternly reminded the majority that even the Commission's experts would not estimate what ore, if any, might lie beyond the one and one-eighth inch core. "Despite the experts' virtually uncontradicted testimony, despite Rule 52(a), and despite the Supreme Court's statement of the law, the majority chose to reject the trial court's findings as to the results of the first drill core, K55-1, and to substitute their own expertise in the mining engineering field," and he followed this by quoting the majority opinion's rather extravagant description of the "mine of vast magnitude."

"Indeed," pursued Judge Moore, "any such conclusions from a first drill core, if so announced by TGS, would undoubtedly have had a substantial effect on the market price of TGS stock and would have immediately brought forth both the wrath of, and injunction papers from, the Commission charging TGS with issuing false, misleading and unsupported statements to boost the price of the stock."

The dissenting opinion found, borrowing the language of the

[9] *Graver Tank & Mfg. Co. v. Linde Air Products Co.*, 339 U.S. 605 (1950).

federal rule, that the premise posted by the majority was itself
"clearly erroneous": there was no knowledge of the existence of a
mine—it was no more than a marginal possibility. Testimony was
unanimous that no estimate of magnitude could be made. The
"large anomaly" did *not* suggest "an extensive region of mineralization" and furthermore TGS did not own or control anything but a
one-quarter segment. Disclosure of the "results"—preliminary visual
inspection of the contents—would have violated the Commission's
own rules and standards. And here he quoted from the Commission's specific declarations regarding offerings under the 1933
Act: [10]

> No claim shall be made as to the existence of a body of ore
> unless it has been sufficiently tested to be properly classified as
> "proven" or "probable" ore, as defined below. If the work done
> has not established the existence of proven or probable ore, a state-
> ment shall be made that no body of commercial ore is known to
> exist on the property.

Under the circumstances and then known facts, the press release implicitly suggested by the majority, declared Moore, would
have been the height of recklessness. Resorting to words taken from
the SEC brief, it would be interesting to know, "what position the
Commission would have taken if TGS had announced that K55-1
was 'one of the most impressive drill holes completed in modern
times' and that it 'is just beyond your wildest imagination.' "

Now tempering scorn with overtones of hilarity, Judge Moore
ridiculed the majority's and the Commission's "full disclosure"
theory thus:

> TGS could have announced by November 15, 1963, that it
> had completed a first exploratory hole, the core of which by visual
> examination revealed over a length of 599 of 655 feet drilled, an
> average copper content of 1.15 per cent, zinc 8.64 per cent, or,
> had TGS waited until mid-December, by chemical analysis 1.18
> per cent copper, 8.26 per cent zinc and 2.94 per cent ounces of
> silver per ton; that TGS would try to acquire the other three-
> quarters of the segment unless the announcement boosted prices
> to unwarranted heights; that if the property could be acquired
> further exploratory holes would be drilled to ascertain the nature
> and extent, if any, of the ore body; that reports of developments

[10] *Item 8(A) (b), 1 CCH Fed. Sec. L. Rep. Pp. 7327.*

would be made from time to time but that the SEC had indicated that TGS should advise its stockholders and the public that there was no proof as yet that a body of commercial ore exists on the property. Such an announcement would, of course, have been of no value to anyone except possibly a few graduates of Institutes of Technology and they, as the expert witnesses here, would have recognized that one drill hole does not reveal a commercially profitable mine.

The majority statement that drilling results on the first hole "might well have affected the price of TGS stock" could have been made of almost any fact related to the company, such as the possible settlement of a strike, said the dissenting opinion. Hourly bulletins to the press from the conference room would not be compatible with common sense. For that matter, scores of day-by-day intra-company situations, in the individual opinions of company officers or employees, might well affect stock prices, with each individual reacting according to his own judgment. However companies listed on a national exchange could scarcely broadcast to the nation on a daily basis their hopes and expectations from developments in progress, such as those in their research departments. While the results from the first hole undoubtedly influenced those familiar with the situation in making their own purchases, Judge Moore attacked the majority holding that such purchases were "the only truly objective evidence" of the discovery, and made the point that the majority were confusing the inducing motive of the individual purchaser with knowledge of material facts which ought to be revealed to the public at large, saying the inconsistency was immediately apparent—the motive for the purchases did not establish the materiality of the facts which influenced them.

The majority's suggestions for improving the news release only disclosed a most remarkable business naiveté to the dissenting judge, and he found that the Commission had failed to prove that anyone was misled. As for the "in connection with" language, he declared that the requirement is explicit in 10(b) and precludes the imposition of liability on the corporation. The SEC and the majority had laboriously and at great length advanced the argument that the requirement was satisfied by the mere fact that the public was purchasing and selling securities on the open market. "However, the fact remains that 10(b) . . . was not passed to protect investors [of this type] . . . but leaves liability for such misrepresentation up to state law, which is well equipped to handle any situation. . . . Section 10(b) was certainly not intended to be a mandate to the Commission to erect a comprehensive regulatory system policing all corporate publicity, as the majority now contend." The long battle over the troublesome words had resulted in sharply contrasting judgments.

Judge Moore went further than did Friendly when it came to the proposed injunction against Texas Gulf Sulphur, devoting one long but lively paragraph to it.

> The remedy of a permanent injunction against the company, its officers and agents, the issuance of which the majority leaves to the discretion of the trial court, would not only be inappropriate but would be destructive of fundamental rights—"inappropriate" because based upon one "too gloomy" press release on April 12, 1964, with no proof of continuing gloominess thereafter. The issuance of any injunction over four years after the alleged violation would place a large company and its many executive employees under the possibility, without even a *Miranda* warning, that anything they said may be held against them and place them under the danger of criminal sanctions; "destructive of fundamental rights" because the restraint constitutes not "double" jeopardy but "perpetual" jeopardy. If, as the majority say, the test of the news release is its impact on the "reasonable" investor (although they indicate that the unreasonable speculator, too, comes under their solicitous wing), to avoid the danger of injunction violation it would be necessary to seek a declaratory judgment from the courts (both trial and appellate because following the majority, Rule 52(a) would no longer apply). As to the sufficiency of the news release the first issue would be what constitutes a "reasonable" investor. After the court has made a preliminary finding of reasonableness, these investors could then testify as to the impact that the proposed release would have on them. Query, as to whether twelve witnesses (akin to a jury) should be required—and would a seven-to-five count be acceptable or would ten-to-two more accurately reflect public opinion? Other situations and problems of an equally *reductio ad absurdum* character can easily be conjured up. They would only point more directly to the conclusion that an injunction here would not only violate fundamental legal principles which for centuries have restricted the injunctive grant but would not be justified by any sufficient factual showing in this case. No clear and present danger, no continuing wrongful acts and no likelihood thereof are to be found in the record before this court.

In his summary conclusions, Judge Moore, who had already provided a rich mine of phrase-making which would undoubtedly materially influence the judgment of future reasonable commentators, declared that the most disturbing aspect of the majority opinion was its utterly unrealistic approach to the problem of the corporate news release. If corporations were literally to follow its implications, every press release would have to have the same SEC clearance as a prospectus.

> Even this procedure would not suffice if future events should prove the facts to have been over or understated—or too gloomy or optimistic—because the courts will always be ready and available to substitute their judgment for that of the business executives responsible therefor.

In addition to the vulnerability of the news release, he was concerned with the dilemma of the large corporation desiring to disclose promising research and development results. If they held back, they would be concealing information. If they spoke out, and the hoped-for results did not materialize, there would always be those with the advantage of hindsight to brand them as false and misleading. Nor did he think it was consonant with reality for the majority to suggest that corporate executives might be motivated in accepting employment by the opportunity to make "secret corporate compensation . . . derived at the expense of the uninformed public." Such thoughts could only arise from unfounded speculative imagination. The dissenting opinion closed:

> And finally there is the sardonic anomaly that the very members of society which Congress has charged the SEC with protecting, i.e., the stockholders, will be the real victims of its misdirected zeal. May the Future, the Congress or possibly the SEC itself be able to bring some semblance of order by means of workable rules and regulations in this field so that the corporations and their stockholders may not be subjected to countless lawsuits at the whim of every purchaser, seller or potential purchaser who may claim he would have acted or refrained from acting had a news release been more comprehensive or had it been adequately published in the news media of 50 states.

In the usually but necessarily dull and careful annals of appellate review, Judge Moore's dissenting opinion was a performance both bravura and virtuoso. It would console some aching hearts and troubled minds, and would be quoted at length over the succeeding months. The only trouble was that the majority opinion was now the law, or would be until further notice. Many in the business and financial world who, up to now, had been just interested spectators as the Texas Gulf Sulphur case unreeled, gradually became aware of a mushroomlike cloud passing over them and their undertakings, and slowly began to worry about fall-out.

# 8
# Et Alia

I

STRICTLY speaking, the Windfall affair could not be classified as even an ancillary legal involvement for Texas Gulf Sulphur Company, since the company was not a party to the hearings. But there was a connection of another sort which justifies the inclusion here of a brief resume of the proceedings in Ontario. It is a fair conclusion that if there had been no Texas Gulf discovery hole in the Timmins area, there would have been no royal investigation of trading in the shares of Windfall Oils and Mines Limited—an investigation that had important repercussions in Canadian government and mining circles and in the lives of certain individuals. The investigation, in turn, *did* have some bearing on the Commission's action against Texas Gulf, which it preceded and slightly overlapped. Jaegerman and some associates from the SEC office attended the hearings during the first half of 1965, as the chief investigator had told a Toronto reporter in March that he was there looking for "anyone from anywhere" who qualified as an inside trader in TGS shares. The complaint against the corporation was brought in April and, as noted earlier, it came as something of a surprise to the company and its counsel, who had been cooperating fully, albeit warily, in the Commission's investigation, and in the course of it had developed a "feeling" that any official follow-up by the government agency seemed unlikely. The conference atmosphere had seemed to justify this belief, and those involved thought they had satisfactorily explained the course of events. Their reading of the green proved faulty, as the April 19 complaint rudely demonstrated.

There is a strong suspicion in TGS circles that the events unfolded during the Windfall hearings encouraged the SEC to take action, or at least hardened its determination to do so. This is not susceptible of proof. In any event, the investigation by the Royal Commission turned up much of interest, especially revealing the connections and activities of Texas Gulf geologist Ken Darke, and others in the exploration team. It presented a useful and illuminating account of the Ontario climate for mining discovery and exploration, which contrasted sharply with that prevailing in the United States, and gave considerable weight to much of the testimony produced later in Foley Square.

Texas Gulf had begun drilling what subsequently became the discovery hole on November 7, 1963, and encountered massive sulphides four days later. As Commissioner Arthur Kelly, on leave from his duties as a justice of the Ontario Court of Appeal, noted in his report, everything sprang from this. With rumors running high and wild in the neighborhood, claims were staked and recorded in all directions at a surpassing rate, as the rush developed, and it was a rush not only to the scene of the discovery and its immediate environs but also a rush to the stock market. A miner's license was available in Ontario to anyone over 18 who had five dollars, and each licensee could stake 90 claims in a year. As for the market prospectors, no license was required. Here a uniquely Canadian phenomenon was described by the Commissioner:

> Many successful mining companies have turned their attention, and devoted part of the return from their operation, to the finding of mines; but even this flow of money and the knowledgeable manner in which it has been expended have not superseded the activities of independent prospectors or lessened substantially their chances of success. Hence, the continuation of the flow of risk capital from the individual investor into the exploration for minerals remains necessary for the perpetuation of the mining industry. Abuses in the handling of this flow, if permitted to divert funds from the purpose for which the investor intends them to be used, can seriously impede the flow; on the other hand, there is a danger that, in removing the undesirable features, the source

on which the industry relies may be destroyed. This would obviously be as harmful as letting the abuses continue.[1]

In short, it was a baby-and-bathwater situation.

Later he was to point out that Texas Gulf had spent about two million dollars in the search which led to the Timmins discovery, and that even at this cost, with the skilled geological and geophysical methods at their disposal, they stood a better chance of gaining some return on each dollar invested than did the majority of the people who, in early 1964, put many times that amount into the purchase of shares of companies which had acquired some interest in an unexplored and unproven mining property.[2]

The feverish activities in Ontario were both sub-climaxed and accelerated by the Texas Gulf news releases of April 12 and April 16, 1964. Somewhat in disagreement with the later findings of the United States courts, Commissioner Kelly held that publication of the story by *The Northern Miner* on the latter date made the public "fully aware of the magnitude of the discovery." [3] What happened after that, and especially what happened in connection with the shares of Windfall Oils and Mines Ltd., peaked in July, and the reverberations were such that the appointment of the Royal Commission followed in mid-August. Hearings were held from February to June of 1965 and the report was filed in September, still several months before the TGS trial would get under way in New York.

It was no accident that the Windfall investigation served to produce far more information about the activities of Darke, the TGS geologist, than would ever grace the record of the trial in which he was a defendant in absentia, especially in connection with his partnership with Bragagnolo and Angus in a venture to stake mining claims as close as possible to the Texas Gulf operation. These activities, however, were found to have no direct bearing on the Windfall matter, and—as the report made clear—they also provided no evidence of disloyalty to his employer, Texas Gulf, or of any action against the company's interests. Nevertheless they rounded out to some degree the picture of one who had emerged as a mysterious figure. Darke surfaced in the Windfall affair in quite another, but equally confusing, manner. The details are relatively

[1] *Op. cit.*, Chapter 2, Note 1, p. 28; see p. 2 of report.
[2] *Ibid.*, p. 121.
[3] *Ibid.*, p. 6.

unimportant. They involved a mis-staked claim made under Darke's direction, a case of innocent error, but the claim *also* attached to lands which later became known as the Windfall claims, and thereby found their way into the Royal Commission's investigation. On such a tenuous thread—the fact that the error had been made by men associated with Darke at a time when he was known to be directing staking operations for Texas Gulf—there arose, apparently, in the minds of many potential investors the conviction that the property in question must be minerally rich. It was true that because of an honest and understandable mistake the desire of Texas Gulf to record the claims had been frustrated, but that was all that was true. Darke and his superior, Holyk, were not greatly concerned over the loss—they had already given these claims a low priority in their planning for the company.

Without question the leading figures in the Windfall matter were George and Viola MacMillan, Toronto husband-and-wife mining promoters who had made a fortune during a long career in Canada. While working together for common purposes, they seem often to have operated separately. For example, George MacMillan, acting under one of his firm names, purchased a large block of Windfall stock in 1961, then sold about 87 per cent of it to his wife in 1963. In the meantime the board of Windfall had been reconstituted to include only nominees of the MacMillans. Mrs. Mac-Millan had no corporate office or position of authority, although eventually she became a large stockholder. Her husband became the president. "The MacMillans," declared Commissioner Kelly, "looked upon all companies with which they were connected as personal activities, to be conducted as they saw fit." At this time they controlled six other companies.

The MacMillans visited Timmins on April 18, 1964, two days after Texas Gulf had publicly confirmed its find from New York, and announced they were going to acquire some property. Within the next few days Mrs. MacMillan purchased 12 claims, which included the four that TGS had given up, with little reluctance, because of the staking error. The deal involved $100,000 plus 250,000 shares of Windfall stock, and it was agreed that the claims were to be optioned to the Windfall company within 30 days. Mrs. Mac-Millan subsequently offered the claims to the company for $200,000 cash, 300,000 shares of capital stock, and payment of a royalty based on profitable production. The offer was accepted by the board, but the Toronto exchange would not approve the Windfall filing statement. After weeks of bitter negotiations, the offer was revised downward so that Mrs. MacMillan received $100,000 in cash, 250,-000 shares (90 per cent of which were escrowed), a specific royalty, and an option to purchase 200,000 shares at 58 cents per share whenever an independent geologist would estimate that a two-million-ton orebody had been discovered. The directors approved *this* on June 15, and later went along on a public release dictated by the MacMillans. The stock exchange, however, demanded another board meeting, and in five minutes on July 13, the directors—who had been kept waiting three hours in an anteroom—approved another letter to the exchange which had been prepared for them. On July 30 the directors met again to receive the results of the assays of the first hole, and these were shown to be completely negative. Anguish was almost, if not quite, universal. Quite a lot had been happening in the meantime. Under "Causes" the Commissioner commented:

> What is remarkable is the way the events combined to produce together results which none of them alone could have produced. It is hardly conceivable that there should again be such an unusual concurrence of incidents as those which contributed to the market action of Windfall Company shares in July of 1964.

On July 3 the closing market price on Windfall shares had been 56 cents, and the opening price on Monday, July 6, was $1.01, with a closing price of $1.95. On July 13 the price reached $4.70 and on July 30 it closed at $4.15. The top price reached during the month was $5.60—and it later dropped back to 80 cents.

There was, of course, the speculative fever in Ontario, and great faith in the possibilities of the Timmins area. There was the remarkable find by Texas Gulf. The public looked on each property in the area as a potential second TGS strike. The airborne anomaly had attracted attention, and there was public faith in the integrity and ability of the MacMillans, among other things. The price paid for the property by them had been one of the highest recorded during the whole of the staking boom, and the public was impressed. The report continues, relating to the remarkable buying splurge on the morning of July 6 which launched weeks of market activity:

> It is impossible to say that these rumors were deliberately circulated by George and Viola MacMillan; but it is a fact that,

due to their interest in companies which held options on Windfall Company shares, substantial benefits could accrue to them by the acceptance of these rumors. Throughout all their conduct was such as to heighten the element of suspense and promote a belief in the rumors. Everyone who had any slight knowledge of mining conditions well knew that a visual examination of the core which had come out of the Windfall claim would have enabled George MacMillan to form an accurate opinion as to whether or not the mineralization in that core was commercial; and the absence of any categorical denial from him was, in effect, a strong confirmation.

Even dissociating the MacMillans from events leading up to the July 6 buying, said the report, it was still true that they had made most advantageous use of the investors' desire to become Windfall owners. The distribution to the public of 900,000 shares held under option by two other MacMillan companies was accomplished with great personal profit. This occurred in a period "in which the trading activities directed by Viola MacMillan indicate a very considerable consciousness of what it was necessary to do in order to support a market and accomplish the primary distribution of shares under option."

The 122–page report of the Royal Commission, with its enlightening appendices, is dramatically rich in details carefully compiled by the investigating staff, although they have no legitimate place in this study. There is, for example, the treatment of John Campbell, director of the Ontario Securities Commission, of whom Commissioner Kelly said: "Because it involved improper conduct by a public servant holding a position of considerable importance, John Campbell's dealing in the shares of the Windfall Company and the loan to him by Viola MacMillan of share certificates in that company constitute the most shocking incident revealed before the Commission." In effect, Judge Kelly recommended that the attorney-general should take a look, since the securities agency was a branch of his department, and then turned his attention to what changes might be made in the laws governing the Commission itself. He was especially concerned that efforts be made to repair the working relationship between the Commission and the Toronto exchange. Another chapter in the report provides an interesting profile of the Honorable George Wardrope, the Ontario Minister of Mines, whose name would be so frequently intruded into the testimony of the SEC case against Texas Gulf. There are brief comparisons of the Ontario Securities Commission with the statutory authority and methods of the U.S. Securities and Exchange Commission, which by then was becoming better known to Canadians.

The Commissioner devoted three pages of the report to a most knowledgeable essay on the practices, functions, and characteristics of the press. It was in startling contrast to the naiveté displayed both by the counsel for SEC and by the majority of the Second Circuit of the U.S. Court of Appeals in the later proceedings in New York. One could wish they had studied it, just for the sake of the record and the evaluative, if less compelling, judgment of posterity.

There were some subsequent actions that could be traced to the labors of the Royal Commission, touched upon only lightly here for the sake of neatness. There were amendments in 1968 to the Ontario statute which had brought the securities commission into being, and the commission prepared guidelines on the subject of timely disclosure, after discussion with the Toronto Stock Exchange, which amended its own guidelines accordingly.[4]

*Canadian News Facts* reported in the spring of 1967 that "Mrs. Viola MacMillan, 63, was convicted in Toronto March 10 of wash trading—the placing of simultaneous buy and sell orders for the same stock in order to create the appearance of activity—in connection with transactions July 10, 1964, in shares of Consolidated Golden Arrow Mines Ltd. She was sentenced to an indeterminate term not to exceed nine months and fined $10,000." Mrs. MacMillan had been released after serving several weeks.

The same publication, on February 15, 1969, was able to report that "Mining promoters George and Viola MacMillan were acquitted in county court in Toronto February 10 on charges of defrauding the public and fraudulently influencing the price of shares of Windfall Oils and Mines Ltd. between April and August, 1964. The court ruled that a rise in the price of Windfall shares could have been due to a major ore discovery by another company near the Windfall property in the Timmins area. The court also ruled there was nothing wrong in withholding the results of Windfall drilling from the public until the MacMillans had their ore assayed."

The "other company" was Texas Gulf Sulphur. Judge Harry Deyman, reported the Toronto *Telegram,* said he could not find anything fraudulent in the MacMillans' press releases. . . . "There was nothing said that wasn't factual." Viola MacMillan, in a pink

[4] *Ontario Securities Commission Weekly Summary,* September 27, 1968, and Toronto Stock Exchange, additions to *Corporate Guide,* September 30, 1968.

plaid suit and hat, "said that mining has been their life. . . . Now that the case is over they can go back and concentrate on business, she said."

The Royal Commission had charged that the MacMillans realized profits of $1,466,000 on trading in Windfall stock.

## II

For Texas Gulf Sulphur Company there was nothing ancillary or peripheral about the Leitch case. It was a direct challenge for the ownership of the Kidd Creek Mine. In short, the plaintiffs would let TGS keep the mine and pay over $450 million, or they could give it up and pay damages of $50 million. The time span of the Leitch trial exceeded that of the main ring action in New York federal court. It grew out of an agreement made in 1963, the writ was served in 1964—hard on the heels of the confirmation of Texas Gulf's spectacular strike near Timmins—and the judge did not release his decision in the matter until almost the end of 1968, more than three months after the Court of Appeals issued its abrasive reversal in the Commission's action.

It will be recalled that 1963 had been a most eventful year for Texas Gulf. Its fortunes had hit the low point in earnings because of the condition of the sulphur market, and it was greatly extended in new ventures which were not ready to pay off. The *Sulphur Queen* had disappeared with all hands in February, and late in August there had been the fatal explosion in the shaft of the potash mine at Moab. The North Carolina phosphate project was still in a pilot stage, and there were rumors of a take-over by outside interests. Then late in the year the long period of exploration in northern Ontario was rewarded, or at least so it might appear to the hopeful, with the drilling of the first hole near Timmins. Security was clamped down and the business of acquiring land began.

In September of 1961 Charles Pegg, the exploration manager of the Leitch Gold Mines Ltd., initiated discussions in Princeton, British Columbia, with David Lowrie, a member of the TGS exploration group. Pegg was experienced in all kinds of prospecting methods and was now intrigued with Texas Gulf's new airborne equipment. He wanted to explore some kind of participation on the part of his company, and this conversation was reported to Mollison in a memo. In January of the following year Lowrie and Pegg pursued the conversation at the Engineers Club in Toronto, and after this Lowrie was empowered to offer Leitch the use of certain airborne physical data and the results of some ground work in specified townships in return for a ten per cent interest in the net profits. Pegg then wrote Karl Springer, the president of Leitch, and discussed the offer.

There is some dispute as to what happened next. To the casual observer it would not seem that the subject of the dispute mattered much either way, but in the trial to come it would be the first factor bearing on the credibility of Pegg in the mind of the court, and as such assumed substantial importance. Walter Holyk, who commanded the active field exploration work for Texas Gulf, said that Pegg telephoned him in January, 1963, while Holyk was in Little America, Wyoming, as to the possibility of obtaining some Texas Gulf data. Later Pegg denied the call ever took place, and declared that negotiations began when he wrote Holyk on February 1 of that year, setting forth the Leitch interest. Holyk's reply was accompanied by a map. He stated that Texas Gulf had performed a number of scattered surveys as indicated by the map, and "would be willing to discuss turning over data in any area with a possibly temporary restriction on some ground north of Timmins." Details were to be left to a later meeting in Toronto, and this took place at the Royal York Hotel on March 11. A few days before the meeting Holyk had received a communication from Royal Trust, executor for the Hendrie Estate, suggesting that the option sought by TGS on a critical area in Kidd Township might be decided within a couple of weeks. It was a significant point, as later developed. After considerable negotiations back and forth between Leitch and Texas Gulf, the contract was finally executed in May, but was back-dated to February 1, 1963.

By February of 1964 the rumors of an exciting discovery by Texas Gulf had begun to circulate, and Pegg heard them first on February 22, but was skeptical. The skepticism had evaporated by early April, and his investigations in Timmins revealed that the find was in the northeastern part of Kidd Township. By April 15 he knew that TGS had a mine, he said, and the best he could do was to stake other claims in the area.

Following the Texas Gulf confirmation press conference in New York on April 16, Fred Hall, then a vice president of the Leitch company, wrote to Stephens offering his congratulations, and adding: "We wrote to enquire as to whether any of these lands are in the 'surveyed areas' . . . subject to the terms of the Agreement made as of the first day of February, 1963. . . ." What might be termed "further correspondence" followed: it included a map, and Texas Gulf took the position that it had acquired no property in the "surveyed areas," but the people at Leitch differed. The writ in the action was served June 5.

The trial did not begin until October of 1966, and it ran for 164 days. Five days before Chief Justice George A. Gale of the Ontario Supreme Court reserved decision, the SEC was already arguing its appeal in the Texas Gulf main case before the Second Circuit in New York. The opinion in the latter would come down in August of 1968, after a very long period of consideration, but Justice Gale's deliberations were even longer. His opinion was rendered in Toronto on November 29. It was in favor of Texas Gulf. Three weeks earlier the Toronto *Financial Post* declared, "The hole in Kidd Township, known as the Kidd Creek Mine, is the center of the biggest legal dispute known in Canada—the now internationally famous action by Leitch Gold Mines Ltd. . . ."

For all of its length and the importance of the astronomical sums sought by the plaintiff, the Leitch case against Texas Gulf seems, in retrospect, to have come down to one very simple matter—a line on a map. That line was the shortest distance between two points of view, and it was certainly examined in the greatest detail. At one point an expert witness in such matters was joined by his lordship in a detailed discussion of the chemical processes involved in the manufacture of a red pencil, while distinguished counsel tapped their feet.

Plaintiffs and defendants were respectively two in number, although this was little more than a formality. Co-plaintiff was Mastodon-Highland Bell Mines Ltd., a Leitch subsidiary with rights in the contract, while the co-defendant was Ecstall Mining Ltd., the newly formed TGS subsidiary to whom the parent company had transferred its lands and mining rights, and which was now operating the mine.

The map which was part of the agreement between the parties was pivotal, as noted, but there were actually many maps, prepared at different times and with quite other purposes in view than becoming exhibits in a half-billion-dollar legal action. The changes, combinations, re-entries, and erasures were minutely detailed in testimony and just as minutely traced by the court in the opinion later. The "contract" map, which in essence had been constructed by Holyk and his associates from existing working records, was one he had sent to Pegg with the letter of February 18, 1963, and it became a trial exhibit. It had its beginnings three years before when Mollison had asked for a map showing areas already flown and those Texas Gulf was proposing to fly. It had been amended from time to time in accordance with need and as *actual* flying took place, often at variance with the *planned* areas.

The trial, and the opinion, presented three highlights in particular—the Royal York Hotel meeting between Pegg and Holyk in March, 1963; the provision in the agreement for the delivery of data to Leitch by Texas Gulf; and the exhaustive treatment of the credibility issue, especially as it affected Pegg. The opinion devoted some 5,000 careful words to the latter issue.

The hotel meeting had been held in the morning hours in the Leitch suite. Pegg had brought the TGS map along, which he had by then examined carefully, and it was spread on a coffee table between the two men. He seemed disinterested in several of the areas as the discussion proceeded, circling them and marking "out" on the map, but the critical conversation concerned areas three and four, and Holyk stated quite definitely that Texas Gulf would consider entering into an agreement only with respect to that part of the 1960 flying which took place over *area three*—or that part falling outside the 1959 flying. He expressed it both ways. He said that he contemplated turning over the A.E.M. maps with respect to any area covered by the agreement, including those showing the anomalies, along with other original data including tapes and films. Again he declared that TGS would agree only with respect to area three as shown on the map before them. "That evidence," said the court, "virtually decided the litigation." The meeting had ended with making a memorandum on hotel stationery of the areas Pegg wished to include in the agreement as Holyk read them from his list. Area *four* was not included in the lists.

The time taken to draft the final agreement was considerable, as might be expected, with changes suggested by each of the parties going back and forth by telephone and mail from March 14 until May 24, when the papers signed by Leitch were put in the mail. The next step would be the delivery of the data, and Pegg was anxious to go to Texas Gulf's Calgary office to receive it. Holyk was equally anxious that this should *not* happen until the agreement had been received. He not only wrote full instructions to Dr. John F. Macdougall in Calgary, but just to make sure that there would be no slip-up, telephoned Macdougall. In any event, the agreement did arrive in New York on Monday, May 27, and Pegg arrived in Calgary to get on with the examination and delivery of the promised data. This consumed four days, and some of the details were the subject of argument at the trial. Inadvertently, and because of earlier labeling of the material, Pegg received some data which properly related to the area four which had been so carefully protected by Holyk during the hotel negotiations and in later exchanges.

The credibility issue arose mainly from the Pegg-Holyk conversations and from the events in Calgary, and Justice Gale approached it carefully but firmly, leaving no doubt as to his conclusions. In his testimony Pegg had "attempted to leave the impression that he was the one who decided to exclude area four from the operation of the agreement. . . . As to the Calgary incident, Mr. Pegg swore that on May 30 Mr. Podolsky [5] sorted and turned over the flight data to him, whereas both Mr. Podolsky and Dr. John F. Macdougall, a Texas Gulf geologist, testified that the former had nothing to do with that feature of the transaction.

"Superficially, at least, the conflict of credibility thus presented has been rather difficult to solve," Justice Gale continues in his opinion. "All of those involved are persons of apparent integrity who testified in what seemed to be a straightforward manner, although at times Mr. Pegg gave me the impression of being rather irresponsible and somewhat insincere. After studying the evidence again, and having weighed the several factors which ordinarily are relevant to an issue such as this, I have come to the conclusion that where the evidence of Mr. Pegg differs in any material respect from that of the others, I should reject his evidence for the reason that he was either mistaken or, on occasions, was deliberately endeavoring to mislead the Court. During the course of the trial, I formed an initial notion that Mr. Pegg was not being entirely frank. . . . It may well be that . . . Mr. Pegg's evidence was, subconsciously at least, influenced by his personal financial interest in the outcome of the litigation."

Pegg's call to Little America, which he denied on trial, bothered the Court, for example, since the denial served no purpose except possibly to cast doubt on Holyk's credibility. Justice Gale found

---

[5] George Podolsky, a TGS geophysicist, then located in the Calgary office.

Pegg's memory as to what was said and what occurred at the Royal York Hotel meeting "either a complete blank or very sketchy." The Leitch exploration manager's evidence in respect to circles he had drawn on the map—refuted without challenge by an expert witness—"represents one of his attempts to deceive the Court because in giving that evidence he must have decided to destroy, if he could, the implication that from the outset he understood that Leitch was not to receive data or rights with respect to area four." The Court unreservedly accepted the evidence of Dr. Holyk as to the hotel meeting.

And so it went, including Justice Gale's painstaking reconstruction of the events at Calgary during the transference of data, over which plaintiff's counsel repeatedly and vigorously attacked the credibility of Holyk, Macdougall, and Podolsky. In conclusion the Court said his finding as to credibility might not be as important as he suggested, since even if Pegg's evidence were to be accepted in all respects, the telephone call to Little America was of no consequence; at the Royal York meeting Pegg knew he was getting no rights as to area four; and even if Podolsky had sorted the material at Calgary, there was no evidence that he had *deliberately* handed over the area four data.

In this action the plaintiff, Leitch, had sought a declaration that Texas Gulf Sulphur Company held as trustee for the plaintiff all lands under the terms of the agreement, including the Kidd Creek Mine, and should now deliver up the necessary conveyances and transfers. As an alternative, plaintiff sought damages of $400 million for breaching the agreement, and damages of $50 million for loss of opportunities to acquire lands, claims, and mining rights. The final half of Justice Gale's opinion bore on the claims and his findings. For instance, prior to argument, plaintiff had insisted that the Kidd 55 anomaly was actually within the boundaries of area three, but the shortest distance between the line and the ground location of any part of the anomaly was at least 7,611 feet. This did not end the matter, however, since even if the mine were in area four, plaintiff felt it had been given development rights. The Court defined the legal problem as consisting, in the first place, of whether there was a "patent ambiguity" on the face of the contract or the map, and second, whether there was a "latent ambiguity" in the language or application of the contract. (The "patent ambiguity" discussion required four pages, while the resolving of any "latent ambiguity" filled 50 pages of the opinion.) After thousands of words devoted to exploring and resolving these matters, Justice Gale declared:

> I have found there is no patent ambiguity in the contract; that there is no relevant latent ambiguity in the contract; that if there is it must be resolved in favor of the defendant; that there is no equivocation in the contract; and if there is, it must be resolved in favor of the defendant. Accordingly I hold that the contract, together with the map, is unambiguous and is definitive of the rights of the parties. . . . These findings mean, of course, that the defendant does not hold the Kidd Creek Mine as constructive trustee for the plaintiff and that the latter is not entitled to damages as alternative relief.

It was a very heavy moment after a very long trial, and after a very long period of study by the Court. The heavens over Toronto and New York figuratively rumbled at the thought of $450 million *almost* changing hands, while up near Timmins the Kidd Creek Mine was completing its second year of operation with the mining and milling of more than 3,600,000 tons of ore, and metals had contributed most of the increase in Texas Gulf's net income—the highest in history. Justice Gale, turning to the ancillary claims for damages, made a slight move in the direction of lightening the moment by noting that, "Rarely will a court have occasion to call 'ancillary' a claim for damages in the sum of fifty million dollars and yet that is the situation here."

After consideration, the Court awarded the plaintiff nominal damages of one dollar for a minor breach of the agreement, indicated that it could have reference to a master to ascertain the amount of its loss, and awarded costs to the defendant. Unofficial estimates of the latter, said the *Wall Street Journal,* had ranged as high as $650,000. The judgment was reached four years and five months after the legal action began, and as *The Northern Miner* observed, if Leitch had won the case it would have been the biggest court settlement in Canadian history. Elaborate security measures were adopted by the chief justice to maintain secrecy throughout the time he was preparing his judgment, and he handed it down not only after all the security markets had closed but at 8 P.M. on a Friday night when the thoughts of most Canadians were concentrated on the Grey Cup football game. He then dined at his club with his wife and a security officer.

During the following week the local market feature, said the *Miner*, was the heavy selling in Leitch and Highland Bell following the week-end announcement of the decision. After a trading delay of two and a half hours, Leitch opened at $3.50, down $8.75 from its Friday close, while Highland Bell opened at $4, off $14.75 a share. Among the sellers, disclosed by inside trading bulletins of the Ontario Securities Commission, were officers and directors of Leitch and Highland Bell.

On December 6, Fred Hall, now president of Leitch, informed his stockholders that the company's directors did not agree with much of the reasoning of the chief justice, retained their full confidence in Mr. Pegg, but had decided not to appeal the judgment on advice of counsel, "because of the limitations on the powers of an appellate court to interfere with findings of fact made by a trial judge." To say the least, this made a nice contrast for Texas Gulf with the handling of the SEC action where, on appeal, at least in the opinion of two dissenting judges, the Second Circuit majority had "usurped" the functions of the trial court.

For his deliberations, Justice Gale's office had been set up in the medical suite of the courthouse because it was almost window-less and easy to secure. A squad of officers spent a week-end check-ing the office and each of the more than 1,100 exhibits looking for bugging devices before the 62-year-old chief justice moved in, the Toronto *Telegram* revealed in a special article two months after the opinion was released.[6] The Canadian Press Service had disclosed on Christmas Day that the judge received four calls threatening his life on the night he had made his decision public.[7] About a month after the trial ended his house was broken into while he and Mrs. Gale were away. Nothing was stolen but security officers believed an electronic listening device might have been planted. The stakes had been very high, and at one point during the trial Leitch stock rose $4 on the strength of a rumor that company lawyers were talking settlement.

The *Telegram* article described the attempt of a man posing as a telephone repairman to tap the line in the judge's office, and an attempt by a supposed window washer on a sixth floor scaffold to peer into the office, as well as letters and telephone calls aimed at influencing the decision. They accused him of a disservice to Canada, and threatened his life.

[6] Toronto *Telegram*, January 25, 1969.
[7] *The New York Times*, December 25, 1968.

Not all of the outside action in connection with the case was directed at the judge, however. A Montreal investment house, Lafferty, Harwood and Company, added a somewhat startling and novel touch to the business of sending financial newsletters to its clients in Canada, United States, and Europe. Fifty-two letters were sent in all, written by Richard Lafferty, senior partner of the firm, and while the communications consistently disclaimed any legal qualifications for the author, they unabashedly plumped for a final decision in favor of Leitch. When the trial passed its 52nd day, Lafferty predicted the outcome in terms of racetrack odds— 85 to 15 with Leitch as the favorite. The story was written in some detail by Robertson Cochrane, a staff writer for the *Toronto Daily Star*,[8] who quoted Lafferty, disappointed but philosophical over the result, as admitting that he had not owned a common stock himself in 20 years—it was against his policy—but expected that his letters would have steered some of the clients into the Leitch stock.

Lafferty attended only a few of the trial sessions and appeared to have been inordinately impressed with John J. Robinette, counsel for Leitch and one of the dominion's best-known trial lawyers. Robinette was also currently representing the MacMillans in their trial. While it took Justice Gale more than seven months to weigh the evidence and write his opinion after the trial ended, it took Lafferty only 47 days to get out his last pre-judgment word to the customers, some of whom might have recalled that the first commentary was issued on Hallowe'en Day in 1966. It might be observed that the whole procedure could have added some colorful touches to the growing literature on disclosure had it occurred within the jurisdiction of the U.S. Securities and Exchange Commission.

Possibly with an eye on the dramatic reversal of Texas Gulf's fortunes, when the SEC appealed the lower court's holdings in New York, Donald MacLennan, a Toronto lawyer and Leitch shareholder, addressed a four-page letter to the other stockholders on the last day of 1968, condemning the judgment of the company's directors in deciding against an appeal "with inappropriate haste." His experiences in trying to communicate with management on this matter, he declared, had left him disillusioned and lacking in confidence, and he included copies of his letters to Hall, now president,

[8] Robertson Cochrane: "Investment Firm Incorrectly Predicted Outcome of Texas Gulf-Leitch Trial," *Toronto Daily Star*, December 13, 1968.

and Springer, the chairman. Subsequently MacLennan and another lawyer, George Fallis, obtained requisitions for a special stock-holders meeting from more than 20 per cent of the shareholders. Early in February Hall stated that the company would not call a meeting. He disputed the accuracy of certain statements in Mac-Lennan's letter, and quoted counsel Robinette as advising that an appeal would be almost hopeless. In view of the ramifications of the entire Texas Gulf affair, another comment by Hall is notable, in that it again had a bearing on the subject of disclosure:

"Had an appeal been launched by the plaintiffs the public would have been entitled to assume that these men had reasonable grounds for believing the appeal would succeed. The result would have undoubtedly had an effect on the market price of the shares of the plaintiff companies. In the absence of reasonable grounds for such belief, the directors consider it improper to launch such an appeal." [9] As has often been said, communications across the U.S.-Canadian border are excellent.

MacLennan and Fallis called the special meeting for March 31, acting under a provision of the Ontario Companies Act, al-though Hall declared that it could have no legal effect.[10] The at-tempt to force an appeal was defeated by an almost two-to-one vote, whereupon the dissidents set about soliciting proxies to be used at the forthcoming annual meeting.[11]

Late in April, Leslie Rowntree, provincial minister for financial and commercial affairs, told the Ontario legislature that he had asked for a report from the Ontario Securities Commission into the activities of an officer of Leitch Gold Mines Ltd., who had reportedly tried to buy a large block of stock in the company immediately before it launched suit against Texas Gulf Sulphur. The minister's statement was in reply to a question from Morton Shulman, a member from High Park, who had asked what action the minister planned, in the light of disclosures that Hall, then a Leitch vice president, attempted to buy 500,000 shares before the suit. As it developed later, Shulman was writing a book.[12]

Perhaps the final note was an announcement from Montreal that Royal Trust Company, who in 1966 had filed suit against Texas Gulf as executor of the Hendrie Estate, was proceeding with

[9] Toronto *Globe & Mail*, February 4, 1969.
[10] *Wall Street Journal*, March 18, 19, 1969.
[11] *Wall Street Journal*, April 1, 1969.
[12] Toronto *Globe & Mail*, May 29, 1969.

its $400 million damage action. The suit was pending in the Supreme Court of Ontario with no trial date set, and although Leitch had originally been named a defendant, the company was dropped after its own action was concluded. Royal Trust was claiming that TGS had made "false and fraudulent" representations to acquire an option in the mining property, and had been aware that the ground was worth more than the consideration paid because work was done on the property without the knowledge or permission of the plaintiffs and while willfully trespassing. There seemed to be no rest for the successful weary.

There was, of course, one best way to resolve issues such as these, and the litigants found it without too much delay. In its regular report to the stockholders covering the first six months of 1970, Texas Gulf was able to announce an agreement to purchase the last remaining outside interest in the Kidd Creek Mine, subject only to the sellers receiving an appropriate tax opinion. The price tag was $27 million in Canadian funds, but for this the corporation would acquire all right, title, and interest of the vendors, and their claims, pertaining to the north half of Lot 3, Concession V, Kidd Township—one of the three 160-acre tracts over which the ore body extended. The purchase included the ten per cent profits interest held by the Royal Trust, and all past net profits due from the property. These had not so far been paid, although the stockholders had been put on notice in 1968. This would dispose of both the claims and the lawsuits between TGS and Royal Trust, as trustee and ancillary administrator of the estate of Murray Hendrie, and the executors of the estate of his later deceased wife, Agnes Rachel, mother of the fortunate Mr. Gilmour of Hamilton, Ontario.

### III

Legally, what might be called the Merrill Lynch affair, was an afterpiece to the Texas Gulf case. It was a significant afterpiece, in the eyes of the Commission, because it served to advance the party line. Unquestionably it was related, but not in any way that would or could affect the fortunes of TGS in its own continuing confrontation with the SEC and the courts. Yet in terms of changes wrought in the life and practice of the business and financial community, it had its place and deserves attention.

Two weeks to the day after the Court of Appeals for the Second Circuit handed down its opinion in *SEC v. Texas Gulf Sulphur,* the Commission began its administrative action against the nation's largest brokerage firm—Merrill Lynch, Pierce, Fenner and Smith—with an order for a public hearing. This was the first such case brought against an underwriter, and was clearly an extension of the argument that had been sustained on appeal against Texas Gulf on August 13, 1968. The essence of the action was that insiders privy to confidential information that might affect the price of a stock cannot capitalize on that information in the market-place. Such information must first be publicly disclosed.

Already, at this time, many lawyers and some judges and legal writers had been maintaining that the SEC should properly come up with a clear set of rules affecting public disclosure of material facts in such cases, and they were about to be joined by others in the securities field, but the Commission continued to argue—in court and on the speaker's platform—that it could never cover every possible set of circumstances in which an insider could be wrong, and that it must rely upon a case-by-case approach to develop the law.

The SEC order of August 27 charged Merrill Lynch, and 14 of its officers and salesmen, with violating the securities laws by passing information to 14 investment companies (the number was later expanded to 15), enabling the latter to avoid losses, or make profits, totaling some $14.5 million in the stock of the Douglas Aircraft Company. The company was subsequently merged into the McDonnell Douglas Corporation.

Two years before, in 1966, Merrill Lynch was in the confidential position of being managing underwriter for a proposed $75 million debenture offering of Douglas, and the latter's president—Donald W. Douglas, Jr.—had telephoned, on the morning of June 20, Dean S. Woodman, a west coast underwriting official for Merrill Lynch. His purpose was to reveal a sharply lower earnings estimate for his company. During the first six months of fiscal 1966 the Douglas earnings had fallen to 49 cents a share, considerably down from earlier estimates. Douglas testified later that he did this because he felt the brokerage firm might now want to eliminate itself from the underwriting. Three days later he telephoned Woodman again and asked if the latter had told anybody, and the Merrill Lynch official in San Francisco replied that he had passed the information along to Archangelo Catapano, vice president in New York of the firm's research department and its specialist on aerospace companies, on the afternoon of the original call.

Douglas then decided to issue an immediate release, on June 24, concerning the decline in earnings. He had met with Woodman on June 21 and given him a copy of the confidential income review, which they "had reviewed in depth." The projection of Douglas earnings for *all* of fiscal 1966 was later revised downward to 12 cents a share.[13]

An interesting sidelight on the above maneuvers emerged during the hearings in 1969 which related to the 15 investment companies, after Merrill Lynch had taken itself out of the action. Woodman testified that he had not spoken with Catapano until June 22, and then Catapano had called *him* to ask what he knew about heavy trading in Douglas. It was then, he said, that he relayed the earnings news, with the request that it not be discussed until it had become public knowledge. Catapano told him later that he had honored the request. But a Merrill Lynch salesman in New York, Lee Idleman, declared that he had received the information on June 21 when Catapano called him, telling him that others had already received it. If anyone asked Idleman where it came from, he was told to attribute it to Kidder, Peabody and Company. He thereupon had telephoned three of his customers.[14]

Douglas stock had been selling on June 22 for around $90 a share. It dropped to $78 on the following day, and to $69 on June 27, the first trading day after the company's news release. Prior to the public announcement, the 14 investment companies that had been alerted had either sold, or sold short, on more than 190,000 shares. The SEC charged that during this same period Merrill Lynch was buying Douglas for some of its smaller customers, and this invitation to private action against the brokerage house was reminiscent of charges in the complaint against Texas Gulf Sulphur which ultimately produced just such a result. The Commission contended that Merrill Lynch's *quid pro quo* for advancing the information was commission business and "give-up's"— commissions directed to it by institutional investors through other brokers. Said *The New York Times:* "For anyone who went short, the trading pattern could not have been better," and it commented that almost half of the 14 investment companies then in the picture were "hedge funds" which often operate on borrowed money, are frequently on the short side of the market, put a high premium on performance, and generate much commission business.

[13] *The New York Times*, November 27, 1968.
[14] *Wall Street Journal*, January 10, 1969.

On September 23, almost a month after the SEC order, Merrill Lynch categorically denied the Commission charges and accused it of trying the case in the newspapers. It requested that the SEC staff be stopped from making further public statements. The brokerage house asked for a dismissal on the ground, among others, that the Commission was unconstitutionally applying new standards, and retroactively, to the conduct of the brokerage business. It desired more time to prepare for the hearing that had been set for October 8, since the SEC case had been two years in preparation. Orval L. DuBois, secretary to the Commission, indignantly denied issuing any releases after the first one, or initiating any publicity. He had been "badgered by the press," he said, for further details.

All of the vigorous denials and assertions of an intent to contest the case notwithstanding, Merrill Lynch settled on November 26. It had been a short war. In its press statement it said the firm and "those of our employees involved . . . have specifically denied any wrongdoing. Our disagreement with the SEC staff was over what actually transpired in the Douglas matter more than two years ago. The staff's charges were not proven, and the judgment concerning the employees was the SEC's, not ours." Unfortunately the two judgments would not enjoy the same effect. "After the most careful consideration," the statement continued, "we decided it would be best not to engage in a prolonged and costly dispute with a government agency."

Said an unidentified SEC staff member: "We went in asking for more than we got, and they came in asking for less than they got." It was obviously a philosophical observation founded on truth. Richard Phalon, of *The New York Times,* writing out of Washington, said the sanctions imposed were about midway in the spectrum of penalties that could have been invoked, ranging from mere censure to revocation of the firm's registration, which would have put it out of business. He guessed that there may have been pressures working on both sides for a settlement that had nothing to do with the effort that would have been consumed by long litigation. It is fair to say that the SEC badly wanted this decision in the record book. It was almost inevitable that the Texas Gulf case would be appealed, and the Commission was here building and improving its weapons on the basis of the Court of Appeals holdings in that action. Facing a new national administration that had indicated a liking for less heavy-handed regulatory attitudes towards

Wall Street, and the fleeting pace of time, the Commission may have felt it advisable not to let the Merrill Lynch action continue too long. It was also thought logical that "several private suits might be pending," the *Times* pointed out. If this were true, the record of a full hearing, now obviated, would have provided opposition lawyers with much more information than could be drawn from the text of the settlement.

The SEC order, based on the settlement offer from Merrill Lynch, commanded these things:

—It suspended the firm's New York institutional sales office for 21 days starting December 5, and its San Francisco underwriting office for 15 days, starting December 11, thus dissociating a number of individuals from income. The Commission estimated the combined shutdown might cost Merrill Lynch itself as much as a million dollars, but the firm had no comment.

—Catapano was censured and suspended without pay for 60 days.

—Phillip F. Bilbao, vice president and manager of the institutional services department, was censured and suspended without pay for 21 days.

—Similar sanctions, of course, applied to the five salesmen dealing with institutional investors.

—Woodman and two other vice presidents—Edward N. McMillan and Norman Heindel—were censured. Censure is the lightest sanction the SEC can apply. McMillan and Heindel consented only to findings that they failed to exercise reasonable supervision; Woodman and the salesmen consented to having violated the law. Charges were dropped against four others originally named.

—The order specified that the firm and the individuals waived a hearing and consented to findings "solely for the purpose of these proceedings and without admitting the allegations."

The Commission's order, incidentally, included a statement of policy from Merrill Lynch along these lines: it generally prohibited disclosure by any member of the underwriting division of the non-public material information about a company obtained in connection with a security offering. But this did not apply to disclosures to senior executives, to the legal department, to persons directly involved with underwriters, to research personnel contacted in connection with a proposed offering, or to members of buying departments of *other* firms who need the information in making decisions to participate. The SEC was not sure that this policy would work, and it again plumped for prompt disclosure of material information.

The settlement broke new legal ground on the obligations of insiders not to capitalize on privileged information in the stock market. As the first underwriter case, it extended the argument sustained against Texas Gulf. The order found that "advance disclosure" to a select group operated as a "fraud or deceit" on public investors who didn't have the same information, and this sounded familiar. It had also been charged originally that customers had violated the law by trading on that information, but none were involved in the settlement.

In many minds the broad legal significance was thought to be that this proceeding might extend the definition of a corporate insider. The Texas Gulf case had appeared to extend that definition, and now brokers could join the assemblage of those unsure as to how to handle corporate information. The SEC had said it believed that *Cady, Roberts* and *Texas Gulf* cases had established the legal principles which governed the conduct of Merrill Lynch—the first with its "inherent unfairness" doctrine, and the second, where the court found it illegal not only to trade on inside information but to pass it along.

The settlement order, opined one financial writer,[15] might not altogether eliminate the uncertainty. Hearings had begun December 16 against the 15 investor companies, one of which had already entered into an agreement with the SEC, and these proceedings were yet to be resolved. At a pre-hearing conference, Irwin M. Borowski, the SEC lawyer, contended that a "tippee . . . stands in the feet of his tipper," and is guilty of fraud. In rebuttal, Samuel E. Gates, representing two of the respondents, declared the financial community couldn't operate if all such information "had to be taken at a peril." His clients, he said, did absolutely nothing with the information from Merrill Lynch, and it was unsolicited. They had already decided to sell as a result of talking with others and making up their minds—and lost $40,000 as a result. At the hearings it was asserted that the word of Douglas' lowered earnings had been

[15] *Wall Street Journal*, November 27, 1968.

circulating along Wall Street for about three weeks before the public announcement of June 24.[16]

It had truly been a short war, but was it over? The winners were not about to abandon the territory they had won while the world talked it over.


## IV

Some of the most lyrical prose gracing the multitude of legal papers which makes up so large a part of the Texas Gulf matter was spun by the various participants in behalf of stockholders. Almost everybody knows, by definition, what a stockholder is, yet this common understanding tends to create a large-size blind spot. Shareholding is strictly a technical qualification presenting many facets.

There is, first of all, the shareowner which the corporation addresses in its annual reports and quarterly statements, occasionally provides with box lunches, and to whom it mails dividend checks. This group, while it actually embraces *all* shareowners, including a host of such institutions as banks, insurance companies, trusts, and investment groups, is not quite this all-inclusive a concept in the minds of either the annual report writer or the presiding board chairman. The latter are thinking, hopefully, of a somewhat more cohesive group of those who *own* the company, generally support its actions, and wish it—and incidentally themselves—well. In his majority opinion, Judge Waterman, of the Second Circuit Court of Appeals, was firm, however, in characterizing the "speculators and chartists of Wall and Bay Streets" as reasonable investors, presumably entitled to the rights and privileges of all stockholders. It must go without argument that the grand lodge of shareowners is of many hues and many dispositions. It must include the sometimes vituperative exhibitionists who so often monopolize the floor at the annual meetings, and the well-heeled operators who are trying through proxies or debentures to take over the company, as well as the rest of the vast army of people's capitalism. And since every army has its sharpshooters, a novel and landmark case such as *SEC v. Texas Gulf Sulphur* invariably produces a hard core of litigants who can be expected eagerly to train their rifles on the corporation itself. At the close of 1968 Texas Gulf noted in its

---

[16] *Wall Street Journal,* January 10, 1969.

annual report that the company was a defendant in a hundred or more of such suits, some of which allegedly were class actions, in which the plaintiffs sought compensatory and punitive damages. In going to court, a very large majority of them were financing the venture with the profits they had already made on the company's stock.

By far the greater number of such actions—but not all of them —had been brought in or transferred to the federal court for the Southern District of New York, where the SEC's case had been tried originally before Judge Bonsal. Four actions were filed in 1966 and 1967 in the federal district court for the Utah Central Division in Salt Lake City. In New York, 62 cases on tap could be divided chiefly into two groups—those who sold their stock *after* the April 12, 1964, news release, and those who sold *before* that date. Some who sold after the date still did not claim to have relied upon the release, but proceeded solely on the basis of non-disclosure.

There would be little purpose in presenting for this record any detailed analysis or running report of these actions. None of them would move to a truly ultimate conclusion in the courts for a long time, although the first damages had been awarded to plaintiffs in the Utah Proceedings by U.S. District Judge Willis W. Ritter late in 1969, who then recommended that the decision be appealed "all the way upstairs." The cases provide a certain amount of interest, however, for the student of corporate legal entanglements in some respects: they put the microscope of public scrutiny on several samples of litigating stockholders and in the process disclose, perhaps, some motivations, attitudes, and methods. They raise some real and unsolved questions for the corporate management which is interested in its stockholder relations, for lawyers and judges, and certainly for such government agencies as the Securities and Exchange Commission, which are in turn the agents of the Congress and all the people. A brief look at some of these actions need not involve still another, and by now undoubtedly wearisome, descent into the drill holes of Kidd Township, or retrace one more time the actions and statements of witnesses, counsel, and court. The facts, and the areas of disagreement with the facts, have been measurably established by trial and review, and presumably will not change much under the stress of private lawsuits, but what is new pertains to the shaping of his instrument by the private litigant. It will usually reveal more about him than it will add anything to the essential elements of the main case.

And since these litigants have voluntarily stepped upon the stage, what they did, what they say, and what they are is now in the public domain, and they cannot honestly complain.

The plaintiffs in the four Utah actions consisted of two individuals and two sets of man-and-wife teams. It could be observed that private litigation revolving around the stock market quite frequently presents the picture of domestic solidarity on attack. Here damages were sought against Texas Gulf Sulphur Company and against Dr. Fogarty, then the executive vice president, which plaintiffs claim were incurred when they sold shares of TGS stock. As might be expected, the charges concerned the exploration activities in Canada and the company's handling of the news of those events.

"Specifically," declared the defendants' post-trial memorandum submitted to Judge Ritter, "all of the plaintiffs allege that they sold shares of Texas Gulf stock to defendant Fogarty, and were defrauded thereby. It is claimed that both Texas Gulf and Dr. Fogarty violated numerous federal statutory and regulatory provisions. It is claimed that both defendants entered into a conspiracy to defraud these plaintiffs, and intentionally depressed the price of Texas Gulf stock for their own benefit and to injure the plaintiffs. It is also alleged that they committed 'common law fraud' as well as breach of common law fiduciary obligations owed to these plaintiffs. It is claimed that these violations were intended to and did injure plaintiffs." These, it must be noted, are facets of the stockholder mind which are all too seldom studied by the corporate relations experts, until blood has been drawn.

On January 7, 1960, the first of these plaintiffs—George Gordon Reynolds—purchased 300 shares of Texas Gulf for 18⅝ per share. He was aware that the company was the largest sulphur producer in the world, and hoped that the stock might return to its previous high of 45. When the stock went down rather than up, Reynolds became concerned, and on May 18, 1962, purchased an additional 200 shares at 15. His total investment at this point, disregarding commissions, was $8,587.50. On April 16, 1964, he sold the stock at 33⅝, receiving $16,812.50, almost doubling his investment. The price of the stock had constantly risen following his second purchase. Almost two years after the purchase Reynolds had been in touch with his broker and at that time read reports of the April 12 "gloomy" release as supplied by Dow Jones and the *Wall Street Journal*, whereupon he decided *not to sell* but to "hold the stock, see what happened." What happened was the company's confirming April 16 news release, and the reports coming into Salt Lake and relayed by the broker had the astonishing effect of then persuading Reynolds to sell. "There was a flurry in the stock, and I decided I'd get out while the getting was good," he said.

Later in the afternoon, when Reynolds had knowledge of the actual TGS announcement, the stock was selling for 37 and he possessed sufficient assets to buy it back but did not do so, believing it might have run its course and not wanting to gamble to get back in. Since Dr. Fogarty bought no shares on the date of the sale, none of the Reynolds shares were sold to him. Possibly the point in the Reynolds case which might have given the Commission pause was that the two disclosures by Texas Gulf had each reached its target of a "reasonable" investor as far away as Salt Lake, but that the investor had reacted positively to the first and negatively to the second—certainly his privilege. However, two years and two months later he sued for damages.

The second action, of Arthur and Mary Louise Stout, involved more money but was simpler in outline. The Stouts purchased a thousand shares in 1962 at 12⅞ per share, making their investment $12,875. They sold them on the morning of April 22, 1964, for 42, more than trebling their investment. Stout testified that the sale was motivated by the first, or April 12, release, yet the fact was that they held the stock for a considerable run. The Stouts gained $12,000 just between the opening of the market on April 13 and the date of their sale, and they offered their shares for sale at a price higher than the closing price on that day—and got it. Although Stout still maintained that his selling was motivated by the first release, ten days before, he did not deny having had notice of the confirmation release four days later, which had been widely distributed in his area by the Dow Jones wire, by a special bulletin from the Stouts' broker, and by various accounts in the *Wall Street Journal,* the *Salt Lake Tribune* and the *Deseret News.* It was again demonstrated here that Dr. Fogarty did not purchase any of the Stout stock. The Stouts sued for damages almost three years after they sold and took their profit of almost $30,000.

Walter A. Mitchell, the third plaintiff, was somewhat more colorful as an individual. A Los Angeles certified public accountant, he presented the picture of one whose tax returns for three years, beginning in 1963, indicated substantial income from his investment portfolio but recurring losses in his accounting business. His investment portfolio's analysis of individual securities, which became an exhibit at the trial, contained such details as Standard and Poor ratings, institutional holdings, pre-emptive rights, long-term debt, preferred stock, convertible bonds, net profits, cash and stock dividends, and price-earnings ratios. His file on Texas Gulf alone comprised 413 pages. He was obviously a careful and unusual man, and it is doubtful if his like had ever moved into the considerations of the company's stockholder relations planning.

The Mitchell shares involved in this action were purchased between December of 1953 and May of 1962. When a drop in the sulphur price had caused reductions in the company earnings, Mitchell wrote TGS requesting an explanation. He was highly aware of the later diversification program and of the increase in sulphur prices. His file contained, for example, the announcement that TGS would spend $45 million to develop a phosphate mine in North Carolina.

Mitchell's broker representative possessed information on the events of both April 12 and April 16 relating to Texas Gulf, but did not volunteer such information, assuming that it was known by his well-informed client, who had the habit of coming into the office almost daily and reading the broad tape. Said the representative in further explanation:

> Mr. Mitchell is so bright that he automatically is aware in terms of his own sagacity and his own research of any occurrence in his own situations. I do no research for Mr. Mitchell in that regard, and all my orders from him are unsolicited. . . . Mr. Mitchell has a habit of collecting his funds and placing orders well below the market to purchase securities that he feels may have major value, and does this based upon his own information, waits until the market declines or is severe before making purchases, and puts his orders in well ahead of the time he actually makes the purchase. . . .

Mitchell was "very much impressed" with the April 12 release. He returned to his office and examined his TGS file, then went to *another* broker and ordered a short sale of 400 shares at 40. It was consummated April 17, although at the time of the order TGS was trading at 34 and a fraction. A week later he sold short his remaining 20 shares—asking 45 but actually getting 46¼. The sale of the two blocks of stock resulted in Mitchell's approximately doubling his money. His close and patient watch resulted in another transaction late in the following year, for on December 12, 1965, he sold short 200 shares of Texas Gulf at 80. This time, rather than fall, the market price advanced to 120 and only then began to decline. When it reached 75 nine months later, he made his purchase to cover the short sale, picking up a profit of about $1,000. During the trial it was proved that Dr. Fogarty did not purchase any of the Mitchell stock. Mitchell sued for damages in April, 1967.

In the fourth action Lawrence and Alice Karlson had purchased 100 shares of TGS for 16⅝ in October, 1963, and sold them in December of the same year for 20⅞. Again it was proved that defendant Fogarty did not buy them. Their profit was about $425. It should be noted that the discovery hole was not even drilled until November of that year, and no news release was made until the following spring. The Karlsons also filed their suit in April, 1967. Their attorney, in line with the evidence, conceded that the stock had not been sold to Dr. Fogarty.

The Karlson claim was based solely on the fact that the company and Dr. Fogarty had not made public the results of the first drill hole. But if they *had* done so, no benefit to the Karlsons would have resulted since it is likely that the property could not then have been acquired, the existing mine would not belong to Texas Gulf, and the rise in price of the stock to which plaintiffs pointed would not have occurred. Rule 10b-5, declared TGS counsel, was not intended to establish a scheme of investors' insurance,[17] but such a scheme would be established if the plaintiffs recovered because their view of the corporate prospects was not borne out. So, of course, could any seller of Texas Gulf stock during the period before the news was made public then recover, and in the case of TGS this would include sellers of more than three million shares.

All of the plaintiffs in the Salt Lake actions based their claims for damages on the allegation that, at the time they sold their stock, it was worth $160 a share, but this was a price that had been reached over four years of subsequent company activity and was due to many factors, not to the Kidd mine alone. The stock was worth, of course, what they received in the market, and in each case they had profited. In all, the plaintiffs in these four actions bought and sold 2,200 shares of stock in lots ranging from 100 to

[17] See Chapter 6, Note 12, p. 150, *List v. Fashion Park Inc.*

1,000, and on their total investment of approximately $32,125 they had shown a profit of approximately $46,775.

Since many more individuals were involved than in Utah, the New York stockholder actions did not present such sharp profiles, but this was about the only difference that was discernible. An analysis of the various complaints attached to the moving papers disclosed that most of the plaintiffs suffered no economic loss whatsoever, having sold at a profit above the original purchase price of their shares. The April 12 news release again served as a dividing line—between those who sold their stock before (or sold afterwards but did not claim their sales were in reliance on the news release), and those who sold afterwards and now asserted that the release was false and misleading. The whole group presented various legal theories—violation of the Securities Exchange Act, common law fraud, violation of a fiduciary duty owed by the defendants, and even misrepresentations in proxy statements and annual reports. Whatever the theories, the basic claim appeared to be that there was some kind of conspiracy among the defendants to suppress information regarding the Timmins drilling in order that they might profit unlawfully through stock purchases.

Again, as in the Utah cases, the essential facts were not in dispute, having been litigated in the original trial, the appeal, and in Utah, with extensive briefing all around by all parties. It seemed fair to state, declared TGS counsel Marden, that few controversies had undergone such thorough factual exploration. He quickly pointed out, in his motion for summary judgment, that while the appellate court may have differed with the lower court in the standards used in judging the April 12 release, it did not disturb the findings concerning its motivating purpose. In fact, thanks to the "fractured opinion" delivered by the Second Circuit judges, *at least a majority* had agreed that no liability in damages should attach to mere negligent preparation, even if negligence were a fact. It was a neat trick in that it forged a rather unfavorable result from the appeal into a useful weapon for the later proceeding. And not once had the Second Circuit majority, he pointed out, characterized the individual defendants' purchases as a fraud or deceit upon *any person*.

It was clearly impossible, Marden argued, to determine any individual or group of individuals in whom the supposed cause of action was created.

Is it those who sold on the day an insider purchased, or
merely the same year? . . . There is no way of answering this question on any logical basis. Judging from the complaints thus far
filed herein, plaintiffs . . . seem to believe that an unlawful
purchase creates a cause of action in all who sold shares during
the period when the material information—in its broadest definition—was undisclosed. The period in the instant case lasted some
five months during the course of which over 2,637,300 shares were
traded on the New York Stock Exchange. Plaintiffs apparently
contend that a defendant who purchased 100 shares at any time
during this period should be held liable to each of these thousands
of sellers . . . each plaintiff here attempts to recover on a basis of
an obligation owed only to society.

The individual defendants in these actions, it was pointed out,
had made no representations to anyone. No seller had made his
decision to sell because of any act of the individual defendants, and
no seller received less because of the purchases of the individual
defendants. In fact, as a former SEC Commissioner had observed,
purchases by the individual defendants, far from causing loss, were
if anything beneficial to the plaintiffs.[18] This had already been
noted by other commentators as well.[19] Since all investors share
the risk that they may act before news is announced, defendants'
purchases here did nothing to increase this risk.

Claims under Section 9 and under other sections of the Securities Exchange Act must fail, the motion argued, because they were
palpably frivolous, because they did not apply, and no liability for
common law fraud arose from the April 12 release because there
would have to be proved "representation of a material existing fact,
falsity, *scienter,* deception and injury," under a leading New York
case.[20]

Again, there was no insurance policy protecting the plaintiffs
against the normal risk all investors must share—the risk that one's
estimation of market movement will turn out to be wrong. "Sound
policy," Justice Oliver Wendell Holmes had declared in 1881, "lets
losses lie where they fall, except where a special reason can be
shown for interference." [21]

[18] J. Whitney: "Section 10b-5: From Cady, Roberts to Texas Gulf: Matters of Disclosure," *21 Bus. Law. 193, 201 (1965).*
[19] *74 Yale Law Journal 658 (1965).*
[20] *Reno v. Bull, 226 N.Y. 546, 124 N.E. 144, 145 (1919).*
[21] Oliver Wendell Holmes: *The Common Law,* Little, Brown, Boston
(1946), p. 50.

On October 17, 1969, giving counsel only two days' notice after a 17-month consideration of the case, Judge Ritter found against TGS in three of the four Utah actions. Whether so intended or not, the memorandum decision exposed the full implications of the Court of Appeals' disposal of the "in connection with" language of 10b-5. Total damages awarded were not large, but they were a grim forewarning to what might happen in hundreds of similar actions. Damages were computed on the basis of the difference between the funds received in the sales and the average high of a 20-day trading period after April 16—amounting to $50.75 per share. The award to Reynolds was $8,562.25; to Mitchell, $4,390; to the Stouts, $8,750. The fourth suit was rejected because plaintiffs sold long before the news release of April 12 appeared. Judge Ritter found the release—in one case—"deceptive, misleading, and inaccurate," and in another "false, misleading, deceptive, and fraudulent; it contained misstatements of material facts with respect to the progress of the drilling." Both 10(b) and 10b-5 had been violated, he said.

Incidentally, on appeal, the Tenth Circuit held that persons who sold their TGS shares after April 20, 1964, more than four days after the issuance of the second press release, could not claim that they relied upon the first "misleading" release in selling their shares. A "reasonable investor" was then aware, and persons who sold thereafter were not truly diligent and could not recover under Rule 10b-5. The appellate court affirmed the determination that the first release was misleading, but overturned an award of damages to an investor who sold his shares five days after the corrective release was issued. Nine days was, in this instance, the reasonable time within which an investor would have made an intelligent investment decision.[22]

Whatever the federal courts might decide was the plaintiffs' due as a matter of fact and law, they could hardly diminish the public profiles of these one-time stockholders seeking damages from the corporation of which they had been a part. There was food for thought at this round table for all who cared to sit down to it.

[22] Fed. Sec. Law Reports No. 367, May 6, 1971.

# 9
# Aftermath:
# Bystanders, Experts,
# and Targets

I

**A**UGUST closed very warm indeed after
the decision in the Texas Gulf case was handed down by the Court
of Appeals, although the temperature was noticeably higher in jour-
nalistic circles than it was among other corporations and the den-
izens of the marketplace itself. The latter were admittedly confused
and somewhat slower to react despite some clarion calls from the
press. The sharpest and most anguished notes issued first from
*Barron's* who devoted eight columns to the matter, taking their
headline of "Perpetual Jeopardy" from Judge Moore's scathing dissent and—just in case the readers should be in doubt—labeled their
treatment "An Angry Note On The Texas Gulf Sulphur Case." It was
that.[1]

A quick round-up by Dow Jones had in fact revealed little
concern among those corporate executives who were *not* in the
mining business and even among some security analysts, one of
whom had said, "We don't live on tips. I don't think it's really going
to hurt us in our work." To which the editors of *Barron's* had para-
phrased Kipling to reply that, "If you can keep your head when all
about you are losing theirs, you probably don't know the score."
They held that the majority opinion had ridden roughshod over
legislative history, legal precedent, simple logic and common sense

[1] *Barron's*, August 19, 1968.

213

in reaching its conclusions, and declared that the consequences to the defendants, the financial community, and the business world were frightening to contemplate if this "shoddy decision" were to stand. The closing blast:

> This is not regulation—it is bureaucracy run wild. For decades Wall Street and Main Street alike have clung to the delusion that the SEC was designed to protect investors. The Texas Gulf Sulphur case should forever shatter that myth. At each fresh aggrandizement of the agency's power, each assault on personal freedom, brokers and businessmen have beat a retreat under the ignoble standard, "We can live with it." Gentlemen, can you live with the police state?

Less angry, a long editorial treatment in the *Wall Street Journal* noted that the business community might seem a little unsure of what had happened, but the potential impact of the court's ruling was nevertheless tremendous. "It is sure going to cut down on conversations around corporate water coolers. . . . And common sense obviously is not served by a court decision that seems written to foster indecision and confusion." [2]

Most of the immediate comment picked for its targets the plight of the company insider and the puzzle of how to handle inside information. The case was by no means closed, said *The Magazine of Wall Street*. "TGS will no doubt fight all the way to the Supreme Court and every company officer and official in the country will be in its corner—at least, in spirit, even if most probably would not want to commit themselves publicly." [3]

Joining this chorus, *Business Week* observed editorially that not only would the strictures of the decision put a corporate official in jeopardy every time he bought or sold stock in his own company, but would apply every time he talked shop with a friend, gave information to a security analyst, or put out a news release. Strictly enforced, they could make free dissemination of information impossible. "The TGS case takes a basically admirable principle—the prevention of deceit—and carries it to a point of absurdity. If the Supreme Court does not reverse it, then Congress will have to reopen the whole question and put some reasonable limits on the open-ended power that the SEC has acquired." [4]

[2] *Wall Street Journal*, "Confusion on the Inside," August 21, 1968.
[3] *The Magazine of Wall Street*, August 31, 1968.
[4] *Business Week*, August 31, 1968.

While *The New York Times* and *Newsweek* both looked hopefully toward the Supreme Court, and Prentice-Hall's *Corporate Report Bulletin* zeroed in on the plight of corporate directors under
the new rules, the growing public relations trade press envisioned
possible disaster for *their* practitioners. The *PR Reporter*, foreseeing
the problems involved in second-guessing both the investors and
the future, and wondering what to do about security analysts,
guessed that some of the financial public relations specialists wished
they had never entered the field, while *Public Relations News* flatly
announced that if the decisions were permitted to stand, "The
practice of financial public relations is threatened with extinction." [5]
The latter continued:

> With dissemination of information subject to indeterminable
> risk, with releases necessarily written by lawyers . . . , with man-
> agement apprehensive about releasing any but cut-and-dried infor-
> mation, with contacts with the financial community to be avoided
> rather than welcomed, and with corporate officials in danger of
> being accused of manipulative practices . . . where could such
> a PR professional sell his services? . . . . [He] would have to re-
> frain from advising use of product publicity; it might expose a
> client company to the accusation that the publicity had been de-
> signed to stimulate higher prices for its securities.

Only *Jack O'Dwyer's Newsletter* managed to find a bright spot
in this special field: the appeals decision had finally given some
recognition to the professional status of the public relations business because, for the first time, a judge wrote that a business executive had exercised good judgment in consulting *both* a lawyer and
a PR man.[6]

There were early evidences of the "we can live with it" school
surfacing within a month or so, as well as other evidence of altered practices. Professional counseling agencies inevitably find it
easier to adjust to new situations (in behalf of their clients) since
the test for such counsel is at least one step removed from their
own chestnuts, whereas the client corporations can be excused for
finding the advice a little glib from their own position nearer the fire.

David Cates, an executive of Loeb, Rhoades and Company,
took pains to point out that banking was different, for example,

<hr>

[5] *PR Reporter*, Vol. XI, No. 34, Meriden, N.H., August 26, 1968, and *Public Relations News*, Vol. XXIV, No. 35, August 26, 1968.
[6] *Jack O'Dwyer's Newsletter*, Vol. 1, No. 7, August 21, 1968.

since it enjoyed "complex stability." A bank was unlikely to find itself mired in the mud of materially unusual business developments, as compared with a mining company, unless it discovered oil under its main office.

> To put it another way, the earnings process in banking—unlike mining—depends on a lengthy "laundry list" of rather steady variables, none of which are crucial yet all together add up to earning power. . . . In sum, banking is very rarely an industry of surprises. On the contrary, its developments tend to be both gradual and marginal. From an able analyst's standpoint, therefore, conversations with a bank official differ profoundly from talks with companies whose lifeblood of news is more apt to be "material." [7]

On the question of whether the TGS decision was a victory for the "little guy," the writer for *Finance* thought it not likely, and for his classical reference turned to Edmund Burke's reflections on the French Revolution. Burke had observed that the first right of every man in civilized society was the right to be protected against the consequences of his own ignorance. The modern problem, said this journal, "is to beware turning the protection into a barrier against the free flow of information—and the free exercise of sensitive discretionary duties." [8]

The annual meeting of the Investment Bankers Association of America, in Miami in December, spent a lot of time kicking around the subject of disclosure in connection with both the *Texas Gulf* and the *Merrill Lynch* cases. In an informal talk to the investment bankers, Chairman Cohen of the SEC had summarized the Commission's position:

"We want to see as much information as possible made available on a nondiscriminatory basis. If people are to be persuaded that the security markets are the place to put their savings, there ought to be the general recognition that markets are fair. What we are discussing here are elementary principles of ethics." But when asked about guidelines from the Commission, he compared the establishment of such black-and-white rules to the formulation of a definition of fraud for legal purposes. "All you wind up doing is putting a premium on some crook's ingenuity."

[7] David C. Cates: "Texas Gulf Sulphur Decision Holds Message on Disclosure for Banks," *American Banker*, September 30, 1968.
[8] Frank Adduci Jr., in *Finance*, October, 1968.

One of the very large mutual fund operators at this meeting posed this question to which he could find no answer under the current decisions: his firm did not seek inside information and seldom got it, but the problem now was what to do with it when they *did* get it. And Al Altwegg, business editor of the Dallas *Morning News*, had an answer for Cohen:

> . . . the SEC should not make new rules by accusation and settlement, creating the rules by precedent. If new rules are needed, they should be proposed to Congress, argued fully, and then set down as law. It is really wrong for the SEC to be both policeman and judge, both player and referee simultaneously. It is totally intolerable for it to be all that and for it also to write the rules— and then say they are too complex to reveal.[9]

Some side effects of the new disclosure "rules" were observed with concern by New York financial writers. Merger talks were now consisting of fast "announcement-withdrawal" techniques which only bewildered Wall Street observers.[10] Meanwhile financial analysts' meetings were growing more imaginative but less informative. When one company showed a color film of a giant squid fighting an octopus, another presented a tape of its funniest radio commercials, and still another showed a 20-minute movie disclosing only its management philosophy, one brokerage house suggested that it might boycott future meetings.[11]

## II

The aftermath of the Second Circuit's opinion, reflected rather quickly in press comments, began a little later to spill over into meetings of the concerned. At the Miami Beach meeting of the investment bankers in December, Chairman Cohen of the SEC had been appearing on a panel built around the subject of the uses and dangers of inside information, and was repeatedly pressed by his worried audience. He responded bluntly that, "I think Wall Street can and will get along without a stacked deck." The chairman had apparently been reading a *New Yorker* article

[9] Dallas *Morning News*, December 7, 1968.
[10] "Market Place" by Robert Metz, *The New York Times*, December 10, 1968.
[11] *Wall Street Journal*, December 19, 1968.

on the subject by John Brooks, which appeared in the November 9 issue. Here Brooks, a business writer whose slant was seldom bent in the direction of the business community, three times employed the expression "stacked deck." "What we are discussing here is an elementary principle of ethics," said Cohen. "There is nothing wrong in this situation that should inhibit an honest man. Really, there isn't anything complicated or anything very new about it."

The other members of this panel were Bert Goss, chairman of the Hill and Knowlton public relations firm, and S. Hazard Gillespie, the Wall Street lawyer who had represented the late Thomas Lamont in the Texas Gulf action. Goss hardly made history by proposing that "the needs of the public be the key to disclosure policy," while Gillespie reminded the Commission that the courts had urged that they bring "some predictability of certainty to this entire business."

Early in October Cohen had written Joseph Guilfoyle, managing editor of Dow Jones, that the argument in *Texas Gulf* "basically involved the question whether the particular discovery was *material* and whether the mere announcement at the press conference was sufficient (prior to actual publication to the public) to permit insiders to trade. There was no disagreement regarding the basic rule that insiders could not, without public disclosure, trade on the basis of material inside information." If these were in truth the basic considerations, it had to be a fair conclusion for the gallery from the apparent reversal of the fact questions by the Court of Appeals that (1) one hole *does* constitute a mine, and (2) a disclosure to the press did *not* constitute public disclosure. This is what the argument was all about.

At another meeting—a New York City communications seminar at the Association of Stock Exchange Firms—Senator Harrison A. Williams Jr., of New Jersey, chairman of the securities subcommittee of the Senate Committee on Banking and Currency, had observed that "there is very little new in the recent court decisions concerning the Texas Gulf Sulphur case." It was then almost election day, however, and Senator Williams had to cut short his remarks to hurry back to Washington for a vote on the issue of debates between Presidential candidates. One thing that seemed to be new, nevertheless, was the question of the timing of disclosure of news, and this case had seen the first attempt to define it as *sometime after* the information had been released to the press. There were other firsts:

(1) It was the first federal court case in which the SEC had charged violation of 10b-5 by any corporate "insider" who simply purchased his company's stock on a public exchange, making no false representations to anyone.[12]

(2) It was the first case in which it was contended that a press release which later turned out to be highly conservative constituted a manipulative or deceptive device even though the issuers had bought no stock.

(3) It was the first case to hold that the acceptance of stock options, even though they were not exercised, had violated 10b-5.

(4) It was the first 10b-5 case defining "insiders" to include lower level employees down to a $750 a month accountant.

(5) It was the first case to charge violation of 10b-5 by lower level employees because they recommended the company's stock to outsiders.

(6) It was the first court case to threaten outsiders who had allegedly received inside information with violation of the rule, although no charges were brought against such tippees.

(7) It was the first case to charge that employees who bought stock in their company necessarily proved themselves to possess material inside information.

(8) It was the first case to extend, through the majority opinion, the SEC's own definition of a "reasonable investor" to include speculators.

There may have been developing some almost imperceptible cracks in the SEC ranks. At a public relations counsellors' session in November, Commissioner Richard B. Smith's definition of material information seemed quite similar to that of Judge Bonsal, and subsequently, in mid-March in Minneapolis, at another public relations practitioners' session, Commissioner Smith would put himself "sympathetically" on the side of some SEC critics who had demanded federal guidelines.[13] By this time Chairman Cohen had resigned, and Minneapolis in March probably seemed farther from Manhattan than it really was. Smith and the new chairman, Judge Budge, were Republican members of the Commission. Smith said he especially understood the uncertainty and fear of legal liability plaguing directors of many corporations because of the insider trading controversy. Judgment was an important factor, "but I'm not persuaded that some guidelines can't be drawn up."

[12] *Harvard Law Review,* Vol. 82, 1969, p. 941.
[13] *Wall Street Journal,* March 19, 1969.

Right after the turn of the year, however, and before his resignation, Chairman Cohen had accepted an important speaking engagement in Baltimore before the Baltimore Security Analysts Society in an apparent attempt to enunciate and reduce to gospel some of the issues, and to package them more attractively, if still firmly, for his professional public.[14] Much of the talk up to this point, he felt, had been uninformed and emotional. It had suggested that the wells of corporate information would now dry up; that business executives had been effectively silenced by the *TGS* decision; that analysts would have to analyze on the basis of the same information everyone else had; that the Commission was sailing into uncharted seas; and that neither it nor the courts really knew much about the security business. It was time for light to emerge from all of this heat and nonsense, he felt, even though there still might need to be some further discussion. Among the points the chairman stressed were these:

(1) *Texas Gulf* was not a departure from previous precedent but a natural and predictable outgrowth of earlier cases, notably *Cady, Roberts* and *Capital Gains*.

(2) The law is and has been clear. Insiders having material non-public information cannot buy or sell for their own benefit or that of friends and customers until the information has been made public. "Some may disagree on what is or is not material," but once the test has been met, the prohibition is clear, covering any employee who hears of it, and others who may be entrusted with it. Any information is material when importance would be attached to it by an investor in reaching his decisions and when it could be expected to affect materially the market price of the security.

(3) Necessary prior disclosure means publication broad enough to inform the investing public fairly. There may be some argument, Cohen conceded, as to when information becomes sufficiently public and what media meet these tests. Effective dissemination means more than just giving it to the press.

(4) Coming out strongly against sin, he declared that corporate publicity should not be misleading.

(5) The acceptance of stock options falls within the ban on insider trading.

In passing, Chairman Cohen recommended to his audience the

[14] *Federal Securities Law Reports,* No. 240-70, February 5, 1969; pp. 83,415 through 83,421, reports the complete text, delivered January 6, 1969, before the Baltimore Security Analysts Society, Baltimore, Md.

New York Stock Exchange's booklet on "Expanded Policy on Timely Disclosures" and several paragraphs of advice that had been given recently by the exchange president to a session of the Financial Executives Institute. He accompanied his recommendations with a renewed declaration that one of the important reasons for the creation of the Commission was the conviction that public and private interests were best served "when more accurate and continuous information is made available to the public . . . I am confident that the trend for the future is *more* rather than less corporate disclosure."

Although, as Cohen said, the Commission has no wish or intention to act as an after-the-fact rewrite man for corporate publicity, he then bent himself to the task of advising how corporate publicity departments should operate, concluding, with not a trace of irony:

"We believe it is inconsistent with the public and investor interests to develop rules or attitudes which would inhibit reliable and useful publicity." Then, as if this might appear too formal a statement, he added: "I suppose that a new legal decision, no matter how venerable its precedents, is often like a new pair of shoes. No matter how long we have been wearing shoes, a new pair may be a little stiff at first. But leather is flexible. Eventually the shoes are broken in and conform to our feet, and we become used to the feel of a slightly different shoe. Then the shoes feel as comfortable as though we had always worn them. I suggest that decisions in *Glen Alden*,[15] *Texas Gulf*, and *Merrill Lynch* afford equal flexibility, and that we will find them equally comfortable."

While nothing was said about it in the press, presumably the audience of analysts arose and hobbled out in their new shoes. The assurances of the chairman apparently did not reach or satisfy, among others, the Banking Law Institute, which in April in New York held a two-day ($135 fee, fully tax-deductible) session devoted to new truth-in-lending legislation, to one-bank holding companies, and to "Texas Gulf Sulphur: Institutions and Inside Information." It was one of many.

[15] *SEC v. Glen Alden Corp.*, see (S.D.N.Y.) Litigation Release No. 480 (August 8, 1968).

The Commission charged that the company had provided certain institutional investors, who were potential purchasers of Glen Alden shares, with important corporate information, including five-year projections, not disclosed to the general public. Without admitting the allegations of the complaint, Glen Alden consented to entry of a permanent injunction prohibiting this practice.

### III

Throughout most of the professional commentaries—even the briefest ones—the writers seemed not content just to report the holdings of the Second Circuit majority. They continued to draw sharp comparisons with the lower court opinion and to quote at considerable length Judge Moore's dissent. The latter, it must be admitted, was very quotable, even though it might not represent the law. The editors of the Prentice-Hall *Corporation Report Bulletin* were quick to spot Judge Friendly's "frightening consequences" language a week after the decision came down and found such questions as the following were left unanswered for corporations, analysts, brokers, and individuals:

1. Must you tell your stockholders about *every* development that comes to your attention? Even say, when a new invention is offered you that, if successful, may increase the value of your company's stock?
2. How do you make the announcement? Newspaper release? Dow Jones announcement? Letters to your stockholders?
3. Suppose you get a report of a new development, but you don't have time to read it. Are you still liable?
4. Can you defend your failure to disclose because it would mean letting your competitors in on an important development?
5. To what extent must you disclose even though you don't trade in your company's stock?
6. If you tell security analysts and not your stockholders, and the analysts trade, are they tippees? If you then trade, are you using inside information?
7. Must you now make your press releases read like prospectuses?

The last word to subscribers from this source was that the position of insiders was "damned if you do, damned if you don't." [16]

"In the *Texas Gulf Sulphur* litigation, the SEC appears to be seeking to bring the existing securities market into the closest possible conformity with a perfectly competitive model in which all investors have equal access to relevant information," said the prestigious *Harvard Law Review*. Basing its treatment of the TGS officers and employees on this duty, derived from *Cady, Roberts,* to disclose material inside information or refrain from trading, "the

[16] *Corporation Report Bulletin,* Prentice-Hall Inc., Vol. XXXVIII, No. 11, August 21, 1968.

Second Circuit took major steps toward implementing the competitive norms the SEC seeks to establish." [17] The case review noted the "ominous dictum" as to tippees, and concluded that if this is followed, decisions on where the loss will fall in private suits would normally be dictated by the plaintiffs. Among the critical comments of the Harvard writers were these:

(1) The court's definition of what information must be disclosed was less satisfactory than its treatment of who must disclose; the holding—all information which *might* affect the value of the stock—was too inclusive and "could inundate the market with information of doubtful utility or . . . drastically reduce insider trading apart from that on regular buying plans." The focus should be on *price*, not value, e.g., an intermediate standard specifying probability or substantial effect on prices would be more helpful.

(2) Instead of sending the case back for findings under its new test, the court had evaluated the facts itself and found the information on the first drill core material. Here it relied heavily on the defendants' purchases—"the act, it seems, outlaws itself." Such an evidentiary practice is dangerous, and the court implicitly contradicted its own concession that greater familiarity with a company's operations does not always foreclose an insider from trading in its stock. The court's approach, said the writers, would treat transactions based on expertise no differently from those based on particular information.

(3) The SEC had argued that there was a beneficial deterrent effect in vagueness as to the time necessary for disclosure; it would be better to adopt a rule based on a minimum waiting period with room for the courts to find violations after the minimum. (Chairman Cohen had said, "A certain amount of uncertainty, of lack of rules, means that people have to continually examine their own positions and make their own decisions about whether what they want to do is legal. If, in the insider area, that means that businessmen decide *not* to buy in borderline cases, I have to think that's all to the good." [18])

(4) When the majority and the dissenters *both* used legislative history to develop their points over the "in connection with" language, the result was a "singularly fruitless argument."

Coming up to forecasting, the Harvard writers found "low

[17] *Harvard Law Review*, Vol. 82, pp. 938–95; 1969.
[18] Carol J. Loomis: "Where Manny Cohen is Leading the SEC," *Fortune*, December, 1966.

probability" that an injunction would issue against the company. It thought it most unlikely, furthermore, under present federal law, in the absence of securities transactions of its own, that a corporation could in any way be held liable for complete nondisclosure, except for specific matters required by statute.

> The most likely result of damages for negligence in disclosure would be dissemination to the public of a smaller volume of information of somewhat greater accuracy and a shift of losses suffered by those who were misled to the innocent stockholders who had not traded. The stockholders, indeed, would be hurt coming and going; if the corporation were held liable for negligent misrepresentation they would bear the loss, and if it were frightened into silence they would be deprived of information from which they might have benefited. And though outsiders would be less often misled, they would have more often to act in ignorance.

The monumental impact of the *Texas Gulf* decision, in the eyes of the editors of the *St. John's Law Review,* lay not only in its unorthodox application of Rule 10b-5, but in the fact that it reached the Court of Appeals, since previous such actions had been disposed of primarily on the pleadings, or had gone no further than administrative or district court levels. *Cady, Roberts,* for example, which had taken up so much of the stage so far and had been leaned on so heavily, never got to court. As a result, there had been a conspicuous absence of what the writers termed "judicial gloss" concerning the rule, and more questions had been raised than answered.[19] Professor Bromberg had said, a year before, "The typical 10b-5 'victory' is only a holding that a cause of action has been stated, good enough to withstand a motion to dismiss." [20] The St. John's comment continues:

> . . . the facts of the *Texas Gulf Sulphur* case are at once so extraordinary, and the disclosure rules laid down by the majority so broadly phrased, that the decision may very well have created more problems than it has purportedly solved. . . . However, the broad sweep attributed by the court to a 10b-5 fraud evidences an intention not only to crystallize existing views as to the scope of the rule, but to extend its reach to heretofore unregulated and unquestioned activities. In doing so, the court may very well have

[19] *St. John's Law Review,* Vol. 43 (1969), pp. 425–55.
[20] A. Bromberg: *Securities Law: Fraud—SEC Rule 10b-5 Sec. 1.3(2)* at 10 (1968).

imposed upon corporate insiders insurmountable burdens of compliance.

This case had provided SEC with the first substantial judicial confirmation of *Cady, Roberts*, it was pointed out. The court did not categorize insiders, but relied upon a touchstone of information-yielding relationships. Although it may have been unwitting, the law review writer here chanced upon a new aspect. Since trading on the part of a tippee lies at the crux of the tipping violation—else the "in connection with" requirement would not be satisfied—two classes would seem to be set up: outside tippees have to trade to establish a violation but insiders do not. The writer suggests that tipping should not be punished if done for a legitimate corporate purpose, to an underwriter, attorney, or public relations counsel. In that case, probably no one would call it tipping.

As an example of how 10b-5 prompts all kinds of surprises, this law review pointed to a Texas case of recent vintage in which the question arose as to whether a tippee (obviously indexed under *dog-in-manger* or *good Samaritan*) could maintain a fraud action against an insider for transmission of false and misleading information.[21] Here the plaintiff had relied upon confidential information provided by the company president, which turned out to be wrong, and had sold his stock at a loss. The court did not think this was a function of 10b-5, a refreshing and startling conclusion in itself in 1968, and held alternately that the doctrine of *pari delicto* would be a valid defense to any such suit.

As with other writers, the Second Circuit's jousting with materiality intrigued the *St. John's Law Review*. Noting that the decision shifted emphasis from the actual investor to the "reasonable man," it highlighted the sharp distinctions between the district and appellate court tests—Bonsal used the date of 7 P.M., April 9, 1964, as a dividing line, while Waterman found materiality as of November 12 of the preceding year, and this difference affected the liability of most of the defendants. "Thus while both courts apparently attempted to apply the standard of reasonableness they arrived at apparently irreconcilable conclusions." The circuit court, it was felt, had been improperly guided by hindsight. As for the future, it appeared that 10b-5, after *TGS*, would also be in the picture when it came to dividend reductions, planned public or private offerings,

[21] *Kuehnert v. Texstar Corp.*, CCH Fed. Sec. L. Rep. Sec. 92,282 at 97,347 (*S.D. Tex. Feb. 27, 1968*).

acquisition programs, preliminary merger negotiations, and proposed tender offers. Some of these would be "problematical"—Chairman Cohen's counsel of calmness notwithstanding.

Any reasonable selection of quotable authorities in the aftermath of the *Texas Gulf* decision would have to include Professor
Alan Bromberg, of Southern Methodist University, who began by
observing that the Second Circuit has jurisdiction over the nation's
financial center and over the federal law which is coming increasingly to be *the* law for corporations as well as securities markets.
In *TGS*, which he dubbed the most important case in a year of landmark corporate and securities decisions, he found hints and remarks
which could be the seeds of more new law. Although the majority
opinion might end in oblivion if the Supreme Court granted review,
"it now stands as a current and crucial statement, of a kind the
Supreme Court itself would probably write." [22]

More significant than any particular holding, said Professor
Bromberg, is the policy which underpins them all. "It is an egalitarian idea . . . that all investors 'shall have relatively equal access
to material information' " and there had been, he found, surprisingly
little effort to justify this general statement of policy in terms of
either economics or history. The court did not come to grips with
the arguments of critics such as Henry Manne [23] and David Ruder [24]
and very likely the court felt that equality was its own excuse for
being. "What the majority was doing was continuing an already
advanced process of telescoping the policies and coverage of a number of different securities law provisions into a general antifraud
provision, 10b-5."

The court was not clear, on the stock options, as to why ratification after disclosure failed to cure the violation, in Bromberg's
opinion, but he guessed the court considered it an offense against
the investing public—cheap stock—rather than against the company. It will be remembered that an earlier observer in this chronicle
had noted that lawyers, judges, and government administrators don't
like options because they never get any.

Bromberg branded the case as a fountain of new law on what
information is material, but said not all of it was consistent. The
result of expanding and stretching "seems to set a very low threshold

[22] Alan R. Bromberg: "Corporate Information: Texas Gulf Sulphur and
its Implications," *Southwestern Law Journal*, Vol. 22 (1968), pp. 731–54.
[23] See note, Chapter 5, p. 93.
[24] David Ruder: "Corporate Disclosures Required by the Federal Securities Laws: the Codification Implications of Texas Gulf Sulphur," 61 *Northwestern University Law Review* 872 (1967).

of materiality." He was bearish on the reasonable investor test when compared to one of market impact. "The most important function of the test of materiality in this context is not the determination of violation or liability in the relatively few cases which will come to court. It is the setting of a standard which business men (properly advised) can use in determining when they may trade securities of their companies in the thousands or millions of cases in which they have some information not known to the public. A test of substantial market impact better fulfills this function."

And what if the media does not carry the news in the mechanics of necessary disclosure? This would be a distinct possibility for smaller companies and smaller transactions. He noted that Dow Jones seems to have a rule of thumb that acquisitions involving less than $3 million will not be reported on the broad tape or in the newspaper. Bromberg's final thoughts:

(1) On underwriting, "While the SEC seems confident that the duty (under 10b-5) not to use material inside information takes priority over duties to individual customers, it remains to be seen whether a court, particularly a state court, would accept this proposition in a private action by a beneficiary against the fiduciary." His practical advice is to bottle up the underwriting department, or withdraw from the market in the company's securities.

(2) The *TGS* decision will probably stop most private meetings between companies and analysts or institutions, or make them harmless, and here he cites the *Glen Alden* case.

(3) Brokers on boards of directors are vulnerable and should probably forego the business.

"*TGS* takes antifraud law significantly farther along the paths traced in recent years," he concluded, "toward negligence and away from intentional conduct, toward misleading information and away from material fact, toward equalization of access to market rewards, and toward greater burdens for the corporate and financial community. Far from a break with the recent past, *TGS* is very much a piece with it. But the recent past is so unlike the beginning as to be almost unrecognizable. So grows the common law."

## IV

Impressions to the contrary, time seldom stands still in the courts of law. It sometimes appears to, as when the bleak drill holes in Kidd Township were surrounded by lawyers and experts in 1964 and then successively became the cynosure of attention as part of a number of investigations, hearings, trials and appeals. Such a stop-motion effect is illusory, of course, as the Kidd Creek Mine went on its way into a full and gratifying production while the briefs were being shuffled hundreds of miles away. By the same token, other things were happening to other people, in courts of law, while *Texas Gulf* lived on its fretful life in argument and print. Some of the paths were due to cross, or at least would run for a time side by side. A few other cases, coming to decision in the last days of the 'sixties, deserve some attention.

One of them was an action brought by the SEC against Great American Industries, some of its officers, and others, and the legal action, at least, took place in the same theater and involved many of the same characters and props.[25] For more than one reason there was brimstone in the air, because two of the three properties about which this litigation centered were sulphur properties, and there was the improbable though unimportant coincidence that one of the news releases complained about was issued on April 12, although two years after its notorious forebear in the TGS case.

The SEC began this action in June, 1966, while the TGS trial was proceeding in district court, seeking a permanent injunction against Great American Industries, certain officers and directors, and others. The chairman and president of the company was a well-known corporate executive, Walter S. Mack. The Commission charged violations of 10b-5, among other things, with respect to certain press releases and reports. Judge Sylvester Ryan, in district court, denied the SEC motion, finding no showing of fraud or deceit "in connection with" the purchase or sale of any securities. He declared that neither the releases nor the reports were false and misleading. The Commission's appeal was argued in March, 1967, and one year and nine months later the Second Circuit reversed as much of the lower court's order as had declined to issue a preliminary injunction. The appellate court now ordered such an injunction— although stating in passing that the degree of the defendants' knowledge was a critical issue and that the record was incomplete and disorganized. As the majority opinion stated, "Since certain conclusions supporting the decision of the majority to affirm ran counter to the majority position in *TGS*, then under advisement, this case was also heard *in banc*." Finally, to complete the rather haunting resemblance to another performance, Judge Moore produced

[25] *SEC v Great American Industries Inc.*, et al. 259 F. Supp. 99.

another explosive dissent attacking the methods of the Commission.

For the purpose of this report the facts in the GAI matter have no great pertinence, but the *connections* are of interest. The company was one of the early conglomerates which, in the colorful phrasing of Judge Friendly, had manufactured rubber goods, soft drinks, and cookies. Having accumulated a tax loss which could be applied against new ventures, it was seeking to diversify, and the subject of this action was three mining undertakings in California, Nevada, and Arizona. The price of GAI stock, which had not exceeded $2 a share in the year or so before 1966, went as high as 14⅝ after the announcement of the first mining venture, while its average daily trading went from 8,500 shares to 185,000. The Commission, which had a sharp nose for such variations, suspended trading not once but twice.

In its complaint, the SEC charged that a series of press releases and reports were either untrue or that they omitted material facts; also that a very large part of the consideration paid for one of the properties went not to the owners but to *intermediaries,* and this had not been publicly disclosed. The point was made repeatedly in the later majority opinion that the payments were not in cash but in stock, which somehow seemed to make all the difference.

In sort of an early distraction to its main holding, the Court of Appeals criticized the practice of "private conferences" such as those which led up to this action, even though all parties may have agreed to them. There had been offered short and long affidavits and excerpts from releases, and not all of the relevant documents had been annexed. Judge Ryan, below, had complained more than once during the trial, and now Appeals said it was handicapped by this disorganized record, although obviously not so severely as to prevent the reversal. "We . . . further place the Commission on notice," said Judge Friendly crossly, "that even when exceptional circumstances may warrant dispensing with an evidentiary hearing on a motion for a temporary injunction or the defendants may agree to that course, the district courts are not to accept the kind of moving affidavit that was offered here; the Commission has sufficient facilities to enable it to present documents in full text." With this out of the way, the majority then held that deficiencies in the releases and reports were not merely negligent but "something more." It said that reasonable traders would be influenced by the knowledge that the sellers of a mining property were willing to pay two-thirds of the price to persons who had produced a buyer, and such knowledge would be material even if the mine later turned out to be a bargain.

The concurrences were provocative. Judge Waterman gladdened the hearts of the SEC by declaring that, "In adjudicating the Commission's regulatory efforts in this area, we must, of course, move on a case-by-case basis, and with care, as in [TGS], but with the Congressional mandate to protect investors always in mind." Judge Kaufman added a caveat: "Those who buy or sell securities may no longer assume that the unmended fences of common law fraud will remain the outer limits of liability under Rule 10b-5." His basic test was that the property was not sold for cash but for securities, and fraud limits under the securities law are not identical with those of common law deceit. Judge Hays wanted to formulate a broader basis for liability—the corporate officers should have known about the finders' fees, and the finders had the duty to tell the purchasers how large they were.

But were the majority opinion to come before the SEC for review, declared Judge Moore with considerable irony, in introducing his dissent, that agency could justifiably condemn its factual statements and omissions of material facts in line with its own rules and regulations. "Officers and directors of corporations are charged primarily with corporate management. If they so mismanage the corporation that damage results to it, the law provides adequate remedies. Congress has not as yet vested in the Commission general supervision over corporations and the business judgments exercised by their officers in conducting their affairs."

Coming to the injunction, Judge Moore accused the majority of reaching "the apogee of misuse, in my opinion, of injunctive power and thereby deprive the defendants of normal rights to say nothing of their constitutional rights. They are placed under a 'temporary' injunction. Temporary until when? Without a date it can be perpetual. Injunction against what? Against violating the law with respect to stating facts or omitting to state facts regarding securities transactions. What facts or omissions? Such facts or omissions as the SEC in its unrestricted (subject of course to court review) judgment may at some future date so determine in the light of hindsight."

The peroration surpassed that in the *TGS* case:

The SEC has advanced "1984" by at least 15 years and casts the ominous shadow of Big Brother over the desk of every executive and over the tables around which directors gather. In a day and age when unreasonable seizures and invasions of privacy give the courts great concern, is it not anomalous that the SEC seeks to pry into the use to which a seller intends to put his sales proceeds? It makes little difference whether it be stock or cash. Is the SEC to have regulatory powers over such use? If so, they should have the power to subpoena every seller to inquire into the intended use of the proceeds. . . . How does such an attitude by an administrative agency differ from that of an agency of a totalitarian dictatorship? . . . . Power to protect—here in theory to protect investors—can so easily be turned into power to oppress. The Congress has not chosen to give the Commission this power— it has been assumed by the Commission. The Commission, in turn, without any showing of threatened danger in the future (in fact, the only transactions involved have been terminated) uses the extraordinary remedy of injunction to place a company, its officers and even individuals unrelated thereto under a sword of Damocles, the thread of which can be cut at any time according to the whim and caprice of agents of the Commission. . . . Even a statement to stockholders and the public that the company hopes to do well in 1969 is fraught with danger if these hopes are not realized. And, needless to say, a prediction that 1969 is likely to be a poor year must obviously be a fraudulent scheme to depress the stock. . . . In short, the Commission would have corporations and their executives march in lock step with the Commission in whatever cadence the Commission sets after the march has begun and subject to change at the Commission's exclusive calling.

The petition for certiorari to the Supreme Court in the *GAI* case held that the appellate decision went far beyond *TGS*, where the "in connection with" words were, in effect, read out of the statute. Here there was no hearing, no trading by defendants, no showing that petitioners did not reasonably believe the publicity to be truthful and complete, but the trial court nevertheless was reversed and an injunction granted because of the "something more." In *TGS* exposure came from allegedly being too pessimistic; here it resulted from not being pessimistic enough. Counsel observed that litigation under 10b-5 at this time represented about a third of all current cases, public and private, brought under the securities statutes.

On May 26, 1969, the Supreme Court declined to interfere, leaving the rule of the case in effect. The next day Mack, now 73 years old, resigned as officer and director of GAI at the annual meeting, as he said he would. He also said the merits of the case had not been tried, obviously putting his faith in the future grind of the law.

What has generally been called the case of Heit against Weitzen, although it involved a number of other parties, was also a part of the Texas Gulf aftermath or context, mainly because it concerned the "in connection with the purchase or sale of securities" wording in the 10b-5 cases, and also because it went before the same appellate court, although the separate actions had originated in the Eastern District of New York. Here plaintiffs Heit, Volk, and Howard had each purchased securities of the defendant, Belock Instrument Corporation, a New York manufacturer of precision instruments, and their complaints arose from their claim that the company's assets and earnings had been overstated in various reports and financial statements; also that the management knew of the alleged overstatements. The district court had consolidated two of the actions and dismissed all of the complaints for legal insufficiency.[26] On October 3, 1968, in the light of *TGS*, the Court of Appeals reversed, remanded, and rendered a single opinion, with Judge Moore again dissenting. Defendant Weitzen was a Belock director; as for the other defendants, Walter Tyminski had been the company president, and Jack Silverstein and Marvin Levy had been vice presidents of finance and operations, respectively. Still other defendants named in one of the actions were the Belock auditors, Lybrand, Ross Bros., & Montgomery, and the firm of Carl M. Loeb, Rhoades & Co., who were alleged to own substantial amounts of the company's stock. Any further sorting-out of the parties would only serve to confuse this brief note without enhancing its point. When the Supreme Court was petitioned for certiorari, it invited the Solicitor-General, Erwin M. Griswold, to file a brief, which he did.

Back in 1965, the Belock company had suffered misfortunes. Most of its business had been with the government, and in June its auditors had confirmed the existence of irregularities concerning the distribution of costs for government contracts. This was reported prominently by the New York press, and the company was under investigation by the Department of Justice. The SEC suspended trading, and in August the grand jury in the Eastern District returned a 41-count indictment against the president, comptroller,

[26] The *Heit* and *Volk* actions are reported at 260 F. Supp. 598, and the *Howard* action at 262 F. Supp. 643.

and operations vice president. These officers were then suspended by the directors and new management put in. One defendant pleaded guilty to one count and the others were tried, one being found guilty while the other was acquitted.

It was against this rather trying background that the plaintiffs had brought their class actions in June and July of 1965. Parenthetically it is of passing interest to note that one of the plaintiffs had purchased debentures on the very day the New York papers reported the company's difficulties with the government—seemingly curious timing, except that what he purchased at 90 traded later during 1968 as high as 550. Another plaintiff had bought debentures at 111, while the third had purchased stock at 5½ which traded up to 26½ during 1968.

Since no securities transactions by the defendants were involved, the pertinent question presented was whether an allegation of false statements, standing alone, would provide a foundation for action under 10(b) and 10b-5, to plaintiffs who subsequently bought securities in the open market. Although the appeals were argued in November, 1967, the Second Circuit decision was deferred eleven months, until after the *TGS* opinion had been filed, with Judge Medina noting the *Texas Gulf* rule and concluding that the plaintiffs had met the requirements of the "in connection with" clause. The contrast with *TGS* was presented by the fact that the defendants did not trade (whatever else they may have done) and the context here was of an action at law for damages, not one for equitable relief.

The petition to the Supreme Court which followed declared that the practical result of the Second Circuit holding was to "cast into discard" all sections of the securities acts except 10b-5. In the future, presumably, nothing else would be needed. In his brief, the Solicitor-General shrugged off the broader aspects of the petitioners' arguments as they might concern the business and financial world generally. He thought that the factual situation of Belock's affirmatively false figures was the main point, and that this narrowed the case. The petition was denied on May 19, 1969, a week before similar action in the matter of Great American Industries. On the same day the highest court dealt with two other related cases.

The *Banff Oil* case posed the question of whether U.S. securities laws apply to foreign companies with no American operations, but whose securities are listed on a U.S. exchange. It was a derivative suit brought by a Banff stockholder and alleged the use of inside information about the company's major oil discovery in Canada in 1965. The drilling took place in Alberta, and this province had enacted a law allowing oil companies to keep discovery details secret for a year—which would presumably be a defense against the insider charge. In a now familiar pattern, the district court had dismissed the suit, holding that U.S. securities laws did not apply to foreign transactions, but saw it reversed by the Court of Appeals. The Supreme Court left this decision standing.

The Supreme Court did raise its voice in a five-to-three decision, however, in the case of Ben Frank, who had been convicted of contempt and sentenced up to six months in prison for violating an injunction against his sale of certain oil interests without having registered them with the SEC. There had been no jury trial. An Oklahoma federal district court had denied the demand for a trial on Frank's part, convicted him, and suspended sentence and placed him on probation for three years. All of this had been confirmed on appeal. In the Supreme Court's opinion, Justice Thurgood Marshall held that "petty" offenses may be tried without a jury, such as those in contempt cases where the law prescribed a prison sentence of up to six months. In dissent, Chief Justice Warren and Justices Black and Douglas asserted that no crime for which a prison term can be imposed can be described as "petty." The facts of the case notwithstanding, it might now be fairly construed that the Commission was not any longer just content to flex its muscles. It could also show its teeth.

Not to complete the picture by any means, but possibly to color it blacker, there was the matter of the Bangor Punta Gorda Corporation, which was the target of a permanent injunction obtained on May 26, 1969, by the SEC. Said *The New York Times,* "The razor's edge that corporations have been treading in the area of timely disclosure has become even finer." [27] Everybody loves the reasonable investor, but it was getting so he might be wearing out his welcome.

On May 8, Bangor Punta issued a news release announcing that it had acquired the holdings of the Piper family in the well-known Piper Aircraft undertaking of Lock Haven, Pennsylvania, and everybody seemed pleased. There were 500,000 shares involved, and Bangor Punta had agreed to file a registration statement with the SEC covering the exchange of a package of securities valued at not less than $80 a share, in the judgment of the First Boston

[27] *The New York Times,* June 16, 1969.

Corporation. The release directly quoted William T. Piper Jr., president of the aircraft concern, as saying that he and the Piper family "would strongly support the merger and would recommend it to all shareholders." The chairman of Bangor Punta, David Wallace, "welcomed the association" with Piper Aircraft, and it was estimated that sales of the combined companies, if their merger became a reality, would reach $450 million in fiscal 1969, with about 40 per cent in the aircraft, recreational and leisure time fields.

SEC thought all of this was tantamount to making a sales pitch for a securities offering that had not yet been registered, and complained that the two companies had violated Section 5(c) of the 1933 Act. This was "gun jumping" because of the sales projections, and because the Piper family was happy about the whole thing. The Commission further stated [28] that its action in obtaining consent to a permanent injunction issued by the District of Columbia district court "should in no way be construed as passing on the merits," but it wanted to be the medium of passing on the offer, rather than leaving it to the companies involved. Bangor Punta was given ten days to file a registration statement with the Commission, or else promptly to issue a statement saying it did not intend to proceed. The Commission considered "gun jumping" a serious matter.

Bangor Punta and Piper agreed, but without admitting any of the allegations in the complaint. The timely disclosure of significant corporate information, said the *Times*, has been a difficult issue ever since *TGS* and *Merrill Lynch*. "Disclosure of merger talks in the future probably will contain only the bare bones, leaving it up to the stockholders to guess what kind of a deal they may be offered."

Despite the soothing syrup of Chairman Cohen, it was now apparent that all was not well in Glocca Morra. In his Loeb Awards speech he had said, "It is my personal view that there is little room for doubt in most cases and, where there may be legitimate doubt, it should be resolved in favor of the investing public and the markets generally." This statement, said one observer, seems to exclude the possibility that the doubtful material information would turn out to be wrong and therefore its revelation would be in favor of only those members of the investing public who acted upon it and brought successful suits.

There was un-Cohenesque doubt, however, in the mind of

[28] Litigation Release No. 4332, May 26, 1969.

Ralph S. Saul who, in 1964 and 1965, when the Texas Gulf case was under investigation by the SEC, had been director of the agency's division of trading and markets. Subsequently he resigned to become president of the American Stock Exchange, and in November of 1968 felt compelled to offer a point of view which could hardly be characterized as either uninformed or agreeable to the Commission: "As a fraud rule, Rule 10b-5 is designed to deal with the flagrant situation. However, it does not always provide a precise guide in making decisions about disclosure. What is material information? When should it be disclosed and how? Rule 10b-5 does not provide answers. Perhaps it is unfortunate that so much of the discussion about disclosure centers upon Rule 10b-5, a fraud rule. The result is a tendency to talk about disclosure problems in abstract and legalistic terms without getting into the more difficult operational problems. . . .

"The difficulty with SEC Rule 10b-5 is that it does not provide a precise guide in making decisions about disclosure. Continuing extension of the reach of 10b-5 by the courts has only served to increase corporate anxieties in the disclosure area.

"Direct government regulation of corporate publicity has inherent limitations," Saul declared. "The volume of corporate publicity; the difficulty of making judgments concerning specific items of publicity, and the proximity of this field to the constitutionally protected right of freedom of expression—all combine to make legal control an imperfect instrument.

"Today attention focuses on the Texas Gulf Sulphur case, which illuminated the entire question but may not provide guidance in specific situations. The case seems to have made the principle of timely disclosure very clear, while leaving questions of procedure, degree and practice unspecified. It is possible," Saul suggested, and undoubtedly his former colleagues were listening, "that the case may reach the Supreme Court, where the legal guidelines will be finally delineated."

To which John P. MacKenzie, who covers the Supreme Court for the *Washington Post*, added gloomily that "Supreme Court refusal to hear the case would mean that the SEC could continue to operate for some time on the assumption that its inside regulations are valid."

Some reasonable time, no doubt, while the web of precedent was spun.

# 10
# Resumption

I

AFTER the big reversal in the Circuit Court of Appeals, things had moved very slowly in the Texas Gulf matter, and they moved both up and down. The first halting steps were taken towards the United States Supreme Court by two of the individual defendants, and the main case settled back under the remand order into the launching pad where it all began—Judge Bonsal and the federal district court in New York. There was a long time-out while both sides examined the ball pitched by Judge Waterman and his teammates. The principal thing that happened during the 18 months following the release of the opinion was a veritable flood of comments, articles, seminars, and speeches—at both the professional and the lay levels—which sought to unravel the decision in terms of the financial and business interests of the country. To strain hyperbole, one effect of this long period of rather heated discussion, of course, was to freeze the holdings of the Second Circuit majority into the consciousness of just about everybody as the new law of the land, and this was exactly what the Securities and Exchange Commission appeared to want. Forgotten now was the fact that almost all of the charges against Texas Gulf had been dismissed the first time up. The possibility that this ageing legal flapjack might turn over once more in the air, under the ministrations of the Supreme Court, seemed remote in time if not in logic.

David Crawford, corporate secretary; Harold Kline, general counsel; and Francis Coates, the veteran director of Texas Gulf, all filed for a rehearing in September after the appellate court decision, and all were promptly denied in October. Lamont, now deceased, and Coates, were the only defendants that had been charged with violations for buying TGS stock, or urging others to buy, *after* the end of the confirming press conference. Crawford and Clayton, found in violation by the district court for jumping the gun, had made their critical purchases *before*. Now Kline, who had not bought any stock but who had received a stock option, and Coates, who had telephoned his broker son-in-law in Houston after the announcement had been made public, were filing a petition for a writ of certiorari with the Supreme Court, in January, 1969.

As had been the case with the various private damage suits, none of the essential facts had changed, but the pitch and thrust of the arguments put forward were sharply different. Both counsel and argument had matured under fire and now, if ever, might be the time to take aim at some of the claims of the SEC which had been at least temporarily made into law by the Second Circuit.

The Coates petition questioned whether a director's purchase of stock on information already announced publicly—and which the director then believed to be available to the public—constituted fraud and deceit under 10(b) and 10b-5. Also, could a director be guilty of fraud for failing to comply with a standard of conduct proposed for the *first time* in the complaint, and did 10b-5, as construed by the Court of Appeals, provide an ascertainable standard of conduct as required by the Fifth Amendment of the Constitution? The appellate majority, finding Coates in violation, had said that at the minimum he should have waited until the news could reasonably have been expected to appear over the Dow Jones broad tape, but added their opinion that he had honestly believed that the news was out. The writ should be granted, said the petitioner, because the Second Circuit had decided incorrectly questions of federal law which were of great importance to all corporate officers, directors, and employees—this was truly the *large issue*, aside from the defendant's personal interest.

The court below had ignored, said the petition, the clear language of the statute and the legislative history of Section 10(b), and it had interpreted Rule 10b-5 not as a rule prohibiting acts which would operate as a fraud or deceit, but as a rule of "fair conduct" in insider trading. Coates did not think the case should become a rule-making proceeding.

There was more. In *Cady, Roberts*, in 1961, the SEC had disclosed for the first time its view that 10b-5 could be construed to prohibit insider transactions without disclosure, but it did not anywhere suggest that anything more was required than a public release of the information. Now, in 1965, it had enlarged its interpretation, first to require also the subsequent report of the announcement on the broad tape, and in 1966, just prior to trial, it had expanded its claim against Lamont for transactions *after* the broad tape communication. It had then gone even further in its appeals brief, stretching the required period to a time after the news had appeared in the morning newspapers and after stockholders had been provided with an opportunity to evaluate the news and consult with their advisors. There was nothing in the rules, or in court decisions, about this. "If the Commission itself, after more than 30 years' experience with the rule, has so much difficulty in deciding what construction to place upon it," said the petition, "it cannot reasonably be said that the rule provides an ascertainable standard of conduct."

In its reply, the Commission brief declared that Coates was contesting on a very narrow ground—whether insiders could trade after an announcement but before publication—and reiterated the fact of his "headstart" on the news, while standing as a fiduciary *vis-à-vis* the stockholders. While the whole case, out of which it arose, was significant, said the SEC attorneys, this petition did not warrant review. They noted that Texas Gulf planned to petition for certiorari "in due course"—which the company, in fact, had never said—and seemed to suggest that the big questions could be left over until such a time. Whether true or not, it was a strategic nudge to the high court.

The Kline petition, except for repeating the constitutional arguments, provided quite a different set of questions, most of them related directly to the new issue of stock options. While other defendants had given up their options before trial, Kline had retained—but not exercised—his. He declared that the majority's definition of materiality was in conflict with regulations adopted by the SEC itself and with the decisions of three circuit courts, including the Second Circuit. He charged that the court below had disregarded the federal civil procedure rule 52(a) in overriding the district court's findings of fact based on virtually uncontradicted testimony. By ordering rescission of Kline's options, it had ignored the stipulation of the parties and the order of the district court, reserving the question of appropriate relief for later, and had thereby deprived the petitioner of his day in court. Moreover, the Court of Appeals had imposed unprecedented and highly uncertain duties on corporate employees and others who deal with securities, raising serious questions of due process and fairness of the administrative procedures followed by the Commission. It had also, in conflict with earlier decisions, ordered ancillary relief which went beyond statutory authority and the exercise of federal equity powers. The court's actions in respect to the options, declared the petition, were an "unwarranted interference with the exercise of business judgment by the directors."

The Commission took a somewhat longer time to reply to this than it had in the case of Coates, asking for an extension. When the reply came along, it repeated the majority finding that Kline was a member of top management. Although he held no detailed knowledge of the drilling progress, he had violated his duty, before accepting the option, to disclose his "material" information. It repeated its nudge that Texas Gulf intended to appeal, and brushed aside the question of standards of materiality as applied by the court as not of sufficient importance to warrant further review. It did recognize, in the case of Kline, that there was a "close question" as to whether his knowledge was material under the standards adopted. As to the constitutional question, it rather grandly said there were "some areas of the law in which it is not possible to anticipate all harmful conduct by specific rules."

Thus prodded, Kline's reply exhibited some signs of higher blood pressure in its forthright responses. The issues relating to him, claimed to be narrow, were not that at all, but "lie at the heart of Rule 10b-5 and they cover substantially all the legal issues relating to the conduct of corporate personnel with respect to purchases of their company's stock, receipt of stock options, and divulgence of information." The inconsistent positions taken by the Commission and the Court of Appeals had generated "massive confusion" and "the use of a rule prohibiting 'fraud and deceit' to establish doctrines of intracorporate responsibilities which go far beyond securities regulation is a development which should receive close scrutiny by this Court."

The assertion that Kline's knowledge had to be material because two officers discussed it with him over lunch went even a step beyond the startling argument of the appellate court that purchases of stock by employees were the best evidence of materiality. Anything imparted, said the petition, thus becomes material because it is imparted. "Such reasoning would make 'material' a luncheon conversation that the company was considering a new style letterhead."

On April 21, 1969, the clerk of the Supreme Court informed the petitioners that certiorari had been denied and, as usual, no reasons were given. Mr. Justice White, however, dissented in respect to the Kline petition: "I would grant certiorari . . . and set the case for oral argument. The issues are of general importance, and the judgment of the Court of Appeals ordering cancellation of the petitioner's stock option has sufficient finality to warrant review now rather than after further proceedings in the District Court."

While it was the considered opinion of some professional reporting agencies and the press that no final judgment had been made, since the Court of Appeals had remanded the whole business to the district court, including the direction to rescind Kline's option, the sporting comment might have been that Texas Gulf was doing its scoring with the dissenters and not with the majorities.

The case, said the *Wall Street Journal* editorially two days later, "leaves the status of corporate inside information just where it was: highly confused. . . . We are just as opposed as anyone else to misuse of inside information but the courts and the commission have really opened a can of worms. When, for example, is information 'widely disseminated'? Must an insider wait until he is, in effect, an outsider?"

## II

Meanwhile, "back at the ranch" on Foley Square, progress in the remand proceedings was making even the Supreme Court resemble a lightning operator. One member of the Texas Gulf staff, who had sat through almost every proceeding in the case from the beginning and was never under any illusion that the SEC litigation would be of brief duration, remarked that he "would not have believed it if someone told me as I sat there in Judge Bonsal's courtroom in May or June of 1966 that there would be men walking on the moon before the judge got to the final hearings on the case." Nevertheless, a meeting in court scheduled for July 21, 1969, was postponed a couple of days while men walked on the moon. It was only a preliminary meeting, anyway, on either planet.

As directed by the court, both the Commission and Texas Gulf submitted pre-hearing memoranda regarding the procedure to be followed on remand, as the slow process got under way again back where it had begun more than three years before. In addition to the corporation, there were ten remaining individual defendants to be dealt with. Lamont was deceased, O'Neill was missing, and Murray, the office manager, had been found not in violation. The remaining issues were the questions of liability, and remedy, so far as the corporation was concerned, and only remedy in respect to the individuals.

The SEC suggested one trial, but with one qualification—it desired all sums awarded against the defendants to be deposited in court, with proper disposition of what was somewhat inelegantly termed "disgorged profits" to abide the court's determination in the private actions of the stockholders now pending. The reason for the request remained obscure to the layman, unless it could be construed as encouragement for getting on with the private suits. The SEC wanted to submit additional evidence and this might take some time. It would include a number of stockholders residing more than a hundred miles from the scene of the trial who had been influenced by the April 12 release. It planned to renew its motion for a default judgment against O'Neill, the missing book-keeper, seeking both an injunction and money.

As for the corporation, there remained the question of whether the release had been deceptive or misleading to the "reasonable" investor, and the additional question of whether an injunction should be granted. The Court of Appeals had in fact inserted a third issue—if the release was found misleading, had there been a lack of due diligence? The SEC believed this had already been decided, although it was "not wholly free from doubt."

The defense was asking for dismissal of the complaint against the corporation on constitutional grounds. Judge Waterman had left matters to the district court, and Judge Friendly had substantially recommended against the injunction process as inappropriate. Waterman had been in error, declared counsel, when he found Judge Bonsal in error, for vindicating the news release *on the facts known to the drafters* and substituting evaluation by a reasonable investor. To whom else could he have been referring, they averred, except reasonable men among the stockholders and the public when he made his judgment? It was firmly noted that the release had produced no unusual market action. Granted, the appellate court had added chartists and speculators to the test, but "the release was surely no more deceptive to a chartist or a speculator than it was to a 'conservative investor' !"

"It is strange indeed," said the defense lawyers, figuratively dropping back a pace and looking at the matter, "that a cautious public statement as well motivated as this one was, specifically designed solely to caution stockholders and the public of the possible dangers of relying on exaggerated rumor, should itself be attacked as misleading and deceptive!"

As for the individual defendants, Texas Gulf counsel charged that there had been no fair warning by statute, regulation, rule or decision to guide them. The SEC had relied upon its own administrative decision in *Cady, Roberts*, generally regarded up to this time as a broker-dealer case under Sections 15 and 19 and indexed as such by the Commission, rather than under 10(b) and 10b-5.

"The holdings of the Court of Appeals are of first impression and have been so regarded by the legal profession and by the business community," said counsel. "In major part, moreover, these findings are contrary to the conclusions reached by the trier of the facts. In these circumstances, the drastic and humiliating remedy of injunction . . . is clearly inappropriate. The Court of Appeals, in this very case, and for the first time, has announced the law applicable to employee purchases of their company's securities; and since the date of that decision company personnel are obliged to abide by the rules thus announced. The possibility of any future violation by these defendants is far too remote to justify injunctive relief. . . ."

The Court of Appeals, said the defense, had no power to rescind Kline's option and the directive was not binding. Due process had been denied. No further penalty should be imposed on Stephens, who had purchased no shares, and who—along with Fogarty—had surrendered his options. Similar judgment should apply also to Fogarty, Crawford, and Mollison, who had sold their stock to the corporation at cost; to Huntington, because the appellate court had drawn inferences of fact not drawn by the trial court; and to Clayton and Darke, because their acts had not been considered illegal when committed. As for Holyk, the "profits" attributed to him should in no event exceed the "value" of his information relating to the first hole. The SEC had withdrawn its claims against the Mollison options, which presumably degraded him from the ranks of top management. The defense lawyers scornfully and completely ignored any rights the sellers of stock might have had.

With the moon and its walkers temporarily disposed of, the first session on the remand was called for Judge Bonsal's courtroom on July 23, with Kennamer and Marden up front and others in the wings. The first item shed a little, but not much, light on the missing O'Neill. Initially representing him, Marden had obtained an extension of time within which to answer the complaint, whereupon O'Neill went back to Ireland, terminated the relationship, and had not been heard from since.

The Court then moved to the more important subject of the news release, and the appellate court's direction to him as to whether it had been misleading and involved lack of diligence by the drafters. There was a mild shaft for Judge Waterman, who had written two somewhat different versions of this direction. As Bonsal observed, "He said it a little differently later on, but that just shows that judges like everybody else have difficulty saying the same thing twice."

Marden could see nothing but a wasteful stand-off if each side brought in more witnesses on the "misleading" point, but was unsuccessful in persuading the Court that his function here had already been discharged. Bonsal replied, and it could have been an omen of things to come, "Yes, but I got a function now to do what the Court of Appeals asked me to do and that is what I want to try to do."

There was considerable argument over the stock options, and Kennamer felt *this* had been settled by the Court of Appeals with its order to cancel Kline's option. Incidentally, Kline had now exercised his option to prevent its lapse, but the company had declined the offer pending litigation, saying it would be accepted later if held to be legal. Judge Waterman had originally disclaimed any intention of ruling upon matters of remedy, but had then proceeded to direct the cancellation. First he was right, said Marden, and then he was wrong, and Bonsal added: "I guess again that is what happens to judges who write long opinions." He noted, however, that the order to rescind was "fairly strong."

There were a few more arguments and a few short speeches concerning the individual defendants. The Court seemed mainly interested in remedy rather than in jousting with the thrust of the appellate court's opinion. This clearly was going to lead to dredging up further details concerning the profits to be "disgorged." It would take some time, summer was at hand, and the judge had been hoping to get a vacation. Resumption was set accordingly for the first court day in October.

Thus the lines were drawn for the next act in district court. In the period of more than a year since the Court of Appeals had acted, however, the aftermath in the press and in the legal, financial, and business communities had been characterized by disbelief, chagrin, outrage, confusion, and latterly a certain amount of "We have to live with it" philosophy.

In summary, the hearings so far had further narrowed the issues from those prevailing in the beginning. The Coates and Kline petitions to the Supreme Court (which were denied) raised nearly all points of law in the case except the sole charge against the corporation of issuing a false and misleading press release. On this Judge Bonsal had taken the testimony, seen the witnesses, and ruled that the SEC had *not* demonstrated that the statement was false and misleading. But he also had held such a ruling to be unnecessary because the release had not been issued in connection with the purchase and sale of securities. The latter holding was overturned on appeal. Now the majority opinion directed Bonsal to go back and apply the standard of the "reasonable investor" exercising due care, and also to determine if there had been a lack of due diligence in the drafting. Bonsal, after some 1,800 words describing the circumstances of the release, had held in his first opinion that TGS executives had exercised "reasonable business judgment under the circumstances" and had been under "considerable pressure." Now he had to distinguish between "reasonable business judgment" and "due diligence."

On the knotty question of timing insider stock purchases after disclosure of corporate information, the SEC had shifted from (1) appearance of the news on the Dow Jones broad tape to (2) enough time for the investing public to evaluate the development and make informed decisions, with a few flourishes in between. On remand, the Commission appeared to have settled its position in this instance to (3) 24 hours after an announcement had been made publicly.

One guideline more related to *policy* than to *time* might have been drawn from earlier statements of Commission spokesmen, but now seemed to have been shelved by mutual consent. On January 23, 1942, just four months before Rule 10b-5 was adopted, SEC Chairman Ganson Purcell had told the Congress that the 1934 act was "eminently wise" in dealing with this problem, "by expressly prohibiting only the most prevalent form of the abuse of inside information—trading designed to take quick profits from short-term market fluctuations." He added:

> Mr. Congressman, under the Exchange Act, they (insiders) are permitted to buy and sell—I should not say permitted—but, rather they still have the right to buy and sell the stocks and securities of their own companies, so long as they report any changes in their positions to the Commission once every month. The only prohibition—and it is not really a prohibition—is the restriction or limitation which rests upon them as a result of Section 16(b) of the Exchange Act. This section provides for the purpose, as it says, of preventing the unfair use of confidential information. . . .

And in 1963 Milton Cohen, director of the *Special Study of the Securities Markets* (praised by the then SEC Chairman William L. Cary as "the most comprehensive of its kind in over 25 years,") agreed that Section 16 had performed well as the basic safeguard against "insider trading abuses." But the SEC, a year later, had chosen to ignore Section 16 and charged the defendants with violation of Section 10(b) and Rule 10b-5, a rule designed to prevent fraud, but which was gradually whittled down to require only negligence.

In fact, when the SEC promulgated 10b-5 on May 21, 1942, its release said: "The SEC today announced the adoption of a rule prohibiting fraud by any person in connection with the purchase of securities. . . . The new rule closes a loophole in the protections against fraud by the Commission by prohibiting individuals or companies from buying securities if they engage in fraud in their purchase."

As for the 13 original individual defendants, Lamont was dead, O'Neill had fled, Coates—as will be later discussed—had settled; Stephens, Fogarty, Mollison, and Crawford had turned in their options, stock, or both; Murray was no longer considered in violation. That left Kline, Clayton, Holyk, Darke, and Huntington. It also left the public, doing business and breathing a little heavily, but not on trial.

III

The hearings were completed on October 8 after three days in court, with each side being given a month to file briefs and another ten days for rebuttal. It would be four months before Judge Bonsal would hand down his opinion—the second in this case—and in the meantime the written submissions would reflect the hopes and fears, to some extent, of opposing counsel, as well as repeat their now firmly-molded convictions and conclusions as to the facts and the law.

Looking back on the remand proceedings, an observer might be struck with the fact that nothing new had really been added in spite of the elapsed time and the parade of witnesses and the dull thud of filed papers. The 1966 trial had summoned and arranged the raw materials which, taken together, had composed the *Texas Gulf* case, and Bonsal's opinion had rung down the curtain on act one, at least. After a nerve-wracking delay, the audience was treated to a thumping reversal in act two, with only a few new characters but quite a lot of suspenseful action. Now, whoever might be considered to be the playwrights, they were certainly having the traditional third-act trouble—how to build the action, move to a climax both logical and stirring, and get the audience out of the theater feeling it has had its money's worth, not been hoaxed, and not left hanging. For the moment they were back to square one— was the news release misleading?

The company, said its lawyers once more, was responsible only for the release—not for the way it was reported, and certainly not for the way some had chosen to interpret it. It had made no representations whatsoever as to the results of the drilling up to the time it was written, because this was not the company's *intent*. It was essentially a wait-and-see statement for stockholders and the public, drafted under difficult circumstances, and designed to combat inaccurate and widespread reports which the corporation could not justify on the knowledge it had. Nothing in the release urged precipitate selling of the stock, or warranted the conclusion that the shares were less valuable than before. If anything, the release indicated that value might be added. There had been no panic selling or wholesale dumping on the market, and for every seller there had been a buyer. As of April, 1966, there were about 60,000 owners of Texas Gulf stock; only a few thousand sold—for whatever reason—immediately before April 16; and it appeared that 99 per cent of the stockholders had not been "misled."

Marden called attention, as had been expected, to relatively recent statements made by the SEC in connection with the *Bangor Punta* case, in which it had condemned the parties for issuing optimistic and evaluative information in advance of a merger, and also in its warnings to oil companies operating on the Alaskan North Slope against stating estimates of potential valuation beyond those justified by the facts available. If Texas Gulf had been appraised of these Commission convictions five years earlier, he declared, the company could not have complied with them more fully than it did in its April 12 release.

There was now no inaccuracy complained of by the Commission, which, proceeding under a fraud statute, was left complaining only of a "gloomy tone." Said Marden: "Such subtle and subjective nuances are best left to the world of arts and letters."

None of the SEC witnesses actually saw or read the release; they only read reports and made their own interpretations, and the TGS counsel thought it "remarkable how many things can be found wrong in the release if one has five years to think about it." The SEC had called it ambiguous, among other things. "If ambiguity means to the Commission 'subject to different interpretations'," Marden declared, "then just about any statement made by human beings is ambiguous. . . . It is for this Court, not disappointed former stockholders, to determine whether or not the press release was misleading." He then quoted Judge Bonsal from the earlier record, as he would do many times in the hearing, as saying that "The Commission has failed to demonstrate that it was false, misleading or deceptive." Nothing had changed.

Coming into court avidly seeking an injunction "for the protection of stockholders" the SEC attorneys found without merit the TGS complaint that the release had been truncated, fragmented, and otherwise misused, since those who found that the release denied an ore discovery were all "skilled editors," whereas the *Herald Tribune* was able to give an optimistic report because it got additional information from Fogarty by telephone. The Commission brief added to the literature on hindsight with this rather astonishing footnote: "It appears that the earlier press reports in the *Herald Tribune* and *The New York Times* of April 11, 1964, concerning rumors and reports of a major ore strike at Timmins, however inaccurate they might have been in specific detail, presented a more realistic picture of the drilling situation."

The SEC cited the Court of Appeals standard in respect to the vulnerability of the April 12 news release as this: ". . . if *any* such person, acting reasonably, could have been misled by it in connection with his securities transactions, whether or not other investors may not have been misled." This would seem to be a rather stringent test for any statement. Marden said it was "anti-thetical" to the rule of law continually applied by common law courts since 1738.[1] The "reasonable man," according to other cita-tions, was an "abstraction," "a fictitious person who never existed on land or sea." The SEC, said the TGS lawyer, would do away with the basic external and objective standard for judgment, would do away with court and jury, substituting a modern version of "oath swearing" and assuming that all of its investor-witnesses are "reasonable investors." This was not supported by logic or by the evidence before the court, he said.

In the SEC's entire 53-page brief, Marden pointed out, there was not a single reference to the Texas Gulf promise to issue a later detailed statement, and he felt this was an omission of significance in appraising the true worth of the Commission's claim of deception. For its part, the SEC described the release as a "plethora of negativism" and scoffed at the idea that due care would require investors to wait and see. The promise of such a future statement, it said in rebuttal, was "tucked away toward the end of a miasma of gloom."

Some of the assertions partook of the "tain't so" variety. Countering the TGS desire to exclude investor-witnesses, the Com-mission simply replied that the testimony of such witnesses was *not* tainted by their opinions or conclusions, while the fact that they had not read the original release was "without merit." In fact all of the *selling* stockholders, said the SEC lawyers, acted as reasonable investors, whereas the Texas Gulf investor-witnesses who purchased stock demonstrated a "canny astuteness." It was a distinction which successfully hid the difference.

In meeting the references to the *Bangor Punta* and North Slope incidents, the SEC declared that in the first instance it was not necessary for Bangor Punta shareholders or the public to know the value of the shares being offered, whereas in the TGS

[1] *Vaughan v. Menlove, 1738, 3 Bing. N.C. 468.*

release material facts were sorely needed because the Court of
Appeals had held that the drilling results in April, 1964, were
"material." They failed to note that this holding not only reversed
the lower court's finding of fact, but occurred four years and four
months after the event itself! The same reasoning was advanced
to brush aside the North Slope release.

At some point Marden asked, "If further drilling had disclosed a marginal deposit, would the SEC now be claiming that
the release misled those who *bought* stock?" Nobody expected a
reply to that, but it bore some relation to his charge on rebuttal that
the SEC briefs were "another effort to create the impression that
this action is other than what it is, that the facts are other than
what they are, and that the law *is* what the Commission wants."
They reflected a spirit of vindictiveness towards the defendants,
since the Commission "persists in suggesting that the release was
intentionally deceptive and born of evil motives. Although its con-
tentions were rejected by this court and by every judge of the
Court of Appeals, the Commission refuses to accept the fact that
its pre-trial conception of this case has not been borne out by the
evidence. . . . The Commission's zeal has led . . . to a per-
version of the facts, the legislative history and the applicable law."

The Commission attorneys supported their claim that the
drafters of the news release had not exercised due diligence by
pointing out that no attempt had been made to determine what
happened at the drilling site between Friday evening and Sunday
afternoon, "although such information was readily available." There
was no problem with the telephone, TGS had a helicopter, it was
a warm day with clear visibility, but Fogarty had not wanted to
take the trouble to obtain such information—and this was labeled
a "clear violation of 10b-5." The charges ignored Fogarty's explanation that the Texas Gulf purpose was chiefly to deny rumors and
not to supply specific drilling details, which he felt would be
meaningless to uninformed investors. With this posture, said TGS,
and with such intent, it made no difference whether the data
represented Friday evening or Sunday morning. And again, Bonsal,
in some 150 words of his original opinion, had found that Fogarty
and Stephens exercised "reasonable business judgment under the
circumstances." Marden continued to combine such reminders with
compliments to the Court as a sort of pleasant lash throughout the
hearings. The several appellate judges who had suggested that
the release should have been deferred or worded differently, he said,

were second-guessing with hindsight, after several months of deliberation, whereas the TGS people had only hours in which to act. He complained that the Commission kept putting forth its "beliefs" of what constituted the appellate court's views—and if these were in truth the views of the majority, there would have been no need for a remand. The best defense of the reasonableness of the decision to make the April 12 release was the Commission's own press release on the Alaskan oil fields. Furthermore, could a decision made in accordance with the guidelines of the New York Stock Exchange be a decision made without due diligence?

The SEC case for an injunction appeared to rest chiefly on the conduct of the individual defendants. They maintained that the Court of Appeals had determined that each individual defendant "knowingly committed serious violations," many of them on repeated occasions, by misusing corporate information for personal advantage. The only requirement for an injunction is that there be a reasonable expectation that the defendant will create a violation in the future—and the SEC lawyers doubted that the defendants could carry the heavy burden of disproving this expectation because their "conduct was both legally and morally improper," —they still maintain they have done nothing wrong, and all except Darke still maintain important TGS positions.

Marden countered by declaring that of all the other news releases placed before the court during the trial, none had been claimed by the SEC to be misleading or deceptive. After five and a half years there had been no charge of this kind made against any public statement by Texas Gulf, and the same people were still in charge. There had been no showing of a course of conduct or a consistent pattern of behavior in violation of the securities laws. Therefore, how could the Commission, in good faith, see a danger of future deception as "quite real"? Such a broadly-framed injunction as the SEC sought here would be improper, and he quoted Justice Holmes: ". . . we equally are bound by the first principles of justice not to sanction a decree so vague as to put the whole conduct of the defendants' business at the peril of a summons for contempt. We cannot issue a general injunction against all possible breaches of the law." [2]

An injunction against negligence of any sort might be considered unusual, declared the TGS lawyers, but where the injunc-

[2] *Swift & Co. v. U.S., 196 U.S. 375 (1905).*

tion is against negligent speech it would certainly violate the First Amendment. The Commission, however, declared that while tolerance of negligence might be necessary for such conduits of information as newspapers, a different rule must be applied where a business entity issues a statement bearing solely on the worth of its properties. Any other interpretation of the First Amendment, it said, "would impose burdens upon the SEC and strike at the heart of the federal securities laws"—the burden of showing deliberate dishonesty as a condition precedent to protecting investors. Nor could the Fifth Amendment be relied upon by Texas Gulf, in its claim that Rule 10b-5 was not sufficiently definite to put the defendants on notice as to their conduct. Their reason dipped into the eighteenth century, thus matching Marden's scholarship: In 1759 Lord Hardwicke wrote in a letter to Lord Kames that strict definitions would "cramp the jurisdiction of equity when faced with the fertility of man's invention." (The SEC had used this previously in the *Capital Gains* case, and its citation gave them their only authority for using it here.) Also, Kline and Coates had raised this question 210 years later in petitioning the Supreme Court, and the petitions had been denied. It seemed a rather thinly-stretched line, but at least it was an answer.

It was a fair deduction, declared Marden on another tack, that in instituting this action the SEC was under the misapprehension that the April 12 release was the product of some Machiavellian scheme.

> The attack upon a typically cautious wait-and-see statement, of a kind that the Commission should bless rather than attack, could not be otherwise explained. Alternatively, it was safe to say that there would have been no complaint about the release if the Commission had not elected to charge the individual defendants with violations . . . because of their purchases of TGS shares. As the facts have unfolded, it has become clear beyond any doubt that there was no connection between the April 12 statement and prior purchases of shares by individual defendants. . . . The SEC's case has now been reduced to insubstantial nit-picking.

In their rebuttal the Commission again complained that the defendants insisted in attacking the Court of Appeals decision and showed not the slightest degree of repentance over their prior conduct—therefore an injunction should issue.

Texas Gulf, said the SEC, setting up a straw man, "suggests

that the public interest requires that it be permitted to disclose important matters concerning its activities without exercising due diligence as to the accuracy of its disclosures." Then, deftly knocking the straw man over, it continued: "They have no such right." The First Amendment does not protect frauds, and "a company making statements bearing on the value of its securities does not require the same need for constitutional protection as does an agency for the press." Thus, a new declaration of unequal rights appeared to be issuing from a government agency. Some might argue with the Commission's conclusion that "the case presents no constitutional problems."

The SEC had few kind words for the individuals, those for whom Marden thought any remedial punishment would be inappropriate and unconscionable. The quotation that the "historic injunctive process was designed to deter, not to punish," [3] stood in sharp contrast, said the latter, to the stated objectives of the Commission: (1) "to drag to light and pillory," which had succeeded; and (2) establishing new rules binding corporate personnel in transactions in their companies' securities, without resort to Congress, which had also succeeded. Any violation of Rule 10b-5, said Marden, was the result, not of a callous disregard for the law, but of the inability of individuals to prophesy the expansion by the judiciary of a rule issued by a regulatory agency.

Fogarty's actions, cried the Commission attorneys, were the most "egregious" because he "leapt into the market" on November 12 for 300 shares, and bought again after the "night shift" developments of March 31 and April 5. "Concealment of the fact of these purchases by Dr. Fogarty while he had inside information could have been the motivation for his creation of the impression that Texas Gulf did not have a discovery until after April 6." In the opinion of the SEC, the fact that Fogarty was now president of the company increased his potential for future violations. As for returning his shares, an attempt to give away the spoils of illegal activities did "not moot the need for an injunction," and the same was true of Stephens, Mollison, and Crawford. Clayton was "another individual who got in early and stayed late," while Crawford, as a lawyer, "in his anxiety to beat the news must have known that such conduct as calling his broker at midnight was questionable." Future violations from all of these could be reasonably expected.

[3] *Hecht Co. v. Bowles, 321 U.S. 321* (1944).

Furthermore, United States investors needed to be protected against such individuals as Holyk and Darke.

As the two top management members of Texas Gulf, said the Commission, Stephens and Fogarty "possess all the ingredients" for future violations, and they, together with Kline, must be prevented from accepting future stock options while possessing undisclosed material information. SEC termed it a 'well-recognized duty" that managers should inform stock option committees of material issues affecting the issuance of options. It had not been well-recognized for very long, as Marden pointed out, since Kennamer had declared, at the close of the first trial, this to be the first case to his knowledge where the Commission had brought an enforcement proceeding involving stock options. The request appeared to be either unbelievably naive or seated in pure hostility, since under the realities of the system no company manager, with or without an injunction, could ever safely accept options.

As for Kline, who had no hearing before the Court of Appeals, the SEC avoided his complaint of denial of due process with the flat assertion that the appellate court had explicitly ordered the cancellation, and apparently the act was sufficient authority. There was the added fillip: ". . . and if Texas Gulf wants to compensate Mr. Kline for his 'loyal services to his company' nothing prevents them from raising his salary or granting him a new stock option." The risk tag to the latter had already been attached. For good measure, the Commission questioned whether the option plan approved by stockholders authorized the directors to ratify Kline's option at all, since it was in violation of the securities laws. If it was deemed that Kline's penalty was greater than that assessed against the other defendants, the court could increase the latter!

In summary, the SEC asked for three orders: (1) that Fogarty, Clayton, Mollison, Holyk, Darke, Huntington, and Crawford be enjoined from violating 10(b) and 10b-5 in connection with the purchase and sale of TGS stock on the basis of undisclosed information, and that Darke be enjoined from tipping; (2) that Stephens, Fogarty, and Kline be enjoined in connection with accepting stock options; and (3) that Texas Gulf be barred from violating the statute and rule in connection with the issuance of future corporate announcements to the public. They asked that Clayton be made to pay $20,010.56; Holyk $35,663.47; Huntington $2,300.56; and Darke $183,613.06, all plus interest. The formula employed in the computation was the difference between purchase price and the average price on the New York Stock Exchange on April 17.

Marden contended that seeking such a monetary penalty was improper and *ultra vires*, under the 1934 Act, which authorized only suits for injunction or restraining orders, and cited the 25-year-old words of the Supreme Court to the effect that a court "may not impose penalties in the guise of preventing future violations." [4] While there had been solid reasons for buying sulphur company stock generally, plus the TGS diversification into other fields, the measure of monetary penalty sought here would charge the defendants with a rise in market values attributable to causes bearing no relationship whatever to the "inside" information they possessed about Timmins. Purposeful wrongdoing, he reiterated, was absent from the record. Furthermore he believed that the SEC had no authority to request, nor the court any power to grant, any order for Darke to rescind his stock transactions. For the Commission to ask a court of equity that Darke make restitution to *people who sold to others* was incredible, a twisted and tortured use of the word. Darke would have been better off in a criminal proceeding where there was a limitation on the amount of fines.

On rebuttal Marden added it all up this way:

> The Commission's position is more than a little anomalous. It has persuaded the courts that in this suit for "equitable" or "prophylactic" relief it need not prove all the elements of fraud or the elements necessary for monetary relief. After carrying a greatly reduced burden of proof in which it need not establish all elements of fraud, such as *scienter*, and thereby obtaining a finding of violation, the Commission then proceeds on remand as if it had proved all of those elements and that defendants have nothing but larceny in their hearts and no motives but evil ones. The Commission has succeeded, in this case, in reducing the substantive elements which must be proved, in reducing the procedural safeguards for defendants, in having its weakest inferences adopted without reservation. It now argues that severe penalties more appropriate to wilful perpetrators of fraud be enforced. The Commission's position is lacking in equity and is without justification in fact or reason. . . . The Commission, it would seem, would have defendants in a Commission suit capitulate upon the threat that the punishment will be worse if they choose to defend. A principle more subversive to our legal system can hardly be imagined.

[4] *Hartford-Empire Co. v. U.S.,* 323 U.S. 386 (1945).

The parade of investor-witnesses invoked by the latest proceedings before Judge Bonsal bore specifically on the point of whether or not the famous news release of April 12, 1964, had been deceptive and misleading to the "reasonable" investor. Whatever the parade might mean to the judge, it was unlikely that it would move the gallery of spectators to any firmer conclusion than that the "reasonable investor" was at best an elusive fish, coming in all sizes and shapes and representing no pattern whatsoever. It might even be that such a fish was only an angler's dream, since almost all of them had got off the hook and fattened on the bait. Furthermore, for the purposes of the lawsuit advanced by the SEC, it would seem that the very failure to prove any hard and fast pattern must redound to the advantage of the defendants. As things turned out later, it did and it didn't, and this was surely par for this course.

Statistically the SEC came off with a slight quantitative edge, since they presented 20 witnesses (16 of them by deposition) to 16 for Texas Gulf Sulphur (seven by deposition). On the other hand, TGS may have had a qualitative advantage—their twelve buying witnesses had traded in a total of 10,000 shares, ranging in lots from 100 to 2,100, whereas the total shares traded by *all* of the SEC's complaining witnesses amounted only to 5,680 shares, and these ranged in lots from 30 at the low point to one of 1,700. For the most part they were small holders. Geographically things were about even, with the Commission's people coming from twelve states and the defense people coming from ten, coast-to-coast and border-to-gulf. As an added note, the smaller the shareholder, the more vivid and emotional was his language.

Apart from their contributions to the Court's evidentiary problem, the investor-witnesses added their unassimilable bits to the colorful, chaotic, and withal challenging mural portraying the composite stockholder. Perhaps it was more of a galloping fresco. Certainly it will not fit into a brief case, but corporate executives would do well to carry it home and give it more attention.

The SEC witnesses, declared the TGS lawyers, were all unhappy that they sold and could only envision the profits that "might have been." They shared a common ignorance of geology and geophysics, which was not unexpected, and many of them were plaintiffs in private damage actions against the company. None had ever seen the actual press release, which was the prime exhibit before the court, but almost all of them had read some of the voluminous press reports in which the SEC had charged the company statement to be "false and misleading" and thus remained convinced that Texas Gulf had practiced a deliberate fraud. They responded predictably, said defense counsel, to grossly improper leading questions. Almost to a man—or woman—they had made substantial profits on the stock they wished they had not sold. At least one of them more than doubled his investment. Another lost on every stock he held *except* his TGS, and would have done even better on that except that he overslept on the morning of April 16. A third complainant actually *sold* his stock after reading the company's statement that it indeed had a mine near Timmins.

Lawyer George C. Zachary, of Beverly Hills, California, was the one who had more than doubled his money—but he had decided to sell 500 shares *before* he received any information on the news release, and had placed his sell order prior to April 13.

Another California lawyer, Daniel M. Feeley, of San Jose, relied on his broker's statement that Texas Gulf officers had denied there had been any sort of an ore strike in Canada—which was not true—and that the stock was overpriced and would go back down. On such reliance, however, he made an eleven-point profit on his investment.

An Oregon cattle rancher, Walter B. Schrock, had bought his stock at 15¾ in 1963. He made his first sale on April 15, he said, without regard to the "gloomy" release and because he made a good profit. The company announcement confirming the mine then prompted him to *sell* the rest of his stock!

Herbert Kuhlmann, of Chicago, had purchased 100 shares in 1959 at 17¼ and in 1962 he acquired another hundred shares at 17⅞ because he was "looking for a stock to invest in that paid a pretty decent dividend and also that was insolvent [sic] and had natural resources figuring on the future." He was highly critical of TGS for reducing its dividend. Kuhlmann thought he had read of a large ore find in Timmins at least a week before the April 12 release, which within the frame of his testimony would not have been possible. He had read *none* of the newspapers where stories had appeared. After reading the April 12 release he got the impression that the stock would reverse itself and go down to about 12, but did not verify this with his broker—"He gives me no advice. I use all of my own." He sold his 200 shares for 29 on April 15, but subsequently sold five other stocks and invested the proceeds in real estate, which might suggest strongly that this had been his purpose in all of the sales.

"The only thing I remember about this company is that I was made a fool of," testified Abraham Staff, an Albany public accountant. Defense counsel tartly observed that this was confirmed by his further statements. Staff owned 300 shares, was plaintiff in a suit against Texas Gulf, and presumably was one more SEC example of a reasonable investor acting with due care. The only reason he could give for buying the stock was the management of the company, but all he remembered of that was "Mr. Lamont."

"The name Lamont sticks in my mind," Staff declared. "Probably because I associated it with a radio program." (Lamont Cranston, "The Shadow"?) He believed Lamont to be president of TGS, and was sure rumors of the Timmins exploration had been making the stock go up, but was unable to specify anything he had read. He steadfastly maintained that articles regarding the sulphur market and the TGS diversification programs were of no interest to him: "I can tell you all of these articles . . . didn't have any effect on my thinking, as far as the stock is concerned, because if it did I wouldn't have sold. I probably saw every article in the paper but it couldn't have had any effect on me." Staff sold at a $2,000 profit on the morning of April 13 when his broker had read him only *half* of the Dow Jones broad tape announcement.

Finally, Irving Weinstein, 73, of Worcester, Massachusetts, purchased stock at 14⅞, read the *whole* Dow Jones release, and sold at 31¼ because he wanted to take his profit. A reasonable man.

In their half of the inning, the defense presented Alan Rhodes, a Cleveland chemistry professor who owned TGS stock in 1963, saw both company releases in 1964, and purchased more stock after seeing the second. He seemed to have interpreted both statements as they were meant by the company to be read. Robert W. Gwynne, a Tennessee cattle farmer who closely follows stock reports, had discussed the April 12 release with friends who also owned TGS shares. They felt that any mineral discovery could simply add to their value, that the release was in fact bullish, and none of them sold. Dr. Harold Doubleday, of Fort Lauderdale, had long invested in mining stocks, had read up on Texas Gulf in *Standard & Poor's*, and considered the release "a conservative statement of good fortune such as I would expect from a well-managed conservative company."

The defense lawyers could point pridefully to James C. Gilbert, a retired petroleum engineer of Cody, Wyoming, because he regularly purchased TGS, usually in 100-share lots timed to follow company news releases, such as those on new highs in free world use of sulphur, launching of the world's largest liquid sulphur tanker, recovered sulphur production in Canada, the increase in sulphur prices, and the phosphate mine in North Carolina. The April 12 release caused him to buy 200 shares, breaking his pattern, plus another 100 on the 15th because "all things looked favorable." He continued to purchase after the confirmation of the mine, and was particularly impressed by the company's diversification program.

The defense pattern was varied with four other witnesses. Robert A. Gilbert, since 1929 an investment research specialist in raw material securities, who now owned his own firm and was consultant to 50 stock exchange houses, trusts, and banks, had issued on April 14 a letter to clients recommending further accumulation of TGS stock. The remaining three had been witnesses at the first trial in 1966. Hyman Bluestein, account executive for Francis I. duPont, Boston, had purchased for himself and his customers and saw the April 12 release as a reason for additional recommendations to clients. Bernard Grishman, of Bache & Company, had been called by many customers on April 13 and had executed TGS buy orders. Herbert G. Wellington Jr., managing partner of Wellington and Company, which purchased 2,000 shares on April 13, felt the later company announcement was just a confirmation of the April 12 release. The parade might well have concluded with such a request as this: Will the real "reasonable investors" please stand up!

## IV

In remanding the *Texas Gulf Sulphur* case, the Court of Appeals had packaged and dispatched to Judge Bonsal a new standard of materiality, including rather forceful instructions for its application. No matter what he thought—and what he thought had been quite clearly disclosed in his first opinion—the name of the game was now compliance. Bonsal therefore had set out in the October hearings to receive further evidence on the way reasonable investors had interpreted the now famous news release of April 12, 1964, and after that to determine remedies sought by the SEC in respect to the defendants who now stood as violators of the statute and the rule. When the new opinion came down on February 6, 1970, it provided readers with an almost pictorial demonstration of the Court picking its way carefully, firmly, and meticulously through a minefield, with only minor hesitations. As he had told Marden back in July, "I got a function now to do what the Court of Appeals asked me to do. . . ."

In the discharge of this function, Judge Bonsal took particular pains to precede his findings by pointing to the sign posts freshly painted by the appellate majority, in effect distinguishing, if not reconciling, the old markers set up by him in 1966. Sometimes the contrast was painful, and this effect would not be lost on the curbstone lawyers, the Monday morning quarterbacks, and the law review editors, but there it was, and they would have to make the best of it until another signpainter came along, with superseding authority.

One of the preliminaries to the opinion, and there were not very many, included a repetition of the Second Circuit's reading of the "in connection with" language of 10b-5—that the rule was violated by false and misleading assertions calculated to influence the investing public whether or not the issuance of the release was motivated "by corporate officials for ulterior purposes." This meant, in free translation, that corporate statements of the character alleged did not have to be accompanied by corporate purchases or sales of stock, even though the rule *did* seem to say otherwise. The Court now wanted to be sure that the authors of this interpretation were clearly pegged. Noting in passing that speculators and chartists had been gathered into the fold of "reasonable investors," Bonsal said the Court of Appeals had directed "an appropriate primary inquiry into the meaning of the statement to the reasonable investor and its relationship to truth," since it had been unable, from the record, and by applying the standard Congress intended, to definitely conclude that it was deceptive or misleading. This determination was to be made in the light of the facts *existing at the time of the release*. With such ground rules stated, he began the task.

Either directly or by deposition the Court then had heard from 20 shareholders who said they had *sold* because of the release, and from 12 who had *retained their stock or purchased more* as a result of the same statement. After citing certain words in the release which had been persuasive to each class of stockholders, Bonsal then held that *all* of them had been reasonable according to the recipe of the Court of Appeals. So far, no blood. But at this point he turned his back for good on those who had not sold.

Were those who sold misled? Judge Friendly and Judge Hays had said they were, and even Judge Ritter out in Utah. Friendly had decided for himself that TGS knew more than the release disclosed. In effect, although the new opinion did not say so, the hindsight jury had successfully second-guessed the company executives, and on remand the present Court had to go along:

> The testimony of the witnesses who sold when the situation in Timmins "seemed to offer good reason for optimism" establishes that they sold because of the press release, and that they were misled by it. It was not necessary that the SEC establish that the selling shareholders were influenced . . . solely because of the press release. It is enough that it materially influenced shareholders' conduct and was a substantial factor. . . .

Having isolated the selling shareholders from the contamination of those who did not sell, the Court now faced the issue of "due care." Texas Gulf had argued that the promise of a definite later statement required reasonable shareholders to wait and see, if they were going to exercise due care. Here Bonsal carefully excised the group once more and cited a single stockholder who had decided to sell regardless of what he heard or read. His next holding: "Since the press release had misled reasonable investors to believe that there was no ore discovery, or if there was, it was not as rich as it was rumored to be, they were entitled to act without awaiting a second release. Therefore, the Court finds that some reasonable investors, exercising due care, were misled by the press release." The minefield seems to have become more precarious at this point, and it was a long jump to the next Court of Appeals signpost.

However, when it came to the question of whether or not the company had exercised "due diligence" the majority opinion had said that TGS could have delayed its statement, or said the situation was in flux, or that the information related to progress as of April 10 instead of "to date": "The choice of an ambiguous general statement rather than a summary of the specific facts cannot reasonably be justified by any claimed urgency," Judge Waterman had said. "The avoidance of liability for misrepresentation in the event that the Timmins project failed, a highly unlikely event as of

April 12 or April 13, did not forbid the accurate and truthful divulgence of detailed results. . . ."

After citing Friendly and Hays again, Judge Bonsal said it appeared that a majority of the *Court of Appeals* were of the view that the framers of the press release failed to exercise due diligence, and on the basis of *that court's standards*, he now found likewise. In short, the press release was now found to be misleading to the *reasonable investor* using due care, the framers had not exercised due diligence, and TGS had violated Section 10(b) and Rule 10b-5. A syllogistic summary might disclose some tenuous threads, but the minefield had been traversed with no fatalities, except perhaps to Texas Gulf.

As to the company's contention that it was responsible only for the news release itself, and not the use made of it by media, the Court offered this comment, a little reminiscent of *Alice in Wonderland:* "Indeed, the fact that the news media emphasized the words which have been found to be misleading to the reasonable investor merely indicates that the news media also deemed them of importance." But, of course, the media had to use them first, or the investors would not have been able to read them.

The schizophrenic cast of the second opinion became notably more apparent as Judge Bonsal approached, and dealt with, the question of an injunction against the corporation, however. Having figuratively beaten the company to the ground in respect to its news release—the only issue on which it stood before the bar—and found it misleading, deceptive, and prepared without due diligence, the Court now denied the SEC's request for a permanent injunction because there had been no showing of a reasonable likelihood of future violations. It was also pointed out that the "due diligence" test of the Court of Appeals was here being applied for the first time. Quoting now from his original opinion that TGS must not be judged by hindsight, and that Stephens and Fogarty had exercised reasonable business judgment under the circumstances, Bonsal declared the issuance of an injunction was inappropriate without a showing of a lack of good faith. All of this was buttressed by Friendly's opposition, on appeal, to any injunction in this case, and by his declaration that the company's motives were laudable and the defect a pardonable one of execution.

Turning to the individual defendants, the Court observed that Darke no longer worked for Texas Gulf, and since he was a Canadian citizen, no useful purpose would be served by an injunction, although "other relief" would be granted. Granting that the discovery was a once-in-a-lifetime affair and that the violations had occurred more than five years before, Bonsal now also refused to issue injunctions against Holyk, Huntington, Fogarty, and Mollison. But Clayton and Crawford were in a different position. They had purchased during the period of non-disclosure knowing "beyond a peradventure of a doubt that TGS had made a very important mineral discovery." At this point in his opinion, the judge felt constrained to comment, somewhat unexpectedly, and indirectly through another authority, on the burden that had been imposed on him by the Second Circuit: "Professor Painter points out that the application of the 'materiality' test by the Court of Appeals represents a considerable extension of the meaning of 'materiality' into new areas.[5] These defendants could not have anticipated this extension at the time of their violations, but they, as indeed all insiders, are now on notice of the scope of Section 10(b) and Rule 10b-5." It was a polite but pointed little shaft.

In spite of the arguments that had been raised against the power of the court to inflict monetary penalties, Bonsal found that such power had been sufficiently well-established to support the SEC demands, "if Congressional purpose is effectuated by so doing," and that he could require the defendants to give up the profits realized in the violating transactions. The Commission formula, first employed in the Coates settlement, was held to be fair—the difference between the mean average price of TGS stock on April 17, 1964—stipulated to be 40⅜—and the purchase price of the shares. Payments were to be made accordingly, to Texas Gulf to be held in escrow for five years, subject to such disposition as the court might direct on the application of the SEC, other interested persons, or on the court's own motion. The payments would include interest at six per cent and any remainder at the end of the period would go to TGS. The SEC's dollar calculations were ordered to be paid in each case except for Darke, and here the Court distinguished between those who had bought on the geologist's recommendation and those who in turn received the recommendation from the tippees. It reduced the award in Darke's case to $90,199.50. Roughly, the "disgorged" profits came to around $157,000, including interest, for the four affected defendants.

The injunction "score" for the Commission was not very

[5] Painter: *Federal Regulation of Insider Trading*, 220 (1968).

impressive. The remedy had been sought against the corporation; against seven defendants in respect to future purchases; and against Stephens, Fogarty, and Kline also in respect to future options. Only Clayton and Crawford drew the penalty, although the Court warned that any future violations would put the others on the spot.

As for Stephens and Fogarty, Bonsal declared that, "There would seem to be little likelihood that these senior officers of TGS would accept future stock options without disclosing what they know to the Stock Option Committee and the Board of Directors." Just how the chairman and president of any corporation could *ever* literally be free of such knowledge somewhat baffles the imagination, in the light of the Commission's revealed position.

Back in 1966 the court had found that Kline did *not* have material inside information, but the appellate majority found that he did and directed rescission and "such restitution as might be proper." Now Bonsal recalled the stipulation that remedies were to have been deferred pending a final determination, as he had been repeatedly urged to do by the defense counsel, and said, "This is the only instance where the Court of Appeals directed a specific remedy as to any of the defendants. . . .While this court believes that the remedy directed with respect to Kline merits reconsideration in the event the matter is again presented to the Court of Appeals, this court is bound by its directions." He reluctantly directed that the option be cancelled, but denied the injunction. The sign-off made everything legal: This opinion, and the previous one, and the Court of Appeals opinions, constitute the court's findings of fact and conclusions of law. And there the matter stood, at least for the present.

It was reported that the Commission attorneys were pleased with the decision and believed a valuable precedent had been set, while the lawyers for Texas Gulf might logically be expected to appeal any adverse holdings. Obviously this was easier said than done. The injunction against the company had *not* been granted, but such a "victory" might effectively shackle any desire or possibility of appeal. The dilemma for the corporation was engagingly agonizing—and the law for the financial and business community was still in considerable disarray.

# 11
# People

IN our time in the United States ordinary citizens go their daily ways secure in the knowledge that they are subject to a considerable body of law, accumulated over the years, decades, and indeed centuries. Most people respect it, some fear it, and many use it. Except for its fundamental premises, however, not many understand it, nor do they feel much compulsion to probe even slightly its multifarious intricacies until such time as it touches their person or their property. The touch may come through a policeman, a jury summons, a subpoena, legal papers, or a judge. Quite often such a touch may materialize through the long arm of the post office, especially if it concerns tax matters, leaving in its wake dismay, confusion, and a sudden sense of jeopardy. Although many of these ordinary citizens, as one of the by-products of their education, will know at least constructively that the law arises from the Constitution, from statutes, from precedents, and from the judgments of courts, the threshold of their awareness is likely to be a low one so far as the *machinery* of legal process is concerned. For them, also, the distinctions between federal, state, and local areas of jurisdiction may be blurred. As human beings they are naturally more attuned to rights than to duties. Almost non-existent is their comprehension of the role played, in the making of law and at an ever-increasing pace, by administrative and regulatory agencies of government. Such matters are even more quickly consigned to the domain of lawyers and similar specialists.

265

Administrative law backdrops, pervades, flavors and over-whelms, at times, this entire chronicle. Like a fearsome space ship, the Texas Gulf Sulphur affair was launched from a hole in the ground, and the propellant was supplied by one such federal agency, established thirty years earlier by statute and now staffed by a non-elected ground crew of eager specialists. The ship is still in orbit and it may remain there for some time. Whether its ultimate achievement may sharply affect the lives and practices of the open-mouthed but often apathetic citizens below, or whether it will simply burn up and disintegrate on re-entry, however, depends not so much on the experts who planned and launched it as on the people themselves, those in whose behalf the venture was purportedly undertaken, those who will pay the bill, and those who will either accept it or reject it in the end, the experts notwithstanding. This philosophy may be cold comfort to those who currently find themselves in the toils, but it is soundly based.

Just as people tend to forget that in every stock market transaction there must be both a buyer and a seller, so they often overlook the fact that a judgment at law or in equity does not emerge unbidden. Unlike the rise of the sun and the moon, the law needs to be summoned, through a very complex process involving human initiative. In short, acts precede judgment. Even the learned and honorable judges of the Supreme Court would have little to occupy themselves but to sit idle and read escape literature, or do water colors, or climb mountains, or just doze, unless issues were placed before them. Such issues, springing from the acts of human beings, duly processed, are the straw for the bricks with which the house of law is built, and rebuilt, and extended, and every brick is numbered.

While due process of law is our glory, and simultaneously our sword and buckler and the priceless possession of every citizen, it is not, in all truth, quite as dramatically and immediately available as was, say, the quickest draw in the West. Neither is it free, in most instances. As a weapon of either offense or defense, due process is sheathed so frequently and so completely in legal printed matter—itself one of the glories of our age—that it fails to meet the demands for instant justice. People talk about it. They are confident it exists, and their confidence is well-founded, but if they are really going to need it, they should be given some advance warning, counseled to be patient, and advised to count their money.

The structure of the law arises, indeed, from the acts of people. The other side of that coin is that the weight of the law descends on people, and often on many more of them than those who instigated the acts. The acts required initiative, but the consequences acquire momentum. All of this, when applied to a complex set of circumstances and events such as was engendered by the Texas Gulf Sulphur matter, from first drill hole to last judgment, sets some unexpected scenes, throws into bold relief some intriguing characters, creates a vast number of unforeseen problems, and raises some provocative and unanswered questions. Not all of them are legal questions, and in the end very few of them may be resolved by commissioners and judges. They may not even be answered in our time, beset with such major distractions as paper gold and walking on the moon.

People came off the reel one at a time, and one of the intriguing characters, for example, is William A. T. Gilmour, a 65-year-old resident of Hamilton, Ontario. His name has thus far barely been mentioned. He was a stepchild of Murray Hendrie, and thereby hangs his tale. The Hendrie estate owned part of the land on which the fabulous copper-zinc-silver deposit was explored and discovered by Texas Gulf. In 1963, it will be recalled, Royal Trust Company, as executors for the Hendrie estate, had given a two-year option to the company to purchase the property for $18,000 *plus* ten per cent of the profit that might be derived from production of a mine. Texas Gulf exercised the option, drilled the holes, and established the Kidd Creek Mine, after trying unsuccessfully to purchase the ten per cent right. While the company's annual statements did not give a breakdown of the profit position of the mine in the Timmins area, other than to indicate that it was responsible for most of the company's increased earnings in the first full year of operation, it had been estimated that the royalty might run as high as $2 million annually—and some claimed $10 million. Just to complicate the picture, Royal Trust had sued TGS to recover either the property or $400 million in damages.

In January of 1969 a judgment of the Ontario Supreme Court named Gilmour as sole beneficiary of the estate of Murray Hendrie, disinheriting about a hundred descendants of Hendrie's ten brothers and sisters who had asked the court for an interpretation of the will. The judgment noted that Hendrie took a very broad, rather than narrow, view of his family and spoke of "my brothers" when in fact they were half brothers. Gilmour was the offspring of the Hendrie widow by a previous marriage, but had been taken into the household and treated as a son. He was eleven years old when Hendrie died.

It is of some contingent interest that Justice D. A. Keith noted, in the Ontario proceeding, that for many decades the land in dispute had no commercial value except a minor one as a timber site. "The value now attributed to it," he declared, "and which may amount to hundreds of millions of dollars, only arises as a result of a mineral discovery made after a failure of countless earlier prospectors to discover the ore body. . . . The trustees, in fact, could never have disposed of the property for what it is now alleged to be its true value, at any time during the life of the life tenant, but were only holding it because to all intents it was unsaleable."

In any case, Gilmour modestly told reporters that he was surprised, and very pleased. He expected that some who lost out might appeal the judgment, and added, "I'll get what's left after the government gets its share." In December of 1970 it was confirmed that TGS had paid $27.5 million to the Hendrie estate in settlement of all claims.

A case such as that of Texas Gulf serves to suggest that much of today's litigation in the business-financial area seems a kind of throwback to the ancient custom of single combat between selected heroes, while armies wait in the wings. But today there often arise clear moral, as well as professional, conflicts between individual participants and the larger background groups who are nominally on the same side of the question. So much of the law affecting all of us happens to be made by one man at a time, or by his attorney. This is traditional, highly and in fact compellingly ethical, and often unfortunate in the outcome, although there would seem to be no other answer. The *best* course for an individual defendant, for example, may not be the one which is in the best interests of his business or professional group, or of society as a whole. If he is a defendant in a corporate action, such as *SEC v. Texas Gulf Sulphur,* (or as were the individual defendants in the federal criminal antitrust proceedings brought against General Electric some years before, which produced prison sentences and fines), his best course may also injure the corporation and its shareowners, not to mention the rest of the interested business community.[1]

[1] Manne, for one, thinks the legal system is not quite suited to handling matters of this sort, because when a lawyer—quite properly—behaves in the traditional manner and confines his efforts solely to the interests of his client, he may be having tremendous effect on the vast numbers of people never represented in the litigation.

In fact, a corporate defendant itself may be faced with a similar question. Settlement before trial, as in *Merrill Lynch* and *Glen Alden*, or a decision not to pursue the matter beyond the point of an unfavorable verdict on appeal, which was clearly one of the options available to Texas Gulf, may often be expedient, less expensive, and more in the interests of the shareowners. The question then may be whether the management even has the right—although it may not admit the charges against it—in the proper discharge of its stewardship, to pursue any but the most prudent, practical, and economical course. Why fight on, why spend the money, in an effort to change the law for the greater benefit of others who are not standing trial or paying the bills? Even more, in the case of the individual defendant who may not have been too badly hurt in his pocketbook or in his standing with the company, at such a stage in the proceedings, does the question of what to do next become a grim problem. And yet, the choice *not* to push on in the hopes of reversing the decision and coming out the victor, when this may concern important questions before the highest court, may have the unhappy result of leaving the law in disorder for all the rest of us and greatly jeopardizing the fortunes of all who come later.

The cases of Coates, Crawford, and Kline—director, secretary, and general counsel of Texas Gulf—lend themselves to interesting examination in this light, and at least suggest some of the motives that contribute to human decision-making. After trial in federal district court Coates stood free of any violation of the securities laws; Crawford was held in violation for purchasing shares and "trying to beat the news" before proper disclosure to the public had been made; and Kline, who had been charged only with accepting a stock option, was held free of a violation, since he had no duty to disclose the little he knew to the option committee. But, on appeal, the majority of the Court of Appeals reversed the finding favoring Coates, affirmed Crawford's violation, and reversed the finding also in Kline's case, also ordering the latter's option rescinded and cancelled. So much for the record, but what were some of the non-legal aspects which might affect or control the courses then to be chosen by each of these defendants?

Francis G. Coates, a 1916 graduate of Yale from Baltimore who then went to Texas to study and practice law, had been a TGS director since 1949. A specialist in corporate and public utility law, he had served as captain in the army in World War I, had been named outstanding alumnus of the Texas Law School and was a lifetime trustee of its foundation, co-founder of a renowned clinic in Houston, director of the American Horse Shows Association, and past president of Houston's Museum of Fine Arts. He also operated two cattle ranches. On April 16, 1964, Coates attended the meeting of the directors and the press conference at which the announcement of the findings in Kidd Township was confirmed. After the meeting had broken up, around 10:20 A.M., he telephoned his broker in Houston, who was also his son-in-law, and ordered 2,000 shares of Texas Gulf stock purchased for the accounts of four family trusts. His children were the beneficiaries. At the trial in district court, Judge Bonsal conceded that Coates had "lost no time in telephoning," but ruled that as the announcement had been made, it was controlling as to the innocence of the director in respect to any violation of the securities laws. The defendant, an experienced corporate lawyer, had said that he believed the standard in the marketplace was that once an announcement was made, insiders were free to purchase stock or recommend it to others. On appeal this finding was reversed, and the case was sent back for determination of an appropriate remedy.

Coates, an elderly man and a distinguished public figure who had been roughly treated in court by the Commission lawyers, resigned his Texas Gulf directorship in 1968 for reasons of health. Having been denied a rehearing, he petitioned for certiorari in January of 1969, and it was denied by the Supreme Court in April. Coming before Judge Bonsal in the remand proceedings later in the year, his attorney, Albert Connelly, reaffirmed the "unfortunate situation" as regards Coates's health, and explained it was for that reason certiorari had been sought. That effort had proved unrewarding, Connelly said, and "as we looked down the road as to the length of time that was going to be required before a final determination and before we came back up to the Supreme Court, we have concluded that there are many reasons which point toward the desirability of a settlement. . . ."

That settlement was reached in October, just before resumption of hearings under the remand was scheduled before Judge Bonsal. Without admitting any of the charges in the complaint, Coates agreed to pay $26,250 to avoid the burden and expense of further litigation. In a stipulation he reiterated his belief that he had been both legally and morally free to purchase the TGS shares and continued to deny any violation of the securities laws. Here the motivation is clear, and the elderly ex-director's decision could hardly be attacked by the fair-minded—but the Commission had another useful settlement. The payment was to be held in escrow for three years subject to final disposition by the court, and here it is also interesting to note certain facts.

The payment represented the difference between the price paid by Coates and his son-in-law on April 16 and the price at which the stock could have been bought on the following day. This hardly clarified the issue of permissible timing for insider purchases following a corporate announcement, however, since the SEC had dropped charges against Lamont after the latter's death, which could be read as indicating that *two hours* after the press announcement supplied another "standard." The difference here would have amounted to six dollars a share. The Commission obviously preferred the longer yardstick, however. When the remand proceedings came along in October it urged adherence to the format established in the Coates settlement and asked that each of the remaining defendants be made to pay an amount measured by the difference between their purchase prices dating back to the recovery of the core from the first drill hole and the mean price on the New York Stock Exchange on April 17, set at 40⅜. Francis Coates died on November 17, 1971. There is irony in the fact that on that date Texas Gulf stock traded at nearly its low point for the post-Timmins period, closing at 12½. Considering the three-for-one split, this was roughly a dollar less per share than the amount involved in the Coates settlement with the SEC. Put another way, this insider's "killing" for the benefit of his grandchildren's trust fund had amounted then to a capital appreciation of a little more than a dollar a share over the eight-year period, and this had been more than wiped out by the $26,250 settlement penalty.

David Crawford, on the other hand, was no senior citizen in failing health but a younger and busier man with his career substantially still ahead of him. A graduate of Cornell, and of Yale Law School in 1941, he had served six years in the navy and obtained the rank of lieutenant commander in the reserve. While associated with a New York law firm he was teaching a seminar in admiralty law one day each week at Yale, and then went with the Economic Cooperation Administration in Washington, serving the general counsel's office in Athens and Paris. Subsequently he joined Socony Vacuum Oil Company for ten years, becoming manager of intergovernmental affairs, and then joined Abbott Laboratories in Chicago as secretary and general counsel. He had barely arrived for his new post as secretary of Texas Gulf and manager of its government and public relations, in January of 1964, when the developments in Kidd Township were coming to a head. On his way to Houston, to make the acquaintance of TGS people and prepare the way for the annual meeting, he learned the Canadian rumors of a rich strike through newspapers purchased in the airport, alerted Stephens by telephone, and continued on his way. Although he had no connection whatsoever with the preparation of the April 12 release, he was, on his return on April 15, asked by Dr. Fogarty to help him and others to prepare the confirming release for the next day's board meeting and press conference. The basis for the draft was an announcement that the Ontario Minister of Mines was broadcasting, in Crawford's belief, on the night of the 15th.

Crawford had then been with the company about three and a half months. He owned some stocks, including shares of Abbott Laboratories obtained through an option—an option which, of course, would no longer redound to his benefit. It was a long night of feverish preparation for the next day's meetings. Among other things, Crawford had telephoned the TGS exploration manager in Calgary and told him of the minister's impending broadcast. After midnight Crawford was about the last to leave. He telephoned his wife and then repaired to the company suite in a hotel. He also made another call, to a broker friend who had also been a neighbor in Lake Forest, outside Chicago, and asked him to purchase 300 shares of Texas Gulf the next morning. In the morning he again telephoned Chicago and doubled the order before going on to the board meeting. Today—as he did on trial in district court—he recalls that it had been a short night with a long and busy day to follow, with little time for reflection, but he was not aware that anything he did had been in contravention of the securities laws. The court, which did have time for reflection, concluded differently, and the Court of Appeals confirmed the finding.

In his petition for a rehearing, having been trained in the law, Crawford both pushed the broad arguments against the applicability of 10b-5, and the restatement of his belief that the news was out when he placed his orders. Before the petition was denied, he had already offered the stock to the company at his cost, and the offer was accepted. Now there was little more he could do as an individual. It was a practical decision but a troublesome and expensive one. Having been found in violation in district court, although the Court of Appeals had not questioned his good faith in believing disclosure had been made, he was in a less favorable position than many of the other defendants to carry the battle to the Supreme Court. As a matter of tactics, this was being done initially by Coates and Kline. He had tried and lost, but was not irretrievably hurt, certainly not with the corporation where his future presumably lay. On remand the Commission declared it sought no monetary relief as to Crawford, Mollison, or Fogarty, since they had sold their "illegally obtained shares" to the company at cost, but suggested nevertheless that the Court prevent them from any future indemnification from the company unless it could be used to satisfy claims of selling stockholders who might sue later. Yet David Crawford, the man, had here been forced to examine soberly and with some anguish his position as a responsible corporate official vis-à-vis his position as an individual, as had the others "out front."

There comes up here another aspect of the same question. Lawyers must be barred from any such unofficial seminar as this since they have their own forums in which to perform and their own game rules. While a corporation may be a fictitious person, with its ground rules only generally described in its charter, its day-to-day decisions will still be made by human beings, computers and other mechanical men having as yet no place in a proxy statement or an organization chart. Men are human, often wise, sometimes foolish or ignorant, creatures of heredity and environment, some cold and some quite warm, and their critical decisions and conduct will usually reflect both their convictions and their prejudices as well as the rules of the game and the pressures put upon them. There must often come times in the lives of most responsible business executives when they are truly puzzled over the ethics of the next move— do they make it as a delegated and accredited servant of the corporation, or as a susceptible but nonetheless upright individual who is on the spot? Where is the division of responsibilities to each of these concepts? The lawyer will have little trouble, as a lawyer, in pointing the way because he identifies his client and acts in his best interest, whether the client is individual or corporate. But this may not do justice to the rest of us who, to be fair about it, are also not in the dock or paying the fee.

Then there was Harold Kline, another fit subject for this speculative examination. He had been hooked on the special question of a judicial attitude towards stock option programs, refined and conditioned to some degree by his own corporate duties, first as corporate secretary and then as general counsel. He had made no outright stock purchases, but neither did he choose to surrender his options, preferring to carry the argument to higher levels. Kline was a graduate of the University of Missouri who had received his law degree at Harvard in 1935 and served as editor of the *Harvard Law Review*. His professional experience, into which wartime army service was sandwiched, had included five years with a distinguished New York law firm, the position of head counsel for the Federal Reserve Bank of St. Louis, and a period as counsel with General Electric before joining TGS in 1958.

Strictly from the outsider's viewpoint, it might be guessed that Kline's course of action arose less from concern with his personal fortunes and more from his convictions regarding the law of the land and infringements upon the right of a corporation to establish and administer an option program free from the harassments of a regulatory agency. His arguments must have given the SEC pause, since they took considerably longer to file an answering brief with the Supreme Court than had been the case with the Coates petition, although in the end the high court declined to interfere, despite urging to the contrary by Mr. Justice White.

On remand Kline's counsel flatly contended that neither the appellate nor the district courts had the authority to rescind and cancel Kline's stock option *in toto* because the securities statute authorized only injunctive relief. There had been denial of due process, and the penalty sought would "far exceed those requested against any other defendant." Refusal of the court to honor the later ratification of Kline's option, said Marden, was unwarranted interference with the internal management of the company and would deprive this defendant of rights fully earned through five years of faithful service during a trying period.

From an examination of the long record of such a case as this, certain propositions seem to emerge which are extra-legal and are perhaps better based in philosophy, since they have to do with human beings. Ours is a government of law, but the law is born of men and beset by them on every side.

1. Law may be controlling, but it does not spring into being unbidden. People must press the button, or nothing happens. Having pressed the button, the pressers and countless others are subject to the consequences.

2. Legal process is a solid constitutional fact, but it is slow, complex, and expensive.

3. Trial—with all that goes on before and after—is a form of

*individual* combat which frequently decides *group* issues, and the group will be bound by the result.

4. The adversary system often operates at the cost of distortion, over-rewarding counsel while penalizing the litigants, and obscuring larger issues in the interminable struggles over small ones. Otherwise innocent witnesses are frequently worse bloodied in the process of doing their duty than are the principals.

5. In such circumstances an individual defendant, and conceivably even a plaintiff, may be faced with painful introspection. The results will then characterize his conduct. Are his obligations *now* to himself or to the group? Who is he? This is hardly a question before the court.

6. In a proceeding such as TGS the shareowner's role is multifaceted and equivocal. He is both plaintiff and defendant, with all of the possibilities flowing from each but with the probability that he may lose coming and going. He is at once part of the company and its putative opponent. He can be an investor for the long haul, or a shoot-from-the-hip speculator calculating his profits in a matter of hours or days without change in his technical status.

7. The corporation's role is troublesomely puzzling, too. It is a composite of shareowners, the directors as their representatives, professional managers, other employees, physical assets and obligations, and it bears an important relationship to its industry and to the national economy. Where does it dig in?

Speaking of people, arrows shot into the air sometimes fall in odd places and with unexpected effects, which is another way of observing that the outcomes of legal proceedings are quite often influenced by people who never enter the courtroom. One curious example of this was afforded by Michael Peter Roche, a brokerage account executive of Toronto, who did not appear in the trial before Judge Bonsal, but whose words were cited twice in the majority opinion of the Court of Appeals on the question of what constituted material inside information, whereas the same opinion chose to ignore, on this question, experts of acknowledged substance and experience who *did* appear. The Roche deposition was taken in Canada, ironically in behalf of defendant Lamont, and not by the SEC, and for a different purpose entirely. It was not even read into evidence in the lower court, but Judge Waterman reached for it and used it nevertheless. One reason may have been that, in its appeals brief, the Commission saw fit to quote Roche, the newly discovered expert, five times, putting him far ahead of such other celebrated references as Bernard Baruch, Judge Elbert Gary, and Learned Hand, and making him a close runner-up even to *Cady, Roberts*.

Having said, early in the opinion, that evidence on the effect of the April 12 release upon the investing public was equivocal and less than abundant, Judge Waterman referred to "a Canadian mining security expert, Roche" and later quoted Roche on the importance of the first hole to investors: " . . . a 600-foot drill core is very, very significant. . . . Anything over 200 feet is considered very significant and 600 feet is just beyond your wildest imagination." The deponent, whose evidence was taken by Lamont's counsel actually to establish the fact that the news of the discovery had been effectively disclosed before the April 16 press conference, also said, "it is a natural thing to buy more stock once they give you the first drill hole."

The question of whether the results of the first drill hole were important to a reasonable investor would seem to be a question of fact upon which expert testimony was proper, but the SEC introduced none at the trial. Among others for the defense, Judge Bonsal *heard and saw* Professor Bellemore, author of a definitive text on security analysis, and Alvin Pearson, president of an investment trust with assets of $450 million and partner of Lehman Brothers and chairman of its portfolio committee. Both declared the first hole results not material to a reasonable investor, although they might have been remarkable or even extraordinary. In the rehearing papers Marden characterized Roche as a dealer "in fifteen and twenty cent stock situations" and said that, "In short, he was a gambler," and could hardly be included in the average prudent investor category.

Roche had a bachelor of commerce degree from the University of Windsor and his professional experience, aside from being an account executive in a brokerage firm specializing in mining stocks, had apparently consisted of working summers for his father, a promoter and prospector.

In contrast to Roche's arrow, a veritable barrage of heavy shells relating to the Texas Gulf matter, both fore and aft, was maintained by another non-witness, who was by all odds the dominant off-stage figure. This was the chairman of the Commission, Manuel F. Cohen. Back in 1940, *Fortune* had described the SEC as "one of destiny's brightest, most contentious children," which had already taken Wall Street into protective custody,[2] but by the close of 1966 the same journal was pointing out that the Commission had emerged as one of the government's most dependable generators of headlines and controversies, and that nowadays its concept of its mission was far different from any that had prevailed a few years back.[3] The reason was clearly Cohen, who after 26 years of service with the agency spoke of it affectionately as "part of my warp and woof—most of my adult life has been spent there."[4]

The SEC had been fairly somnolent in the 'forties and 'fifties, but the new action really began in 1961 with Chairman William Cary's projected special study of the securities markets. The 172 separate recommendations eventually created what was called an "agenda for the future" and made major pressures for change the prevailing climate at the agency.

At the very least Cohen, a warm and engaging man, a vigorous activist, and a highly regarded civil servant who has remained outside partisan politics, is one bureaucrat who can speak the language of Wall Street even while he is busy overhauling its practices. Under his influence and direction, the SEC has substantially concerned itself with more and better corporate disclosure, with defining and enlarging the category of inside traders, and with improving the efficiency and business practices of the business community. There are few who would find such objectives wrong in the broad statement, but they have often pinched in specific application. Most of the opposition to the Commission in the '60's has been founded in its super-aggressive methods, its willingness to change—or invent— the rules to advance its broad authority, its frequent resorts to expediency in order to speed up the game, and its increasingly superrogatory tone of voice towards the federal courts. While accepting the necessity in a complex and far from perfect age, most Americans seem to have a basic distrust of administrative law, and the question of constitutionality arises more and more often throughout the land as the Commission lays on the horses.

Born in Brooklyn, a graduate of Brooklyn College in 1933, Cohen obtained his law degree upstate from St. Lawrence University in 1936, having done interim work as a research associate for the

[2] See "SEC," *Fortune*, June, 1940, p. 91.
[3] See Chapter 9, Note 18, p. 223.
[4] "Speculating About Manny Cohen," *Business Week*, February 15, 1969, p. 108.

Twentieth Century Fund. After five years of private law practice he joined the SEC in 1942 and spent the next 26 years there until his resignation early in 1969. He had been named chief counsel for the division of corporate finance in 1952 and became director of the division in 1960. He was appointed a commissioner by President Kennedy the following year, and was made chairman in 1964 by President Johnson, following in the footsteps of such other notables as Joseph Kennedy, James Landis, William Douglas, and Jerome Frank, but also making footsteps of his own.

Cohen understands that the securities industry must make a profit, but he believes unrelentingly that it should not be at the expense of public interest, and again this would call for no argument. It can hardly be denied that in four years he made a deep and lasting impression on securities regulation. Under him, it was said, life at SEC "turned furious," whereas previously, especially in the 'forties, the Commission seemed a sedate and retiring body, like many other federal commissions, while problems mounted. Under Cohen the staff was youthful and dedicated, striking hard on several fronts. It was said that more actions were brought in 1968, for example, than in the previous 34 years, and many of them raised the hackles of Wall Street and the business community. The chairman has been proud of the Commission's record, and it was at no time more evident than in the months following the introduction of the Texas Gulf case and in the weeks which preceded his retirement and the appointment of Judge Budge as his successor. He expressed confidence that "most thinking, responsible people in the long run" would back the agency's policing activity even though "sometimes people affected by it feel hurt." [5]

Cohen was not by any means the most popular chairman of SEC, and while he was highly regarded, many critics thought he was the wrong man for the job, objecting to his headlong pace and charging him with an overweening desire to build a record. But he replied that SEC was simply "doing what it must." It was frequently noted that in the cases presented to the Commission, Cohen very often came up with unanimous votes, but that he effectively *made* it happen through his personal tactics.

Cohen uses arguments in discussing conglomerates, *Fortune* observed, that can be applied to most large companies. He feels investors should know just where the profits come from in diverse operations. The corporations, on the other hand, are hardly en-

[5] *Ibid.*

thusiastic over such disclosures because of the difficulty of allocating costs, because of help to competitors, because of unions and anti-trust charges, and because stockholders would be provoked into unwarranted criticisms. Moreover, he believes the corporate accountants are too congenially passive in their practices.

In grappling with the *Texas Gulf* and *Merrill Lynch* issues, the SEC undoubtedly raised the fears and doubts of the business and financial community over new dangers in dealing with the troublesome questions of inside information. The decision to appeal the *TGS* case within three weeks of the Bonsal decision must have been difficult because Bonsal, in dismissing the action against the corporation and most of the individual defendants, had also made rulings that were basic to the SEC ambitions, such as enlarging the category of insiders, and equating purchases on a public exchange with those made face-to-face. After the Court of Appeals had reversed almost all of the lower court findings, Cohen spoke often and widely in an attempt to counter the feeling that corporate disclosure machinery had become a chaotic mess. Addressing the University of Connecticut's Loeb awards luncheon on May 21, 1968, he had anticipated the decision in respect to the apparent strictures of 10b-5 by telling the press that, "I doubt that this is an area in which it will ever be possible to lay down comprehensive and precise guidelines as to what must be done. . . . Such a code would only enhance the substantial premiums guile and subtlety already command." Denying that certain enforcement actions taken by the Commission had inhibited the flow of financial information, he declared that alarmists had overstated the situation and that there was no valid basis for such assertions. "The decisions now pending in the Court of Appeals will, I am sure, provide significant guidance on several of these questions."

As late as mid-January of 1969 Cohen prefaced his remarks to the annual Institutional Investors Conference in New York with the observation that his speech would be neither a valedictory nor a farewell address, but the question of his continuing under the Nixon administration was the Street's—and obviously his—favorite topic. "Replace proud Manuel Cohen with a business-oriented administrator and vitality could die quickly at the SEC," declared Wayne Green, in the *Wall Street Journal*, at the end of 1968.[6] Green added:

[6] "Would a New Chairman Slow the SEC?" *Wall Street Journal*, December 26, 1968.

Manny Cohen would have you believe it's not about to happen. He publicly proclaims—naively, some securities experts feel—that the SEC can't be slowed, no matter who's running the show. Meanwhile, Mr. Cohen will hardly let anyone think about a new chairman; he doesn't want his critics savoring the idea that he may not be around much longer. . . . He has always been cocksure, and he has relished the limelight that bathes his SEC chair. It delights him to confound his critics and maintain public attention during what could be the waning weeks of his chairmanship.

Meanwhile the staff thought that the momentum of the securities industry (26.4 million individual buyers plus institutional holdings of 34 per cent of all outstanding equities) in crucial directions was so great that any chief regulator would have to perpetuate the Cohen policies. The opportunity for comparison was about to be afforded.

Closer to the date of his bowing-out, the chairman's tones were a little sharper, as he addressed the Economic Club of Detroit on January 27, 1969, and advised business to rein its power:

The corporation as an institution is, in fact, invested with political power. . . . Any totalitarian institution—public or private or semiprivate—can be run by well-meaning men, but the overwhelming fact remains: it is still a totalitarian institution. . . . I suggest that the exercise of political power, whether by government or business, cannot be legitimate unless it is non-authoritarian—that is, unless it is subject to free and systematic analysis and criticism. To some extent federal regulatory agencies have provided this function.[7]

He had another rather startling suggestion, that corporate directors would be well-advised to develop procedures of their own for institutional criticisms of important corporate decisions, perhaps through internal review committees that are independent of on-line corporate decision-making and possibly through public disclosure of proposed actions. Incidentally, this doctrine of distrust in corporate management was echoed repeatedly in the SEC's insistence, during the remand procedures in district court, that an injunction issue against Texas Gulf and its top men because they would obviously continue to violate the law and could not be trusted.

On Washington's birthday, however, the White House cut down

[7] *The New York Times,* January 27, 1969.

one cherry tree by disclosing the appointment of Hamer E. Budge as chairman of SEC. Cohen's resignation, for "personal reasons," was immediately effective, although his term as a Commission member would have had some time to run. Budge, a former Idaho state judge and Republican member of the House, had been named to the Commission by President Johnson, and supposedly had gone along wholeheartedly with those SEC actions, such as *Texas Gulf* and *Merrill Lynch*, which had most upset Wall Street. Whatever the new chairman's philosophy might turn out to be, and it was rumored that he had a soft spot for small business, he was moving into an overwhelming load of work and headaches. One of the latter consisted of his decision, in June, to turn down an offer to head the biggest company in the mutual fund business, at a reported $80,000 a year. Noting that the times would seem to call for a tough-minded decision-maker as SEC chairman, *Time* commented several weeks later that Budge is a "tranquil, kindly administrator who has a penchant for delay." The week before Senator William Proxmire had accused him of "gross, clear, conspicuous, transparent conflict of interest" for considering, and taking two months to turn down the offer.[8] But whatever the future might hold for him, it would not appear that the new chairman could be cast for any major human role in the Texas Gulf affair, which was now playing out its climactic scenes in another theater.

Another SEC personality, however, had earned program mention almost from the time the curtain went up, and that was the chief investigative counsel, Edward C. Jaegerman. Back in 1940, *Fortune* had said of Jaegerman, then trial counsel, and Tim Callahan, assistant general counsel, for SEC, that they didn't object to being called the "Rover Boys" because they had a roving commission to prosecute securities law violators wherever they could find them. "They have chased crooks across the borders into Canada and Mexico, hauled them back to face the music. . . . Bachelors, they live in suitcases, travel thousands of miles a year." Callahan had been an All-American guard at Yale in 1920, and Jaegerman was one of Bill Douglas's bright young men. In 1964 he was a bachelor no longer, however; he had six teen-age children, two of them in college.[9] Callahan retired from the agency in 1966 at the age of 70.

Jaegerman, after more than three decades at SEC and participation in more than 500 investigations, might fairly be said to

[8] *Time*, August 8, 1969, p. 65.
[9] *Op. cit.* Note 2, this chapter; p. 276.

have made the case against Texas Gulf Sulphur, picking it up from a Washington telephone call after the confirmation of the Timmins discovery and performing most of the spadework for the government which led to the complaint. A tenacious investigator, he pursued the key witnesses in the United States and Canada in what one columnist had described as the "authentic witch-hunting spirit of the late Joe McCarthy" and put the SEC "in the position of reversing the spirit of the common law and the Constitution and branding private persons guilty as charged unless they prove their innocence to the satisfaction of their government prosecutors." [10] While Jaegerman could justifiably deny any philosophical coupling with McCarthy, the accusation might have some support in respect to the vigor and enthusiasm with which he conducted his chase, and to his rough-and-tumble technique with witnesses, and to his dedication to the proposition that the Commission was properly holding the gun to malefactors of either great wealth or undeserved profit flowing from an unfair position as corporate insiders. His tendency in examination appeared to lean towards multiple repetitions of guilt and improper motivation regardless of the replies and explanations of witnesses, and he was not above browbeating the more humble victims. The total effect was to create an impression that all—from Lamont and Coates to the most far-flung of the tippees—were acting in concert in some dark and shameful conspiracy. Presumably this is the function of the gun squad, complemented when the issues came to trial by the cutting edge of California-based prosecutor Kennamer, with his announced intention of dragging to light and pillorying the individual defendants. In the Texas Gulf affair the two opponents who most often seemed to be in center stage, both attracting and repelling each other, were Jaegerman and Fogarty. Both were loquacious, filled with conviction, and confident—and both had large families. Without question each polarized the cumulative issues: in Fogarty's case it was the integrity of the corporation and its devotion to the best interests of all the shareowners; for Jaegerman it was his conception of the right and duty of the Commission to punish the rascals and defend the public against wrongdoers, as well as to advance the regulatory power of the SEC to new, and as yet unadjudicated, positions. There was a sort of religious fervor present in each, although each had also a high sense of humor.

[10] Eliot Janeway in the *Chicago Tribune*, November 4, 1968.

The Jaegerman task was finished with the filing of the complaint, for all ordinary purposes, but he added an intriguing chapter two months after the Second Circuit handed down its decision on the appeal by resigning from the SEC to become a managing partner with Charles Plohn and Company, a well-known member firm of the New York Stock Exchange. "I really made a coup," declared Plohn, a former Dartmouth swimmer, while the former Rover Boy was equally enthusiastic in his explanation, giving Callahan's retirement as one reason ("We had been such great pals and no one could ever replace Tim.") and his need to finance the college education of his children as another. He loved the new job and intended to speak "with the voice of authority." The new salary was "fantastic." [11] One of the odd but unimportant by-products was that Jaegerman's office would now be under the same roof as that sheltering the Texas Gulf executives in the Pan-Am building.

The press added a few things to the story then and later. Jaegerman first met Plohn in 1967 when SEC began an investigation into the latter's firm in a matter involving the sale of certain electronics shares. Subsequently the firm was suspended for three weeks from doing business in unlisted securities, consenting to the action without admitting or denying the allegations. Late in August, 1969, the New York Stock Exchange levied fines of $50,000 against Plohn himself and $100,000 against the firm, for an alleged failure to exercise proper supervision over the firm's business. The action broke some new ground in that it was said that these were the largest penalties ever laid against a member firm by the exchange, and that such actions are not usually publicly disclosed. Jaegerman pointed out that the action related to "conditions that existed nearly two years ago," while his own connection with Plohn was only one year old. He also noted that he had joined the firm at the urging of both the SEC and the exchange, although a spokesman for the latter declined comment.

If it were not for circumstances such as these, said consulting economist Eliot Janeway in his *Chicago Tribune* column, there would be no need for a code of ethics for SEC investigators. If the government would only pay its policemen more money, the "tone of the SEC's current crusade to impose a new morality on the securities business would be relieved of the suspicion that the ghost of Joe McCarthy is riding again, this time bedecked in a liberal

[11] *The New York Times*, October 22, 1968.

garb." Perhaps, said Janeway, if adequate pay cannot be arranged, securities people should voluntarily undertake not to hire Commission personnel for a two-year cooling-off period. "The circumstances and, above all, the atmosphere, in which Jaegerman chose to exercise his right to increase his income by going private happened to be less private and more sensitive to the intangibles of public morality than could apply to any other government investigator in the limelight or, particularly, to any other custodian of the SEC's arsenal of brass knuckles." [12]

On the second Friday in June, 1971, the governing board of the New York Stock Exchange permanently barred Jaegerman from any connection with a member firm, and again Jaegerman, once so loquacious, could not be reached for comment. While he had been managing partner of Plohn and Company, said the exchange announcement, he had also been an officer of a corporation outside the securities business, receiving personal compensation without exchange approval. Also, he had violated a regulation of the Federal Reserve Board by borrowing the money for purchasing the corporation's securities on better terms than the Plohn firm could provide. Finally, the exchange charged that Jaegerman, while holding substantial interests in the unidentified corporation, used his Plohn position to have favorable recommendations on the company's stock issued by the Plohn research department and salesmen. There were a few other charges, all adding up to the melancholy conclusion that the policeman had been policed.

Unfortunately matters did not rest here for either Jaegerman or Plohn, as the vigilant machinery of both the exchange and the SEC continued to operate with seemingly impersonal concern for the characters involved. Documents on public file at the regional SEC office revealed that, as of April 24, 1970, an annual "surprise audit" by Plohn's accountants, Arthur Andersen & Company, confronted the firm with disciplinary action for apparent violation of the New York Stock Exchange's net capital rule—that a firm's indebtedness must not be any larger than 20 times its net capital. Late in July Jaegerman, as managing partner, declared the company was "in compliance" with the rule as a result of taking emergency steps. Part of an impressive silver collection belonging to Mrs. Fay Plohn had been sold at auction at Sotheby's in London, for $592,579,

[12] *Op. cit.*, Note 10, this chapter.

and the second part would be sold later. Shares of the GAC Corporation, which had been counted as capital, were sold for approximately $590,000, according to the closing price on that day. One of the two Big Board memberships had been sold for $144,000, while the other seat and the two seats on the American Exchange were waiting in the wings. Ten of the firm's eleven branch offices had been closed, a costly business, and the bookkeeping for customer accounts had been transferred to another firm. On August 18, Plohn & Company was suspended by both exchanges, and the New York Stock Exchange announced that the house was in such financial condition that it could not be permitted to continue in business with safety to the creditors or to the exchange. Plohn employees had dwindled from 350 to less than 50, with most of the registered representatives said to be leaving. The New York regional office of the SEC had begun an investigation to determine the reasons for the company's financial troubles—and Jaegerman had resigned as managing partner. For once he could not be reached for comment, as it appeared that the erstwhile Rover Boy had been clipped by the blades, sharper than a serpent's tooth, of the lawnmower he had left behind him at the SEC.

Unlike the SEC, which was represented onstage by relatively few leading personalities—Jaegerman, Kennamer, and the two mining experts—the chief actors for Texas Gulf were all treading the boards as defendants, and their characters, decisions, and motivations were not only on display but were a matter of record. As such they were naturally subject to both fair and unfair comment, as has been the custom in all times and most places in history. Uninhibited by either direct or cross examination, or even by personal interview, a writer for such a non-legal journal as *The New Yorker* was free to add color to the scene by describing Fogarty and Stephens as "vigorous and harried corporation nabobs" and the elderly and distinguished lawyer Coates as "a Texas wheeler-dealer." Lamont was "a polished Brahmin of finance": the geophysicist Clayton became a "hot-eyed mining prospector" and Kenneth Darke a "cigar smoker with a rakish gleam in his eye, who looked a good deal more like the traditional notion of a mining prospector than like the organization man he was." [13]

As chief executive officer and next in command, respectively,

[13] John Brooks: "Annals of Finance," *The New Yorker*, November 9, 1968, pp. 164, 179.

Stephens and Fogarty were bearing the official brunt of speaking for and defending the corporation's course of action. Because he had purchased no stock during the critical period under examination at the trial, and had appeared only temporarily on target as the recipient of a stock option which he subsequently surrendered, Stephens's role partook mainly of the shepherd, whereas the others —including Fogarty—were fending off much more personal blows. Quiet-spoken, extremely courteous, and undoubtedly knowing more than anyone else in the sight and reach of the court about the affairs of Texas Gulf Sulphur, at which he had spent his entire business life, Stephens came off as somewhat less colorful and provocative than other witnesses, and while this may not be as much fun, it is a state that can be extremely enviable in a legal action. While he may be a nabob—whatever that is today—and his third of a century climb to the top of a hazardous and rough-and-tumble industry must testify to his vigor, he shows few signs of being harried. Fogarty, on the other hand, does not mind being colorful and probably can't help it.

Mining and geology are not only Fogarty's background, as he said on trial, but even more markedly his foreground, which he continues to explore on a round-the-clock basis with both love and ambition. Claimed by the head of the Denver Catholic Charities on the death of his parents, he was, at the age of ten, one of seventeen foundlings in a boys' school at Fort Logan, Colorado, and later was able to attend college on a *Denver Post* scholarship. He chose the Colorado School of Mines when the dean told him he would need only one pair of pants. From a South American jungle, where he found employment as a senior geologist on the conclusion of his war service, he negotiated a return to Colorado and earned his doctorate in what is still thought to be the shortest time on record. That led him to Texas Gulf in Houston, and eventually to its presidency. Fogarty is a man of simple absolutes, most of them positive and upward-slanted, arrived at very often through prayerful reflection. He is clearly against sin and, unlike Calvin Coolidge, will go to any lengths to explain why. His capacity for aggressive and documented bounce-back often caught his prosecutor-tormentors off balance and frequently bemused Judge Bonsal. If Texas Gulf did anything wrong, it is a sure bet that Fogarty was at the center of it because he is seldom found off-center, but it is an even greater cinch bet that *he* didn't think it was wrong.

Going down the chain of command, all of those in the exploration team were important in the discovery of the mine, but not necessarily important to proving or disproving the case brought by the Commission, except as they were swept into the net of alleged inside purchasers. Clayton, hot-eyed or not, was not faced with any decisions such as were Crawford and Kline which would offset his own interests to his duty to the corporation, and neither was Holyk. Both had more or less gone along doing their jobs, but the *effect* of what they did varied substantially with the frame of reference. Holyk, whose geology doctorate was derived from prestigious Massachusetts Institute of Technology, but who was a native of Revelstoke, British Columbia, and had done war service as navigator and flying officer with the Royal Canadian Air Force, was clearly the pivotal man in the unsuccessful attempt of the Leitch company to wrest $450 million from Texas Gulf. His negotiations, his actions, and his credibility were critical in the action brought against TGS in Ontario Supreme Court, and weighed so heavily with the court that Justice Gale's decision stood without appeal on the part of the plaintiff companies. In short, what he did and said apparently saved the mine for the company in the one case, while in the action tried in New York, Holyk appeared more in the role of narrator of on-site exploration and drilling and corroborator of the acts of others. Counsel for SEC was mainly intrigued with the 550 shares of stock and the calls on 1,200 shares purchased between November 12, 1963, and March 30, 1964, and with the fact that Mrs. Holyk had done the buying. On the remand, SEC would demand that Holyk "disgorge" $35,663.47 plus interest. It also thought an injunction should issue because United States investors "clearly needed" to be protected against his probable future violations of the law.

Clayton, the Welsh-educated geophysicist, absorbed far more of the court's time in his New York testimony than did Holyk, probably because he evolved as the authoritative interpreter of the Canadian Shield, the concept of an anomaly, and of much of the methodology of exploration and discovery. He had served with the Royal Air Force. Clayton bought his own stock—1,260 shares between November 15 and April 15—but had the added distinction of being married to a Texas Gulf consultant. Much of his time on the witness stand was spent in watering down many of Kenniamer's attempts to magnify the significance of the findings in the Kidd-55 sector, and the duel was not without its humorous side, except that the SEC thought he should be made to cough up $20,010.56 of his gains because he was "another individual who got in early . . . and stayed late."

Mollison, the exploration manager who would later become vice president of Texas Gulf's metals division, could hardly be classed as a big plunger in the SEC's netful of insider investors, since between November 15 and April 8 he had purchased a total of 300 shares with an investment of about $6,700.[14] When he went with the company six years after his graduation from the University of Minnesota, all of the exploration staff was busy trying to find essential sulphur in the Gulf Coast area, and he was the first to be given the assignment of finding some metallic sulphides. As the Kidd Creek Mine came into being he stood between Holyk's field group and Fogarty, and if that was not sufficient to make him a key man for the investigation and trial period, other things did. In fact he was a participant in each act of the Commission's scenario—he bought stock, he was awarded a stock option, he supervised the field work for the high command in New York, he provided the factual basis for the battle-scarred April 12 news release, he was responsible for *The Northern Miner's* article, and he flew with the Ontario Minister of Mines and drafted the contentious dispatch which was *not* broadcast on the night of April 15 but was released the next morning in Toronto to the press gallery of parliament. Like Holyk and Clayton (but unlike Stephens, Fogarty, Crawford, Coates, and Kline) Mollison was faced in the aftermath with no schizophrenic decision-making, although he might be some day.

A well-controlled matter-of-factness was usually Mollison's shield against the sarcastic and provocative questions put by the SEC counsel, and this streak in his character shows in the following exchange with Kennamer:

> Q. Mr. Mollison, did you intend to be so discourteous to the members of the board of directors of Texas Gulf that they should learn of this enormous discovery for the first time through a broadcast late at night emanating from Toronto, Canada?
> A. I had no intention to be discourteous.

[14] Seven of the individual employee-defendants, between November 12, 1963, and April 16, 1964, purchased a total of 6,160 shares at an approximate cost of $141,875. Of this amount Fogarty bought 3,100 shares and Clayton 1,260, leaving 1,800 divided among the other five. Four employee-defendants also purchased in this period calls on 4,700 shares totaling in the aggregate $112,025 if all were taken up. These figures exclude the 2,000 shares purchased by Coates and the 3,000 purchased by Lamont, both directors, on April 16 after the press announcement.

Q. Was it your intention, sir, that the members of your board of directors should at last learn this secret by means of a broadcast emanating from Toronto, Canada, late at night from a source not connected with the company?

A. I had no knowledge of the affairs of the board of the company.

Q. That isn't my question, Mr. Mollison. I want to know whether you intended that the members of the board of directors of Texas Gulf should learn for the first time of this discovery through a television or radio broadcast emanating from Toronto, Canada, late at night before the meeting of the board at 9 o'clock the following morning.

A. My intention had to be within the scope of my responsibilities, and my responsibilities did not include any reporting to the board.

The theoreticians of professional management should have been delighted with the final rejoinder. It was clear that he could be trusted to hold the horses.

It is, of course, pushing the obvious to describe as important onstage figures at least some of the judges who figured in the Texas Gulf affair from the beginning. To ascribe any undue influence upon the results as a by-product of their backgrounds or characters or personalities would verge on license rather than fair comment. Yet it would be unrealistic to pass over completely the dominant effect, upon both the matters and the human beings paraded before them, either live or by deposition, of Bonsal, Waterman, Friendly, and Moore, of the federal bench, as *personalities*. The same might well apply to Chief Justice George A. Gale of the Ontario Supreme Court, who presided over the Leitch case, and to Justice Arthur Kelly of the Ontario Court of Appeal, who sat as a commissioner in the Windfall hearings.

To the layman the dilemma of a Judge Bonsal seems even more perplexing than it may have seemed to him, with all respect to the learned bench. Having done his duty and made his findings in the first instance in district court, he had not only been reversed by the appellate majority but seemingly been invited to reverse himself the second time around. This draws the line rather agonizingly between man and judge, and it can only be concluded that the judiciary has resources to call upon unknown to ordinary mortals. In due course, Judge Bonsal delivered his second opinion in the Texas Gulf matter. It would be commonplace to say that it met with a mixed reception, composed of equal parts of dismay, wonder, cynicism, head-scratching, and retreaded jubilation on the part of the Commission. Laymen can speculate, where officers of the court may not with impunity, and it has been suggested, no doubt capriciously, that the most widely-read and provocative law review article on the subject might be one written by Mrs. Bonsal.

Somewhere ahead in point of time during the latter half of 1969 there loomed the United States Supreme Court. When, as, and if it came to review *Texas Gulf Sulphur* and any of the concurrent related cases in respect to some of the remaining and more demanding issues raised on trial and appeal, the roster of the high court would include not only a new chief justice but, in fact, three new associate justices, not to mention one veteran associate justice who had served as chairman of the Securities and Exchange Commission, and who had never been regarded as exactly colorless by press and public. Sufficient unto the day would be the ceremonial parting of those curtains.

While it is customary to regard court records and opinions as cast in predominantly dry legalese, a close look or thorough reading more often than not will disclose here and there the revealing and welcome encroachment of human sympathy, antipathy, or other vestiges of the non-mechanical man. Even a judge that falls asleep, with some justification, during protracted passages of soporific testimony, strikes a small blow for vitality in the judicial system and delays the day when evidence might be fed into a computer. Judge Dudley Baldwin Bonsal, sitting on the Southern District of New York bench since 1961, was not seen to nod even once during his long postgraduate trial course at the hands of the experts who described in infinite detail how to find, drill, and evaluate a mine. Bonsal seems a model of the no-nonsense school but without overtones of animosity or irritability, and like a bright pupil he would cut into the occasional murky periods of expertise with intelligent questions which put the show back on the road. He seemed always firm and occasionally funny, although not at the expense of any of the parties. With great patience he would examine, explore, and discuss the assertions and viewpoints of the most abstruse and longwinded witnesses and the sharpest eruptions of counsel until he seemed satisfied that he—and they—agreed on what the record should show. And when much of his findings—even of fact—was rejected by the appellate majority, he was meticulous in expressing his awareness of, and respect for, the instructions coming down from the Court of Appeals.

Sterry Waterman provided a flash of the man inside the robes in releasing the majority opinion when he told the *Wall Street Journal* reporter that it was "going to have a hell of an impact on the financial world," and added that "Everyone in the United States has been waiting for this." It had been twenty months since the filing of the district court's decision, and no one would have blamed all of the judges of the Second Circuit for jumping up and down and clapping their hands at finally being free of their task, but the impression prevailed that Judge Waterman was elated to find himself first up at bat. Appellate judges are denied whatever refreshment and exercise trial judges may derive from the immediate conflict provided by witnesses and counsel and are forced to flex their minds and muscles for the most part in arguing with their colleagues. Presumably they should be pardoned the very human desire to throw open the chamber windows and re-establish contact with the waiting crowd. The concurrence of Judge Friendly did not keep him from seizing the opportunity to temper the forthright blows struck by Judge Waterman by setting forth his own philosophy and law in regard to stock options and the complained-of news release, and his crystal-clear advice to the courts below in regard to the use of the injunction. It was what might be called a "Yes, but—" concurrence, from one whose interest was not only in the law but in the possible economic consequences.

When his turn came at the window, Judge Moore exercised his considerable capacity for eloquent and wrathful dissent, although not scorning the documentation which underlay his position. Judge Moore left nothing to chance. There was going to be no one in the rear of the crowd who could complain of not hearing or of not following the argument. Moreover he supplied the vivid words, the memorable phrases, and even the biting caricatures. He even came close to getting the best press, although no measurements were taken. What came through was not only his conviction but also a sense of pleasant fulfillment. Another man, with the same arguments but a different temperament, might not have been heard.

The judges of the Second Circuit enjoy a certain amount of variety even in the performance of their official duties. Some three months after the culmination of their labors on the *Texas Gulf* case, they were called upon to review the decision of a federal district court jury which had found the Swedish film, "I Am Curious —Yellow," obscene, and which Judge Thomas F. Murphy had ordered confiscated. Showing a certain consistency, which was in its way reminiscent of the majority in *TGS*, Judge Hays found that the jury's holding of obscenity was not an issue of fact but "rather an issue of constitutional law," while Judge Friendly, once more in the back-up position, declared that "our individual happiness or unhappiness is unimportant, and that result is dictated by Supreme Court decisions." Judge Hays explained that "several scenes show sexual intercourse under varying circumstances, some quite unusual," but the majority found that the sex scenes were part of an artistic whole and that the film was not utterly without redeeming social value. In a strong—and this time not silent—dissent, Chief Judge Lumbard chided his associates for taking away from the jury "the power to pass on these not too difficult and complicated questions. . . . With due deference to the very considerable intellectual attainments of my colleagues, I submit that when it comes to a question of what goes beyond the permissible in arousing prurient interest in sex, the verdict of a jury of twelve men and women is a far better and more accurate reflection of community standards and social value." [15] And so it goes.

Looking at judges as people in terms of what they may have said or done on a past action is one thing. Projecting this already precarious technique into the future has almost no justification at all. Nevertheless, the act carries no penalty for the ordinary citizen and is good practice for the professional. One may be very certain that both the plaintiffs and the defendants in *SEC v. Texas Gulf Sulphur*, plus a great host of their contemporaries in business, finance, law, and government, have cast a most interested eye, and perhaps an apprehensive eye, in the direction of the "new" Supreme Court, where the balance may well have been altered by the departure of Earl Warren and Abe Fortas and by the advent of Warren E. Burger as chief justice. *TGS* is not just a matter of inside trading, corporate disclosure and communication practices, the transformation of a fraud law into one that requires no fraud, growth of a new federal common law, the validity of stock option programs, working definitions of materiality, and the propriety of seeking injunctive relief against a "once in a lifetime" event. The big issue concerns the challenge issued to the courts by a federal administrative agency, perhaps even to the Congress, and undoubtedly to the people.

Warren and Fortas were liberal stalwarts of a five-man activist majority, and in the words of *The New York Times*, the new court

[15] *The New York Times*, November 27, 1968.

"could be a vastly different institution from the one that changed American life so profoundly over the last 15 years." [16] Back in June, before President Nixon nominated him to succeed Warren, Burger had suggested, and then participated in, a seminar sponsored by the scholarly Center for the Study of Democratic Institutions, at Santa Barbara, California. Here he made some rather unexpected observations, considering that he had presumably been picked for his new post as a strict constructionist, one who had criticized the entire philosophy behind many of the Warren court's liberal decisions, and who might want actually to "turn the Court around."

In all fairness, it should be pointed out that at the Center Judge Burger's frame of reference was criminal law, and he announced that he was overstating his opinions in order to evoke a challenging response. Nevertheless his suggestions seemed to confirm his conservatism: end the jury system and use panels of judges instead; adopt the European system of trial by inquiry with free questioning by judges in place of the American adversary system, which is "certainly inefficient"; abolish or sharply modify such traditional trial concepts as the presumption that the accused is innocent, his right to remain silent without prejudice, and putting the burden of proof on the prosecution.[17] While none of this bore much relation to the questions raised in the Texas Gulf matter, it afforded a rewarding glimpse of the thinking of the new chief justice.

Although his nomination was struck down in November, the reception accorded the naming of Judge Clement Haynsworth in August was considerably colored by the immediate and probably overstated complaints of some civil rights and labor leaders, who distrusted the South Carolina Court of Appeals jurist. *The New York Times* editorially found the choice disappointing but added this note which might have turned out to be prophetic, or at least somewhat relevant:

> While Judge Haynsworth's record does not seem to us quite as consistently or truculently unsympathetic to the cause of civil rights as some of his critics suggest, it has surely been marked by an extremely cautious reluctance to interpret the Constitution in the light of changing conditions. . . . The real and more subtle line is drawn between the concepts of justices who favor "judicial restraint," as Felix Frankfurter did, and those who, like William O.

[16] *The New York Times*, August 19, 1969.
[17] *Newark Sunday News*, June 1, 1969.

Douglas, are thought of as "activists." It is an old and honorable difference.[18]

And Douglas, of course, was still around, having come to the Supreme Court in 1939 after serving two years as chairman of the SEC. This fact, plus the advent of four new justices and presumably a change in the balance of the court, made the game of speculation more exciting.

In due course, after unhappy experiences with two nominees, President Nixon had seen the confirmation by the Senate of Harry A. Blackmun. Then, following the retirement and death of both Justices Black and Harlan, the Supreme Court received on January 8, 1972, the 99th and 100th members of the high court in the persons of Lewis F. Powell Jr., a 64-year-old Virginian and former president of the American Bar Association, and William Rehnquist, 47, from Arizona, a former Assistant Attorney-General. Both had been labeled judicial conservatives. The two new justices would not join the Court, however, until after disposition of a petition for certiorari in the TGS case had been acted upon, in December of 1971.

Evolution had been inevitable, so far as the securities business was concerned, with the coming of the New Deal and with the hearings that preceded, and then resulted in, the major legislation represented by the Securities Act of 1933, the Securities Exchange Act of 1934, and the Public Utility Holding Act of 1935. The fireworks which celebrated the birth of the SEC were touched off by a group of brilliant men with a bias—such as Louis D. Brandeis, Felix Frankfurter, Sam Rayburn, Benjamin V. Cohen, Thomas G. Corcoran, James M. Landis, Ferdinand Pecora, and later Douglas, Jerome Frank, and Leon Henderson. It was Landis, while doing his homework as chairman, who insisted that the Commission look at its every move through the eyes of the Supreme Court. Douglas had come to Washington, now the stamping ground of the brain trust, from Washington State, the home of sheep and apples, and he had a westerner's distrust of eastern slickers. His assignment, under Chairman Joseph Kennedy, was to take over certain studies important to the SEC's administrative organization problems in connection with corporate reorganization. Out of his performance flowed an appointment to the Commission. When Landis left the

---

[18] *The New York Times*, August 19, 1969.

chairmanship in 1937 to become dean of Harvard Law School, Douglas became the new chairman, dropped the conciliatory tones of his predecessor, set his course on the letter of the law, and began to crack the whip, using his own studies as background material. He was desirous that the exchanges learn to regulate themselves, but finally decided that the SEC would have to move in and do the job, even if it didn't know how. But he received unexpected help from a new faction that succeeded in turning out the old guard. The new faction also produced William McChesney Martin as president of the New York exchange. Martin and Douglas got along well, the administrative problems under the 1934 Act seemed on their way to solution, and Douglas went on to the Supreme Court, to be succeeded by Frank, the intellectual. Both of them contributed to the continuing tradition that every SEC chairman, up to the present day, would be described as an enigma. There was no question but that the 1934 Act had already helped to professionalize the securities industry, even though its procedures were cumbersome and expensive and its nuisance value sometimes unbearably high.

The real enigma in the Texas Gulf affair, as in any comparable legal proceeding, or in fact in any kind of human undertaking, is people—what they are like, what they will do and say and feel. While this may not be a very startling statement, it still signifies the greatest difference between the Anglo-American system of case law based on precedents and the strictures of codification preferred by other countries and other civilizations. The administrative practices and rules of such a federal agency as the Securities and Exchange Commission, or of such another agency as the Internal Revenue Service, carry the aura of codification and arbitrariness across the frontiers and into the territory of the common law, but when the chips are down must still justify themselves under the traditional system—or at least until further notice. And that is why people are more important than lawyers.

# 12
# The People's
# Business

I

WATCHMAN, what of the night? It had
been a fat and provocative seven years since the discovery hole
and the Kidd Creek Mine had kicked off the Texas Gulf story and
then seen it spread out in ever-widening circles. What were some of
the effects on the business of all the people?

In Eden, it has been reported, there was both insider trading
and full disclosure, and in some form or other these subjects have
been cropping up ever since over an extended period. Given the
sense of mission possessed by the SEC under Chairman Cohen
in 1964, and the zeal of the dedicated and for the most part
youthful staff who were committed to the ideal of complete equality
in the marketplace, what happened to Texas Gulf could have
happened to anybody in roughly similar circumstances. Brushing
aside the vigorous and somewhat purple accusations of the Commission's counsel at the opening of the trial, there was nothing
personal or vindictive in this SEC swoop. Texas Gulf was little
more than an unfortunate bystander who happened to be standing
on a busy corner, minding its affairs, when the cops came along
bent on action. Its business, at that particular moment, among
many other activities, included the finding and development of a
rich mine, and some of those most closely connected with the
effort had also been buying the company's stock. While it might

seem to be over-simplification—considering the morass of compli-
cations that followed—it is not too far from the truth to say that
the federal agency's squad car was cruising around the neighborhood with a John Doe warrant looking for somebody to fit the
description, when the call came in from the station house in
Washington. Even then it looked like a minor complaint hardly
worth investigating—two news releases four days apart, plus some
market action—but from just such acorns grow the mighty oaks
which shade the courthouse.

There is a recurrent temptation to liken the *Texas Gulf* case
to a theatrical production whose plot revolved around the twin
themes of insider trading and full disclosure, to judge from the
attention lavished upon these subjects by the critics after the
play opened. After leaving the theater almost everybody was ob-
sessed with the sharp musical score, which was set in 10b-5 time
and came upon the audience unexpectedly. The producers had been
intrigued by the subject matter for quite some time but never had
been able to assemble just the right talent and the right script
until now. Their only significant previous attempt, an off-Broadway
effort entitled "Cady, Roberts," had never reached the big time,
although the experience and modest return had paid off well. It
now appeared that they had a hit on their hands. The only questions
were who was being hit and how hard.

In the 16 months of investigation and trial, and during the
succeeding two years before the majority opinion of the Court of
Appeals was handed down, the *Texas Gulf* case was a matter that
seemed to concern only Texas Gulf, but then suddenly all of this
was changed. It became evident that the chestnuts of the corporate
community as a whole were in the fire, and so were those of such
related private sectors as banks and brokerage firms, analysts,
lawyers, underwriters, financial public relations practitioners, and
all sorts of institutional traders, not to mention the exchanges themselves. What had begun as a drama involving a specific number of
characters that could be counted on perhaps three hands now
reached out to envelop in some way almost the entire audience.
The only spectators left in their seats were the shareowners, who
were already beginning to stir and evaluate their new positions.
The national scene broke into an interminable series of discussion
groups, which were faithfully, or at least vividly, reported by the
professional, industry, and lay press.

Somewhat typical was the experience of Professor Harold

Marsh Jr., of the University of California at Los Angeles, who had been invited to address a group of lawyers in a continuing-education-of-the-bar program in San Francisco in 1968, and who had sought the advice of friends in the profession. His subject was to be what lay ahead under Rule 10b-5. One friend suggested that he stand up and say "Chaos!" and then sit down, while another described the assignment as quite simple—under the rule, whenever stock is sold and the price goes up, the seller could sue the buyer; if the price goes down, the buyer could sue the seller; and if the price remained the same, each one could sue the other. Actually Professor Marsh did a somewhat more thoughtful job. In the course of it he suggested that the newly-discovered chaos proceeded from increasing federalization, the tendency of the judiciary to assert complete supremacy in the structure of government, and the "disgraceful" unwillingness or inability of the states to enact fair laws protecting traders and stockholders. For his audience, the only cheerful note he could dredge up was the prospect of more legal fees.[1]

## II

Some actively benign effects had accrued, however, and could be observed in close-up when the camera was adjusted. The same month, a Canadian writer declared that, "When Texas Gulf discovered its huge base-metal mine in late 1963, it opened up a new era for the small Ontario town of Timmins. It took it out of the uncertain here-today-gone-tomorrow atmosphere of gold mining and gave it a future rooted in the more lasting world of industrial metals. Already Timmins is shrugging comfortably into its new coat." [2]

It was now a community of about 41,000 and was rapidly diversifying as it became the service center of a mining and forest products area with a 200-mile radius. Air Canada had put in three flights daily linking Toronto, with more air service to come. So far the population was up only about 500, but this was the first increase in 20 years as gold trickled from the depleted mines. Gold mining, this writer pointed out, was a transitory business, with each mine having about a three-year full life. It had come to be a depressed

---

[1] Harold Marsh Jr.: "What Lies Ahead Under Rule 10b-5," *The Business Lawyer*, November, 1968, pp. 69–76.
[2] Frank Kaplan, Toronto *Financial Post*, November 9, 1968.

industry, subsidized for the past two decades by the federal government to cushion shutdowns. But base-metal mines had longer terms, because copper, lead, zinc, and silver adjusted to economic conditions. The reasonably permanent future for the community brought by the Kidd Creek Mine was clearly evident in new suburban housing, a new 300-bed psychiatric hospital on a northeastern Ontario college campus, new office buildings and merchandise outlets. The railway and the Timmins-Porcupine Development Commission had each appointed full-time officers to develop agriculture and tourist potential.

But Timmins was only a spot—a rewarding spot—in the total picture. Appearances to the contrary, that part of the mining industry in which Texas Gulf found itself did not limit its governmental interests to the thrusting policies and practices of such a federal agency as the SEC. It had a variety of fish to fry, holes to drill, and problems to solve.

On April 14, 1969, in a statement before the House Committee on Interior and Insular Affairs, Hollis M. Dole, the new Assistant Secretary of the Interior for mineral resources, had declared that the United States was in jeopardy with respect to its long-range mineral position. He advocated a massive program to upgrade minerals and mining technology, almost on a crash basis, or the country would face the grim possibility that growth in its standard of living would be limited within 20 to 30 years. The country was not running out of mineral resources, he said, but it was short-changing the science and mineral technology needed for their discovery, profitable production, and processing. The reasons lay in the wasting nature of mineral deposits, declining grades of ore at home, increasing competition for high-grade deposits abroad, and a growing shortage of mineral specialists and engineers.

With only six per cent of the world's population, the United States consumes one-third of the world's minerals. Twenty years ago, said Dole, the country had 9.5 per cent of the world population and used half of all minerals, and there was a 9 per cent domestic production deficit with a 20 per cent deficit forecast for 1975. But that projection had already been exceeded and the gap was widening at a frightening rate. Growth in population by the year 2000 forecast a fivefold increase in global demand for minerals, with a domestic demand three and a half times larger than at present. He concluded: "Meeting the national need for minerals is a function of private enterprise, but the government has a variety of obligations and a significant supporting role. . . ." Presumably one of those obligations was also being discharged by the SEC, although it could hardly be described as helping to meet the national mineral crisis. The trouble is that government is many-faced and multi-tempered. It lacks the time and talent to put the necessary pieces together.

Even without the regulatory "assistance" of the Commission, mining could be a chancy business. Many years ago Herbert Hoover had written in his memoirs that ". . . if all costs are included— prospector's and subsequent equipment and operation of the more favorable prospects—gold mining is an unprofitable business in any country. Taking the world as a whole, the gold produced costs more than it sells for. It is certainly no business for amateurs." Other experts and veterans in the business had pointed up the same fact, for all minerals, that the *total* costs of finding new deposits exceeded the *total* returns. Stephens, at the TGS annual meeting in 1965, noted that from 1959 through 1961 his exploration department had flown 15,000 miles of airborne geophysics. They detected several thousand anomalies, inspected several hundred, drilled about 60, and then came up—on the sixty-sixth anomaly drilled—with the one-in-a-million Timmins mine. F. C. Kruger, chairman of Stanford University's department of mineral engineering, recently put some of these thoughts together in his Henry Krumb lecture,[3] asking how successful was all of this exploration in terms of profit. *The Northern Miner* had reported that only eight-tenths of one per cent of all Canadian incorporated mining companies had paid dividends. The overwhelming majority of 7,000 mining units registered in all provinces and territories have never paid anything. In any case, Kruger drily comments, ample financing is required to support an adequate effort, long enough to cover a big enough area and to give the law of averages a chance to be effective.

So concerned is the Commission with the investor's prospective golden eggs that it has almost no time or concern for the health of the goose, showing little inclination to diagnose the latter's problems or worry as to whether or not the treatment might be fatal. In the fall of 1969 the SEC submitted [4]—although that is not the word the Commission would be likely to use to describe its actions—its

[3] Published in the September, 1969, issue of *Mining Engineering*, as "Mining: A Business for Professionals Only," pp. 83–8.
[4] Securities and Exchange Act of 1934, Release No. 8681, September 15, 1969. Notice of Proposed Revision of Form 10.

notice of an intention to revise certain forms to be required henceforth from mining companies under the Securities Exchange Act of 1934. It was asking for quite a lot—total tonnage, for each of three years, of ore produced and estimated reserves; average grades of ore; average direct and additional costs, and dollar amount realized, per ton produced; changes in ore bodies or mining conditions; and a number of other details up to now considered to be matters of confidential concern only to management. The response of one of the recipients, the American Mining Congress, was not submissive.

The information sought constituted highly discriminative treatment of the extractive industries, said J. Allen Overton Jr., executive vice president. If sought from manufacturing companies, it would be so detrimental as to be strenuously resisted. "If this attempted inroad against the mining industry is successful, the foot will be in the door for the regular disclosure by all public corporations of their confidential data, a critical setback for the survival of our competitive, free-enterprise system." He added that the information would be of extreme interest to domestic and foreign competitors, suppliers, customers, labor unions and "political subdivisions." Despite his tendency to splutter in print, Overton added that the information would in fact, for many smaller companies, go to the heart of their ability to survive. He struck at what should have been the weakest link in the SEC proposals:

> The best interests of stockholders are not served by the disclosure of information vital to the successful conduct of the business. Corporate management should retain the prerogative of maintaining corporate security. . . . Those who would opt for more disclosure at any price usually urge that the benefit to the public outweighs the disadvantages to the corporations. We submit that in this case there is no redeeming benefit to the investing public to put on the scale to offset the discrimination and anticompetitive aspects to the mining industry. . . .

*Barron's* had been hitting close to the same mark the previous year in the course of taking a searching look at U.S. farm policy. One of the editors, Dr. Kurt Bloch, contrasted such revolutionary developments as computer technology and atomic fission as a source of power with the "new economics" of the past eight years:

> Increasingly the nation tends to be victimized by the false perspective of Washington, to the extent of ignoring the relentless dynamics of U.S. business, which supplies the continuity and sub-

stance of the national welfare. What happens in business leaves its mark not in official reports but in the annals of corporations and in the market for their equities. What is recorded there, however, rarely makes the front pages—a new mine, e.g., becomes noteworthy when officers of the corporation finding and developing it are smeared by a federal agency—so that business is seen as some kind of special interest group rather than as the great mover of affairs and the generator and beneficiary of innovation.

In moral philosophy, Dr. Bloch concluded, we learn about ends and means. "A laudable end rarely can be achieved by ignoble means. Moreover, if an end is improperly defined, it will never be achieved, and means designed to achieve it ultimately will turn into ends themselves." [5]

The closest the presidential campaign of 1968 came to the TGS affair was in the matter of the famous Nixon letter sent to 3,000 business leaders in the final weeks. It was entitled, "The Role of the Securities Industry in the National Economy," and it sent *The New York Times* and its stable of political writers into a shaking frenzy. To be fair, Nixon was the Republican candidate for President of the United States, and presumably he was entitled to make his position clear on this and other subjects. Granting that the problems arising from the fantastic growth of the securities industry were sophisticated and complex, he declared his belief in the securities laws and their full enforcement to insure protection for the investor, and said that the federal government should be continually sensitive to the needs for improvement. He then characterized the action of the Johnson administration in these matters as the "same tired old cure-alls" of the Democratic party, and said its philosophy was that government could make decisions better than could the investor for himself. Nixon called for an independent, comprehensive *economic* study of the role of financial institutions in the economy *before* steps were taken which might seriously hurt the country. As a sort of footnote to the last point, he noted that Congress had authorized an SEC study covering "some" of these issues, but before it could be initiated, both the Justice Department and the Commission had advanced proposals involving drastic changes, smelling of rate-fixing, and dangerous to small independent businessmen. [6]

The reaction of the *Times* filled most of the following two weeks. Nixon was charged with sending a secret letter to Wall

[5] Dr. Kurt Bloch: "What Price Parity?" *Barron's*, December 9, 1968.
[6] *The New York Times*, October 2, 1968.

Street, with denouncing the mutual funds legislation which had already been killed in the House, with not having seen the letter at all, with intending to dominate the independent regulatory agencies of government, with trying to produce immediately after his election a Republican majority in the Commission itself, which was hardly possible (although it happened), with attacking the New York Stock Exchange, with not knowing that his views were really *not* shared by the securities industry, and so on. Both Eileen Shanahan, in her Washington column, and Terry Robards, writing from New York that "politics had thundered into Wall Street," [7] offered numerous critical comments about the letter from "leaders" of the industry but failed to mention any names. Even the editorial page went along on the charge of a "secret" letter in the face of a Nixon comment that it was silly to label anything secret when it was addressed to 3,000 people, and offered the conclusion that the candidate "looks with favor on the enhancement of private monopoly power."

On the same page, and surely a coincidence, a letter from former chairman William L. Cary, now a Columbia law professor, went along with the act to charge irresponsibility, a desire to "gut" the SEC and shrink its budget, and claimed that the Commission had been vigorous in the protection of the public interest, citing the *Texas Gulf Sulphur* case as proof. Professor Cary declared in his closing, as noted earlier, that securities regulation in the United States was considered the best in the world and was being copied abroad.[8]

The principal notable reactions to all of these outbursts were a booming reaction on the New York Stock Exchange producing the second highest level in history, and a reasoned and somewhat deflating editorial in the *Wall Street Journal* [9] which raised the question of whether the candidate's critics had ever read the letter. In Washington Manny Cohen again declared that government regulation had created prosperity for the securities business. "We must be the voice of the investor for, as the recent defeat of the mutual fund bill demonstrated, the investor has no real organized voice." [10] But a week later, Albert Kraus wrote in the *Times* that the SEC's support might be waning. He quoted still another unnamed

[7] *The New York Times,* October 6, 1968.
[8] *The New York Times,* October 7, 1968.
[9] "Review and Outlook," *Wall Street Journal,* October 11, 1968.
[10] *The New York Times,* October 9, 1968.

observer: "The SEC is fighting a holy war. Its big trouble is that it can't seem to enlist any crusaders." [11]

With the shooting all over, except in Vietnam, and the new administration well into its first full year, everybody's best guess seemed to be that a "Nixon Commission" was unlikely to reverse any such major precedents as had evolved from the *Texas Gulf* and *Merrill Lynch* cases, but that comparable actions might not be brought along very fast. By September, SEC Chairman Budge was making what amounted to his first policy statement, before a conference of 450 brokerage firm executives in New York, and in it he expressed the opinion that both the government and industry were prone to forget that the primary responsibility for regulating the industry lay with the industry itself.

Perhaps a more reasonable comment on the Commission methods and problems had been voiced almost two years earlier, before the heat of a presidential campaign partially obscured the issues, in a review of the SEC report on mutual funds.[12] Here the observer found the report, although it had many virtues, provided relatively little in the way of economic justification because the SEC's orientation is legal rather than economic. "Its heart is in the right place," said the reviewer. "It would be in a far stronger position, however, if its head possessed the right answers."

The SEC's special study of the securities markets also suffered from the same economics gap, according to such supporters as Professor Irwin Friend, of the University of Pennsylvania, who deplored its failure to provide information and insight into the economic performance and significance of the securities industry.


### III

The business of all the people, not just that of a single corporation, was affected by the findings of the court in *TGS* and by the theories and practices of the Commission which followed. Not all of the business affected was that conducted by lawyers, but it appeared that more of it *might* be, and the whole process of distributing corporate information was the first to come up for examination and debate. Despite its frequent and apparently sincere claims that it favored complete and continuous revelations of information from corporate undertakings on almost any subject

[11] *The New York Times*, October 16, 1968.
[12] M. J. Rossant, in *The New York Times*, December 7, 1966.

deemed worthy of mention, the SEC had nevertheless laid a heavy hand on the machinery designed to perform such tasks. The agency was primarily concerned with information to investors, but that meant everybody, and all types of media.

Prior to the 1930's company publicity men and company news bureaus performed a useful service, but usually in a very low key. Their connection with management was at best a one-way channel, direction downward, and if they thought of themselves as being part of an echelon, it was obviously not a very lofty one. Anyone who was so bold as to speak of the function of "public relations" did so on his own time or at least with a cautionary look over his shoulder, to make certain the boss was not listening. The best practitioners were sensibly aware of the importance of their function when properly performed, and were not unaware—especially in a depression era when business enjoyed no great popularity and was often caught with its foot in its mouth—that communication and clarification of industry's role must eventually deserve more consideration at the policy level. In short, the boss had to be educated, but it was going to be a slow process, with plenty of skeptics and scoffers.

The essential factor in the true coming-of-age of public relations as a practice and as a profession during the last 30 years, has been the abandonment of press agentry in favor of a careful and efficient study of the working channels of communication, the needs of the media for timely and truthful information whether the news be fair or foul, and of the priceless virtues of reliability and accuracy at the sources. With attention of this kind given to the receivers and distributors of the news, the foundation was in place for an elevation of the function within the company, based on professional competence and demonstrable good judgment. To a very considerable extent this is what has happened in the business world. To consider just one category of the public, the investor, it can be said that he gets more and better information than ever before in history, and than in any other country in the world.

In 1866, when the officers of the New York Stock Exchange sought to obtain a financial statement from a well-known company, they were told that "the company made no reports and published no statements and had not done anything of the kind for the last five years." Such an anecdote provides the only light touch in the exchange's "Expanded Policy on Timely Disclosure" published in 1968.

In the nineteenth century most corporate undertakings preferred to walk the streets fully clothed and muffled in secrecy, and in the succeeding decades were weaned from the practice only gradually, not so much because of the pressure of official demands as from the growing need to talk about themselves in order to enhance the distribution of their goods and promote their growth with the public. The official demands came later, and as might be expected, were the result of abuses of public information. For some time now corporation executives have quit getting under the desk on the approach of a newspaperman. New arteries of information have been developed, as the stock exchanges continue to pry more facts out of their listed companies. Financial houses have developed batteries of security analysts, and the latter have formed their own societies and grown in prestige. There is an almost unbelievable amount of financial news generated, distributed, and read with avidity. It filters down to the investor by what the late Harold Fleming, a veteran business and Wall Street correspondent, terms a process of information osmosis. While it is true that some get the news ahead of others—which especially irks the SEC—and some are better able to digest and interpret it than others, nevertheless it is a question whether the results can be matched in speed and detail by any imagined direct distribution not now in effect.

The danger, insisted Fleming, is that the SEC, in trying to force utopian and unthought-out ideas on the information streams volunteered by the financial world, may harden the existing arteries of news, causing them to transmit either less information, or more information imperfectly interpreted. The hypertension that may now be induced in corporate officers and their expensive outside counsel, as a result of the recent developments, will be due to fear of the later hindsight of disappointed investors and retrospective SEC staff lawyers. And this will apply particularly to press releases and interviews. As the appellate court minority in *TGS* said, "If press releases have to read like prospectuses to guard against possible 10b-5 liability, it is safe to predict that they will quickly fall out of favor with corporate management."

The analysts may be in a special quandary, as their business speakers arrive for luncheon accompanied by counsel, or worse yet, veto an appearance at all. Many publicly-held companies are so worried by the recent court decisions and government rulings covering disclosure of financial information that they have dried up the traditional flow of such data,[13] while others have, in the

[13] *Wall Street Journal,* February 11, 1969.

confusion, decided to tell all and flood the news media and the analysts with speeches and announcements. In the opinion of one writer, even the market letters issued by analysts might be brought into question as violations of the SEC rules.[14]

In 1970, before his own retirement as SEC chairman and the succession of lawyer William Casey, head-man Budge told a Washington meeting of investor relations specialists that discussions with financial analysts should be limited to information already published in the registration statement. After being nudged from the floor, he conceded that other matters might be discussed provided they were "not material." But, as a result of the Texas Gulf case, it could be argued that any fact would be "material" if it *might* affect the desire of *any* speculator to buy, sell, or hold a company's securities. The same handcuffs would fit analysts and corporate news releases.

For longer than anyone in the business cares to remember, corporate public relations departments have had to battle corporate law departments, over the desks of company executives, for comparative freedom from excessive legal caution in dealing with the news. There was a time not so long ago when practically all of such arguments were summarily decided in favor of the lawyers, whose expertise in their own field was unquestioned, but whose sense of the company's responsibility to the public was diminished through lack of exercise or an inability or an unwillingness to evaluate the climate of opinion or the corporation's total interests. For months during the final checking of this study, to give one example, even the TGS lawyers fought against publication of the book on the rather naive ground that it would unduly influence the courts in decisions still pending. That could be termed a sort of inverted contempt of court. It requires a brave or foolhardy chief executive to override the commands of a famous law firm when his alternative is simply to brush aside the pleas of an intra-organization subordinate. Being on the payroll instead of on retainer sapped the persuasiveness of the company advisor all too often. This hard-won ground is again in danger of being abandoned if future press releases are to be second-guessed by skeptical and—in respect to business—not too expert judges having the benefit of hindsight. With all due respect to the lawyers, corporate information on critical subjects can too easily revert to being flat, stale, unprofitable,

[14] *The New York Times,* August 28, 1968.

and even dangerous, or it might vanish completely, if the decisions in such matters are left to legal departments.

And now also, everybody was eager to help business handle its communications, it seemed. The Second Circuit judges had included, in the *TGS* majority opinion, suggestions on writing news releases, and the SEC frequently contributed its advice on this subject. In a commendable effort to cooperate with both the Commission and the business community, the New York Stock Exchange revised and expanded, in mid-1968, that portion of its company manual devoted to timely disclosure of information. The difficulty here, however, lay in the fact that most of the new suggestions made were those with which most companies heartily agreed and were already seeking to practice, whereas the proof of the pudding under the current decisions remained in the *ex post facto* deliberations of the courts or in the too often expedient or unpredictable actions of the SEC. The *TGS* opinion had pretty clearly demonstrated that almost nobody could decide safely what was a "material" fact, for example, until the judges had spoken, and the ordinary citizen was left to guess what that might be, and then take his chances.

In effect the Exchange's suggestions as to the internal handling of confidential corporate matters came down to a warning to be fair and careful—if unusual market activity should arise during such a period, the company should be prepared to make an immediate public announcement. Such advice, of course, raises the question of priority for any management. It might not be in the interests of the corporation and its stockholders to supply the details, as in the case of a land acquisition program or a proposed merger, and to do so might well destroy the benefits envisioned for the doubtful result of enlightening some potential speculators. (Such an announcement might also run contrary to the SEC's policy and create new perils.) It could well develop that the speculators themselves might be led into an unprofitable venture. Management's prudent course might well be to withhold comment in the overall interest of the company and its owners—but there is little guarantee today that whatever course it chose would protect it from a violation action based on 10b-5.

In the matter of the relationship between company officials on the one hand, and analysts and institutional investors on the other, the Exchange's advice is companionable but not too helpful. It holds that annual reports, quarterly statements, and interim releases cannot provide all the information that the investing public desires

(but why not?) or all that it should have, in the fairness concept
so dear to the Commission's heart. The company should therefore
preserve an open door policy for analysts, financial writers, and
others—but it should not disclose anything which is not "publish-
able." The two suggestions would seem to cancel out each other,
although the new policy leans a bit when it says that nothing should
be withheld in which analysts or other public investors "have a
warrantable interest." In this case, "warrantable" turns out to be
about as reliable a guide as "material." Who issues such warrants?
The business of the company is to provide products and services for
sale, presumably, while the business of analysts is to provide information, also for profit, and any doubt would necessarily have to be
resolved in favor of the company, or the management should turn
in its suit.

Considering the sophistication of most of the companies listed
on the exchange, the rather lengthy instructions given in the manual on how to write a news release, and where to send it when
written, are downright naive, especially when they neglect to point
out that the release may well be ignored by the media, leaving the
sender in the shoes of a non-discloser. The writers go even further
in this direction when they discuss the appropriate times to award
stock options to key executives, and how and when officers and directors should purchase stock in the company, adding, however,
that hindsight is remarkably keen and accusations can always be
made that inside knowledge was employed. The manual then recognizes that, "This theory, carried to its extreme, might suggest that
a corporate official should never buy or sell stock in the company
he represents"—an unhappy footnote to people's capitalism. A great
deal of print might have been saved if the exchange authors had
simply skipped to the final conclusion offered the reader, which
was that "the final decision of each officer and director with respect
to securities transactions must be his own."

The New York Stock Exchange does have a duty to maintain
a market which will protect, so far as possible, the interests of investors, and its chief instrument is the stock list department, which
monitors trading. When unusual activity occurs, trading can be
suspended, companies can be contacted for announcements, and
investigations can be launched which may discipline members.
Through the device of the stock listing agreement, companies are
bound to comply with this department's requirements, and the company's chief executive is held responsible. It is this state of affairs

which underlies the issuing of the timely disclosure policy, an honest attempt to improve a chaotic situation.

### IV

Disclosure, in the common understanding, and disclosure as it may now be examined in a court of law, or even earlier in a Commission proceeding, are possibly two quite different animals. While stubbornly resisting all suggestions that it supply the business, financial and legal communities with any practical rules or guidelines relating to the timing of insider trading, the SEC has on a number of occasions contemplated taking a hand in the procedure of disclosing information. In 1966 it announced that it might make a major overhaul of its regulations for disclosing corporate information to the investing public, one which could lead to significant changes in the informal procedures now employed by many companies.[15] Chairman Cohen's remarks hinted at the reason—the Commission did not seem to be getting as much information from corporations as was some of its competition, the analysts and the institutional investors. That the latter were "able to obtain from the issuer, because of their economic power or for other reasons, information that is not available to those with whom they are trading in the public market, raises serious questions of law and propriety."

Realistically the Commission's problem here was that it was already glutted with information in the form of required reports but was just not very handy in processing and digesting it, and in getting it out. The data was also rather expensive for the customers. Reading between the lines of various staff comments, one could guess that the SEC would like to lay down the rules on what should be disclosed, and when, and then put the costly job of widespread distribution on the corporate machinery itself, with the lubrication for this effort supplied by the threat of 10b-5 penalties in the case of failure to satisfy. "This is a real problem," declared still one more unnamed official. "The information is filed here but how do we get it into the hands of the public?" Physician, heal thyself.

Everybody can define disclosure, just as everybody can define such other specific abstractions as business, war, and love. The troubles arise, and the circumlocutions begin, when even those who agree on the principles try to apply them, at which point complica-

[15] *Wall Street Journal*, November 17, 1966.

tions begin to extend and alter the definition. This does not stop almost everybody from giving advice to the corporation.

Philip A. Loomis, SEC's general counsel, defines insider information as any corporate news which would have a sharp and immediate effect on the company's stock if given in confidence, but this is a definition which requires the exercise of judgment without benefit of standards or guidelines. The judgment is not even that of a particular class, such as officers and directors, because it can apply to any employee plus their relatives and friends. No one can really know how the market will react, and only when it does is there the semblance of a test. Contrary, perhaps, to the popular picture, very few responsible people in a business corporation shape their day-to-day decisions and communications with an eye on the ticker. They are too busy doing their job.

Senator Harrison Williams, of New Jersey, chairman of the banking subcommittee on securities, planned to hold hearings to determine whether new legislation was necessary to insure equal access of information to all of the nation's investors, thus in one stroke adopting the Commission's egalitarian principle but skipping the practical question of whether it might be *possible* to enforce such a principle. And one of the country's largest public relations firms advised business *not* to play it safe by clamming up, since this would expose them to as many dangers as talking too much—not very helpful, as advice goes, and considering the source possibly self-serving. Ralph Saul, then president of the American Stock Exchange and a former SEC official, came closer to summing up the dilemma when he said, as noted earlier, that cases such as *TGS* had made the principles of timely disclosure very clear but left the questions of procedure, degree and practice unspecified. Or, as another observed, it appeared that principle had scored a thumping triumph over reality.

One of the chanciest areas of business affected by what now appeared to be the Commission's policy on disclosure was bound to be that of proposed company mergers, which are especially difficult to negotiate in a goldfish bowl. Informal conversations which *might* lead to action can originate on a golf course or over a luncheon table, and even subsequent exploratory studies and preliminary conversations would not, normally, prompt or justify formal disclosure. In point of fact, such early stirrings, if known outside the group of principals of either company, could lead to confusing and chaotic market reactions which might never be underwritten by a consummation. Some such dance, for example, took place in the negotiations between Xerox and C.I.T. in 1968, where too early discussions of a projected merger, possibly in apprehension over penalties for lack of disclosure, broke up the wedding.

In a lengthy open letter to Chairman Cohen, printed in the *Wall Street Journal* on December 12, 1968, Milan G. Weber, president of a firm whose business was acting as a catalyst in mergers and acquisitions, complained bitterly over the fear and uncertainty created by both government agencies and stock exchange administrators, in their recent attempts to explain and establish a policy of full disclosure. Weber felt strongly that it was in the public interest that acquisitions and mergers be achieved where the facts justified them, and where they effected an improvement in the business community: ". . . but when such disclosure comes to the point where business is seriously hampered and the interests of stockholders are jeopardized, it is time to call a halt. . . . We do not feel that the management of responsible corporations should be obliged to report to your agency, or to a stock exchange, or to anybody else, every time he is obliged to consider several possibilities for the purchase of materials, parts, components, airplanes, automobiles, or . . . companies."

Weber pointed out that one of the fruits of too early disclosures of an acquisition was that key employees began looking for new jobs, and he described the fears of publicly-held companies "inherent in their attempts to walk the thin line between premature disclosure and belated informing of the public." He called for standardization of procedures and clear definitions of what the Commission and the exchanges expected from a company contemplating a merger. Finding a high degree of integrity in the business community, the writer believed that it should have the fullest power to make decisions without having to announce to the world, during discussions, every new factor leading to those decisions.

Whatever the quality and utility of the suggestions made to the business world might be, in the effort to shore up the corporate walls against the perils of disclosure, business was booming for the public relations firms who made a practice of advising them.[16] One prominent agency had set up a "client selection committee" to make certain that prospective clients possessed good performance records and a management that could be reasonably measured on its integrity. In the tail-wags-dog business this set a new record for

[16] *Wall Street Journal*, January 30, 1969.

presumption. In others, both the amount of business and the staff had doubled during the past year, fees had been increased on the average of ten per cent, and most of the increase was going for salaries, since good men seemed to be in short supply. According to a vice president of Carl Byoir and Associates, the job called for a systems engineer with Wall Street experience who could write like Shakespeare. The big news, he said, was that corporations were at last realizing that information was an asset.

It could also be costly, in a number of ways. The taxpayers were footing the bills for the regulatory body which made full disclosure necessary, whether or not it proved useful to the investing public. The mechanics of providing the SEC with information were reflected in substantial added operating costs and overhead for the companies, and there was the additional possibility that information so expensively supplied would benefit competitors and interfere with the objectives of mergers, land acquisition, and new financing projects. Ironically, the timeliness and completeness of the news would necessarily diminish its value to those who produced it and make them less eager to bestow future bounties and windfalls, while its very completeness might put it beyond the understanding of the ordinary investor and mislead the speculator. Truth in securities could be not only costly but self-defeating in many circumstances.

When Mobil Oil Corporation completed its first exploratory well on the Alaskan North Slope early in 1969, it declined to disclose results, to protect its competitive position, although it planned to drill as many wells as possible to protect its stockholders and to acquire further information prior to an expected lease sale by the state of Alaska later in the year. There had been repeated rumors in the oil industry and in Wall Street that Mobil and Phillips Petroleum Company had discovered oil in this territory and the stock in both companies was actively traded upward.[17]

In May the highly sensitive weekly, *The Northern Miner*, in Toronto, volubly took to task the conduct of the Gulf Oil Corporation of Pittsburgh because a wholly-owned subsidiary in Canada was being close-mouthed about a uranium discovery six months earlier. The company had done considerable drilling since the discovery but left the mining industry guessing with only the observation that the find was "significant." The publication made the point that the market value of a group of oil companies, all with Canadian

[17] *Wall Street Journal*, March 10, 1969.

listings, had gone up by approximately $100 million on the strength of the Gulf find, although they stood to share only 10 to 20 per cent of any profits realized in Saskatchewan's Wollaston Lake area. "It is high time," said the editors, "Gulf got off its high horse and told the Canadian people just what it has come up with in Saskatchewan." [18]

Meanwhile a new feature on the securities landscape appeared early in 1969 with the advent of a new television service in New York. Whether it was in response to the Commission's desire to spread the news to all as fast as possible, or simply to demonstrate —at a profit—the unique features of electronic newsgathering as compared to newspapers, is not known. During the business week, from 11 in the morning to 3 in the afternoon, station WOR-TV was providing everybody, including housewives, with an uninterrupted flow of information on securities, commodities, indices, and trends, with the help of a team of commentators who were proved experts. Under an agreement with Dow Jones, there was a 15-minute lag between the time a stock price appeared on a brokerage house ticker and its appearance on a television screen. Jack Gould, of *The New York Times*, declared the program was not for amateurs but for old hands at the game, since the quotations moved quickly and required both close attention and experience from the viewer. The program already had its first sponsor. In less than a month the station had received 20,000 inquiries on how to use ticker tape in the parlor, and women dominated the first sample analyzed by a two-to-one margin.[19]

The public relations business was not the only one cashing in on the spell thrown on the financial community by the SEC. Liability insurance for officers and directors was also booming. Readers of the *Wall Street Journal* on a day in January, 1969, were startled to see a full-page paid advertisement with almost half of the page devoted to the headline: "I might just sue every company director reading this newspaper." The copywriter serving the interests of American Home Assurance Company led off in this manner: "I'm not a madman. This is not a joke. If you are a director of a major company, I've got you where I want you. At my mercy. All I have to do is own a few shares of stock in your corporation and I can sue you and every other director and officer in the company.

[18] *The Northern Miner*, May 29, 1969.
[19] *The New York Times*, March 4, 1969.

What can I sue you for? What can't I sue you for!" And then he told them, adding for good measure that he was not alone in this advantageous position in respect to "our company" since there were 24 million others just like him.

In five years director-and-officer liability insurance had gone from almost nothing to more than a billion dollars, and rates had increased as much as 400 per cent. Even accounting firms were being sued. While the number of suits brought has increased to a frightening extent, any student of the modern corporation should perhaps be more alarmed, or impressed, by the fact that the courts seem to be found increasingly on the side of the shareholder, and by the additional fact that most of the actions involve stock transactions rather than some other type of alleged misfeasance. Instead of being brought in state courts, they are occurring with greater frequency in federal courts, under 10b-5, and here—as general counsel Loomis of the SEC has pointed out—it is not necessary to prove a deliberate intent to deceive. Carelessness is sufficient. Under the rule no security is required for a so-called representative suit in behalf of a class of stockholders, the statute of limitations is longer, and the stockholder does not have to be in the same state as the defendant. Today the Supreme Court has required that federal judges must decide at the beginning of a trial whether or not the shareholder represents a class, a ruling which also helps to guarantee the lawyer's fee.

Professor Bromberg, clearly an authority in this field, may have had tongue in cheek when he observed that "Rule 10b-5 has allowed judges to infuse their ideas of fairness into the securities law. Courts are always making new law. It is a very democratic process where individual investors go into the courts and help expand the boundaries of the law." If so, it is a democratic process that is making business executives more than a little jumpy. The cost of pioneering can be painful.

There are probably some questions, also, about the eventual efficacy of insurance for officers and directors. For one thing, the company generally pays most of the premium. If the corporation is moving against an officer or director in a derivative suit, the fact that a losing defendant can pay the damages out of a policy largely financed by the company justifiably confuses some people and makes others think that it only helps officers and directors to be careless. Nobody really knows as yet what the insurance covers, and will not until enough courts decide the questions.

Some of the current problems of capital and conscience, as posed by the editors of *Time*, can be these:

> A banker sits on a company's board and also has a place on the investment committee of his bank's trust department. Almost simultaneously he learns that the company's profits will be disappointing and that someone in his trust department wants to buy the company's stock. Should he warn the bank not to buy?
> A lawyer on the board of another company finds out that the firm will soon market a profitable new product. But one of his law partners is an adviser to several estates and intends to unload the company's shares. Should the lawyer dissuade his partner?
> A corporate executive lunches with his firm's president and discovers that hard times are ahead. Would he be wrong to dump his own holdings in the corporation's stock? [20]

The answers in the first and second cases would be clear in the minds of most lawyers—a director's first *legal* responsibility is to the corporation and its stockholders. The decisions would obviously not endear the decision-maker to either the bank or the law partner nor enhance his personal financial or professional future. The third case rests entirely on a personal decision, and while it might in today's theater run the risk of a securities law violation, it does not appear to raise much conflict between individual and corporate interests.

When Howard Butcher III, a Philadelphia broker who was also a director of Penn Central Company and about 70 other firms, was sued in 1968 for using "secret information" because his brokerage firm had sold railroad stock before an earnings decline was announced, he decided that the potential liability of being a director was too great for an active businessman. He quit *all* of his directorships, and so did his partners, on the theory that anybody who had any business at all was bound to have conflicts of interests.

The same doughty appellate court for the Second District recently opened up either some new perils in corporate relationships, or another can of worms, in connection with a case involving the Martin Marietta Corporation. It said, in effect, that a corporation can be barred under certain conditions from profiting in another corporation's stock. Among other side-effects, this might make it even harder to persuade outside executives to serve on a corporate board. The part of the 1934 Act invoked here was Section 16(b),

[20] *Time*, October 18, 1968.

which prohibits "short swing" profits to directors, officers, and ten per cent stockholders, but until this case there had been no restriction on a *corporation* dealing in the stock of another company unless, of course, it owned ten per cent of the shares. The decision of the appellate court was somewhat narrow in its application, setting forth that in certain circumstances the outside director is merely an *agent for his own company*, thus binding that company to the same standard of performance as the director himself.

In this case George M. Bunker, the president of Martin Marietta, had joined the board of Sperry Rand Corporation following the purchase by his company of about $10 million in Sperry Rand stock. A few months later Bunker resigned and Martin Marietta began selling the stock with no qualms, since the amount had never equalled as much as ten per cent. The amount of profit involved was slight, but a stockholder sued to have it turned over to Sperry Rand under the short-swing provision of the law.

What ensued had a familiar ring. The federal district court threw out the suit, ruling that Martin Marietta was not subject to Section 16(b), but the Court of Appeals reversed on the *facts*, contending that Bunker had been named a director because of his company's purchase of the stock. It cited Bunker's letter of resignation to General Douglas MacArthur, then the Sperry Rand chairman. One sentence had read: "When I became a member of the board in April, it appeared to your associates that the Martin Marietta ownership of a substantial number of shares of Sperry Rand should have representation on your board." And so it now appeared, to many lawyers, that if a corporation can become a director and an insider, through its deputy on the board, for the purpose of short-swing profits, then it may also become a director for many other purposes and subject to a whole host of perils and liabilities. The decision, incidentally, closed another loophole, because it specifically extended the short-swing rule to *former* directors who sell within the six months period.[21]

It would seem that the advantages and prestige attaching to a corporate directorship must now be sharply evaluated in terms of the disadvantages and the dangers, and most of this change in climate can be traced back to the *Texas Gulf Sulphur* case. The president of one west coast conglomerate described an invitation to serve on his board as an invitation to be blackmailed through the nuisance suits of shareholders. The shortage of competent men

[21] *Wall Street Journal*, February 24, 1969.

appears in such peripheral developments as smaller boards and increased pay for directors. It has been said that many large companies now set the figure at $10,000 or more a year. A 1967 survey by the National Industrial Conference Board disclosed one company paying $18,000 and another $20,000. One small company even placed a classified advertisement for directors, while two businessmen have capitalized on the situation by establishing a head-hunting agency and will try to find competent directors for a fee. There are always some silver linings in such situations, however, and it is reported that directors are attending more meetings and are doing a better job of keeping informed. They had better. The task must be almost insurmountable in the case of a director of a conglomerate.

Former SEC chairman Cary had once bragged that U.S. securities regulation was the best in the world and was being copied abroad, but this declaration was one that required a little parsing. The Canadians, for example, having observed and participated in some of the bruising aspects of the *TGS* case, its related actions, and its aftermaths, were not so sure that they wanted to import this product across the border without a few changes. *The Northern Miner,* which had been sitting rather close to the ringside, declared itself "all for reform where reform is needed, but we subscribe to the belief that people in this country are quite capable of providing their own remedies, and it disturbs us to see how such false gods as the SEC are held up as the answer to Canadian problems." [22] A representative of the *London Financial Times,* Harold Wincott, had visited Washington to take a closer look at the SEC and reported that "Oddly enough, I came back from the U.S. feeling that in some ways we run things better than I had thought. And certainly it would be quite wrong if we in this country got the impression that all is for the best in the best possible of worlds in the U.S., where the conduct and regulation of companies and the securities business is concerned. . . . [It] has not made plaster saints out of American businessmen and financiers, nor has it saved the American investor from the consequences of folly and greed." Despite the fact that British financial reporting standards were probably better than any in Europe, the record was flawed by a number of scandalous episodes in the 'sixties, not all of them at the expense of the small shareholder.

The 29-year-old grandson of the founder of the Boy Scouts,

[22] *The Northern Miner,* December 8, 1966.

Lord Baden-Powell, was surprised to learn from friends, in 1966, that the controlling interest in the insurance company of which he was board chairman had been sold to a real estate group by another director who had not thought it necessary to inform him of the fact. Lord Baden-Powell was very angry, and resigned. And a large electronics company, Pye of Cambridge Ltd., had recently admitted to stockholders that the income from an Irish subsidiary, over a long period, had been credited to a private account not known to the parent company's auditors.

Things were somewhat murky on the continent, as the *Wall Street Journal's* correspondent pointed out.[23] A new German disclosure law was the means of revealing, not much to anyone's surprise, that holdings in the vaults of the three biggest banks controlled West Germany's two biggest department stores, large blocks of stock in Daimler-Benz, the auto maker, and in mining, power, chemical, shipping, and brewing companies. In France and Italy new legislation was prepared to enforce disclosure, although the standards were not as rigid as in the United States. Most European firms were in the habit of reporting a profit figure without explaining how it was calculated. Because its shares were traded in America, Montecatini, a big Italian chemical producer, had to issue detailed financial statements—but did not do so in Italy. Italians had to read them after they had been reprinted from American newspapers. Rather grudgingly, European financial and industrial circles were beginning to give up their secrets and there is little doubt but that one of the compelling reasons lay in the standards being enforced across the Atlantic.

The Commission's standards and practices are not without their critics, however. Many have complained that corporate securities regulation to date has suffered from being almost the exclusive province of lawyers, and that if economics scholars have not been barred, they at least have not seen fit to contribute their thinking to this field. At a recent Washington conference of economists *and* lawyers, Professor George J. Benston, of the University of Rochester, suggested the general ineffectiveness of the SEC financial data disclosure practices, charging the agency with not using its powers to develop helpful innovations, such as probability reporting—a device roughly similar to weather forecasting. Frankly he found the SEC requirements not only expensive to utilize but not worth the

[23] *Wall Street Journal*, November 30, 1966.

cost, indicating that no significant use was made of the material and that it had only limited relevance to investors.[24]

The professor also took issue with the argument that, even if the data was not significant, it was better than the mass of allegedly fraudulent data foisted on the public prior to the SEC:

> A careful examination of the Senate hearings that preceded passage of the Securities Act of 1933, and the voluminous Pecora hearings that preceded the Securities Exchange Act of 1934, fails to turn up more than one citation of fraudulently prepared financial statements. . . . Thus the need for the financial disclosure requirements that are the "heart" of the Securities Act of 1933 appears to have had its genesis in the general folklore of turn-of-the-century finance rather than in the events of the '20's that preceded the legislation, insofar as fraud and misrepresentation are concerned.

Although prime interest in disclosure as a *concept* may have been set off by the writings of Brandeis, it gained great momentum through the writings of Adolf A. Berle Jr., and certainly became official with the acts of 1933 and 1934, developing a connotation of its own as an antidote to fraud, and one which was dogmatically accepted. Brandeis had written *Other People's Money* after the Pujo Committee, in 1912, had put the spotlight on Morgan partners and interlocking directorates. The pure Brandeisian doctrine was against bigness, both in business and government. It paved some of the way to the New Deal and led straight to the depression-born Senate resolution 84 to investigate short selling, introduced December 14, 1931, and more or less prompted by President Hoover's warnings. That led in turn to Pecora, Charles E. Mitchell, a midget on Morgan's lap, and the securities legislation. By 1940 all business seemed suspect and the TNEC hearings brought the liberals into full blast. The securities laws were inevitable, and after the surprise appointment of Wall Streeter Joseph P. Kennedy [25] as the first SEC chairman —he solved the problem of bringing the parties together—Landis,

---

[24] George J. Benston: "The Effectiveness and Effects of the SEC's Accounting Disclosure Requirements"—a paper presented before a conference on economic policy and corporate securities regulation, sponsored by the American Enterprise Institute and George Washington University National Law Center (1968).

[25] At a private dinner early in 1971, before William Casey's confirmation as chairman of the SEC, Senator Edward Kennedy observed that Casey's background clearly made him the second most outrageous choice for chairman in SEC history, the first being Senator Kennedy's father.

Douglas, and Frank made their personal marks in the top spot prior to the advent of Cohen. In the beginning the law did not authorize the registration of stocks, although the Commission could prohibit trading on the national exchanges, but under Kennedy's administrations almost everybody came into the fold. The period of good fellowship, it was said, ended with Kennedy, and there would be rough days ahead for the financial community. This was true. For the first time in history, with the passage of the 1933 act, disclosure was not at the discretion of management.

## V

Intertwined with the whole disclosure concept is insider trading. One of the great mysteries of our time, says Henry Manne, who wrote the best-known work on the subject,[26] is why the Commission, the courts, and even some businessmen accept so unquestioningly the thesis that insider trading is evil. He says flatly it is surprising that an independent federal agency should push so assiduously for a position it has never studied, and one which has not been justified in theory or fact. Believing that no one would be seriously injured were the insider trading limitation abandoned, Manne points out that the long-term investor receives full value when the information has been disclosed or exploited, and therefore does not care whether prices go up sharply or gradually. Stockholders do not have to be aware of developments to share the benefits; they are not in conflict with insiders who purchase. To the short-term trader or speculator, however, insiders represent *competition* for the same profits, and the gambler would be more at home with the abrupt fluctuations which are more likely with a full disclosure rule. In short, the full disclosure philosophy seems to benefit all the wrong people. In this connection it is useful to remember that the appellate majority in *TGS* took pains to include these "wrong people" in the investing public and to extend them equal protection. It could be interposed at this point that it was all very well for Judge Waterman to throw the egalitarian mantle over both the average investor and the speculator. The fact remains that a speculator will take, if he can get it, and use, for his own purposes, a fact which would not be at all material to the average investor, and which he would have great difficulty in utiliz-

[26] *Op. cit.*, Chapter 5, Note 2, p. 93.

ing even if he knew it. The *rights* of each party may be the same, but the methods and objectives are as different as day and night. The techniques and methods of the speculator thus make it possible for the Second Circuit majority to label as material facts those which would never be so under heaven for average people. Does the end justify the result? It is extremely doubtful.

In his writings Manne seizes the thistle with enthusiasm and develops the argument that a rule *allowing* insiders to trade freely may be fundamental to the survival of the corporate system: "Only the dynamic model of a competitive economy comprehends uncertainty about the future, and it is the existence of this uncertainty that gives rise to the concept of profits and the entrepreneur." [27]

Joseph A. Schumpeter, the eminent Austrian economist who became an American citizen, thought that the entrepreneur must disappear in the total bureaucratization of the large corporation, and that the disappearance of this function would lead to the death of the corporation, a conclusion widely criticized in view of the persistence of innovation in the evolution of the modern business undertaking. Schumpeter believed that any indiscriminate assault on bigness and market power, taken out of their evolutionary context, would deprive the capitalistic process of its source of progress —throwing out the baby with the bathwater. Because he thought intellectuals were incurably socialistic and that private property would lack effective defenders against their attack, he would probably have looked askance at the SEC attack upon insider trading, or seen it as evidence of his prediction, although it has seemed to many that he was lacking in his assessment of the adaptive vigor of the corporation. To Schumpeter the entrepreneur was the central figure in economic life in America. Later economists observe that once innovation has been firmly established, profits level off to create continuing pressure on the entrepreneur to press on with more innovation.

Manne insists that the entrepreneur must be rewarded and that a crucial theoretical difficulty has been finding an appropriate, not illegal, method of compensating for these services, which would differ from the interest paid to the capitalist and the salary paid to the manager. Salary is inadequate to this task as it purchases a known service in the labor market. The operation of a profit-sharing plan fails to meet the conditions, merely making the recipient an investor or capitalist. *Ad hoc* bonuses are not unilateral, are deter-

[27] *Ibid.*, p. 118.

mined by someone else, and must be calculated on an annual basis. While stock options appear to be a desirable device for compensating entrepreneurs, they are expensive and cumbersome and the employee is limited to a specific reward, given in advance, no matter how great his innovation. There is no such limitation on the effectiveness of insider trading, proclaims Manne.[28] It is an engaging theory, and refreshing for its brashness in the face of government opposition on a fairly grand scale. The opposition, Manne holds, is inspired by lawyers, who always see things in terms of individual confrontation, whereas the economists, who think more in scientific and objective terms, hold back.

In this connection it is interesting to recall that the arguments *against* insider trading usually come down to three: (1) shareholders must have adequate information on which to base their decisions; this is closely connected to the concept of shareholder democracy so tenaciously held by the SEC; (2) information developed within the corporation belongs to all shareholders equally, which would make insider trading a form of extra compensation, or a taking of wealth which should go to all shareholders; again, Manne names this a concept beloved by lawyers but says it was devised to function within a legal system and not as a guide to economic policy; (3) disclosure helps public officials and private litigants to discover violations, making regulation easier. These are the SEC arguments behind the drive for a basic *per se* rule against insider trading which they are asking the courts to adopt. This could well be more significant in the long run than whether the individual defendants in the *Texas Gulf* case were guilty or not—except, of course, to that corporation and those defendants.

One of the mildly intriguing sideshows attending the insider trading issue arose in a Foley Square courtroom in New York during the later phases of the Commission's administrative action in the *Merrill Lynch* case. Two dozen attorneys representing the 15 financial institutions charged with receiving and acting upon advance information of a sharp earnings decline in Douglas Aircraft stock—before the public had been told—apparently set out to weaken the SEC position on tippees. There was a time when the only damage that might result from acting upon a stock market tip would be financial loss if the tip proved wrong. But now the SEC contends that acting on a tip is against the law if the source of the information is unimpeachable—that is, if it came from the

[28] *Ibid.;* the argument is developed in pp. 131–8.

horse's mouth, from a company officer or similarly authoritative spokesman. What the lawyers for the respondents seemed to be attempting was to write still another definition of materiality. They kept surprising Warren E. Blair, the hearing examiner, by attacking the accuracy of the information that passed from Douglas Aircraft to Merrill Lynch, and thence to the financial institutions, on the theory that wrong information could not be considered material information. Since the hearing was only a quasi-judicial proceeding, these tactics may have been aimed at subsequent actions, when the matter could come before both the full Commission and the appellate courts. The reed would not seem to be a very strong one in the light of past holdings on what is material, however.[29]

Eventually, on the last day of June, 1970, Blair ruled that twelve of the investment company management concerns had violated anti-fraud provisions of the federal securities laws by selling Douglas shares after being tipped off by Merrill Lynch. Although these firms were to be censured, this could be interpreted as little more than a slap on the wrist. The examiner found there had been no deliberate intent to flout the law, and no previous misconduct. He felt that publicity on the case had in itself acted as a further sanction, and rejected the more severe suggestions that had come from the SEC staff, to revoke registrations or bar association with broker-dealers. The Blair decision, which was subject to review by the whole Commission, would require not only insiders, but anyone who knowingly gets inside information from insiders, either to disclose it to the investing public or to refrain from trading on it as long as the information is confidential. This case marked the first time, he declared, that so-called tippees have been so charged, but this did not excuse the SEC from taking action because the Commission had long been concerned with the "concept of unfairness."

There are clearly at the present time no indications that the game of insider trading can ever be endowed with a set of rules by which all the players can abide and set their courses of action in complete safety. The stakes and the perils for the business and financial community are very real, and no one can be blamed for wanting to know the rules before committing either himself or his organization to the game, but there is not even this kind of choice. In our complex economy the game must go ahead even without rules, and participation is not optional.

[29] *The New York Times*, December 22, 1968.

It is doubtful whether the SEC, or the courts, could ever clarify the situation sufficiently to guarantee safe conduct to any corporation, bank, investment firm, or individual trader, even if it was willing to do so. It could *try* a little harder, as many of its victims and a number of judges and professional observers have pointed out repeatedly. It could try for guidelines that might at least sketch in the boundaries of permissible action, but guidelines are not necessarily lifelines and the law will continue to be applied in specific cases when a matter comes to litigation. It could also try to mature its economic research and bring to its own philosophy and practice the same degree of expertise that it has applied to administration and regulation. It could do worse than listen to its tone of voice now and then, editing out some of the shrillness and militance and arrogance, and perhaps not scorning some grace notes, in recognition of the fact that it is an agent of a reasonable citizenry. The Commission, or any independent federal agency, has at least one thing in common with a corporation. It is a fictitious person moved and animated by human beings and penalized by human limitations, not the least of which is the inevitability of change. Like kings, Congressmen, and business executives, commissioners move along and die and are replaced by others.

The mechanics of disclosure, not the morals of disclosure, prevent hard and fast rule-making, and staring up at everybody from the bottom of every barrel is the critical factor of materiality, which is up for grabs with every changing set of facts and circumstances. Of course the securities industry, and every business undertaking, would like safe-conduct rules even at great expense to its freedom and traditional methods of operation. But not even the Supreme Court, with its molasses-like deliberate speed, is ever likely to supply such rules. The average man and the average company will have to do the best they can with prudence and good judgment, perhaps aided now and then by the Constitution if the weather is right for it. Probably the best that can be expected will be rules telling the insider what he cannot do. Beyond that he will be on his own, not an entirely strange situation in a capitalist society where enduring profits must be earned.

Since the 1930's the attitude of the American public towards the buying and owning of a company's stock by its employees, at any level, has wavered between a feeling that it is a good thing for insiders to have a stake in the corporation which employs them, and another feeling that there is something sinister attaching to the term "insider." The adjustment of the Congress to this situation was Section 16(b), which removed the prospect of quick-turn profits by those most in the know—officers, directors, and ten per cent shareowners. It then remained for the interpretation of 10b-5 thirty years later to throw the net over *all* employees who might, through hindsight, turn out to have possessed inside information. On the present scene many believe it is time for Congress to take another look and impose some solid new rules, rather than leave the game to the case-by-case attack by the Commission and the courts.

As the more directly affected portion of the whole public, the business and financial communities have not exhibited any spectacular willingness to challenge the fundamental issues, shrugging off one development after the other as additional bits of bureaucratic regulation involving for the most part higher legal fees. The ramifications of the *Texas Gulf* decision, which as of the date of the Court of Appeals opinion in 1968 comprised the whole law on insider trading, came at them slowly and as something of a nasty surprise. In the ensuing seminars and professional debates, lawyers and SEC staffers tossed the ball back and forth in an extraordinarily minute examination of 10b-5, but nobody seems to have raised the questions of what might be desirable or appropriate for the survival and growth of the economy itself. There has been very little righteous indignation over the larger issues and a notable lack of crusading, except on the part of a handful of editors. It was *Barron's* who cried out "Police state!" but no vigilante meetings followed.

If Congress is so disposed, it might detect an ominous pattern in what has been happening, and would not have to look too far over its shoulder to draw the parallel with the noble experiment of prohibition. The SEC can hardly police all insider trading, and has in fact admitted frankly that it has not the resources or the budget to do so. In doing what it can, it will obviously pick and choose its targets and concentrate its firepower, thereby discriminating and undermining any claim to across-the-board regulation. Vast profits from knowledgeable trading, involving billions of dollars each year, will prove as persuasive to the trader as were the vast profits obtainable in evading the prohibition laws, and the attitude of the "consumers" towards enforcement could well be similar for the two eras. The breakdown of law begins when the rewards of evasion outweigh by a large margin the possibility of getting caught, and the prospect is not a pretty one. With illicit profits at high levels, corruption is generally not very far away. A thoughtful and intelligent re-examination of the securities laws, acknowledging the growing intrusions of federal statutes into the common law, might not only be timely but in the hearing process would draw into the arena a wider and sounder sample of both legal and economic scholars than has been utilized by the SEC alone, in determining its philosophy and practice.

In what amounted to his first public statement of policy, SEC chairman Budge seemed to signal a slow turn to the right when he repeatedly plumped for greater self-regulation on the part of the securities industry. "Self-regulation," he declared, "if properly implemented, can best serve the needs of the brokerage community as well as the needs of the investing public. . . . One of the principal reasons self-regulation was put in our statutes was that it was believed the securities industry might be in a better position to evaluate and resolve its own problems in a changing environment than might be the case with direct and pervasive regulation by a government agency which necessarily could not be on the scene every business day." The Commission's regulatory responsibility, he indicated, should be in an overseeing capacity.[30] It had been a wet summer in New York, and the olive branches were blossoming in September.

Actually there were blooms of change from the same branch a month earlier when Budge wrote Bert C. Goss, chairman of the public relations firm of Hill and Knowlton, suggesting that guidelines be developed by the business community itself in terms of ethical behavior and proper business conduct rather than by the Commission as interpretations of the law. "This approach has the additional advantage of affording a greater degree of flexibility than if we were to attempt to 'lay down the law,' " Budge wrote.[31]

Back in November, 1967, the Commission had authorized a study to reappraise federal administrative policies under the 1933 and 1934 acts, under the direction of Commissioner Francis M. Wheat, a former Los Angeles attorney with five years of experience with the agency. The "Wheat Report," as it was called, was released to the public in mid-April of 1969. The 500-page document is essentially a technical memorandum.[32] It does not confine itself to matters of broad policy, pointing out that while recodification of

[30] *Wall Street Journal* and *The New York Times*, September 5, 1969.
[31] *Jack O'Dwyer's Newsletter*, August 5, 1969. Vol. II, No. 31.
[32] "Disclosure to Investors: A Reappraisal of Federal Administrative Policies Under the '33 and '34 Acts—The Wheat Report," Commerce Clearing House, Inc., April, 1969.

the securities laws, as had been widely suggested, was probably a proper course, this might take 20 years, whereas the study group sought the humbler way of being as practical as possible. Problems arising under 10b-5, however, were expressly excluded:

"Questions which have recently excited the greatest interest," the introduction set forth, "such as the obligation of so-called 'insiders' to make appropriate disclosures of unpublished material information in connection with their purchases or sales of securities, are beyond its scope; such questions, arising largely under rule 10b-5, involve disclosure in the context of federal policy aimed at the prevention of fraud and manipulation in the securities markets."

From the outset, said the Wheat report, disclosure had been a central aspect of national policy in the field of securities regulation, the emphasis resting on two considerations. One relates to the proper function of federal government in investment matters, while the other rests on the belief that appropriate publicity tends to deter questionable practices and to elevate the standards of business conduct—the ritual bow to Brandeis. Apart from the prevention of fraud and manipulation, the authors of the report maintained that the draftsmen of the 1933 and 1934 Acts viewed their responsibility as being primarily one of seeing to it that investors *and speculators* had access to enough information to enable them to arrive at their own rational decisions. Aside from this rather pointed attempt to embrace the doctrine of the Court of Appeals in the *Texas Gulf* case, the report confined itself to a number of practicable suggestions and appeared to have been well received by the financial community.

Observing that historically the SEC efforts in the disclosure field had concentrated on the new issue market, the report suggested that now greater attention should be paid to disclosures in the trading markets. This must involve improvement in the existing means of disseminating reports under the 1934 Act, as well as improving the reports themselves. Considerable attention was given to the recently installed microfiche system by SEC, centering upon a small sheet of film containing as much as 60 pages of printed material which can be projected on a screen. The microfiche system has been described by one unkind critic as doing no more than transferring to subscribers the SEC's own filing problems. Nevertheless it has cut down on cost, and prior to its introduction relatively meager use had been made of reports because of the expense and their limited content. Among other matters covered in considerable detail in the Wheat report were these:

—There should be a greater effort to intervene constructively by stimulating dissemination of information to trading markets.

—Simplifying prospectuses.

—Reaffirming SEC efforts to require reporting of sales and earnings by line of business for diversified companies.

—Liberalization of the "gun-jumping" restrictions to accommodate problems such as those which arose in *TGS*.

—Additional guidelines for more uniformity in annual reports.

—Attention to alteration of forms, and their timing.

Establishing the philosophy of disclosure under the securities acts, and citing Brandeis as one of the chief architects, the study group said the fundamental aim was to provide information, not to shield the public from dubious ventures. Filtering down information from the more aware professionals to the ordinary investor helps to strike a pragmatic balance. The group had reviewed past criticisms of the policy, it said, and taken them into account.

The authors believed that the policy relating to projections of sales and earnings should not be changed, although this had been suggested by experienced analysts (and by Manne with "probability forecasting"). It was felt that the problems of civil liability in connection with any such change might be insurmountable if the projections were not granted specific immunity; also the facts change rapidly. Since such documents are designed to elicit material facts, investors should be left free to make their own projections.

In a thorough and generally kindly review of the Wheat report, Robert W. Taft, a public relations executive, lawyer, and investor relations teacher, commented that the various company reports filed with the SEC were notoriously inaccessible and relatively expensive to obtain. To the extent that the Commission's current reporting requirements act as a "backstop" for the timely disclosure policies of the stock exchanges—and the report said they did—Taft said the SEC may be a solid backstop but the ball game is being played on a different field. He thinks the agency might well take itself out of the communications field entirely since its activities are not accomplishing their intended purpose.[33]

Five months after the Wheat report was transmitted, two events occurred. On September 2 the Commission announced that it was about to take its first major step toward overhauling company dis-

[33] Robert W.. Taft: "The Wheat Report," *Public Relations Journal,* August, 1969.

closure regulations with a package of sweeping changes, some of which could be controversial. For the most part they would follow the recommendations made in the report. On September 3 President Nixon announced from the White House West in San Clemente that he would nominate a conservative Democrat, A. Sydney Herlong Jr., of Florida, to replace Commissioner Wheat, who had resigned. Herlong had served 20 years in the House, much of the time on the Ways and Means Committee, and had retired voluntarily.

A significant portion of the SEC proposals dealt with increasing the amount of information that must be reported under the 1934 Act, including a breakdown of sales and earnings contributed by separate lines of a company's business. The reaction of the mining industry to this move has been earlier noted. While the first package was being submitted for public comment before final action, there was a strong indication that more would follow.

In October the Commission issued a policy statement which adhered closely to some of the Wheat report's recommendations and dealt with the potential conflict between two SEC disclosure regulations—one which *bars* publishing information which might influence the outcome of a securities offering, and another which *requires* prompt disclosure of important corporate developments. The SEC said any such conflict was "more apparent than real," but indicated that the disclosure of a "material event," so long as it did not include predictions or opinions, would be permitted.

## VI

Not all of the SEC's ventures were met with success, of course, and when it had applied in 1968 to the federal district court in New York to enforce an administrative subpoena against the *Wall Street Transcript* it may not have been aware that attacking the press was not quite as safe a pastime as attacking a business corporation, which one long-ago wit had likened to "kicking pigeons." Judge Harold R. Tyler Jr., ruled that the Commission had exceeded its constitutional authority. The eloquent militance of an affidavit submitted to the court by Donald I. Rogers, veteran newspaperman and financial writer who was now associated with the *Transcript,* was such that it prompted the equally militant editors of *Barron's* to reprint it in its entirety on the journal's front page.[34]

"I consider it a shocking invasion of freedom of the press,"

[34] *Barron's*, December 2, 1968.

said Rogers, "for the Commission to seek to investigate the *Transcript* on the notion that it should be registered with and licensed and regulated by the Commission. What is worse is that the Commission seeks nothing specific according to its subpoena, but seeks to inquire into the general newsgathering facilities, sales facilities, operations, names of subscribers and prospective subscribers as well as correspondence with them. . . . Not even the strongest and mightiest publication could avoid damage both financial and to its reputation in the face of such investigation. . . . The very prospect of such an investigation is frightening to and destructive of a free press."

Rogers then invoked references to the Iron Curtain, the state of Alabama, the N.A.A.C.P., Torquemada, Hitler and Goebbels, and John Peter Zenger, among others, and asked the court to remove "that club."

Judge Tyler's decision showed that he had been listening, and declared that neither the First Amendment nor the powers conferred by Congress upon the SEC permitted an inquiry which could only lead to restraint of expression by a newspaper. He stayed the hand that held the club, also pointing out that "by reason of their broader and more varied jurisdiction, federal district courts are better equipped than administrative or regulatory agencies to vindicate constitutional rights." It was quite a day for the opposition, although it did not cut much mustard for the corporations who were not equipped with a similar arsenal of weapons. Perhaps hoping that history would repeat itself, the Commission chose to appeal to the Second Circuit. After a modest wait, the reward was not long in coming. On February 2, 1970, the Court of Appeals ruled two-to-one that the SEC could enforce its subpoena against the *Transcript,* thus reversing the 1968 ruling by Judge Tyler. And on June 16 of the same year, the U.S. Supreme Court let this decision stand, denying an appeal by the publisher of the newspaper, Richard A. Holman. Interestingly, Holman had made the files of the Commission on an earlier occasion. The registration of his broker-dealer firm had been revoked in 1965 and the company was expelled from the National Association of Securities Dealers. These events, presumably, could have had little bearing on a question of freedom of the press.

The jeopardy which Judge Moore had labeled "perpetual" in his dissent in the *Texas Gulf* case was necessarily limited to the defendants in that action, but the fall-out was very persistent. Rule 10b-5 resembled a small, well-defined tropical disturbance which overnight had come up out of nowhere and developed into an unpredictable hurricane. Nobody, except possibly the SEC, knew where it might strike next, or what might be contrived in the way of effective protection. At the very least it was a long and stormy season across the landscape occupied by the securities industry and its financial and business neighbors. There was undeniably a lot of wind, although much of this was generated by the human voice. Lightning struck here and there, many got wet, and some took advantage of the widespread confusion to turn the situation to their advantage, following a predictable human pattern. By any estimate there was certainly a lot of jeopardy in the air and well-meant attempts at cloud-seeding had produced scanty benefits.

The Southern District of New York, housing the federal court of the same name, seemed especially storm prone. One day might see Judge Tyler's incidental defense of the greater competence of the federal district courts in the *Transcript* matter, while another day would find the Commission, not at all daunted by such rebukes, addressing the judiciary in what could only be characterized as a high-handed manner. In the *Gerstle* case,[35] a class action was brought by a disgruntled stockholder to recover losses allegedly resulting from a failure to make full disclosure in a proxy statement. The SEC employed an *amicus curiae* brief to effect a striking shift in one of its oldest accounting concepts. The arguments must have been compelling since the judge found for the plaintiff on all counts and awarded substantial damages, but the language directed at the court was bound to raise some eyebrows, as here:

"The Congressional purpose was to elevate standards in the securities field above those generally prevailing. In applying the Commission's command that proxy solicitations be neither false nor misleading, *the court is admonished to keep that goal in view. . . . The words to be interpreted here are the language of the SEC, exercising its power to prescribe standards, and the meaning of those words is illuminated by the intent revealed in their application by the SEC itself.*" Emphasis has been added, although it seems hardly necessary.

The defendant corporation, Gamble-Skogmo, was trying to bring about a statutory merger with General Outdoor Advertising, which meant that a vote of the shareholders of both companies was required. This involved the proxy solicitation rules of the SEC. Company executives consulted the Commission's staff in respect to

[35] *Gerstle v. Gamble-Skogmo CCH Fed. Sec. L. Rep. 92,367 (EDNY 1969).*

the proxy materials, and were apparently met with the advice that it would be contrary to the SEC's historic policy for them to include any statements about the market values of the assets, although it was known that true value considerably exceeded the book value. This assurance was given by a branch chief in the division of corporate finance. Since its inception the SEC had steadfastly ruled out as speculative and unsubstantiated all references to the appraisals of assets carried at book value, or the prospect of their sale.

What astonished the accountants and lawyers, in the *Gerstle* case, was the court's holding that the companies were *required* to disclose in their proxy statements an appraisal of the true value of the assets. The fact that this was contrary to the rigidly enforced past accounting practice of the SEC was nullified by the Commission's own brief, changing the rule. In short, the law had once more not been made until the defendants were already in court. After the game started, the policy was changed. Said the SEC brief to the court: "When a proxy statement containing financial statements is attacked as creating a false or misleading inference, it may be no defense that proper accounting procedure has been followed with respect to the financial statements." The rules for the game of disclosure were beginning to stump even the experts.

"In its crusade against the worst outbreak of inflation in 18 years," proclaimed the editors of *Time* in the summer of 1969, "the government has been struggling for months to create a climate of uncertainty among businessmen, consumers and investors." [36] The dog's eye view was that the campaign had been something of a success, and one criterion was all too certain. The market was down, and nobody seemed to know just how far down. In business circles such a development is a substantial attention-getter, swinging the spotlight away from the more debatable causes and effects and the perils and triumphs of individual corporations and regulatory agencies. Conceding, as it had earlier, that harassment—like beauty —was only in the eye of the beholder, according to an anonymous commentator, the editors of *Barron's* now added morosely that moral indignation has rarely commanded a premium, and in a bear market it goes begging.[37] They were inclined to find Wall Street less a street of fear and more an avenue of apathy. Chairman Cohen had departed the SEC for private practice, and both the Commission and the Supreme Court had undergone shifts and changes, the results

[36] "Wall Street's Season of Suspense," *Time*, August 8, 1969, p. 59.
[37] "Street of Fear?" *Barron's*, September 1, 1969.

of which were yet to be demonstrated. The Texas Gulf defendants had to return to an autumnal court before Judge Bonsal to renew the contest and face possible penalties. Merrill Lynch had thrown in the sponge for practical reasons, and the institutions to whom it had passed information were still awaiting the outcome of their own hearings. The SEC had stood off the urgings of the judiciary to lay down some guidelines on insider trading, and was still engaged in the more rewarding game of playing one case at a time and even changing its rules, as in *Gerstle*, whether they concerned "material" information or accounting practices. Within a year, of course, some of these observations would be severely edited by time, the courts, and the investing public. Perpetual jeopardy appeared to be one policy that could be depended upon, and brought to mind still another paragraph from Judge Moore's dissent in *Texas Gulf:*

> The resolution, if such be possible, of the many problems presented in this field should be by rule, as definitive as possible, formulated in the light of reality and not retroactive in effect as here. . . . Presumably the Commission will make recommendations to the Congress to give that body an opportunity to accept or reject after thoughtful debate such proposals as may be made. The companies, the securities of which are listed on exchanges, their employees and the investing public alike should have some knowledge of the rules which will govern their actions. They should not be forced, despite an exercise of the best judgment, to act at their peril or refrain *in terrorem* from acting.

Apathetic or not, spectators along financial way were fascinated by such capers and banking headaches as were posed by the forthcoming bidding for oil leases along Alaska's petroleum-rich North Slope. The Bank of America, which had been employed to collect and invest a money windfall that might exceed a billion dollars, had chartered a jet to take the deposits on bids back to California in order to clear checks and start earning interest at the earliest possible moment. The difference in interest would be considerably more than the cost of the jet plane.

In many ways the most fascinating piece of news that surfaced in the late summer of 1969 concerned a copper-lead-zinc-silver prospect in Western Australia—certainly the most engaging within the frame of reference of this chronicle. Once more the company involved was Texas Gulf Sulphur. Before the press flurry subsided momentarily, the names that made news carried a familiar ring—

Dr. Leo Miller, chief executive Stephens, general counsel Harold Kline, and even corporate secretary David Crawford. The first and chief instrument of communication was the Dow Jones broad tape, which somehow managed to make a ten billion dollar error on the first run-through of the estimated dollar value of the mineral deposits. Texas Gulf, in New York, was once more somewhat frustrated in its attempt to issue a clarifying and deflating news release —this time because the elevators in the Pan-Am building suddenly went out of service during strenuous efforts of the staff to compose the release. And finally, Texas Gulf stock jumped some 20 per cent in the trading. The only thing lacking, to create a feeling of "Here we go again!" was that so far the SEC had not unleashed its investigators.

As usually happens—in fact, just as it happened in the Timmins affair—explanations followed. Apparently an Associated Press reporter in Perth was engaged in a round-up feature on Australian mining, and as part of the job held a conversation with Miller, the man who was responsible for much of the early evaluation and planning of the Ontario venture in 1963. Subsequently the company had established a new subsidiary, Australian Inland Exploration Company, and Miller became president. When queried he had referred the reporter to TGS statements regarding the prospect at Mons Cupri, made in April at the company's annual meeting, but which had attracted no notice from the press. In keeping with company policy, Miller refused to put a dollar value on the prospect, which had already been estimated as indicating 36 million tons of ore. It could only be assumed that the reporter made his own calculations based on current mineral prices. In any case, the first Dow Jones announcement placed the value at more than *eleven* billion dollars—a figure that was corrected in the second take to something over *one* billion.

Apart from the initial gross error, Texas Gulf was irritated because Miller had been put into the position of making an "announcement" instead of merely responding to questions. The resulting news story indicated that the company had formed another subsidiary, the Mons Cupri Mining Company, to develop the deposits, actually first reported two years before. To compound the company's irritation, the Associated Press market story two days later attributed the trading activity to a statement by a market analyst, rather than to its own reporter. And the *Wall Street Journal*, presumably protective of *its* corporation, failed to mention the ten billion dollar error on the broad tape.

It is to be noted that TGS president Fogarty's kitchen table did not figure in this latest go-around. The company very carefully framed its news release to say that the dollar figures in press service reports had not originated with them. It called attention to its most recent quarterly report to stockholders ten days earlier, in which it said a feasibility study on the prospect was continuing, along with some other exploration and drilling work. It also re-ran a portion of the annual meeting report to stockholders on April 24, which had given the Mons Cupri story in such detail as should have warmed the hearts of the Commission's mining specialists, specifying mineral percentages, tonnage estimates, and indicated operating possibilities. The real irony here of course, lay in the specific details, which were just what the Commission had, on trial, demanded in order to endow the investor and speculator with the whole truth, nothing held back. And the result, as could have been forecast by any reporter, was that nobody except the *Mining Journal* picked up the story.[38] The news, when it finally came to the trading floor, arrived on the wings of error and prompted a five-point rise. It was a piquant comment on the SEC's disclosure policies.


Chronicles must come to an end, for various practical reasons, but they do not necessarily conclude. Conclusions are for those who are willing to gamble, for those whose subject matter lends itself to a neat outline with terminal points clearly marked, or for those who have somehow convinced themselves that there is no tomorrow. The lucky concluders are transposed by time into prophets, while the less fortunate, like MacArthur's old soldiers, merely pass out of the picture unnoticed and unheralded. The reporters of events, such as those associated directly or indirectly with the Texas Gulf Sulphur affair, are little more than stringers of beads. They have the opportunity to search for patterns and perhaps to process and bring some order to the raw material—again, thanks to hindsight. But how long is a piece of string?

On December 20, 1971, Texas Gulf Sulphur Company and nine individual defendants were denied a hearing by the Supreme Court, without comment, although Justices Potter Stewart and Harry A. Blackmun said they felt some of the questions raised should have been heard. The appeal had said the case was of seminal importance in the interpretation of federal securities laws,

[38] *Mining Journal*, July 25, 1969, p. 71.

and that the Second Circuit had placed impossible burdens of compliance on responsible corporate officials.

Ten days later Texas Gulf announced that it had agreed to settle the bulk of the private damage litigation brought by former stockholders arising from the Timmins discovery, including a pending class action brought on behalf of those claiming they sold TGS stock in reliance upon the press release of April 12, 1964. The agreement had been submitted to Judge Bonsal for hearing on its fairness and reasonability, and it would require the payment of $2.7 million into a fund to be administered by the Court. It provided for a general dismissal of claims against the defendants. The action was taken, said the company, to put to rest all the controversy and to avoid all further expense, inconvenience, and distraction of what had become, in eight years, burdensome and protracted litigation. All too true, but it would take more than this to put the controversy to rest. The company and the individual defendants would continue to deny all charges of wrongdoing or liability asserted in all of the complaints filed in all of the actions in question.

In what would seem, to most laymen, a forlorn and foredoomed attempt to persuade the Supreme Court to reconsider and reverse its action taken at the close of the year, counsel for Texas Gulf and the individual defendants filed petitions on January 14, 1972, for a rehearing. Filed at the same time was another request for a rehearing, in behalf of the company and Fogarty, in the matter of two of the "Utah" former stockholders, Walter Mitchell and George Gordon Reynolds. Certain pertinent happenings, and certain points raised in the petitions, perhaps justify extending the piece of string a bit further before knotting it firmly to conclude the chronicle.

One of the happenings has already been alluded to—the addition of Justices Powell and Rehnquist to the high court bench *after* the December refusal to review the TGS case. Another was a decision handed down on January 11 in *Reliance Electric Co. v. Emerson Electric Co., 40 U.S.L.W. 4125,* described by the press as opening a large loophole in the securities laws as these affect insider trading in the stock markets, and described by an indignant Justice Douglas in his dissent as a "mutilation" of the law.

In asking the Supreme Court to vacate its previous denial of certiorari, Marden asked for consideration by the full court of nine justices, pointing to earlier provocative comments on the case by Justices White, Stewart, and Blackmun, and again stressing the significance of the issues to all affected areas of the public. The pending Reynolds and Mitchell petitions, he pointed out, which arose from the same case, would be before the whole court. He suggested that the extent to which the SEC, over a 30-year period, had encouraged and insisted upon a conservative approach in statements regarding mineral exploration had not been properly stressed before the Court. It was against this background that the disputed news release had been drafted, and now TGS had been condemned for not taking the opposite approach. Moreover, the burden of proof had been shifted from the Commission, where it properly belonged, to the defendants, first to show that no selling stockholder had been influenced by the release, and second, to prove their own "due diligence." The creation and application of a new and unique standard of materiality under section 10(b) was totally unworkable in the context of the securities laws, he contended, and "would serve only to entrap." Within a matter of days, concluded Marden, the Court in the *Reliance Electric* case had instructed the SEC to proceed by administrative or legislative means, not by judicial proceedings, if it seeks to change the long-standing prohibitions of the 1934 act.

Crawford and Huntington prepared their own petitions, also asking for review by the whole Court, as did the counsel for Holyk, Darke, and Clayton. The new element in all of these was that almost for the first time the plight of the *individual man,* previously obscured by the great and complex issues of the case, was set out.

"The end appears close at hand," said Huntington. "The chances of success in any petition for rehearing must be extremely small. And yet the effort is made. Why? Because of the belief that a wrong has been done and that the Supreme Court may right it." His early fears in this highly publicized case were that judges might ascend to the pulpit and preach morality, he said, and that facts, law, and procedure might be bent accordingly. These fears were justified. "Rough-shod treatment was given to the facts by the majority of the Court of Appeals. The law was bent beyond former recognition."

Asking each Justice to put himself in the petitioner's place, David Crawford again recited the facts relating to his own actions, for which, in a case of first impression, he was found to have violated a statute sounding in fraud and deceit and was enjoined for life. Punishment was what the Commission sought, he declared, and punishment was what the lower courts decreed. It began when the Commission counsel cast him and the other defendants in the role of criminal types and announced that the Commission's objective was to "drag to light and pillory."

Crawford asked the Court to recognize that lives of respectable citizens, of which he believed himself to be one, can be destroyed by interpretations of the securities laws which ensnare the innocent in ways never intended by Congress. "This Court devotes much time," he said, "to protecting the rights of individuals in criminal proceedings and similar protection should be accorded the rights of individuals in an equity proceeding under the securities laws." He thought this merited the Court's review.

Counsel for the three Canadians concentrated, in his petition, mainly on the case of Kenneth Darke, "a relatively insignificant individual in the entire complex and exhaustive proceedings." Darke had been ordered to "restore" $48,404.58 to TGS, representing the profits made by others purportedly on his recommendation to only two of them to buy TGS shares. Other tippees were unknown to him. Terming this a staggering sum, counsel said that if required to pay it, Darke would be indentured to TGS for life. Before the indenture became a reality, such a mandate should be closely scrutinized by the Court. This was especially applicable, he said, where an average person is caught in the gossamer web of governmental and judicial pronouncements in a rapidly expanding and highly sophisticated area of law; where liability is imposed without any direct evidence and upon only the flimsiest of circumstantial evidence; and, where the court's stated justification for the remedy created has no application to the facts of the case.

Finally, as Marden pointed out in his petition relative to the Mitchell-Reynolds matter, just 12 days after Texas Gulf had offered its agreement to settle "the bulk" of outstanding stockholder suits pending, another alleged class action had been filed in Utah seeking at least $10 million for the plaintiff, Fox, and members of his class who had sold after 10:55 A.M. on April 16, or later. The juxtaposition of these two events, declared Marden, demonstrates the hazard to which the management and shareholders of a publicly held company may be subject for an innocent act under the rules of law announced by the courts below.

It would be irresponsible and foolish to suggest that the people of Texas Gulf, or the corporation which they bring to life, have arrived at the end of the venture which began in the Kidd-55 sector, because they are only at a point on a curve. The curve had its beginnings long before the discovery hole. Nor have the Commission, or the courts, or the host of others who touched and were marked by their contact with those events, been presented with any ringing conclusion.

It often seemed as though the operative word in this chronicle was "jeopardy," and perhaps that is the string which supports and displays the beads. Jeopardy is indeed perpetual, whether it is that of defendants and plaintiffs in a legal proceeding, that of the prudent investor in our economy, or the speculator, or the reasonable man, or the government agency, or the managers of business and finance, or even that of the judges and courts themselves. There is always enough jeopardy to go around, and more where that came from. Men somehow learn to live with it and occasionally even learn from it. Jeopardy is the certainty of change.

As January of 1969 came along, James P. Dixon, the president of Antioch College, was exploring the problems of change, and while the frame of reference for him was the college and the current troubles of all educational institutions, his thoughts seem applicable to the present subject.[39] He produced two witnesses. In an editorial in *Science* [40] Philip Abelson had written about society's "great growth kick," contrasting the growth in the complexity of human life (three per cent a year) with the growth of electrical power capacity (six to seven per cent a year). Under these circumstances, Abelson had said, the ecologic catastrophe produced by air pollution, thermal pollution, and nuclear dangers was inevitable. This declared, Dixon, was a pointed example of the problem of not being able to apply known truth to the solution of human problems.

Then there was John Gardner who, as president of the Carnegie Corporation, as Secretary of Health, Education and Welfare, and then as head of the Urban Coalition, had come to know something about human institutions. The modern belief, says Gardner, that man's institutions can accomplish just about anything man wants, when he wants it, leads to the contemporary phenomena of bitterness, anger, and cynicism. We feel enormously frustrated by our institutional forms. We expect our institutions to perform utopian miracles. We expect them to provide the environment in which each of us can be operational; at the same time we habitually deny the adequacy and integrity of almost every human institution that we have yet invented.

It is unlikely in the extreme that the president of Antioch College, attuned to the nearer clamors of his campus and milieu, was giving much thought to the events recorded here. Dixon thinks the case for radical change can well be made, but that at the

[39] James P. Dixon, in *Antioch Notes,* January, 1969, Vol. 46, No. 4, Yellow Springs, Ohio.
[40] *Science,* October 11, 1968.

moment in American culture it does not have adequate power to change institutions *in ways that the human beings in them want them to be changed.* It is cowardly, he insists, to depend altogether on criticism of proposed change—"Somehow we must find ways to institutionalize the need for change in both our structures and our programs."

People will not wear indefinitely a harness that chafes and binds. It would be folly to suggest that what the courts and the statutes say is not important and generally binding as of a given date, and the same in some measure applies to what other experts and quasi-official sources say, such as governmental agencies, legal authorities, volunteer regulatory bodies of securities exchanges, and even the corporations. One should give all of these his best attention. Nevertheless it should be kept in mind that everything is open to change, and in the end it is what the people say that counts.

"Judicial process cannot finally resolve a dispute when the public interests involved in a decision are far *wider* than the interests of the litigants," says Martin Mayer, in the admirable final chapter of his book about the legal profession.[41] "The *ratio decidendi*, the reason for the decision, affects only one facet of a social system. Rebuffed by the Court at this point in the maze, a vital social system with popular support will simply hunt out a new path to the same Objective."

And again, commenting on "justice,"—"Justice dies with its beneficiaries, while the law remains. Justice is always in large degree anarchic, dependent on the individual situations of the parties to the case. The only possible operational definition of the word says that justice is the visceral reaction of informed people." Both comments would appear to hold something of comfort for those directly concerned in the Texas Gulf Sulphur affair, and for the multitudes along the sidelines.

Courts will continue to experience difficulty in applying the standards of the reasonable man, who may not even exist. If he exists, he is extremely volatile, as well as a lot of other things. He can change his mind, and he can be as stubborn in the face of findings by his peers as was Herman Frasch in 1894. Emerson, neither miner nor investor, counseled the individual to trust himself, since every heart presumably vibrated to that iron string, but it would be well, also, for the individual who contemplates a course

---

[41] Martin Mayer: *The Lawyers*, Harper and Row, New York (1966), pp. 542 and 545, respectively.

of action in the marketplace to keep his eye on the people, that vast assemblage of reasonable men. There is nothing fixed or monolithic about reasonableness. It is a state that rests upon the probability, and possibly the inevitability, of unregimented cerebration and unpredictable action. Of such things are chronicles born.

# Index